DEVELOPMENT AS A HUMAN RIGHT

DEVELOPMENT AS A HUMAN RIGHT
LEGAL, POLITICAL, AND ECONOMIC DIMENSIONS

Edited by
Bård A. Andreassen and Stephen P. Marks

Foreword by
Louise Arbour, United Nations
High Commissioner for Human Rights

A Nobel Symposium Book
Nobel Symposium 125

Published by the
Harvard School of Public Health

François-Xavier Bagnoud Center
for Health and Human Rights

Distributed by
Harvard University Press
Cambridge, Massachusetts
London, England
2006

Design, layout, and production coordination: Lynn Martin

Copy editing: Ann Barger Hannum and Lynn Martin

Proofreading: Randall Albright

Library of Congress Control Number: 2006933703
Data available on www.loc.gov
ISBN: 0-674-02121-5

Contents

Foreword
Louise Arbour, UN High Commissioner for Human Rights

This book is a timely collection of excellent scholarly writing on the right to development and the related concept of human rights-based development. It is all the more welcome as the signs of purposive engagement and a gradual convergence of positions are becoming more and more manifest among the various actors — the Member States, international institutions, and civil society — on different aspects of development of relevance to the implementation of this right. I see this in the global consensus articulated in the 2000 Millennium Declaration, the 2002 Monterrey Consensus of the International Conference on Financing for Development and in the 2005 Summit Outcome. This convergence is even more palpable in the work of the UN human rights bodies that deal with this right, in particular, the Commission on Human Rights, its Working Group on the Implementation of the Right to Development and the High Level Task Force. Political responsibility has now passed to the newly created Human Rights Council to propose critical steps to make the current process of globalization work towards improving the well-being of people, in every corner of the world.

After twenty years of reaffirming its value, the right to development should be a high priority on the human rights agenda of governments and civil society everywhere; however, it continues to be more a matter of political commitment than of practical policy and action that can affect people's lives. I believe that two challenges need to be met before this right can be taken seriously in policy and action. The first is to create a robust the concept of development, capable of incorporating the principles that underlie the right to development; the second is to identify the practical steps to implement this right, similar to the rights that are operational in the law and administration of Member States.

A Robust Concept of Development

The concept of development has become more robust in recent times and it is more widely recognized that human rights and human development share a common purpose. Development has evolved from material attainments and economic growth to a broad based notion of human development. As the essays in this book clearly bring out, economic growth is only negative to the extent that it impedes rather than enhances the freedom, well-being and dignity of all people everywhere and threatens the resources on which we depend. Similarly, the increase in exchange of ideas, images, goods, people and money, which we call globalization, is not necessarily negative if it can be harnessed to reduce rather than increase disparities, and to empower communities rather than alienate them from the process of development.

The real purpose to the right to development is to secure the harmonization of the aspirations toward the material improvement of the human condition with the aspirations of freedom and dignity. Neither objective is possible under conditions of poverty. Poverty often results from willful neglect and discrimination. Lack of adequate development or development that permits exclusion and discrimination in access to and allocation of resources paves the way to increased inequality and marginalization of the poor and the vulnerable. It denies them their human rights. Economic and social inequalities create differences in access to political power, access to justice and access to basic goods and services, all of which are essential for the full realization of human rights.

The process of development must strive to realize all human rights entitlements of all rights holders. This is particularly relevant for the poor and the marginalized. For them it is necessary that the development process move away from a needs-based exercise in charity and assistance to one that creates and sustains genuine entitlements that span all aspects of their life — economic, social, and cultural, as well as the civil and political.

Putting Concepts Into Practice

The second challenge the essays in this book underscore is to translate political commitment into development practice. The key here is to anchor the process of empowering people to exercise their choices and freedoms within the human rights framework. While human rights standards and principles have to provide the parameters for the articulation and the conduct of the development policies and programs, the process has to lead to enforceable human rights and the relevant political, legislative and administrative institutions to ensure that the benefits of this process will reach the poorest and the most vulnerable.

Development with social justice cannot be achieved in the absence of respect for human rights. Indeed, the possibility for people themselves to claim their rights through legal processes is essential so that human rights have a meaning for those most at the margins, a vindication of their equal worth and human agency. International human rights law emphasizes judicial remedies for violations of rights, though administrative remedies can also be acceptable if they are "timely, accessible, affordable and effective." Potentially, all human rights have justiciable elements. Effective judicial enforcement depends more on courts being granted the authority to hear claims, than on the inherent nature of the rights. Similarly, litigation and examination of individual and group petitions at the international level can both help to develop understanding of the substantive content of international norms and lead to real change for individuals by helping them to take charge of their lives.

All human rights must be given effect at the national level. The States have the primary responsibility for economic and social development and the role of national policies and development strategies cannot be overemphasized. There has to be an enabling environment — legal, political, economic and social — sensitive and reflective of the local context for the realization of the right to development. The creation of such an environment hinges critically on the individually and collectively motivations of States to apply, observe and adjudicate, in the process of development, the human rights standards and the principles of participation, accountability, non-discrimination, equality, empowerment and international cooperation. The principles should guide national development initiatives and inform and inspire the international efforts to "make the right to development a reality for all," in the words of the Millennium Declaration.

The moral and ethical motivations of collective responsibility for development, and even for humanitarian assistance, are not always translated into firm commitments or concrete actions. This gap between intention and action has undermined the credibility of the international community in the eyes of those who must rely on international support. The recent international response to natural catastrophes has been a display of swift practical solidarity in times of crisis, but it has also been too slow and too limited, as has been the global commitment and efforts to scale-up the treatment and care programs for malaria, tuberculosis and HIV/AIDS. We must ensure that collective action based on genuine partnerships and cooperation is mobilized to overcome development challenges and create the necessary conditions for effective and sustainable local action.

By addressing duties and responsibilities at both the national and international levels, this book provides context, background, normative frameworks and policy recommendations that merit the careful consideration of scholars, practitioners, diplomats, and activists. We are grateful to the Nobel Institute for convening the Nobel Symposium on the Right to Development and Human Rights in Development. It fell to Professors Marks and Ardreassen to collect in this volume the views and experiences of the worlds leading authorities on the topic, who participated in the Symposium. Their own contributions and those of the outstanding group of authors they brought together combine the highest level of theoretical reflection with a concern with finding practical ways, based on experience, to make progress on the implementation of the right to development and human rights-based development. My Office is committed to using the ideas and analysis contained in these contributions in its own efforts to identify and advocate strategies that will move the right to development further toward the daily reality of human rights practice. In the end, the right to development informs our quest for dignity at home, and our vision of globalization for the world.

Introduction
Stephen P. Marks and Bård A. Andreassen

Since the adoption of the Universal Declaration of Human Rights (UDHR), the relationship between human rights and economic development has been one of nearly parallel tracks of international diplomacy and action that have rarely intersected. In the last decades of the 20th century, development thinking shifted from a growth oriented model to a human development model, defined as a process of enhancing human capabilities. This approach acknowledged intrinsic and mutually reinforcing links between development and human rights. Such is the premise of the Declaration on the Right to Development, adopted by the UN General Assembly in 1986. The 1993 Vienna Conference on Human Rights called the right to development "fundamental,"[1] and delegates to the 1998 General Assembly celebrating the 50th anniversary of the UDHR proposed that the Declaration be on a par with the UDHR.[2] Despite enhanced attention to this right in the early 2000s, many questions remain unanswered.

The Nobel Symposium on the Right to Development and Human Rights in Development (Oslo, Norway, October 13-15, 2003) brought together experts in economics, international law and relations, and social sciences to look at these unanswered questions. The Symposium was sponsored by the Nobel Foundation through its Nobel Symposium Fund. The participants, from universities, international institutions, and governments, explored the implications of the theme for development economics and international human rights law. The results of these reflections are presented in the following essays by 15 scholars and international officials who attended the Nobel Symposium. They explore the meaning and practical implications of thehuman right to development and the related term of human rights-based approaches to development, and ask what these conceptions may add to our understanding of and thinking about human and global development. This introductory essay sets the following chapters in the context of that larger question.

This volume takes as its basic structure four sets of issues: First, it discusses the conceptual underpinnings of human rights in development (or human rights-based approaches to development) and the notion of the right to development as a right

---

1   The Vienna Declaration and Programme of Action reaffirms, "the right to development, as established in the Declaration, as a universal and inalienable right and an integral part of fundamental human rights." Vienna Declaration and Programme of Action, UN GAOR, World Conference on Human Rights, 48th Sess., 22d Plenary Meeting, pt. 1, UN Doc. A/CONF.157/23 (1993), reprinted in 32 I.L.M. 1667 (1993); also available at http://www.unhchr.ch/html/menu5/d/ vienna.htm.
2   The G-77 sponsored a proposal, on the eve of the 50th anniversary of the Universal Declaration of Human Rights in 1998, to have the General Assembly proclaim the Declaration on the Right to Development to be on a par with the Universal Declaration. Notwithstanding her support for the right to development, the High Commissioner for Human Rights discouraged this initiative, and it did not find its way into the resolution adopted on the 50th anniversary.

related to, but different from, human rights-based development. The process to which both of these conceptions refer is one in which all human rights are progressively realized, and where the process itself is conducted in conformity with the human rights requirements that they be participatory, non-discriminatory, transparent, and accountable. Second, the contributors explore the issue of the duties and responsibilities to ensure human rights in the processes of development. They generally support the principle that the state has primary responsibility for the realization of human rights and clarify how this responsibility involves both national and international obligations and constrains policy choices and priorities of national and international actors, whether public (state) or private (non-state). Third, the essays examine mechanisms for the implementation of the right to development at the national level. Until and unless national governments and civil society find that the right to development defines their aspirations, it will have no traction in the critical decisions on resources for and processes of development. Finally, significant attention is given to the roles and responsibilities of the international community acting through multilateral agencies, including human rights bodies, development agencies, and financial institutions, to contribute to the realization of the right to development. Without their engagement, there is little chance for consensus on principles and mechanisms for an operational model for implementing the right to development.

Conceptualizing the Right to Development

The right to development was reaffirmed in the Declaration on the Right to Development of 1986 and the Vienna Declaration of the 1993 World Conference on Human Rights as a human right, thus creating the expectation that it can be made operational and implemented with the same vigor as other human rights. However, such a formal pronouncement says little about the controversies regarding the content of the right to development or about ways in which it relates conceptually to other human rights. The first part of this book, on conceptual underpinnings, opens with an essay by Amartya Sen, which explores the skepticism around the cogency and viability of the concept of a right to development. He views human rights in terms of social ethics and public reasoning more than as legal entitlements. Addressing the criticism that the right to development is neither justiciable nor feasible, he considers it "a conglomeration of a collection of claims, varying from basic education, health care and nutrition to political liberties, religious freedoms and civil rights for all," the legal protection of which is less appropriate than political and social advocacy and agitation. According to Sen, the fact that the rights contained in this "conglomeration" may not be fully realizable under current circumstances is not adequate to deny that they are rights: Ambiguity of obligations, including imperfect obligations, does not exclude cogency and legitimacy of the right to development, which is part of a larger challenge of human solidarity and freedom.

David Beetham, whose chapter on "The Right to Development and Its Corresponding Obligations" appears in Part II on duties and obligations, also addresses the ambiguities of the definition of the right to development by considering the putative antithesis between collective and individual rights. He resolves this antithesis by considering development (and hence, the collective right to it) as a necessary condition for other individual human rights. Conceptually, the added value of the right to development is that it imposes human rights-based conditions on development, which is reasonable in theory but perhaps an exaggerated claim on institutions. Beetham, for one, questions the "inflationary tendencies" of the right to development, whether it is to extend it to "personal development of the individual" or to over-emphasize the non-economic dimensions of development. This over-emphasis renders even more difficult the task of identifying when this right is infringed upon by international economic arrangements or domestic policies and determining what should be done about it.

In his reports to the UN and in his contribution to Part I, Arjun Sengupta, the former Independent Expert on the Right to Development, describes the right to development as a "vector" of all the different human rights, explaining that this right protects a particular set of goods and values that are realized in a way consistent with a rights-based approach. The value of the vector improves if at least one right improves and no right deteriorates. If any right is violated, then the vector deteriorates and the right to development is violated. Drawing on the Preamble and Article 1 of the Declaration on the Right to Development, Sengupta has defined the right to development as follows: "The right to development, which is an inviolable human right, is the right to a particular process of development in which all human rights and fundamental freedoms can be progressively realized."

His approach assumes, as do most governments, international institutions, and scholars, that development is a comprehensive process not only of economic growth but also of social, cultural, and political change. The ultimate goal is progressive, equitable, and constant improvement of well-being. This view contrasts with conventional definitions of economic development, which focuses on a simple expansion of GNP, industrialization, export-growth, or capital inflows. After defining the right to development as a process, Sengupta explores what he refers to as rights-based economic growth, the nature of rights and their correlative obligations, as well as the definition of the rights-holder. He addresses the principal challenges for the operationalization of the right to development in terms of economic growth, international legal standards, and reciprocal obligations.

The process of development, as defined by the 1986 Declaration, must be genuinely participatory, promoting the "active, free and meaningful participation" of "the entire population and of all individuals."[3] The intent is clearly to avoid technocratic determination of policy and to achieve implementation of programs that integrate local knowledge and aspirations into the process either at the initiative of the central government or with the support of the international community. It would, however, be nonsensical to take literally the reference to the participation of the "entire population" and "all individuals"; yet the terms "active, free and meaningful participation" call for a degree of community involvement adequate to ensure

---

3   Declaration on the Right to Development, Article 2 (3).

that there is a "fair distribution of the benefits"[4] of development. Participation also must result in the progressive improvement of the well-being of all people, and not just a class, political elite, population stratum, or geographic region.

While the principal aim of this book is to sharpen the understanding of development as a human right, the right to development is not the only — or even a necessary — way of looking at the issue. For many, human rights in development are more a matter of defining and applying "rights-based" or "human rights-based" approaches to development. Jakob Kirkemann Hansen and Hans-Otto Sano review the emergence and scope of such approaches, as well as operational strategies for their implementation. They introduce and analyze four constituent elements of a rights-base approach, namely, values and application of norms of justice, governance institutions, the rule of law, and the integration of law in development processes and in analysis of poverty.

Duties and Responsibilities

Like other human rights, the right to development has to create rights and obligations with a sufficient degree of justiciability and feasibility to meet the conditions that Sen sets out in his chapter. He is careful to note that the legitimacy and cogency of a human right such as the right to development does not require full incorporation into legislation and judicial enforcement nor complete feasibility. The obligations involved in human rights impose moral and sometimes legal duties to protect the rights-holders by preventing violations of their rights, and to promote their rights by acting positively to fulfill them. Any discussion of human rights in development must address the meaning and scope of claimed duties and responsibilities of prevention and promotion. The three essays in Part II focus on both preventive and promotional duties and responsibilities. The state has the primary responsibility to frame and implement the laws and procedures that enable the enjoyment of human rights. The cogency, legitimacy, and practical value of any human right, however, are not settled by its formal adoption in domestic and international law. Nor is the matter settled by the theoretical claim that concerned states and the undifferentiated international community have a duty to cooperate. Several chapters address the complexity of philosophical, political, and legal claims of a duty to adopt measures to protect and promote these rights.

In his essay on "Obligations to Implement the Right to Development: Political, Legal, and Philosophical Rationales," Stephen P. Marks assesses three sets of rationales that are implied by the Declaration on the Right to Development and are relevant to determining corresponding duties and responsibilities. His central concern is to explore the rationales behind the 4 explicit duties and 21 imperative statements in the 1986 Declaration. Notwithstanding ambiguities and a reluctance to transfer notions of justice from the domestic to the international system, elements of these obligations may be found in naturalist, contractarian, and consequentialist theories of law, finding their strongest justification in institutional cosmopolitanism. Political

---

4   *Id.*

fault lines tend to limit the potential for translating commitment at the highest level into development practice and legal obligations. Considering the political foundation of law, Marks concludes that the legally binding character of this right is a function of political shifts in power relations that are consistent with ethical considerations, practical feasibility, and legal arguments.

In addition to the conceptual points referred to above, Beetham defines the essential obligation of the right to development as one of not causing damage or harm. In other words, governments must not "initiate or support policies or institutional arrangements, whether domestic or international, which systematically damage any country's economic development, or encourage a markedly unequal form of that development." He minimizes the importance of the more positive formulations of obligations to provide assistance because they reinforce "one-sided dependency" and "convey an image of benevolence," and explains why it is preferable to emphasize infringement rather than assistance.

In her essay, "International Human Rights Obligations in Context: Structural Obstacles and the Demands of Global Justice," Margot E. Salomon develops a similar concern for unjust economic arrangements. She posits collective duties of the international community under existing international human rights law, as interpreted by the treaty bodies. According to Salomon, the redressing of global inequities, which the right to development implies, has become part of the legal system that has emerged from Articles 55 and 56 of the UN Charter and Article 28 of the Universal Declaration of Human Rights. She identifies obligations both within the jurisdiction of states and extraterritorially and builds on the legal argument of an obligation of the international community to act in ways that alter unjust institutional structures. Salomon finds support not only in the UN Charter, human rights treaties, and political documents but also in the pronouncements of treaty bodies, whether in general comments or in concluding observations on states parties' reports. These bodies have increasingly been identifying the impact of global financial and trade structures on the fulfillment of human rights obligations. One of the obligations that she examines in detail is that of due diligence in preventing, investigating, and punishing violations. Accordingly, Salomon stresses, states have a negative duty to avoid hindering the right to development and a positive duty to ensure international enabling environments favorable to this right.

States are not the only duty-holders in the context of the right to development. Bård A. Andreassen explains in his essay, "Development and the Human Rights Responsibilities of Non-State Actors," that international law involves both indirect and direct obligations of non-state actors. Indirect obligations mean that states have obligations to ensure that national law and regulations effectively enforce international law in relation to non-state actors. International law may also impose direct obligations on non-state actors to respect international law. Andreassen raises critical questions about the nature of business enterprises and their moral responsibilities, if any, to respect human rights in their undertakings and businesses. It might be argued that they have certain moral obligations, corresponding with the statement in the

UDHR's Preamble that "every organ of society" should contribute to secure the effective recognition and observance of human rights. Andreassen reviews several initiatives to enhance companies' voluntary adoption of ethical and human rights standards, but he emphasizes that non-state actors' human rights responsibilities are still a matter of soft law. He also argues, however, that these responsibilities may, step by step, be taken to a next level of legal obligations where national legislation has incorporated and courts have applied human rights instruments and related provisions to cases involving business behavior. Can it be argued that transnational corporations (TNCs) are (or should become) responsible, under international human rights law, to respect and contribute to the implementation of the right to development? We are obviously at a stage of the development of international law where this question is unsettled. Should sustainable human development emerge as a peremptory norm of international law having the character of *jus cogens*, the case could be made that investment agreements and other treaties concerning TNCs should not contravene the right to development. The moral and political case could be made for the right to development to reflect a categorical imperative; however, a considerable number of obstacles need to be overcome before the legal case can convincingly be made. As emphasized by Andreassen, however, there is a trend among a growing number of TNCs to adopt voluntary guidelines and codes of conduct that refer to human rights standards; the effectiveness of these provisions largely depends on civic engagement and the pressure that people and popular movements can put on companies. In spite of the lack of clear human rights obligations of non-state actors, such engagement may reflect important principles of participation and public engagement in national development, and hence contribute to rights-enhancing and rights-conducive development.

Voices are still heard among representatives of governments and academics, as well as front-line development practitioners, that the right to development is not clearly defined. Article 1 of the Declaration on the Right to Development implies that there are several different ways a country can develop, but that only a process "in which all human rights and fundamental freedoms can be fully realized" would qualify as the object of the right to development. In theory, protecting and promoting human rights trump other policy objectives in society and, in principle, have priority in the use of resources and institutional arrangements in that society. The right to development, considered as a full-fledged human right, should determine many policy and resource allocation decisions. However, this somewhat straightforward approach to the meaning of the right to development has proved to be too simple. Specifically, the operationalizaton of the right has not kept up with theory. The prospects and difficulties of bridging this gap between rhetoric and reality, between theory and practice, are addressed in Parts III and IV.

Operationalizing the Right to Development

The use of the term "development" has evolved over the last 60 years, and this evolution provides the context for operationalizing the right to development. In the initial post-World War II years, development was identified with the growth of per capita real income, which was taken as the index of average well-being representing the standard of living of the population, both as instrumental in achieving the different objectives of living and as an end in itself. When increasing real income was found insufficient (even if necessary) to secure the fulfillment of certain minimum requirements for improved living conditions of the people, development economists and several UN institutions extended the measure of well-being to include indicators of basic needs and adapted development policy accordingly. The human development approach could be regarded as an extension of the "basic needs" approach by moving from the indicators of "basic needs" in the commodity space to the indicators of human development in the space of capabilities and functionings, such as life expectancy, infant survival, and adult literacy, supplementing the indicators of per capita real income.

The capability approach goes one step further. The capability of a person reflects the various combinations of functionings (doings and beings) that he or she can achieve. According to Sen, it reflects a person's freedom to choose among different ways of living.[5] If aggregative indicators could be designed to represent the freedom to choose from alternative combinations of functionings, each achievement indicator in the space of functionings would correspond with an indicator of freedom in the space of capabilities. When these freedoms are claimed and recognized as rights, the well-being of people is identified with their level of enjoyment of all these rights.

Indicators for each right are essential tools to operationalize this definition. An increase in the value of a particular indicator would imply an improvement in the realization of its corresponding right. At the same time, development logically entails a process or a change over a period of time, when all the rights are sequentially and cross-sectionally related to one another. They are interrelated in such a way that the value of one right depends on the value (or realization) of one or several other rights.

In the North-South debate on the New International Economic Order of the 1970s, the right to development was sometimes described as a right of the developing countries, the assumption being that the "peoples" who would benefit from this right were represented by the governments that emerged from the process of decolonization.[6] However, developing country governments are not always fully representative of the "people" inhabiting the state territory and therefore are not always seen as being the legitimate rights-holder of the right to development. Moreover, these governments may not be willing or able to ensure that the rights they claimed to promote are in fact enjoyed by the entire population.

According to the definition given by Sengupta, the right to development is considered a collective right, simultaneously enjoyed individually by the citizens of a country and exercised collectively through policies and institutions. If the govern-

---

5   Amartya Sen, *Commodities and Capabilties* (Amsterdam: North-Holland, 1985); *Development Is Freedom* (Oxford: Oxford University Press, 1999).
6   Mohammed Bedjaoui, "Le droit au développement," in Mohammed Bedjaoui (ed.), *Droit international: bilan et perspectives* (Paris: Pedone, 1991), pp. 1247-1273; Bedjaoui, "Unorthodox Reflections on the Right to Development," Snyder and Slinn (eds.), *International Law of Development: Comparative Perspectives* (Abindgon: Professional Books, 1987).

ment of a developing country claims the right to development against the international community on behalf of its citizens, the legitimacy of such a claim depends on the existence of appropriate mechanisms to ensure that the entire population enjoys the benefits of the right, rather than it being a source of elite privilege.

From this conceptualization of the right to development, specific concerns arise with respect to national level application of a human rights-based approach to development, on the one hand, and international measures and mechanisms to fulfill the obligation to cooperate with a view to realizing the right to development, on the other.

Rights-Based Development at the National Level

The most evident obligation for the state arising from its recognition of the right to development is to begin implementing a human rights-based approach to development at the national level. Part III contains three chapters, which examine the realities and challenges of rights-based development in national contexts.

Yash Ghai, in his chapter on "Redesigning the State for 'Right Development'," addresses the role of the state, and especially of state policies and national constitutions, which he believes should be "redesigned" to comply with right to development obligations. He pays particular attention to how right to development principles can assist in the search for people-oriented governance and development in processes of formative constitutional reform and examines the recent constitutional reform process in Kenya as a case in point. Through this case, he shows that a participatory process consistent with a rights-based approach may be a mixed blessing. Participation may, in fact, be hijacked by sectional political interests motivated by a thirst for power. The risk of this is particularly high in societies deeply divided by communal interests. The otherwise commendable vision of the right to development can be exceedingly hard to put into practice, and Ghai's chapter alerts us to the pitfalls that accompany the promise of implementing the right to development at the national level.

Sandra Liebenberg addresses the South African post-apartheid experience and demonstrates how a national legal commitment to human rights can bring about positive achievements in terms of social policy and legislation. However, even if such commitment exists in the national system, a rights-based approach stands an even better chance of success if it is backed by social action and mobilization, typically demonstrated in the NGO Treatment Action Campaign in South Africa. Liebenberg's analysis emphasizes, in other words, the non-legal dimension of human rights advocacy and reminds us how central the right to organize and the right to take collective action is for human rights respect and fulfillment.

However countries approach implementation of the right to development at the national level, their efforts must be subjected to some form of monitoring and evaluation. Central to any monitoring are the indicators used and the rigor of the method by which they are established and applied. Rajeev Malhotra argues in his chapter that right to development indicators are useful to the extent that they capture the rights attainment levels of the people concerned and at the same time measure the effort being made by the duty holders to realize those rights. In practical terms, he is attentive to the need to select specific human rights indicators for gauging implementation levels of the right to development, which would correspond with the development priorities and aspirations of the people of each country. In his view, right to development indicators would also need to measure the extent of operationalization and the conformity of the process to the principles of the right to development. He further suggests that two sets of indicators would be necessary, one meant to capture the quality of a process compliant with the principles of rights-based development (participatory/inclusionary, accountable, non-discriminatory, sustainable, or empowering), and the other contextually specific to the rights attainments of individuals in all areas critical for the right to development. He sees these two sets of indicators as complementary and covering both the conduct of the process and the outcomes that it generates.

It will ultimately be necessary to establish an international committee to review the implementation of this composite right and to make recommendations. The current reform of the treaty bodies, aiming at establishing a single unified standing treaty body — preferably with effective participation of NGOs and other civil society bodies — may offer the opportunity to introduce such indicators, monitoring, and recommendations. For the moment, there is no reporting mechanism for states or for NGOs to assess progress made and difficulties encountered in implementing the right to development.

Numerous methodological difficulties arise at the national level to define and apply such policies and practices. Some of these relate to the practical implications of the idea that human rights should be treated as a comprehensive system and in an integrated and holistic fashion. Others relate to resource constraints and competing paradigms for development. Indeed, the incentives are greater to define and implement poverty reduction strategies (PRS), comprehensive development frameworks (CDF), and similar programs linked to development financing than to define and implement the right to development. In contrast to PRS and CDF, the right to development does not have concomitant resources. It is therefore necessary to focus on international policies, beginning with the implied obligations.

International Institutions and Global Processes

One of the premises of human rights thinking has been the expansion of the capabilities and freedoms of the poor and vulnerable. That expansion implies altering priorities in the allocation of resources. Measures taken toward that end, however, must not be at the expense of the freedoms of more fortunate persons, beyond what is strictly required to protect the rights of others and the general welfare in a democratic society.[7]

---

7   Article 29 of the Universal Declaration of Human Rights (UDHR) states, "In the exercise of his rights and freedoms, everyone shall be subject only to such limitations as are determined by law solely for the purpose of securing due recognition and respect for the rights and freedoms of others and of meeting the just requirements of morality, public order and the general welfare in a democratic society."

This perspective facilitates the understanding of the interrelation among the rights contained in the Universal Declaration of Human Rights. Traditional freedoms defined as civil and political rights range from the most basic integrity rights (everyone's right to life and to be free from slavery, forced labor, and arbitrary deprivation of liberty) to the freedoms of autonomy of action (freedom of movement and residence, freedom of expression and information, freedom to practice one's own religion and belief, freedom of assembly and association, freedom to participate in the cultural life of the community, and freedom of scientific work and creative activity.) The individual's capability of making use of these freedoms of action depends on the degree to which other rights are ensured — primarily economic, social, and cultural rights. Among these that are particularly instrumental to freedoms of action are the right to education,[8] the right to an adequate standard of living, including food, health and housing,[9] the right to work,[10] and the right to social security,[11] including effective, functioning, and affordable social insurance.

Fulfillment of economic, social, and cultural rights, in general, is required for the free and meaningful exercise of civil and political rights, and vice-versa. The interrelationship among these rights is illustrated by the fact that the right to education is essential for freedom of expression and information, for scientific and creative work, and for participation in the cultural life in society, while the right to food is essential for the enjoyment of the right to education, the right to health, or the right to life. Similarly, the realization of the right to health depends on the freedom of information, as we have seen for years in the spread of HIV-AIDS and, more recently, of SARS.

These rights are both cross-sectionally and sequentially inter-related: The level of realization of a right depends on the levels of realization of other rights, and the level of realization of a right today influences the level of its realization tomorrow. The process of development captures this interdependence over time and across the sectors when all the rights are to be realized together. At any given time, the extent of the realization of the rights to be claimed is clearly defined. Such claims for the realization of those rights, however, have to be consistent with one another and with their realization over time.

Despite these complex interrelationships, the ideological divisions of the Cold War partially explain the artificial — and certainly unhelpful — wedge that was driven between the two major categories of rights. Contrasting this historical experience, the right to development requires the integration of civil, cultural, economic, political, and social rights through rights-based development, eliminating any need or justification for the traditional dichotomy of rights.

State obligations concerning human rights should reflect this interrelationship among rights and guide the process of their operationalizing. Interpreting state

---

8   UDHR, Article 26, and the International Covenant on Economic, Social and Cultural Rights (ICESCR), Article 13.
9   UDHR, Article 25, and ICESCR, Articles 11 and 12.
10   UDHR, Article 23, and ICESCR, Article 6.
11   UDHR, Article 22, and ICESCR, Article 9.

obligations is complicated by the fact that human rights are often spelled out in very broad terms, and their corresponding duties are not always clear. Many general rights, in fact, consist of a bundle of rights, which need to be unbundled before the specific obligations can be defined. The right to development is a highly composite right, and its components, therefore, need considerable specification in order to determine the content of the correlative obligations. The notion of "imperfect" obligations can to some extent refer to composite rights that have not yet been sufficiently unbundled.

Once unbundled, the components of the right to development include all human rights and key economic and social processes but attach particular importance to the rights to food, health, work, and education. Consequently, the right to development is vulnerable to the same misconceptions that attend these rights regarding progressive realization and the role of resources, as defined by Article 2 of the International Covenant on Economic, Social and Cultural Rights (ICESCR), which requires states to take steps to the maximum of the their available resources to "achieve progressively" the full realization of the economic, social, and cultural rights in that Covenant.

The words "achieve progressively" have often been misinterpreted to imply a weak or nonexistent obligation by states. In the interpretation of the Committee on Economic, Social and Cultural Rights, however, full realization of all economic, social, and cultural rights will generally not be achieved in a short period of time. Thus, the concept of progressive realization must be seen in light of the overall objective of the Covenant, which is to establish clear obligations for states parties to move as expeditiously as possible to realize these rights.[12] Other widespread misunderstandings are that economic, social, and cultural rights must be provided by the state, that they are costly and lead to an overgrown state apparatus, and that they must be fully justiciable to have the status of rights. This view results from a very narrow understanding of the nature of these rights and of the corresponding state obligations. In fact, state obligations to respect, protect, and fulfill economic, social, and cultural rights do not always require significant resources or an immediate judicial remedy. State obligations must be seen in the context of the individual as the active subject of all economic and social development, as stated in Article 2 of the Declaration on the Right to Development. Individuals are expected, whenever possible through their own efforts and resources, to find ways to ensure the satisfaction of their own needs, individually or with others. States must, at the primary level, respect the resources owned by individuals, their freedom to find a job of preference, and their freedom to take the necessary actions and use the necessary resources — alone or with others — to satisfy their own needs. For example, the obligation to respect these resources requires official measures to recognize and register the land rights of indigenous peoples and land tenure of small-holders whose title is uncertain.

---

12   General Comment No. 3 (1990) on the nature of state obligations under Article 2(1).

At a secondary level, the state has obligations to protect the freedom of action and the use of resources against threats of predatory actors, such as powerful economic interests. This obligation also entails protection against fraud, against unethical behavior in trade and contractual relations, and against the marketing and dumping of toxic or hazardous products. This protective function of the state is the most important aspect of state obligations with regard to economic, social, and cultural rights, and it is similar to the role of the state as protector of civil and political rights. To the extent that legislation institutionalizes the obligation to protect and provides for judicial remedies, the justiciability of economic and social rights is no longer subject to question.

At the tertiary level, the state has the obligations to assist and to fulfill economic, social, and cultural rights. This duty includes the obligation to assist, for example, by taking measures "to improve methods of production and distribution of food by making full use of technical and scientific knowledge, by disseminating knowledge of the principles of nutrition and by developing or reforming agrarian systems," as required by Article 11(2), of the ICESCR. The obligation to fulfill also involves the direct provision of basic goods, such as food or the means to obtain it, for instance, during periods of high unemployment, crisis, or disaster. The obligation to provide also refers to direct assistance for people who are marginalized by factors such as structural transformations in the economy.

In light of all these elements of state obligation, it is a gross oversimplification that economic and social rights differ from civil and political rights, in that the former require the use of resources by the state, while the latter do not. The argument is tenable only when the focus on economic and social rights lies on the tertiary level (the obligation to fulfill), while civil and political rights are observed on the primary level (the obligation to respect). This scenario is, however, arbitrary. Some civil rights require state obligations at all levels, including the obligation to provide direct assistance.[13] Economic and social rights, on the other hand, can in many cases best be safeguarded through non-interference by the state, with the freedom and use of resources of individuals.

The Right to Development — Process and Outcome

The distinction between the right to a process of development and the right to certain outcomes of development, both of which form part of the right to development, corresponds to the distinction between obligations of conduct and obligations of result, well known in international law.[14] In fact, most human rights must be met

---

13   General Comment No. 6 on the right to life, adopted by the Human Rights Committee (UN Doc. A/37/40), refers, *inter alia,* to widespread and serious malnutrition leading to extensive child mortality, as a non-fulfilment of the right to life. Remedies to counteract child malnutrition often require government organized provisions. In a field better known to lawyers, equal access to justice (which is essential for the protection of civil and political rights) requires legal aid to those in the lowest income brackets, another illustration that the state may have to be a provider in order to complete its range of obligations also in regard to civil and political rights.

14   The distinction was notably discussed by the International Law Commission. See *Report of the International Law Commission* on the work of its fifty-first session (May 3-July 23, 1999), UN Doc. A/54/10, para. 145-180.

by obligations of both conduct and result. The right to life, for example, requires not only an obligation of states not to deprive persons of their life (except for capital punishment under very strict and limited conditions in states that have not yet banned it), and an obligation to enforce prohibitions of homicide, but also an obligation to create or ensure conditions under which life is not widely endangered by endemic or epidemic illnesses or hunger.

In light of the complexity of the issue and the need for flexibility to respond to different situations, it now becomes understandable that the basic provisions of the ICESCR (especially Articles 2 and 11) were drafted more in the form of obligations of result rather than obligations of conduct. It is also understandable that these obligations, taken at their highest and most general level, cannot easily be made justiciable (enforced through judicial remedies). Nevertheless, obligations of conduct are fundamental to human rights and require further elucidation as states gain experience complying with their treaty obligations.[15]

The above analysis has several implications for the right to development. As in the case of its component economic and social rights, the right to development itself is not synonymous with increased resources, but instead relates resources to the respect and protection of the individual's ability to utilize those resources in rights-enhancing ways. Furthermore, the right to development requires that implementation of both traditional categories of rights at the national level be pursued in an integrated way.

Unfortunately, national policies rarely go beyond lip service to the right to development and almost never use this right to set priorities and allocate resources. Although ministries of foreign affairs may instruct their delegates to the Human Rights Council and the General Assembly to vote for the right to development, these foreign policy positions have little significance for national develop- ment policy and practice. Bridging this gap will take leadership at the highest level to change the priorities, incentives, and training of key officials.

At the international level, the interpretation and specification of obligations or responsibilities of states to comply with the normative content of the right to development are a matter of considerable controversy. The underlying premise of the Declaration is a dual set of responsibilities. On the one hand, the General Assembly recognized "that the creation of conditions favorable to the development of peoples and individuals is the primary responsibility of their States."[16] On the other hand, "States have the primary responsibility for the creation of national and international conditions favorable to the realization of the right to development . . . and the right and the duty to formulate appropriate national development policies . . . ."[17] The former appears to apply primarily to developing countries, which have responsibili-

---

15   The Committee on Economic, Social and Cultural Rights provides illustrations of the conduct expected from states parties in its general comments. For example, in its General Comment No. 12 on the right to food, adopted in May 1999, the Committee clarified states' obligations, violations, and national and international implementation of this right. The specific obligations were further spelled out in the *Voluntary Guidelines to Support the Progressive Realization of the Right to Adequate Food in the Context of National Food Security.* See IGWG RTFG, Final Report, Annex I, September 23, 2004.
16   Declaration on the Right to Development, Preamble.
17   *Id.*, Article 3.

ties to elaborate and implement development policies in accordance with the principles of the Declaration on the Right to Development, while that latter appeals mainly to developed countries, which should reduce resource constraints in order to create the required "international conditions favorable" to this right, and have "the duty to take steps, individually and collectively, to formulate international development policies with a view to facilitating the full realization of the right to development."[18] To be even more explicit, notwithstanding the language of diplomatic compromise with which the Declaration is replete, "effective international cooperation," (that is, support from donor countries) is described as "a complement to the efforts of developing countries" and as "essential in providing these countries with appropriate means and facilities to foster their comprehensive development."[19] Thus, the Declaration presupposes that donor countries will facilitate the efforts of developing countries to advance the right to development by relaxing resource constraints, including in areas such as trade, debt, technology, and finance, when such action would facilitate their development.

International Mechanisms: Toward an Operational Model

The idea of reciprocal responsibilities is essentially what the Independent Expert proposed in the "Right to Development-Development Compact" (RTD-DC) approach, building on the idea of "a compact for human development."[20] The Independent Expert defined a development compact as "a mechanism for ensuring that all stakeholders recognize the 'mutuality of obligations', so that the obligations of developing countries to carry out rights-based programmes are matched by the reciprocal obligations of the international community to cooperate to enable the implementation of the programmes."[21] There is little in the way of state practice that follows this model, although the development policies of several major donor countries show a willingness to be forthcoming with resources for countries that adopt a human rights-based approach to development, if not an explicit right to development approach. This is true for countries like Denmark, the Netherlands, Norway, Sweden, the United Kingdom, and Canada. The same could be said for the Millennium Challenge Account (MCA), originally proposed by President Bush at the Monterrey Conference on Financing Development in March 2002, when he said, "Developed nations have a duty not only to share our wealth, but also to encourage sources that produce wealth: economic freedom, political liberty, the rule of law and human rights."[22] The Conference adopted a consensus document enumerating among the elements for sustainable development, "respect for human rights, including the right to development, and the rule of law, gender equality, market-oriented policies, and an overall commitment to just and democratic societies."[23]

---

18   *Id.*, Article 4.
19   *Id.*
20   The concept was originally proposed by UNDP in the *Human Development Report 1994* (p. 77).
21   Arjun Sengupta, *Frameworks for development cooperation and the right to development,* Fifth report of the independent expert on the right to development, E/CN.4/2002/WG.18/6, September 18, 2002, para. 14 (c).
22   Remarks by US President George W. Bush, Monterrey, Mexico, March 22, 2002.
23   Monterrey Consensus of the International Conference on Financing for Development, Annex, para. 11

The MCA turned out to be more focused on economic growth and promotion of markets than on the integration of human rights into development, as explained by Marks in his chapter.

Should such state practice develop over time with enough consistency and with evidence that it is based on an understanding that there is an obligation to do so, it might be possible to talk of the emergence of a customary rule of international law to cooperate in the realization of the right to development. To be consistent with this right, such a new customary norm would link relaxation of resource constraints by developed nations to developing country policies that comply with the six principles of the right to development (an integral approach to human rights, equity, non-discrimination, participation, accountability, and transparency). The reality is that, today, no state implements such policies based on the belief that there is a legal obligation to do so.

It is indeed this latter point regarding practice that requires closer scrutiny. Most contributors to this volume argue that the recognition of the right to development as an inalienable human right confers at least a moral — and, several claim, legal — duty on states and other agencies of society, including individuals, to implement that right in their international relations.

Assuming that countries do formulate and implement a set of appropriate policies based on the right to development, what specifically should other states do to enable such policies to succeed? Several answers to this question are suggested in the chapters of Part V on international institutions and global processes.

Asbjørn Eide focuses, in his chapter, "Human Rights-Based Development in the Age of Economic Globalization," on responsibilities of states for the realization of human rights in an era of prevailing neo-liberalism, the debt crisis, the Washington consensus, and the power of the international trade regime, all of which challenge the values and content of rights-based development. Based on the responsibility for rights-based development — which the Declaration on the Right to Development reaffirms — he formulates ten propositions to underpin a strategy for such development.

In the chapter by Siddiq Osmani, the claims on international and national policy are extended to the broader issues of a rights-based approach to development in the context of globalization. After analyzing some of the constraints (especially regarding labor, fiscal policy, and the structure of production and employment) and opportunities (primarily relating to growth) posed by globalization, he examines what a rights-based development policy should include. He argues that the formulation of such a policy should be participatory and that the goals should be based on international human rights law, recognizing the indivisibility and non-retrogression of rights whenever trade-offs are necessary, and the need for effective monitoring and evaluation.

In his chapter on "Advocating the Right to Development Through Complaint Procedures Under Human Rights Treaties," Martin Scheinin demonstrates that several universal and regional courts and treaty bodies have decided cases that at least implicitly hold states accountable for the right to development. The paths to pro-right to development outcomes are various — including claims based on privacy, property, and minority rights — but the interdependence of human rights results in the vindication of development-related claims through these complaint procedures.

Addressing the role of international financial institutions (IFIs), Sigrun Skogly focuses on one of the most critical features of the international dimensions of human rights-based approaches to development. She identifies "a strong convergence between a rights-based approach to development and the right to development," both requiring the fulfillment of human rights in the process of development. This process implies the full commitment of IFIs to allocate financial support, leverage other resources, and set trends in international finance and development thinking. To accomplish this, IFIs should be guided by the human rights treaty obligations of their members, both debtor and creditor states. She argues further that human rights enhance the efficiency and effectiveness of efforts of IFIs to advance human development.

Multilateral lending offers opportunities to promote the right to development and bilateral international cooperation opens up new possibilities for realizing the right to development. These possibilities radically transform international economic relations, especially between developed and developing countries, based on equity and partnership. One of the principal motivations of the human rights movement leading up to the formulation of the right to development was establishing equity and empowerment in international economic transactions between developed and developing countries. Much of the logic of the North-South conflict that was behind the demand for a New International Economic Order in the 1970s has now lost its relevance and, in particular, its tendency to overemphasize international relations at the expense of institutional and political conditions and requirements at the national level. It can be argued, however, that the rationale for equitable treatment and participation in decision-making and access to the benefits of development at the national as well as the international levels remains as strong today as it was then. Within this perspective, it may be further argued that the human right to development provides scope for a cooperative relationship between developed and developing countries based on partnership rather than on the confrontation of earlier years. A main challenge is to develop mechanisms and institutional frameworks that can facilitate such development.

The right to development is premised on the integration of civil and political rights with economic, social, and cultural rights. Thus, freedom of information and association, democratic decision-making, participation, and nondiscrimination are essential to realizing economic, cultural, and social rights. Similarly, health, education, and other rights in this category provide the social conditions under which civil and political rights can flourish. More important, as a result of this interdependence and reciprocity, monitoring mechanisms for the right to development will have to be different from those used for traditional categories. The United

Nations treaty bodies monitor each of the rights contained in the respective instruments. Monitoring the right to development should focus on the realization of all the specific rights as well as on policies that deal with these rights in a composite manner. It also has to address the extent to which the process of development promotes economic growth with equity.

Such a monitoring mechanism can in principle be established even without a convention — for example, if the committees under the two Human Rights Covenants took up the examination of each of the rights in light of their inter-linkages. In fact, the committees have on occasion referred to how the enjoyment of some rights facilitates or detracts from the enjoyment of others. To expand their monitoring to the right to development, they would need to examine more than the interrelatedness of rights and introduce elements of national development policy and criteria of equity, both within and between states.

Each of the authors in this volume grappled with the elusive concept of the right to development and provided either a much needed clarification of the content and significance of this right or practical guidance on how the right to development can become a tool for the advancement of human rights in national and international development policies and processes. Their role was to elucidate the issues rather than to reach common conclusions. After reflecting on their valuable contributions and on the deliberations of the Nobel Symposium, we have ventured some conclusions of our own, which we offer in the final chapter. The right to development will remain part of international human rights discourse for some time to come; we hope these reflections will help breathe new life into the concept and move it closer to its avowed goal of the betterment of the human condition.

Part I. Conceptual Underpinnings

1 | Human Rights and Development [1]
Amartya Sen

Human rights is an intensely evocative idea. There is something deeply attractive in the presumption that every person anywhere in the world, irrespective of citizenship and residence, has some basic rights to which others must pay serious attention. The concept can also be intellectually powerful if it is used with adequate discernment and critical assessment. To give the idea its due, we have to examine what is entailed by the recognition of some claim as a human right. What difference can such a recognition make? And what makes human rights a viable and useful concept?

Doubts: General and Specific

These issues, among others, must be addressed for understanding and scrutinizing the cogency and relevance of a "human rights based approach to development." It is necessary to split the exercise into two parts, dealing with the cogency and viability, respectively, 1) of the idea of human rights in general and 2) of the concept of the human right to development in particular.

Serious doubts have been raised both about the general framework of human rights and its specific application in terms of the right to development. Human rights activists are often impatient with such conceptual questioning, given the tremendous urgency to respond to terrible deprivations around the world. This proactive stance has its rewards, and it has helped to contribute to the defense and safeguarding of human freedom and security — at the global as well as national levels. And yet the conceptual questions must also be adequately addressed if the idea of human rights is to command reasoned loyalty on an enduring basis. As the world moves uncertainly from one crisis to the next, in one theater of action to another, it is critically important to try to match the stirring appeal of human rights by reasoned justification and defense.

Consider the general framework first. Despite the tremendous appeal of the broad idea of human rights, it is also seen by many as intellectually frail and lacking a solid foundation of the kind that legally enforceable rights have. If a putative claim is not legalized, then (so the argument runs) where is its bite? How can it be a "real" right? More than two centuries ago, Jeremy Bentham articulated this basic skepticism — indeed, dismissal — in his "Anarchical Fallacies," written in 1792, in denunciation of the French Declaration of the "rights of man": "Right, the

1   Presented at the Nobel Symposium on the Right to Development and Human Rights in Development, Oslo, October 13-15, 2003. This essay draws on my Gilbert Murray Lecture ("Why Invent Human Rights?") given in Oxford on November 14, 2002, commemorating the founding of OXFAM 60 years earlier.

substantive right, is the child of law; from real laws come real rights; but from imaginary laws, from 'law of nature' . . . come imaginary rights."[2]

On this reasoning, a proposed right has to be legalized for it to be a real right.

However, if a right is in fact legalized, then even though that right would have legal validity, that viability would be entirely confined to the domain of the relevant legislation (such as nation states). No matter what we call such legally validated rights ("human rights," or whatever, it does not make any difference), they are, then, just legally instituted rights, dependent on national legislation or international conventions, rather than on the basic "humanity" (or "human-ness") of the persons involved. Thus, on this reasoning, the concept of human rights is either an empty noise (Bentham called it "bawling upon paper") if the right is not legislated, or an altogether redundant demand, if it is already legislated. Various versions of this kind of dismissal of the concept of human rights have been aired over the past two-and-a-quarter centuries, starting from Jeremy Bentham, who found the idea of "rights of man" to be "simple nonsense" (and argued, further, that the notion of natural and imprescriptible rights" was just "rhetorical nonsense, nonsense upon stilts").[3]

In addition to this type of general skepticism, more specific doubts have been aired about the notion of the right to development in particular. In addition to general questions about how precisely the right to development should be formulated, we have to distinguish between two specific kinds of doubts, related respectively to issues of justiciability and feasibility. First, it is argued that the right to development can hardly be made into a "justiciable" right. Even though a government can be castigated for failing to do what is needed, say, eliminating hunger, there are difficulties in pressing this in a court of law with penalties for non-fulfilling governments. And if a right is not justiciable, then what is the point, so the argument runs, to see something as a right, rather than simply as a desirable goal.

Second, some political and legal theorists have taken the position that no claim can be seen as a right unless it is entirely feasible. Maurice Cranston used this famously to argue against economic and social rights, suggesting that the orbit of rights be confined to the so-called "first generation rights," like liberty, freedom of speech, or non-interference in personal lives.[4] If this position were correct, then the idea of the right to development would be mistaken, since its content would have to go beyond the "first generation rights" (involving such claims as the right to receive basic schooling, to have the opportunity of basic health care, not to be hungry, and so on).

I begin by addressing first the ecumenical doubts about human rights in general, and then proceed to take up the specific doubts about the right to development, connected with the possibility of unjusticiability and infeasibility.[5]

---

2   Jeremy Bentham, "Anarchical Fallacies; Being an Examination of the Declaration of Rights Issued during the French Revolution" (1792); republished in J. Bowring (ed.), *The Works of Jeremy Bentham*, Vol. II (Edinburgh: William Tait, 1843), p. 523.
3   *Ibid.*, p. 501.
4   Maurice Cranston, "Are There Any Human Rights?" *Daedalus* (Fall 1983).
5   I had an earlier opportunity to discuss the relation between human rights and development in my address ("Development and the Foundation of Freedom") at a Symposium on Poverty and Development, arranged by the Royal Norwegian Ministry of Foreign Affairs, in Oslo, March 4, 2002.

What Are Human Rights?

What, then, are human rights, and why are they important? I would argue that human rights are best seen, foundationally, as commitments in social ethics, comparable to — but very different from — accepting utilitarian reasoning (advocated by Jeremy Bentham and others). Like other ethical tenets, human rights can, of course, be disputed, but the claim is that they will survive open and informed scrutiny.[6] The universality that these claims have is dependent on their survivability in unobstructed discussion. The validity of these rights can be questioned only by showing that they will not survive open public scrutiny, but not — contrary to a common temptation — by pointing to the fact that in many repressive regimes that prevent open public discussion in one way or another, these rights are not taken seriously.

In this sense, the viability of human rights is linked with what John Rawls has called "public reasoning."[7] But it goes beyond Rawls's inclination, particularly in his later works, to confine the domain of such public confrontation within the boundaries of particular nations or "peoples."[8] On the contrary, the discussion has to include, if only to avoid local prejudices, views also from "a certain distance," the need for which was powerfully identified by Adam Smith:

> We can never survey our own sentiments and motives, we can never form any judgment concerning them; unless we remove ourselves, as it were, from our own natural station, and endeavour to view them as at a certain distance from us. But we can do this in no other way than by endeavouring to view them with the eyes of other people, or as other people are likely to view them.[9]

This view of human rights in terms of social ethics and public reasoning contrasts with seeing human rights in primarily legal terms, either as consequences of humane legislation, or as precursors of legal rights. Human rights may well be reflected in legislation, and may also inspire legislation, but this is a further fact, rather than a defining characteristic of human rights themselves.

Consequent Legislation and the World Beyond

It is, of course, true that many acts of legislation and legal conventions (such as the "European Convention for the Protection of Human Rights and Fundamental Freedoms") have clearly been inspired by a belief in some pre-existing rights of all human beings. In his classic 1955 essay "Are There Any Natural Rights?" Herbert Hart has argued that people "speak of their moral rights mainly when advocating their incorporation in a legal system."[10] This is certainly one way in which human

---

6   I have examined the ethical interpretation of human rights in "Consequential Evaluation and Practical Reason," *The Journal of Philosophy* 97 (September 2000).
7   John Rawls, *A Theory of Justice* (Cambridge, MA: Harvard University Press, 1971), and *Political Liberalism* (New York: Columbia University Press, 1993).
8   Especially in John Rawls, *The Law of Peoples* (Cambridge, MA: Harvard University Press, 1999).
9   Adam Smith, *The Theory of Moral Sentiments* (1759; revised edition, 1790; republished, Oxford: Clarendon Press, 1976), III, 1, 2, p. 110. The Smithian perspective on moral reasoning is pursued in my paper "Open and Closed Impartiality," *The Journal of Philosophy* 99 (September 2002).
10   Herbert L. A. Hart, "Are There Any Natural Rights?" *The Philosophical Review* 64 (April 1955), reprinted in Jeremy Waldron (ed.), *Theories of Rights* (Oxford: Oxford University Press, 1984), p. 79.

rights have been invoked, and Hart's qualified defense of the idea and usefulness of human rights in this context has been justly influential.

Two points are particularly worth noting here. First, to the extent that Hart is right, human rights are the "parents" of law, rather than only "the child of law," as Bentham had argued. Social ethics can generate legislation, rather than being generated by it. Second, while inspiring legislation is one of the uses of the social ethics of human rights, it is not its only use. The idea of human rights can be — and actually is — used in several other ways as well. In this sense, Hart's interpretation of natural human rights is too limited. Indeed, if human rights are seen as powerful moral claims, as Hart himself suggests by seeing them as "moral rights," then surely we have reason for some catholicity in considering different avenues for promoting these claims. The ways and means of advancing the ethics of human rights need not, thus, be confined only to making new laws (even though sometimes that may indeed happen to be the right focus for action). For example, the monitoring and advocacy activities undertaken by such organizations as Amnesty International, or Human Rights Watch, or OXFAM, or Médecins Sans Frontières, or Save the Children, or Action Aid, to name just a few, can themselves help to advance the effective reach of the social ethics of human rights. In many contexts, legislation is not at all involved.

Indeed, sometimes legislation would be quite the wrong thing to invoke in support of human rights. For example, the entitlement of a wife to be consulted on family decisions is an important right to assert and agitate for in male-dominated societies, and yet it may well be a mistake to make the right of such consultation a legal requirement (perhaps taking the husband to prison if he refuses to consult his wife). The social change has to be sought in other ways, not primarily through punitive legislation, but through feminist movements, political agitation, expansion of female education and employment, and so on.

The rights that are advanced through social and political activities may or may not have any legal status in the country in question, but their promotion is not rendered useless by the absence of legal backing. Also, the agents of promotion may or may not have any special legal status, and yet they can make a difference to political, social, and administrative practice. For example, unlike the Indian and South African Human Rights Commissions, which are recognized in the respective national laws, the Pakistan Human Rights Commission is basically just a nongovernmental organization (NGO), and yet it has, under the visionary and courageous leadership of Asma Jahangir, I. A. Renman, and others, been remarkably effective in identifying and resisting violations of human rights and defending vulnerable persons, including religious minorities and ill-treated women.[11]

The effectiveness of human rights depends not only on specific legislations, but also on social behavior patterns. Indeed, even such pioneering figures as Tom Paine

---

11　A fine discussion of the reach of their monitoring activities can be found in *The State of Human Rights, 2001* (Lahore: Human Rights Commission of Pakistan, 2002). The remarkable work of Shirin Ebadi in Iran, to whom the 2003 Nobel Peace Prize was awarded, may also fall in the same important category.

and Mary Wollstonecraft, who can be rightly seen as being among the founders of the approach of human rights, were intensely concerned with social practice and behavioral priorities. Paine's *The Rights of Man* and Wollstonecraft's *The Vindication of the Rights of Women,* both published in 1792 (just when Bentham was engaged in denouncing the "rights of man" in "Anarchical Fallacies"), were aimed at social change and considered a variety of means of changing the world, of which legislation was only one.

Development, Justiciability, and Feasibility

I turn now to the specific case of the right to development, and in particular to the objections arising from its possible unjusticiability and infeasibility. From the preceding discussion, it should follow that justiciability is only one of the ways of making a human right effective. Indeed, coercive legislation may not often be the most effective way of advancing the right to development. That right can be seen as a conglomeration of a collection of claims, varying from basic education, health care, and nutrition to political liberties, religious freedoms, and civil rights for all.

Some of these claims are indeed appropriate subjects for coercive legalization, and it is entirely right to seek legislation that would prohibit torture or arbitrary arrest, discrimination against women, or suppression of free speech. The route of law and justiciability would be appropriate in many such cases. But even here, social and political activism is bound to have an important role, both in generating social pressure for undertaking such legislation and in providing monitoring and scrutiny to ensure the effectiveness of the laws that are enacted. But on top of that, even when no such law exists, there is room for social and political action through naming and shaming, and other ways of bringing public pressure on violators of human rights. And this would, of course, be particularly the case with economic and social rights. These are often appropriate fields for political and social advocacy and agitation, and the recognition of human rights can make a very positive contribution to these activities as well.

I turn now to the objection of infeasibility. This criticism is based on the presumption — often implicit — that recognized human rights must be fully feasible, in the sense of being accomplishable for all. This presumption immediately puts many so-called social and economic rights, which can be very central to the right to development, outside the domain of possible human rights, since it may not indeed be feasible right now to guarantee them for all, especially in the poorer societies.

Maurice Cranston, who defends the first-generation human rights (for example, against torture or arbitrary incarceration), firmly draws the line against the inclusion of economic and social rights.

> The traditional political and civil rights are not difficult to institute. For the most part, they require governments, and other people generally, to leave a man alone . . . The problems posed by claims to economic and social rights, however, are of another order altogether.

> How can governments of those parts of Asia, Africa, and South America, where industrialization has hardly begun, be reasonably called upon to provide social security and holidays with pay for millions of people who inhabit those places and multiply so swiftly?[12]

It is certainly true that many economic and social rights that may figure prominently in the broad basket of the right to development may not be immediately feasible for everyone right now.

In assessing this line of reproach, we have to ask: why should complete feasibility be a condition of cogency of human rights when the objective is to work toward expanding both their feasibility and their actual realization? The understanding that some rights are not fully realized, and may not even be fully realizable under present circumstances, does not, in itself, entail anything like the conclusion that these are, therefore, not rights at all. Indeed, the promotion of human rights proceeds on the understanding that there is much to be promoted, including the expansion of feasibility of the recognized rights. That can, in fact, be an important part of the motivation for focusing on the right to development.[13]

It is important to note, in this context, that the question of feasibility is not confined to economic and social rights only; it is a much more widespread problem. Even for liberties and autonomies, to guarantee that a person is "left alone" has never been — contrary to what Cranston claims — particularly easy. That elementary fact cannot but be more clearly recognized now, at least since September 11, 2001, than it used to be. If the feasibility of guaranteeing complete and comprehensive fulfillment were made into a necessary condition for the cogency of any right, then not only economic and social rights but also liberties, autonomies, and even political rights may fall far short of cogency.

Conclusion

This discussion has been mainly dialectical. Even though I began with a constructive view of human rights as commitments in social ethics defended by public reasoning, most of the arguments have been aimed at disputing various critiques, in particular the legalist dismissal of human rights, in general, and more specific condemnations — particularly applicable to the right to development — based on the insistence on justiciability and full feasibility. To conclude, I return to the constructive program.

Just as freedom is a social value, so, it can be argued, is the importance of solidarity among human beings in understanding the need to support each other's freedoms, and the need to consider what one can reasonably do. Indeed, a refusal to do anything at all to help prevent the violation of human rights can be seen as both a functional neglect and an intrinsic moral failure. However, the duty of any third person in support of human rights cannot but be somewhat inexactly perceived,

---

12   Cranston, *supra,* note 4, p.13.
13   On this, see Arjun Sengupta, Asbjørn Eide, Stephen Marks, and Bård Anders Andreassen, "The Right to Development and Human Rights in Development," presented at the Nobel Symposium, October 2003.

since much will depend on what others are doing and what can be effective and how. For the sake of comparison, it can be mentioned that there can, in fact, be a similar ambiguity even in the application of actual laws, when the duty to help others exists within a legal system. A good example is the "criminal liability of omissions," as it exists in French law, related to a failure to provide reasonable assistance that one person is expected — indeed, required — to provide to another. There are, not surprisingly, deep ambiguities on the scope and coverage of this legal liability, as the literature on its experience has brought out.[14]

Ambiguity of obligation, however, whether in law or in ethics, does not indicate that there are no obligations at all and that one simply need not bother. Indeed, such loosely formulated obligations belong to the important category of duties that Immanuel Kant called "imperfect obligations," to which he attached great importance.[15] They can co-exist with other — more fully formulated — "perfect obligations."

Let me illustrate. Consider a real-life case that occurred in Queens in New York not long ago: a woman, Kitty Genovese, was fatally assaulted in full view of others watching the event from their apartments, but her cry for help was completely ignored by the non-acting observers. It is plausible to argue that three terrible things happened here: 1) the woman's freedom — and right — not to be assaulted was violated; 2) the assaulter violated the immunity that anyone should have against assault (a violation of a "perfect obligation"); and 3) the others who did nothing whatsoever to help the victim also transgressed their general — and "imperfect" — obligation to help (which they could reasonably be expected to provide). These failings are interrelated and bring out a complex pattern of rights-duties correspondence in a structured ethics, which can be seen as supporting the evaluative framework of human rights.

The concept of rights not only focuses on particular freedoms; it also demands some corresponding obligations. This applies to the basket of claims that can sensibly fit under the broad umbrella of the right to development. In some cases, the obligations may be perfectly specified — for example, the duty of the state to refrain from torture, or even to provide opportunities for elementary education on basic medical care to all. But in many cases, the obligations are imperfect. There may well be differences of views about the extent to which, say, citizens of one country may rightly feel the duty to help remove deprivation in another — possibly far away — country. What is obligatory, I would argue, is not any specific externally given level of assistance, but the need to consider these issues through open public discussion. What is demanded is nothing like an automatic agreement on some pre-determined formula, but a commitment to participate in a process, which includes an exercise of social ethics, within each country and across borders.

---

14 Andrew Ashworth and Eva Steiner, "Criminal Omissions and Public Duties: The French Experience," *Legal Studies* 10 (1990); Glanville Williams, "Criminal Omissions: The Conventional View," *Law Quarterly Review* 107 (1991).
15 Immanuel Kant, *Critique of Practical Reason* (1788; translated by L. W. Beck, New York: Bobbs-Merrill, 1956).

The reasoned basis of human rights lies in the importance of human freedom and the need for solidarity. That far-reaching recognition demands engagement — both at the local and at the global level. The right to development has to be seen in the context of this much larger challenge.

2 | The Human Right to Development
Arjun Sengupta

Introduction

The Declaration on the Right to Development, adopted by the United Nations in 1986, introduced a totally new perspective to the discourse on development by recognizing the right to development.[1] The realization of that right by all individuals in developing countries, like the realization of any other human right, became a standard of achievement and a policy-priority of all nations. The world community debated the ideas behind that right quite extensively for several decades prior to reaching an agreement. Conceptual differences were mixed up with political positions of the different countries, reflecting the tensions of the Cold War period. Some rights were identified with the position of the so-called First World, others with the socialist Second World, and the right to development, rather tenuously, with Third World developing countries. Finally, towards the end of the Cold War, these rights were synthesized in the Declaration on the Right to Development of 1986 — an agreement between nations with all the compromises and ambiguities of the language of a negotiated document.

The Declaration was adopted by a very large majority, with only one dissenting vote (that of the United States) and eight abstentions. Still, for quite some time, questions were raised about the international recognition of such a human right to development.

However, by 1993, there was consensus among the nations affirming the right to development as a human right when even the United States officially supported it at the Vienna Second UN World Conference on Human Rights. This was further reiterated at almost every international and intergovernmental conference since then.[2] As a result of this broad-based support, the right to development can now be said to enjoy a general international recognition.[3]

The author is grateful for comments and criticisms of this chapter to Amartya Sen, Stephen Marks, Asbjørn Eide, Thomas Pogge, Bård Anders Andreassen, Siddiq Osmani, Manimay Sengupta, Margot E. Salomon, and Rajeev Malhotra. Parts of this chapter were published in the *Oxford Development Studies*, Vol. 32, No. 2, June 2004.

1   The Declaration on the Right to Development, adopted Dec. 4, 1986, GA Res. 41/128 UN GAOR, 41th Sess., at 3, Annex, UN Doc.A/Res/41/128 Annex (1987) [hereinafter Declaration (1986)].
2   1994 International Conference on Population and Development; the 1995 World Summit for Social Development; the 1995 Fourth World Conference on Women; the 1996 World Food Summit; the 1996 Second UN Conference on Human Settlements; the 2001 World Conference against Racism, Racial Discrimination, Xenophobia and Related intolerance; the 2000 Millennium Summit; and 2002 World Social Summit.
3   Recognizing the right to development as a human right by a declaration or resolution, expressing the consensus of the international community on the meaning of that right contributed to the norm-creating process, which may eventually generate legally binding obligations related to that right. The reaffirmation

note continues on following page

However, there were still major differences in the interpretation of the Declaration on the exact content of the right to development. Several working groups of experts have been involved in interpreting and analyzing the instruments. The most recent of these initiatives is a series of my reports as the Independent Expert on the Right to Development to the Human Rights Commission.[4] These reports provide, on the basis of the different articles of the Declaration, a definition of the right to development, its content and method of implementation, and the obligations of the different agents responsible for implementing this right, along with illustrations of its application.

The purpose of this chapter is to analyze the content of the right to development in terms that can be operationalized and discuss what the right to development is, how it could be implemented, and what the advantages are of implementing it in line with human rights laws. This chapter argues that looking at the process of development in terms of the right to development adds significant value to the development discourse as practiced today. The recommended method of implementing this right is discussed in the chapter as a more effective way of realizing economic development. Further, approaching it as a part of the system of international law improves the prospects of implementing the programs of development.

The first section of this chapter focuses on the definition of the right to development by summarizing the content of the right to development as elaborated in reports during my tenure as the UN Independent Expert on the Right to Development. This sets the basis for the subsequent sections about the international law of human rights, the nature of human rights, and their obligations and implications for implementing the right to development.

---

note continued from preceding page
of the principles behind the right in many subsequent international pronouncements must be accompanied by consistent state practice in order for the norm to gain the status of customary international law. So even if the Declaration on the Right to Development cannot be described as binding on all states because it is not yet a part of an international convention or established customary law, one could claim that there is a presumption that the principles embodied in this declaration law. See Arjun Sengupta, "On the Theory and Practice of the Right to Development", *Human Rights Quarterly*, Vol. 24, No. 4 (November 2002); and B. Sloan, "General Assembly Resolutions Revisited Forty Years Later," *British Yearbook of International Law* (1987). In the case of the right to development, as is discussed later, its legal force is strengthened by the fact that the obligations relating to its constituent rights have already been recognized by international treaties, such as the International Covenants on Civil and Political Rights and on Economic, Social and Cultural Rights.
4   Reports from the Independent Expert (1999-2001): First Report: E/CN.4/1999/WG.18/2, July 27, 1999; Second Report: A/55/306, August 17, 2000; Third Report: E/CN.4/2001/WG.18/2, January 2, 2001; Fourth Report: E/CN.4/2002/WG.18/2, December 20, 2001; Fourth report of the independent expert on the right to development — Mission, E/CN.4/2002/WG.18/2/Add.1, March 5, 2002 ; Fifth report: E/CN.4/2002/WG.18/6, Sept. 16, 2002 and E/CN.4/2002/WG.18/6/Add.1, December 30, 2002; Preliminary study of the independent expert on the right to development on the impact of international economic and financial issues on the enjoyment of human rights, E/CN.4/2003/WG.18/2, January 27, 2003; Review of progress and obstacles in the promotion, implementation, operationalization, and enjoyment of the right to development, E/CN.4/2004/WG.18/2, February 17, 2004. Available at http://www.unhchr.ch/html/menu2/7/b/mdev.htm. Reports of the Working Group (1993-1998): Report on its 1st session, UN Doc. E/CN.4/1994/21; Report on its 2nd session, UN Doc. E/CN.4/1995/11; Report on its 3rd session, UN Doc. E/CN.4/1995/27; Report on its 4th session, UN Doc. E/CN.4/1996/10; Report on its 5th session UN Doc. E/CN.4/1996/24. All these reports, together with some critical and explanatory comments on these reports, were reproduced in *The Right to Development: Reflections on the First Four Reports of the Independent Expert on the Right to Development* (Geneva, Switzerland: Franciscans International, January 23, 2003).

Definition of the Right to Development

The definition of the right to development provided in the Independent Expert's reports on the basis of the Preamble and the Articles of the Declaration[5] can be presented as follows:

> The Right to Development, which is an inalienable human right, is the right to a particular process of development in which all human rights and fundamental freedoms can be fully and progressively realized. (Definition 1)

This definition contains a number of elements derived from the text of the Declaration that can be elaborated in light of the discussions on the human rights instruments in general.

Development, as articulated in the Preamble of the Declaration, is a process that is comprehensive — going beyond economics to cover social, cultural, and political fields and aiming at "constant improvement," meaning progressive and regular improvement of well-being. This differs from the conventional definitions of development in terms of a simple expansion of gross national product (GNP) or industrialization or exports-growth or capital inflows. The process of development here must be genuinely participatory, with a fair and equitable distribution of benefits that results in the progressive improvement of the well-being of all people, and not just certain economic groups.

Participation in development and equitable distribution of benefits thereof to all are two main characteristics of a process that is called rights-based, meaning that it is consistent with human rights standards. Many such characteristics have been identified in different human rights instruments as well as the Maastricht Guidelines; General Comments of the Committee on Economic, Social, and Cultural Rights; and the statements of international and human rights organizations. In my reports as the Independent Expert to the Commission on Human Rights, I summarized the characteristics of a rights-based process in terms of five principles: equity, non-discrimination, participation, accountability and transparency — all of which contribute to making the process consistent with human rights standards.

It should be noted that a *rights-based process of development* is not the same thing as *the right to development.* Any process of development, or for that matter any activity, can be rights-based, if it is carried out in a manner consistent with human rights standards. When that process of development can be and is claimed as a right, it can be the object of the right to development. There may be several different ways a country can develop. Only some of these ways may be rights-based; that is, conforming to the standards of human rights and consistent with the definition of development given in the Declaration.

---

5   Article 1 says: "The right to development is an inalienable human right by virtue of which every human person and all peoples are entitled to participate in, contribute to, and enjoy economic, social, cultural and political development, in which all human rights and fundamental freedoms can be fully realized." The Preamble says: "Development is a comprehensive economic, social, cultural and political process, which aims at the constant improvement of the well-being of the entire population and of all individuals on the basis of their actions, free and meaningful participation in development and in the fair distribution of benefits resulting there from."

It would follow from Article 1 of the Declaration that, among the different rights-based processes of development, only that process which "aims at and realizes all human rights and fundamental freedoms" qualifies to be regarded as the object of claim as the right to development.[6] The outcomes of the process are human rights, but the process itself would also be claimed as a human right.

As the Preamble defines it, development is a process of securing a "constant improvement of well-being." This definition extends the notion of well-being to the realization of human rights and fundamental freedom through a rights-based process. The evolution of the notion of well-being reflects the evolution of development thinking in the post-1945 period. From the beginning, development was identified, at least in principle, with the improvement of well-being of all people. Differences arose when such development had to be defined in operational terms so that appropriate development policies could be designed. In the initial years, development was identified with the growth of per capita real income, which was taken as the index of average well-being, representing the standard of living of the people, both in being instrumental in achieving the different objectives of living and in being an end in itself as an index of "aggregate preference satisfaction."[7] In the next stage of development thinking, when increasing real income was found not sufficient, even if necessary, to secure the fulfillment of a certain minimum requirement for improving the living conditions of the people, the well-being function was extended to include some indicators of basic needs. The corresponding development policy aimed specifically at increasing the provision of basic needs as well as per capita real income.[8] The Human Development Approach could be regarded as an extension of the "basic needs" approach by moving from the indicators of basic needs in terms of commodities to the indicators of human development in terms of achievements, such as life expectancy, infant survival, and adult literacy, supplementing the indicators of per capita real income. Sen, who had inspired the human development ap-

---

6   As the Nobel Symposium Background paper states, "If development is carried out in a manner that causes widespread unemployment, increases inequalities, impairs empowerment, encourages discrimination — all the elements that are inconsistent with human rights standards — it will make it difficult, if not impossible, to realize the different human rights. A rights-based process can be described as one that is consistent with human rights standards. Based on human rights instruments, these standards can be summarized as equity, non-discrimination, participation, accountability, and transparency. Indeed any activity in a world that respects human rights should be carried out in a rights-based manner. But that does not make it, or its outcome, a right, unless it is claimed as a right and qualifies as a right. The right to development is a claim to a rights-based process of development." Arjun Sengupta, Asbjørn Eide, Stephen Marks, and Bård Anders Andreassen, "The Right to Development and Human Rights in Development: A Background Paper" for the Nobel Symposium Organized in Oslo, October 13-15, 2003" (Oslo: Norwegian Centre for Human Rights, 2003), p. 9.

7   That is how Partha Dasgupta stated it in his *Economic Journal* article of 1990. Partha Dasgupta, "Well-Being and the Extent of Its Realization in Poor Countries," *Economic Journal*, Vol. 100, Issue 400 (1990), p. 3. Arthur Lewis, among other leading development economists, as early as 1955, talked of growth of GNP as the objective of development because it "gives man greater control over his environment and thereby increases his freedom." Arthur Lewis, *The Theory of Economic Growth* (London: Allen & Unwin, 1965), pp. 9-10, 420-421.

8   This approach was associated with the McNamara-World Bank's "minimum needs" program and the International Labour Organization's "basic needs" for development programs where policies for accelerating the growth of per capita income were supplemented and adjusted with policies for increasing the provision of basic needs and for re-distributing income and changing institutions to make it possible for the poor to satisfy these basic needs. Paul Streeten, et al, *First Things First: Meeting Basic Human Needs in the Developing Countries* (Oxford: Oxford University Press, 1981).

proach, describes these human development indicators as achievements in the space of "functionings," where commodities are converted into "doings or beings" that are valuable.

Sen's capability approach goes one step further. The capability of a person reflects "the various combinations of functionings" (doings and beings) that he or she can achieve. It reflects a person's freedom to choose between different ways of living."[9] When these freedoms are claimed and recognized as rights, the well-being of people then reflects their level of enjoyment of all these rights and development as improvement of well-being takes on the meaning of expansion of freedom and realization of rights. In a rights framework, the well-being function can then be represented by indicators of the different rights properly designed. It may also include the level of per capita real income as an indicator[10] of other development objectives not reflected in rights and standards of living in general. The indicators of real income must be suitably adjusted for consistency with rights standards, so that the improvement of the rights must complement the increase in real income. In other words, the notion of well-being extends, in a rights framework, the usual notion of availability of goods and services to a rights-based access of all individuals to some of the goods and services related to enjoying fundamental freedoms which are claimed as human rights and also a rights-based process of generating real income. The level of well-being can then be described as the level of realization of the fundamental rights and of the rights-based per capita real income or the standard of living. Development then would mean improvement in that well-being.[11]

Based on these discussions, it should now be possible to rewrite the definition of the right to development given above (Definition 1) in a form that can be suitably operationalized. It will first be necessary to construct appropriate indicators for each of the different rights, so that an increase in the value of that indicator would imply an improvement in the realization of that right. The construction of these indicators is not only difficult, but is also an exercise in approximation based on judgment and informed agreement about how best to represent the different aspects of a right. Still, such indicators need to be constructed to assess whether a program to improve the

---

9   Amartya Sen, "Development as Capability Expansion," *Journal of Development Planning* Vol. 19, pp. 41-58.

10   Depending upon our ability to design appropriate indicators to represent these variables, these well-being functions can be effectively operationalized. The best example of such an exercise is Dasgupta's study of the aggregate well-being in poor countries. (See note 7.) The ingredients of his well-being index were six, including per capita national income and life expectancy at birth, infant survival rate, and adult literacy rate, which to him represent welfare and positive rights, and two indices of political and civil rights, reflecting negatives rights. He does not adjust per capita income to make it rights-based, but it may not be difficult to do that at least partially with some indicators of equity or participation or accountability. Dasgupta has discussed the issues of aggregation, valuation, and identification of rights in much greater detail in a notable recent contribution. Partha Dasgupta, *Human Well-Being and the National Environment* (Oxford: Oxford University Press, 2001).

11   The notion of well-being indicated above focuses on freedom and rights, emphasizing the aspects of agency or the capacity of people to do what they want to do. But it also extends to the notion of welfare and happiness, or well-being grounded on utility. Per capita real income stands for average welfare, and rights stand for what Sen calls "agency freedom" as well as "well-being freedom." Amartya Sen, *Inequality Reexamined* (Oxford: Oxford University Press, 1992), pp. 56-72. They are not the same, but are often complementary, and their policy implications usually reinforce each other. Dasgupta has made extensive use of such well-being indicators to assess the distribution of well-being among many poor countries. See Dasgupta, *supra*, note 7.

realization of the rights is being successful or not, taking into account the impacts of the different policies and the mutual feedback of the interdependent rights. The basis of estimated resource costs of the incremental value of the indicators must also be considered. Suppose there are 'n' such rights, which are built on some basic freedoms that qualify to be recognized as rights, by passing what is described later in this chapter as Sen's tests of legitimacy and coherence, and which are actually recognized through due process of national and international norm-creating procedures. Then if Ri is an indicator for the level of enjoyment of the 'n'ith right, a rights-based well-being (WR) can be defined as a vector (R1, R2, …..Rn, y*), where y* stands for general standard of living, measured by per capita real income adjusted by rights-based norms.[12] Development, which can be claimed as a human right, can then be described as a vector:

$$DR = d\ (WR) = (dR1, dR2, …….dRn, g^*)$$

when dRi is the improvement of the right Ri over a period, and g* is a rights-consistent (or a rights-based) process of economic growth during that period, and DR is the process of development as progressive improvement of rights-based well-being.[13]

So an operational definition of the right to development, derived from Definition 1, given above, will then read as:

> "The right to development is the right to a process of development, consisting of a progressive and phased realization of all the recognized human rights, such as civil and political rights, and economic, social, and cultural rights (and other rights admitted in international law) as well as a process of economic growth consistent with human rights standards." (Definition 2)

It may be noted that while other elements DR are human rights, g* need not be recognized as a human right. In effect, g* would represent the improvement of all other elements of well-being not covered by the recognized rights, or in terms of Arthur Lewis' definition (see note 7), all other freedoms that cannot be claimed as human rights.

---

12   An example of such adjustment is y* = y (i - gini), where the data on gini-coefficients are available to indicate the level of inequality. There may be some double counting involved in this process because, as the determinants of some of the rights may also affect the value of y*. For instance, if Ri represents the right to food, of which the production of food is a determinant, and where an increase in its value would also increase y*. But this is not really a drawback. Between two situations of the same level of y*, if one is attended by a higher value of that Ri than another, then it should be recognized as a situation with a higher value of rights-based well-being. The rights-based standard of living y* remains the indicator of the command over resources and the other substantive elements of the rights-based well-being. The realization of the different rights complements that and enhances the value of the level of well-being.
13   More precisely, the Ris should be represented by Rijt, when there are 'n' rights, i = 1,2,…..n, for 'm' individuals, j = 1, 2, …..m, over a time period T, (t = 1,2,……T). In this presentation Rit would stand for an aggregative indicator for all the individuals, j = 1,2,…..m, as it abstracts from the problems of aggregation. (A simple assumption would be Ri is the sum of the rights i, for all individuals js. See Georges Abi-Saab, "The Legal Formulation of a Right to Development" in René-Jean Dupuy (ed.), *The Right to Development at the International Level* (The Hague: Hague Academy of International Law, 1980), pp. 159. Incremental realization of rights, over a period T, would be dRit, t=1,2,…..T). Dropping the time subscript and using dRi as the indicator of the improvement of right would mean that dRi is the average rate of increase of Ri over the period.

A variant of this definition would drop economic growth or g^*, as a constituent element of the composite right, and the right to development would be simply the right to "a process of development, consisting of a progressive and phased realization of all the recognized human rights or dR = (dR1, dR2, …….dRn)" (Definition 2a). Economic growth carried out in accordance with human rights standards has an instrumental rather than a substantive role in facilitating the fulfillment of all the rights. This can be reflected by adding to this definition the conditions $dRi = f(g^*, Pi)$, indicating that the improvement of each right depends upon a rights-based economic growth, g^*, and a program of policies specific to each right, Pi.[14]

Definition 3, more in line with Amartya Sen's approach in Development as Freedom and consistent with the wordings of the Article 1 of the Declaration as dR = (dR1, dR2, …., dF1, dF2, dFs),, where Ri's are recognized rights and Fj's are fundamental freedoms, which have not yet been recognized as rights. Development then means a process where all (recognized) human rights and fundamental freedoms are realized. For Sen, freedom in the sense of capability is the extent to which the person is able to choose a particular combination of functionings — what a person is able to do or be — and development means an expansion of capabilities. But all freedoms cannot automatically become rights. For freedom to become rights, some "threshold conditions" of importance and social influence ability have to be satisfied.[15] Further, in terms of the international law of human rights, these freedoms have to be recognized as human rights through appropriate procedures. Definition 3 captures this condition: development is a process of expansion of freedoms, some of which have been recognized as rights and others waiting to be recognized but nevertheless of sufficient importance to be counted as substantive elements of people's well-being. In Definition 2, all these freedoms, not yet recognized as rights, were expressed by the proxy of g^*, assuming a close, one-to-one relationship between them. If all these freedoms could be enumerated and represented by appropriate indicators, they could be included as constituent elements of the development vector as given in Definition 3, and the rights-based economic growth g^* could then be just instrumental, as in the condition, $dFj = F(g^*, Pfj)$ where $Fj(j=1…s)$ are freedoms, not yet recognized rights, and Pfj are programs and policies specific to freedoms j. For operational purposes, however, it may be much more convenient to use the proxy of g^* as a substantive variable as in our Definition 2, and concentrate on the policies to realize the different rights and promote rights-based economic growth.

All these definitions would fully accommodate the three characteristics of inviolability, interdependence, and indivisibility of human rights that are considered to be basic in all human rights discourse. Inviolability implies that in the course of the re-

---

14 Operationally, these two variants of the definition do not conflict with each other. It will be necessary to construct indicators of the different rights, as well as of the rights-consistent economic growth; assess the determinants of each of the rights, their interdependence, and their interrelation with economic growth; and work out a program to realize them. But the obligations corresponding to these two variants would be different and when g^* is considered only as instrumental, it is possible to concentrate on realizing the different rights, irrespective of any value of economic growth.

15   Amartya Sen, "Elements of a Theory of Human Rights," *Philosophy and Public Affairs*, Vol. 32, No. 4, (2004°, p. 319.

alization of the right to development, no individual right can be violated. That is, $DR > 0$ implies $dR_i > 0$ $i = 1, \ldots..n$, or the increments of all indicators of rights must be non-negative.[16]

Two rights are interdependent if the level of realization of one right depends on the level of realization of the other (that is, $R_i = f(R_j)$ $i = j$). Two rights are indivisible, or integrated, if the violation of one right leads to violation of the other right (i.e. $dR_i > 0$, $i = j$).

These two conditions can be expressed in terms of our definition of the right to development, as $R_i = f(R_j, g)$, $j = 1,2\ldots..n$, $i = j$ and $¥R_i > 0$, and $¥R_i > 0$, $j = i$. With these conditions, an improvement in the vector of the process of development, reckoned as the right to development, that is, $DR > 0$, or $(dR_1, dR_2\ldots\ldots dR_n, g) > 0$ implies that $g > 0$, and that there is at least one i, such that $dR_i > 0$, and all other rights $dR_j > 0$, $j = i$. Further if for any right, i, $dR_i < 0$ implying that it is violated, then $DR < 0$, or the right to development is violated. This follows from the integrity of the right to development.

Two characteristics of this right to development become apparent when it is expressed as a vector. First, the right to development is a composite right, where all the rights are realized together, recognizing their interdependence and not just their aggregation. The whole is greater than the sum of the parts, or, as Dasgupta would articulate it, the parts of the component rights are related in a non-linear way with positive feedback.[17] As G. Abi-Saab, one of the original proponents of the right to

---

16   This principle of inviolability is upheld very strongly in all human rights movements, so that any program of public action must not be allowed to violate any human right. This also rules out the possibility of a trade-off between rights, even when some drop in the realization of a right might be compensated by an adequate increase in the realization of another right. Indeed, this is supposed to be the characteristic that distinguishes a human right from all other forms of rights or claims of advantage. In the legal texts, there are special and exceptional cases where such violation can be condoned or regarded as a justifiable derogation, such as during an emergency or when one person's right can be detrimental to another person's right. But otherwise, for most cases, human rights cannot be violated. See "Maastricht Guidelines on Violations of Economic, Social and Cultural Rights," *Human Rights Quarterly*, Vol. 20 (1998), pp. 691-730. Economists are often uncomfortable with this principle because, if rights-fulfillment absorbs resources, whether they are financial, physical, or institutional resources that are of limited supply, the fulfillment of one right could quite possibly violate another right, and a tradeoff between them would frequently be necessary. However, this may not be much of a problem in the case of the right to development, which is a composite right of the process of increment of all the rights. Even with the condition that no right can be violated (that is, $dR_i < 0$) or the level of realization of any right cannot decline, it is possible to choose between the magnitudes of the increments of the different rights and work out a mechanism of trade-offs between dR_i's and dR_j's. People may have slightly more of the right to food against slightly less improvement of the right to education, depending upon the constraints on institutional and financial resources. This is also a way out of the problem faced by some developing countries, which have a poor record of performance regarding some of the rights. They could still plan for increasing the realization of the right to development, if they do not let the performances with regard to those rights get worse. If the number of people held without trial is used as an indicator of the fulfillment of civil rights, the country may still achieve some progress in the right to development as long as the realization of other rights improves and the number of people held without trial does not increase.

17   Dasgupta, *supra*, note 10, p. 14. Note that while each of the rights, R_i, can be represented by an indicator of numerical index, the right to development DR need not be represented by a scaler, as a function of the constituent rights, when what we want to know is whether DR is improving or is being violated and not how much over time or over others. For that, DR, treated as a vector of improving rights, constrained as above, would be sufficient. However, it is possible to convert the fulfillment of the individual rights into a scaler index of DR by weighting these rights or making $DR = F(g, dR_i, i = 1,2,\ldots..n)$. But that procedure may be highly controversial, even more than the attempt made by Frances Stewart to combine the basic needs indicators of food, health, education, shelter, and water into a measure of the

note continues on following page

development,[18] believed that this right could be seen from the collective perspective, "without going through the process of aggregating individual human rights." It is a composite of all the human rights implemented together in an integrated manner, as a part of a development program in the context of the growth of resources.

Secondly, the right to development can improve only when at least one right is improved and none violated. Since the component rights are all civil, political, economic, social, and cultural rights, if any one of these rights is violated, the whole right to development is violated. This implication of the integrity of the right to development as a composite right of all the recognized rights is a distinct value addition to treating the improvement of any of these rights, individually and separately. Realization of no right can be increased if measures are not taken simultaneously to protect, if not also to improve, the realization of the other rights. The right to development, thus, effectively reconciles the earlier conflict between the countries that championed only the civil and political rights, and the countries that emphasized the fulfillment of economic, social, and cultural rights, even at the expense of some of the civil and political rights. The international human rights movement seems to have come full circle to what it began with in the Universal Declaration of Human Rights of 1948, which enunciated the unity of all civil, political, economic, social, and cultural rights.[19]

The Process of Development

Another element of the definition that needs elaboration is the notion of the process of development. The right to development is a right to both the process and the outcomes of the process. Development is not a finite event but a process over time. It consists of a phased realization of the outcomes of improved enjoyment of the different rights, as well as the growth of resources or GNP and changes in technology and institutions in terms of the extended definition. The process is no less a tangible object than the different rights themselves. At any point in time, the targeted increments of realization of the rights are well-defined, maintaining their intersectoral and intertemporal consistency because the enjoyment of any one right depends on the fulfillment of any other right and the level of realization of one right today determines the realization of other rights tomorrow. The process itself has to be carried out in a rights-based manner, with all the outcomes realized with equity and accountability and through the policies and actions taken by the

---

note continued from preceding page

achievement of a "full life" through a meta-production function. Frances Stewart, *Planning to Meet Basic Needs* (Hampshire, UK: Macmillan, 1985). But even in the context of planning, there may be no need to combine the dRi's into an overall index just to judge whether national policies are conducive to the realization of the right to development or in violation of that right, and the extent to which they target the incremental improvement of at least some rights without violating any others, in accordance with the interdependence of rights and the implied growth of resources.

18   Abi-Saab, *supra*, note 13.

19   For an historical account of the development of the concept of human rights, see Johannes Morsink, *The Universal Declaration of Human Rights: Origins, Drafting and Intent* (Philadelphia: University of Pennsylvania Press, 1999).

state and other agents following the human rights standards in a participatory and non-discriminatory manner. Economic growth will also relax the constraints on and facilitate the realization of the outcomes. The right to development has, thus, both a substantive role as a composite of goals and an instrumental role characterizing the way these goals are achieved.[20]

Human rights are normally claimed both for their substantive and instrumental value. They are desirable in themselves, and they are desirable as they help realize other desirable objectives. But they qualify as human rights, not just because they are intrinsically or instrumentally desirable but because they are recognized through an appropriate norm creating process and the claims for them satisfy the tests of legitimacy and coherence, as discussed later in this chapter. The right to development, as argued, passes these two tests. Contrary to the views of some critics, a process of development, just because it can be also instrumental to realizing some of the outcome of rights, does not disqualify itself to be a right.

Economic Growth

The significance of including rights-based economic growth (or g*) as a constituent element of the right to development is not always fully appreciated. All other rights, as elements of the vector whose improvement is regarded as development, have been recognized as human rights in the various international treaties, except growth. But when these rights are to be realized together progressively over a period of time, as the right to development, it is only logical to include a process of economic growth consistent with human rights standards (that is, rights-based) as an element of the right to development vector relaxing the resource constraints and representing all other freedoms associated with development, which cannot be claimed as rights.

The realization of all these interdependent rights depends on the availability of, as well as access to, goods and services necessary for the fulfillment of each right. This is true not only of the economic, social, and cultural rights but also of civil and political rights. The former are often regarded as positive rights for which corresponding social development indicators must improve with increasing availability of relevant goods and services and appropriate public policies. Civil and political rights, on the other hand, are usually regarded as negative rights because *respecting* them may only require the duty-bearers to abstain from action without using many resources. However, *protecting* them by the duty-bearers (states) would invariably require resources (goods and services and also institutions). The availability of any one of these goods and services cannot be increased indefinitely without decreasing

---

20   This conforms to what Sen has noted in the context of decision theory and rational choice, "The importance of paying particular attention to 'comprehensive outcomes' (including actions undertaken, processes involved and the like, along with the final outcomes), instead of confining attention to only the 'culmination outcomes' (what happens at the very end)." Amartya Sen, "Consequential Evaluation and Practical Reason," *The Journal of Philosophy* (September 2000), pp. 491-492. It also means that the nature and the extent of the final outcomes may be affected by the value attached to the process, and that a preferred or optimal state of affairs has to be determined by both the final outcomes and the processes leading to those outcomes. On this, see Amartya Sen, "Maximization and the Act of Choice," *Econometrica*, Vol. 65 (4), (1997), pp. 745-779.

the availability of another, especially if the country's resources do not increase. Similarly, access to the relevant goods and services would depend upon public policy, including public expenditure, which cannot expand indefinitely without an increase in public revenue, which in turn would be related to an increase in the country's national income. It may be possible to improve the realization of some rights through the availability and access to the corresponding goods and services, separately and individually, for a limited period and to a limited extent without economic growth. But sustainable realization of almost all of these rights requires relaxation of resource constraint through economic growth. A policy of reallocation of resources from one use to another alone cannot succeed for long in fulfilling a right without reducing the availability or resources for others, and therefore the realization of some rights, and thereby violating the composite right to development. Without bringing economic growth explicitly into the picture, the right to development would be confined to the possible realization of only some of the rights.

For economic growth to be included as an element of the claims representing the right to development, as noted earlier, it must be consistent with the conditions of realizing all the other claims as human rights. Such a process of economic growth must be carried out with equity and justice, in a non-discriminatory and participatory manner and with accountability and transparency, making it rights-based or consistent with human rights standards. It should be possible to design appropriate policies to enable the realization of such a rights-based process of economic growth, clearly identifying the agents responsible for carrying out those policies, nationally and internationally, which would ensure the coherence of that process. So admitting that growth is a constituent element of the right to development is justified not only because it is implied by the simultaneous and progressive realization of all those rights but also because it can be as legitimate and coherent as other rights. However, it is not necessary that such economic growth (which has not been recognized as a right) be a human right itself in order for it to be regarded as a constituent element of the right to development.

The characterization of economic growth as enabling the realization of all human rights follows from its instrumental role in the right to development. But a rights-based economic growth with equity and justice is also desirable in itself. It stands for the improvement of all other elements of well-being which are not captured by the realization of the recognized rights, as would follow from the definition of well-being discussed above. It is desirable also because it represents for most developing countries life with dignity for their people, liberated from the quagmire of underdevelopment, and fair and equal treatment by other countries. This is precisely why developing countries have always championed the right to development as more than the sum of specific rights and as including economic growth under an international order and social arrangement that enable them to enjoy this right.

The understandable and legitimate urge of developing countries for such economic growth has sometimes been misconstrued as supportive of only the economic, social, and cultural rights at the expense of civil and political rights. Similarly, the pressure of some countries to recognize only the civil and political rights as legitimate human rights claims has been resented by most developing countries as a rejection of their demand for economic growth in an equitable international order. The right to development as formulated here can help reconcile these competing approaches. Civil and political rights, and economic, social, and cultural rights can be seen as fully integrated within the demand for the rights-based economic growth when they are all perceived as constituent elements of the right to development. None of these elements can be allowed to deteriorate and the policies of the national and international duty-holders would aim at maximizing the realization of at least some, if not all, of these rights, depending upon the context and the prevailing conditions of a country, as well as the preferences of the people.

To appreciate the difference that is made by a rights-based approach to development leading up to the recognition of the right to development and the resulting value-addition to the whole discourse and practices of development, one has to understand what is meant by "rights", how do those "rights" entail some specific obligation of social actions and when such "rights" are taken as "human rights." These issues are discussed in the following sections.

Recognition of the Right to Development in International Law

The idea of human rights has a long history, but the form in which it serves as the basis for the Declaration on the Right to Development stems from the post-World War II system of international law. That system was the outgrowth of the international human rights movement, born during World War II, as Louis Henkin put it, "out of a spreading conviction that how human beings are treated anywhere concerns everyone, everywhere."[21] All individuals, anywhere in the world, were recognized to have some indispensable human rights and fundamental freedoms, the protection and promotion of which was the purpose and concern of all societies, irrespective of the states or institutions to which those individuals belonged. In the UN Charter, which was the first international agreement after the war, "the peoples of the United Nations" gave themselves these fundamental human rights, which the governments of all nations agreed to accept as appropriate for international concern. Member States cooperated among themselves to define these rights and incorporated them into the Universal Declaration of Human Rights, as a "common standard of achievement for all peoples of all nations." By adopting the Covenant on Civil and Political Rights and the Covenant on Economic, Social, and Cultural Rights in 1966, they assumed the obligation to respect and promote these rights and submitted themselves to some form of international scrutiny over compliance with those obligations. For any state, these norms have become the common standard by which the performance of all governments is measured and evaluated.

If the national protection of human rights is deficient, then, as Henkin puts it, "international human rights laws are designated to induce states to remedy those de-

---

21   Louis Henkin, "International Human Rights a Rights," in Morton E. Winston (ed.), *The Philosophy of Human Rights* (Wadsworth, California: 1989), p. 129.

ficiencies" and to submit to international "machinery that would monitor compliance."[22] In other words, laws and institutions of international human rights complement the protection of rights afforded by national laws.

It is this characteristic of the international recognition of human rights that makes the current deliberation on the right to development in different international fora an important milestone in development discourse and practice. Although the right to development has been recognized as an international human right, very few countries have incorporated the corresponding rights and obligations adequately in their national legal and constitutional systems. Nor are they usually reflected in the international policies of most states or in the practices of the international institutions. Their actual incorporation in the domestic legal system and in international practice will significantly change the principle and practice of development.[23] One implication of the recognition of the right to development in international law is that this right can be translated into legal rights in a legal order and the rights-holders can legitimately demand that the duty-bearers, once identified, be held accountable for carrying out their obligations and be subjected to a mechanism that monitors and adjudicates their performance, prescribing remedies in case of failures.[24]

This way of looking at human rights as a moral entitlement or a moral right that becomes translated into a legal entitlement or a legal right is not the only approach to human rights. Indeed, those who regard human rights as a part of positive law would be satisfied if they were recognized by an appropriate norm-creating mechanism (such as legislation, constitutions, judicial pronouncements, and international treaties), even without any references to the prior inclusion in a moral order. Their view would be, as Sen put it, "human beings are no more born into human rights than they are born fully clothed; rights would have to be acquired through legislation, just as clothes are acquired through tailoring. There are no pre-tailored clothes, nor any pre-legislated rights."[25] Similarly, there are human rights protagonists who would like to see these rights as essentially moral rights, a set of ethical claims, the benefit of which everyone should have in a just social order. These are grounds of social and political mobilization and possibly need not be identified with legislated legal rights. As Sen wrote in his article on "Consequential Evaluation and Practical Reason," "The importance of human rights need not lie only in their being putative proposals for legislation . . . Human rights can have their own domain of influence and importance without being parasitic on — or even being wisely reinforced by — subsequent legislation."[26]

22   Louis Henkin, *The Age of Rights* (New York: Columbia University Press, 1990), p. 17.

23   This process of incorporation would of course not be automatic, even after the recognition of the human right to development by all nations. It would involve States parties and other duty-bearers changing their policies by accepting the related obligations, resolving the conflicts of interest and of political and social power relations, both within a nation and between the nations. That would require major domestic efforts and mobilization of public support across the nations. Commitments to international law would greatly help that process and induce the nation-states to behave as legitimate members of the international community.

24   Henkin, *supra*, note 22, pp. 1-42.

25   Amartya Sen, *Development as Freedom* (New York: 2000), p. 228.

26   Amartya Sen, "Consequential Evaluation and Practical Reason," *The Journal of Philosophy*, Vol. XCVII, No. 9 (September 2000), p. 498.

The approach followed in this chapter does not dispute that there are human rights that may not be translated into legal rights. The claim here is rather that the right to development is a legal human right, grounded in moral norms but reaffirmed as a legal right in international law — though the extent to which it constrains states is still evolving. The international agreements, practices, and customs have created the enhanced expectation that governments will move from political commitment to legal obligation for which they will be held accountable. For that, it will be necessary to establish that the right to development satisfies the characteristics of a human right and to identify precisely the duty-bearers and specify their obligations and the corresponding national and international legal monitoring, adjudication, and enforcement mechanisms.

Rights and Obligations

Rights have been described and classified in many different ways, but their essential characteristics can be summarized by the definition provided by Morton E. Winston who edited the influential book, *The Philosophy of Human Rights,*[27] incorporating the elements of definitions proposed by different contributors to that book. "An agent A has a right R to a particular good G if and only if the possession of R by A provides the basis of a justified claim that society has a duty to protect (and promote) A's enjoyment of this good G."[28]

Winston further elaborates this definition as follows. The particular good G, which is the object of the right, can range over many different things such as "interests, liberties and powers or access to the necessary means of satisfying one's interests or exercising one's liberties or powers." The claims derived from rights R, which may be either moral claims or legal claims or both, call forth duties from other members of society (for example, governments, individuals, or, in some cases, nongovernmental organizations, private agencies, or corporations). "What is important about rights is that they give their holders a basis for claiming that other agents within society have certain duties which they are bound to fulfill with respect to their [the rights-holders'] enjoyment of certain goods. Rights, in short, are grounds of duties of others which benefit the right-holders."[29]

If the right R provides the basis for making "justified" claims, which are grounds of duties of others within society, it is essential to establish this justification. Members of society — national or international — must be persuaded to

---

27   Morton E. Winston (ed.), *The Philosophy of Human Rights* (Belmont, CA: Wadsworth Publishing Company, 1989). The contributors to this book included Joseph Raz, Joel Feinberg, Henry Shue, Ronald Dworkin, Louis Henkin, and Reiza Martin.

28   Winston's definition refers to only the duty to protect; but in his discussions, he includes clearly the duty to promote especially the economic, social, and cultural rights, as well as the rights of minorities and Indigenous peoples, and even their civil and political rights. See Morton E. Winston, *On the Indivisibility and Interdependence of Human Rights,* HRHD Lecture Series (April 1999). Available at http://www.bu.edu/wcp/Papers/Huma/HumaWins.htm.

29   Id. It may be noted that in conformity with our earlier discussions, rights in the definition have both intrinsic and instrumental value. Interests, liberties, and powers are claims for their intrinsic values. Access to the means for satisfying those interests, liberties, or powers are claims because of their instrumental value. Both qualify as rights.

accept the right as a moral or legal claim on society. That justification has to be both normative and procedural. The normative justification may be derived from a set of moral and legal principles that members of the society are willing to accept as their standards of achievement. The procedural justification has to be based on following appropriate norm-creating procedures acceptable to most if not all members in a society so that the abstract principles of what is good is translated into concrete norms of social behavior. The procedures justifying legal norms creating legal rights are not necessarily the same as procedures justifying moral norms creating moral rights. The moral rights have to go through appropriate legal processes, such as legislation, constitution-making, and judicial decisions, as well as institutional lawmaking procedures, in order to be recognized as legal rights.[30]

This characteristic of the rights (that create grounds of duties on the other agents of society to fulfill the claims of the right-holders) has two implications. First, it should be possible to demonstrate that such claims require carrying out these duties. The exact nature of the duty would depend upon the exact nature of the right and every right will have at least one (if not more) correlated duty. The performance of the duty may not always be sufficient to fulfill the rights; there may be many other factors, foreseen and unforeseen, that would prevent such fulfillment. But if the duty is obligatory for fulfilling the right, its performance must be a necessary condition in the sense that without it the right cannot be fulfilled. However, identifying such a duty presumes its feasibility of realizing the right. For if it was not feasible, there could be no duty that would realize that right. So, in order to convert an aspiration or something that is desirable into a right with correlated duties, it would be necessary to establish that it is a "feasible" right that taking some measure or creating some conditions, by some agency in society could feasibly realize these rights.[31]

It is quite possible that at a particular point in time or in a given state of affairs a right is not feasible to be realized unless appropriate changes in the institutions and social arrangements are introduced. Feasibility would then imply that there exists a set of actions or policies adopted by the duty-bearers that will change the institutions and make it possible to realize the right. In other words, changing the institutions,

---

30   It is important to remember this point especially with regard to the right to development, as is discussed later in this chapter. The goals of development may be accepted very widely as laudable and desirable objectives that governments, and international agencies, should follow. But they become rights with specified and accountable obligations when they are recognized in international law and in national practice based on legislative and institutional arrangements. Both the civil and political rights and economic, social, and cultural rights, went through a long process of normative justification by human rights movements and by intensive discussions about the moral norms of a society in terms of human dignity and the principles of a just society. They were then adopted as the International Covenants on Economic, Social and Cultural Rights and Civil and Political Rights in 1966 following an internationally accepted norm-creating process. The process of ratification and incorporation in the domestic legal system makes them fully established legal rights, although it is still not complete in several countries.

31   If development as a process of realizing all the rights and fundamental freedoms as defined above is to be reckoned as a right, it must be "feasible;" that is, it should be possible to design a social arrangement to enable the claimants to enjoy those rights. Obviously, such development has to be "progressively" realized as a process in time, as the instantaneous or immediate realization of all (or even most) of the rights will not be feasible. The obligation of the policy-makers or the state-authorities would be to expedite, to the maximum extent, this process of progressive realization of as many rights as possible, depending upon the constraints of resources and institutions in a country.

or what is sometimes referred to an institutionalizing the right, would be a part of the obligations of the duty-bearers.[32]

The second implication relates to the identification of different duty-bearers to specific duties. It is not always the case that identifying a duty with respect to a right would automatically lead to recognizing the bearers of that duty. Sometimes more than one agency may need to perform the same duty in parts or in complement with each other. Sometimes one agency may be the primary duty-bearer, having the primary responsibility of carrying out the duty while others may have shared responsibility. All of that would depend upon the institutional arrangements for exercising the rights. But until the duty-bearers can be specified and the duties corresponding to a right can be assigned to specific agencies, a right-holder's claim cannot be regarded as a right. Rights are grounds of duties of others, but the act of claiming by a right-holder must be matched by ascribing obligations to specific duty-bearers.[33]

Establishing this relationship between a right-holder and one or more duty-bearers is important for all rights — moral, legal, contractual, or any other — because rights imply accountability. Someone should be responsible for satisfying the claims of the right-holders. In the case of legal rights, accountability implies remedial action by those not meeting these obligations. Even if culpability or willful neglect of duty cannot be established and the duty-bearers may not be liable to penal sanctions, they have to be identified at least to share the burden of remedies.[34]

For a claim to be regarded as a right, it has to pass two tests that are related to the normative and procedural aspects of a right, namely legitimacy and coherence of the right.[35] Passing these two tests would qualify the right to withstand what Sen calls "the legitimacy critique" and the "coherence critique," and accordingly these can be

---

32   Onora O'Neill objected to the recognition of "welfare rights," which include economic, social, and cultural rights, saying that, "some advocates of universal economic, social, and cultural rights go no further than to emphasize that they can be institutionalized, which is true. But the point of difference is that they *must* be institutionalized; if they are not, there is no right." Onora O'Neill, *Towards Justice and Virtue* (Cambridge University Press: 1996), p. 132. But this is too narrow a view of the scope of human rights, which provide "grounds of duties" on other agents, which, if carried out, would most likely realize the rights. If they are not institutionalized, as O'Neill puts it, the rights would most likely not be realized. But so would be the case if any of the corresponding obligations are not fulfilled. Claiming a human right would entail that all corresponding obligations should be fulfilled by the duty-bearers, whether the obligations are for institutionalizing the rights or for carrying out any other required measures.

33   In this case of development, the primary duty-bearer will have to be the state-authorities who are in the position to design appropriate development policies and implement them. There will be other duty-bearers who will have responsibilities with respect to different aspects of development — taxpayers must pay taxes, multinationals must follow the appropriate conduct, and the international community must cooperate. But the states have the responsibility to ensure that these other duty-bearers fulfill their obligations. When these duty-bearers are subject to their domestic legal and administrative forces, the states could hold them accountable. When the duty-bearers are other sovereign states and institutions, the states will have to persuade them to cooperate to carry out those duties. But in either case, the exact responsibilities with respect to the different aspects of the development policies will have to be assigned to these duty-bearers. The design of the development policies must incorporate such assignments of specific responsibilities to all the different agents and methods of monitoring and enforcement.

34   In situations where the right-duty correlates do not lead invariably to the matching of rights-holders to specific duty-bearers, such identification has to be made by law or institutional arrangements to make a claim a valid right. In most human rights law, this is done by making the states or the government of the rights-holder the primary duty-bearer responsible for making institutional, legal, and other arrangements to satisfy the claim of the rights-holder.

35   In the literature on rights, it was Wesley Hohfeld who in 1919 first enunciated the notion of a legal right as an "advantage" for an agent correlated with a "disadvantage" for some other agent in a society. He

note continues on following page

termed as "Sen's tests." The legitimacy critique raises questions about the status and authority of the right, or from which normative order that authority is derived and what legitimizes the claim. The coherence critique relates basically to questioning a right when one is not able to specify exactly the duty-bearers and the corresponding obligations that make the right feasible in practice.[36]

Human Rights As Rights

The distinction between human rights and rights in general becomes clearer as they are put through the legitimacy and the coherence tests. Human rights like all rights should pass these tests. But they are more basic and fundamental than other rights in the sense that they are foundational norms of society — the standards that bind the agents of a society. They are inviolable, because if they are violated the society disintegrates. Therefore, the tests they have to pass have to be broader and more stringent than other rights. The legitimacy of human rights has to be established on the basis of a justification of a higher order than that of other rights in general. The rights-duty correlation implied in establishing coherence must also have a much broader scope with a greater reach on the agents of the society.

The foundational characteristics of human rights and the power of the use of rights language in a political society are now widely accepted. As Philip Alston put it, "the characteristics of a specific goal as a human right elevates it above the rank and file of competing social goals, gives it a degree of immunity from challenge, and generally endows it with an aura of timelessness, absoluteness, and validity."[37] By implication, the fulfillment of such human rights gets an overwhelming priority in the

---

note continued from preceding page

identified four such rights, each associated with second-party correlations: to a claim, a liberty, a power, and immunity. For a claim-right, the correlation element is a duty of some second party, and it is this claim-right, which is considered as the basis of the modern theory of legal rights, enforceable within a system of laws. The philosopher, Joel Feinberg, has been credited with the development of the most influential account of claim-rights Rex Martin, "Human Rights and Civil Rights," *Philosophical Studies*, Vol. 37, No. 4 (1980); and Joel Feinberg, "The Nature and Value of Rights," *Journal of Value Inquiry and Social Philosophy*, Vol. 4, Englewood Cliffs, Ch. 4 (1973). According to him, a right has two dimensions; a claim to something and a claim against someone, both recognized according to moral norms and legal orders. A claim is complete, or as Feinberg puts it, becomes a "valid right," when both dimensions merge. In terms of Sen's tests, establishing "claims to" a right would satisfy the legitimacy test, and "claims against" would relate to the coherence test, and satisfying both the tests, "claims" become "rights."
36   Sen, *supra*, note 25, pp. 228-233. Interestingly, this test is a good way of preventing the proliferation of human rights to all kinds of aspirations and political goods that are often proposed in the different institutional fora. Philip Alston proposed criteria that would amount to spelling out in great detail both the normative and procedural justification of our legitimacy criteria. Philip Alston, "Conjuring Up New Human Rights: A Proposal for Quality Control," *The American Journal of International Law*, Vol. 78, (1984), pp. 607-621. It may not be very useful to go into such detail because ultimately the choice of such rights is subject to political discussion. It might be better to concentrate on some broad tests as proposed and persuade the international community to discuss thoroughly the qualification of these rights according to these tests in the international fora. Indeed, the study of Professor F. G. Jacobs that Alston himself quotes on the Council of Europe's discussions about basic economic, social, and cultural rights for inclusion in the European Convention of Human Rights suggested criteria very similar to that presented here. They were the following: 1) the rights must be fundamental; 2) the rights must be universally recognized and guaranteed to everyone as human rights; and 3) the rights must be capable of sufficiently precise formulation to give rise to legal obligations. F. G. Jacob, "The Extension of the European Convention on Human Rights to Include Economic, Social, and Cultural Rights," *Human Rights Review* (1978), p. 166, cited by Alston.
37   Philip Alston, "Making Space for New Human Rights: The Case for the Right to Development," *Harvard Human Rights Yearbook* (1988), pp. 3-40.

use of resources and public policy.[38] Human rights would "trump" other obligations, command the priority in the use of resources for implementing the rights, and in-fixing responsibilities for appropriate actions on different agents in the society. Holding those agents accountable for their actions and setting up mechanisms for monitoring and enforcing their obligations effectively, change not only the process of development but also the method of their implementation when development is regarded as a human right. The specific problems of development would vary from country to country but policies for overcoming those problems, within a framework of rights and obligations both nationally and internationally, would not only have a clear focus on the goals of development, but also a high likelihood of successful im-plementation.

In putting the claims for human rights through the tests of legitimacy and coher-ence, one must not, however, ignore the strength of political processes that spear-headed the human rights movements. The tests are seldom conclusive in the sense of a definitive or a unanimous verdict in favor of a claim qualifying as a human right. But they can at least bring out carefully all the characteristics of the claim relevant for that purpose and for guiding the political process considering that claim. It is the political process, which ultimately determines if a claim can become a right, or reach the status of human right. The procedural justification of the human rights must of course include all the norm-creating requirements of admissibility of the usual rights. But in addition, these norms should be discussed and examined in wider forums with public participation. The recognition of these rights as binding norms of the so-ciety must be acceptable to broad sections of the society. Legislative action may not be able to ensure the realization of these rights without such a broad consensus.

The relationship between moral and legal rights is significant in the case of the right to development since it has been only been recognized as a human right through inter-governmental and international declarations and one regional treaty. In order to become a legal right, states would have to accept more precise treaty ob-ligations and adopt appropriate legislation in their national systems, which would be legally binding regardless of how they are supported by any particular moral argu-ment. If a right is incorporated in the legal system that is, if it is legislated, it has a standing whether or not it is morally justifiable. On the other hand, if a right is fully morally justified, it may not still be accepted as a legal right. It should then call for persistent campaign to attain appropriate legal recognition. The foundation of the right to development remains its recognition by the international community, and it

---

38   That a violation of human rights could be the ground of a social revolution has been recognized in the human rights movement from its inception. The American Declaration of Independence (1776) talked about the right of the people to "alter or to abolish" the form of government that became destruc-tive of such human rights. The Universal Declaration of the Human Rights (1948) states in the Preamble that human rights should be protected to prevent people from resorting to rebellion. Ronald Dworkin refers to the "background rights" of every person, a violation of which would justify a whole people amending the Constitution by rebelling and overthrowing the government. See Ronald Dworkin, *Taking Rights Seriously* (Cambridge, US: Harvard University, 1977). Dworkin is also credited with the notion that a government may have a number of policy goals, such as promising general welfare, maximizing the common good, or satisfying the will of the majority. Human rights claims would "trump" all these poli-cies and be the first priority in fulfilling that claim. See Ronald Dworkin, "Rights As Trumps," in Jeremy Waldron (ed.), *Theories of Rights* (Oxford: Oxford University Press, 1995), pp. 153-67.

is therefore necessary to press the case forward for its legal recognition, justified both in terms of its legitimacy and coherence.

The Rights-Holder As Individual and As Group

If an agent A has a right R, A must qualify as a candidate for R. A must be an agent whose interest or well-being would be recognized as vital or substantially important in the society to bind other agents to do what is necessary to improve that agent's well-being or interest. Also, A must be an individual, or a collective that behaves like an individual that can identify clearly a state of affairs to be better, or improved in terms of its well-being or interest, compared to another state of affairs. This requirement is crucial for ascertaining whether a policy P taken by the duty-holder is improving the realization of the right. This is also a reason why human rights are taken as individual rights because the individuals are expected to have a notion of well-being (reckoned in terms of preference, utilities, happiness, or interests), which can be improved through the enjoyment of rights. For a collective of individuals, all with different well-being functions, it is difficult to state unequivocally if one situation or state of social arrangement is better than another, and therefore it may not be possible to ascertain any improvement in the realization of rights.

For the notion of a group right (or a collective right or a people's right) to be plausible, it must be based either on the specification of the right that can be enjoyed individually by the members of the group, but is exercised collectively, when an individual can enjoy these rights together with other members of the group. (For example minority rights, linguistic rights, religious rights, or many of the Indigenous people's rights). Alternatively, the group itself may have an identity, defined by history, law, or territory independently of and above, the identity of individual members of the group, with a clear procedure for ascertaining the realization of the right.[39]

In the North-South debate on the New International Economic Order, the right to development was sometimes described as "a right of the developing countries." States can have rights under law, if duly recognized. But they cannot have human rights and such claims of developing countries could not be justified. The developing countries of the South could not be given an autonomous group identity, nor was it possible to establish that the states would be fully representatives of the citizens of the developing countries so that these individuals would unequivocally enjoy the rights claimed and realized by the states. Insistence by the developing countries on the right to development being the right of developing countries deflected such claims from the mainstream of the international human rights movement. On the other hand, in terms of the description given above, the right to development would still be recognized as a collective right, which is to be enjoyed individually, by the citizens of a country, but which is to be exercised collectively so that it can be enjoyed

---

39   For an examination of this argument, see Margot E. Salomon with Arjun Sengupta, *The Right to Development: Obligations of States and the Rights of Minorities and Indigenous People* (London: Minority Rights Group International, February 2003).

by all the citizens together. If the state of a developing country claims the right to development against the international community on behalf of the people of that country, appropriate mechanisms have to be established to translate the benefits from the exercise of that right to the citizens of the state.

The Notion of Meta-Rights and Basic Rights

The distinction between legal and moral rights leads to the possibility that some rights that meet the legitimacy and coherence tests may not be actually realized or may even be unrealizable within a given time. The actions or policies to be taken to maximize the likelihood to realize the right and agencies to carry them out may be fully identified. Still there may be exogenous developments that can frustrate these policies. The interconnection between the different segments of policy-results may not work out as expected. The constraints of resources and institutions do not allow sufficient progress to be made in the immediate or near future. As a result, the right may not be realized, and no agent would be held responsible. The right remains unfulfilled as a "background" moral right, influencing the behavior of the agents without becoming a justiciable and enforceable legal right. Sen gives the example of the right to food (the right not to be hungry) as such a right that can remain unfulfilled or unrealizable until it is progressively realized through the relaxation of resource constraint and policies that would make the freedom in question real.

Sen then invokes the notion of a "meta-right." "A meta-right to something x can be defined as the right to have policies p (x) that genuinely pursue the objective of making the right to x realizable."[40] Even if the right to x remains unfulfilled or immediately unrealizable, the meta-right to x, p(x) can be a fully valid and realizable right, if all the obligations associated with p(x) can be clearly specified, with the identification of the agents to carry out those obligations, and held accountable for non-compliance. The right to x may remain a moral right or an abstract, background right of general political aim providing justification for political decision but a right to p(x) can be a real, legal right to make x achievable in the future.

For the right to development, the outcomes of the process of development are human rights, as is the process of development that leads to these outcomes. In spite of establishing the legitimacy and coherence of these rights, the final outcomes of evelopment may remain unfulfilled within a target period of time. But the process of development that leads to those final outcomes may be effectively realized. Such a process of development entails a program of policies and phased realization of the target rights, executed over time maintaining consistency and sustainability, with a high probability of leading to the realization of the final outcomes. The agent-specific obligation for carrying out that program of development policies can be identified and subjected to monitoring and proper legal enforcement. It is that program of development policy that can be regarded as a meta-right.

---

40 Amartya Sen, "The Right Not to be Hungry," in Alston and Tomaševski (eds.), *The Right to Food* (The Netherlands: SIM, 1984).

The notion of meta-right is useful for rights that are not immediately realizable. If people can claim a valid right — valid in the sense of its passing both the legitimacy and the coherence tests — then they can also demand that the state and other duty-bearers carry out their obligations. So if, the right to development, with both the outcomes and the process are accepted as legitimate and coherent, therefore feasible and valid, the adoption of the corresponding program of development policies would also be accepted as inviolable obligation of all states that have endorsed this right.

The right to development is still not accepted by many as valid or realizable. However, if the right to the program of development policies is accepted as a meta-right, it will mean that these policies would make the right to development realizable, even if that objective is not immediately achieved. So the focus of attention should be on development policy, whether as an obligation corresponding to a valid right to development or as a meta-right to an objective of development as a human right that cannot be immediately achieved.

The right to development, as the right to a process of development, can however be usefully described as a "basic right" in the sense that Henry Shue used this term.[41] The term refers to the minimum set of rights that any civilized international community would consider as the standards of achievement of a civilized society. A basic right is essential to the enjoyment of all other rights. A basic right is not necessarily superior or preferable to other rights. But if the point is that people should be able to "enjoy" or "exercise" other rights, then, "the basic rights need to be established securely before other rights can be secured." Further, "when a right is genuinely basic, any attempt to enjoy any other right by sacrificing the basic right would be quite literally self-defeating cutting the ground from beneath itself."[42] The right to a process of development can in that sense effectively be described as basic relative to all the other rights, civil, political, economic, social, and cultural. Without the realization of the basic right, none of the other rights can be enjoyed effectively and in a sustained manner.

Implementing the Right to Development

The recognition of the right to development as an inalienable human right confers on it a claim to national and international resources and obliges states and other agencies of society, including individuals, to contribute to its implementation.[43] According to the Declaration on the Right to Development, the primary responsibility for implementing the right to development belongs to states. The beneficiaries are individuals. The international community has the duty to cooperate to enable states to fulfill their obligations under Articles 1, 55, and 56 of the UN Charter. Accordingly, the Vienna Declaration calls for effective implementation of the right

---

41   Henry Shue, *Basic Rights* (Princeton, NJ: Princeton University Press, 1980), pp. 19-20.
42   *Id.*
43   The Vienna Declaration and Programme of Action, in fact, states categorically, "Human rights and fundamental freedoms are the birthright of all human beings; their protection and promotion is the first responsibility of Governments." Further, "enhancement of international cooperation in the field of human rights is essential for the full achievement of the purposes of the United Nations."

to development through policies at the national level with equitable economic relations and a favorable environment at the international level. The identification of the corresponding obligations at the national and international level would therefore be the first step in implementing the right to development.

National Obligations

National obligations should begin with the formulation of a set of policies applicable to the implementation of each of the constituent rights of the right to development individually, as well as in combination with each other as a part of a development program. They should be categorized as measures that prevent violation of any right and measures that promote the improved realization of all rights. According to our definition of the right to development, violation of any one right would mean violation of the right to development itself. The design of any program for the promotion of a right therefore must ensure that any other right will not be adversely affected.

To operationalize these rights, and to know when they are or are not realized, these rights, R_i's must be represented by some indicators whose value would increase, as R_i is increasingly realized. Constructing such indicators may be difficult, posing different problems for different rights. In the case of many civil and political rights, where the rights are either violated or realized, the corresponding rights could have the value 0 or 1, although for a country as a whole with many individuals, the construction of an aggregative index may become very complex. In the case of economic, social and cultural rights, which are supposed to be progressively realized, the value of the indicators should be able to increase monotonically with the progressive realization of the rights. That will be the case if these indicators are indexes represented by real numbers. For simplifying the operational procedures to implement a right, attempts should be made to combine the different characteristics of a right by suitably weighting them into a single index.

Indeed, most of these rights will have a number of characteristics or dimensions. For example, the economic rights will have to combine the availability of the corresponding economic goods with the access to those goods in a manner that is consistent with the human rights standards. Those standards have been defined in terms of at least five characteristics as discussed earlier, so that the access should be at least equitable, non-discriminatory, participatory, accountable, and transparent. All these have to be ascertained and reflected in an indicator that combines it with the indicator for the availability of goods and is represented by an index for the realization of the right. For instance, the index of the right to food should reflect both whether sufficient food is available and whether everybody or the target-population of the poor or the vulnerable will have access to that good in, say, an equitable or non-discriminatory manner. All these exercises, of course, in actual practice, may not be very precise, giving only approximate answers. But they must be sensitive to the relevant issues and aware of the purpose of the exercise for assessing the comprehensive outcomes of not just what is achieved but also how it is achieved.

It may not be easy to build up an overall indicator for the right to development. This is because to convert a vector comprising a number of distinct elements into a scalar or an index would require a process of averaging or weighting the various elements that would be open to fundamental objections. However, expressing the right to development as a vector of all the rights would make it possible to establish whether there has been an improvement in the realization of the right to development; it would not, of course, allow comparisons to be made between the achievements of two or more countries, or even within the same country over time. The only way to do this is to build a consensus through open public discussions about the relative importance of the different levels of achievement.

This, however, would not prevent the formulation of a program for development that takes into account the interlinkages between the objectives of realizing the various rights including, as mentioned above, the right to the need to expand resources, GNP, technology, and institutions. What differentiates the program for realizing the right to development from other conventional programs of development is not only the differences in the objectives to be realized but also the manner in which they are to be realized. This type of development imposes additional constraints on the development process, such as maintaining transparency, accountability, equity, and non-discrimination in all the programs. In addition, the program must ensure overall development with equity, or transformation of the structure of production, which reduces inter-regional and interpersonal disparities and inequity.

Like all other development programs, such a program would be subject to constraints in resources, technology, and institutions. The importance of the constraints is not as apparent if one is seeking to achieve individual rights in isolation. But as a part of a country's overall development program, the right to development is very much a matter of modernization and technological, as well as institutional, transformation, which relaxes the technological and institutional constraints over time. Therefore the right to development is also related to increasing resources over time by making the most efficient use of the existing resources through proper fiscal, monetary, trade, and competitive market practices and by promoting the growth of resources and expanding the opportunities for trade. Achieving the right to development requires the same fiscal and monetary discipline, macroeconomic balance, and competitive markets as any other form of prudent economic management. The basic difference is that prudent management in furtherance of achieving the right to development is expected to bring about a more equitable outcome of the economic activities that make possible an improved realization of all the components of that right.

International Cooperation

No state in today's globalizing world can follow any policy independently — that is, without considering the effects of its policies on other countries or without taking into account the impact of the behavior of other countries on its own policies. The impact of the policies and practices of the developed countries on those of the developing countries, and vice versa, was recognized in the concept of international cooperation emphasized in the International Covenants and the Declaration on the Right to Development. Just as these impacts are reciprocal, so, too, are the obligations of international cooperation.

When these rights are to be realized as a part of a country's development program, as is the right to development, all the constraints of resources, technology, and institutions can be seen as dependent upon the extent and nature of international cooperation. The international community, which could supply foreign savings and investments, technology, and access to markets, as well as institutional support, can facilitate the realization of the rights. International cooperation need not be confined to the supply of foreign savings, or the transfer of resources, although transfer of resources is necessary. The poor countries are short of domestic resources, which need to be supplemented by flows of foreign savings. Any discourse on the right to development cannot therefore avoid reminding the international community of its pledge to reach its target of devoting 0.7 percent of its gross national product as foreign aid, and that only a handful of countries have come anywhere near meeting the target. However, in the context of fulfilling the right to development, the obligations of the international community would extend to international cooperation for supplying technology, providing market access, adjusting the rules of operation of the existing trading and financial institutions and intellectual property protection, and creating new international mechanisms to meet the specific requirements of the developing countries.

Such international cooperation would usually have two dimensions, which are not mutually exclusive. First, cooperation measures should be conceived and executed internationally in a multilateral process in which all developed countries, multilateral agencies and international institutions could participate by providing facilities to which all qualifying developing countries could have access. Secondly, bilateral facilities or country-specific arrangements would supplement them to deal with problems requiring measures adapted to particular contexts. There are multilateral facilities dealing with the debt problems of developing countries, structural adjustment, and concessional financing by international financial institutions. There are bilateral programs supplementing the multilateral process for providing market access, and supporting national projects to solve the many problems of inadequacy and instability of trade and financial transactions. All of these require intensive review from the point of view of meeting the obligations of international cooperation to realize the right to development. It should not only be transparent and non-discriminatory but also equitable and participatory — both in the decision-making and in the benefits-sharing process. The quid pro quo for the industrial countries and the international institutions of accepting this human rights framework is that their obligation is matched by the obligation of the developing countries to facilitate the realization of the human rights as constituent elements of development. That itself would improve not only the cost-effectiveness of such cooperation but also lead to a more equitable and mutually beneficial order of the international economy.

Both these multilateral and bilateral dimensions of international cooperation open up new possibilities for realizing the right to development, radically transforming international economic relations — especially between the developed and developing countries — on the basis of equity and partnership. One of the principal motivations of the human rights movement leading up to the formulation of the right to development was establishing equity and empowerment in international economic transactions between developed and developing countries. Much of the logic of the North-South conflict that was behind the demand for a New International Economic Order in the 1970s has now lost its relevance. However, the rationale for equitable treatment and participation in the decision-making process and access to the benefits of the process remains as strong as before. The human rights approach to the realization of the right to development provides scope for building up a cooperative relationship between the developed and developing countries on the basis of partnership rather than the confrontation of earlier years.

Monitoring Mechanisms

In the right to development, the realization of civil and political rights is integrated with the fulfillment of economic, social, and cultural rights and vice versa. Any program for realizing civil and political rights as a part of the right to development must clearly specify how they facilitate the realization of economic, social, and cultural rights, such as through freedom of information, association, democratic decision-making, participation, and non discrimination. Similarly, a program for realizing economic, cultural, and social rights must be dependent on the promotion of civil and political rights, both at a point in time and over time. More important, as a result of this interdependence, the monitoring mechanisms for the right to development will have to be different from those for monitoring civil and political rights and economic, social, and cultural rights. The United Nations treaty bodies monitor the rights contained in the respective instruments individually and separately. A mechanism for monitoring the right to development will have to review the implementation of the various rights, both individually and in a composite manner, as a part of the process of development and in the context of economic growth with equity.

Such a monitoring mechanism can in principle be established, even without a convention, on the basis of the consensus that has been built up around it and the analytical provisions that can be introduced into the concept of the right to development. To begin with, the committees under the two International Covenants should examine each of the rights in the light of their interlinkages and should determine whether the exercise of one right is facilitating or detracting from the fulfillment of others. But that will not be enough, because, as we have noted, it will also be necessary to examine their implementation taken together as a composite whole against the background of a program of national development promoting growth and technological progress. It will also be important to assess how such national development promotes equity both within a state and between states through a rights-based approach to international cooperation. It will ultimately be necessary to establish an international committee to review the implementation of the integrated right to development and to make recommendations thereon in terms of the international consensus. Non-governmental organizations (NGOs) and other civil society bodies may submit reports for its consideration. It should also be possible for individual states to submit reports about their grievances or the difficulties faced in implementing the right to development, and the international community may invite the concerned states and international agencies to respond to the review of these reports.

Development Compacts

In my reports as Independent Expert on the Right to Development to the Commission on Human Rights, I proposed "development compacts" as a practical model of international cooperation to implement the right to development and to set up a system of monitoring within the countries engaged in that cooperation.

A development compact is a mechanism for ensuring the recognition among all stakeholders of the "mutuality of the obligations," so that the obligations of developing countries to carry out these rights-based programs are matched with reciprocal obligations of the international community to cooperate to enable the implementation of the programs. The purpose of development compacts is to assure the developing countries that if they fulfill their obligations, the program for realizing the right to development will not be disrupted due to a lack of financing. The process of instituting a development compact involves several steps:

- Focusing on realizing a few rights, or poverty reduction, in a way that is consistent with human rights norms, without violating any other rights;
- Designing a national development program by countries requesting a development compact;
- Developing the program in consultation with civil society;
- Adopting legislation to incorporate human rights in domestic law;
- Establishing a national human rights commission where such bodies do not already exist;
- Specifying the obligations of both the national authorities and the international community;
- Organizing a support group for the concerned developing country comprising stakeholders who, inter-alia, would scrutinize and review development programs, examine the obligations specified, and decide on burden-sharing among the members of the international community in meeting their respective obligations under the compact;
- Assessing and implementing appropriate measures at both the bilateral and multilateral levels (for example, debt relief, trade, investment);
- Determining the residual financing requirement of a particular development compact after the implementation of all other measures of development cooperation and after taking into account the possible contributions of multilateral and bilateral donors having a special interest in the country;

- Setting up some financial facility with contributions in the form of "callable commitments" from the donor community; and
- Establishing a mechanism with the help of the support group to invoke the "callable commitments" according to agreed-upon principles of burden-sharing to finance those residual requirements.

The development compact can be an effective international mechanism complementing the treaty bodies to monitor the right to development. It would have to assess the implementation of the various rights both individually and in a composite manner and facilitate the implementation of the right to development, as well as to consider the financing of specific measures.

Conclusion

The right to development has by now been established as an international human right. The international community has recognized it as a right that can be claimed by individuals and peoples. It has also recognized the obligations that such a claim would impose on states and the international community. What remains now is to work out programs and measures to implement it in practice, making it possible by all the rights-holders to enjoy this right.

3 | The Implications and Value Added of a Rights-Based Approach
Jakob Kirkemann Hansen and Hans-Otto Sano

Introduction

The past seven years or so have seen a remarkable growth in the interest in and promotion of what has been termed a "rights-based approach," (RBA) in which goals and processes of international assistance reflect the principles and norms embodied in the international human rights instruments.

Rights-based approaches are not necessarily confined to development activities, but they have received particular attention within this sphere. Efforts to reinforce human rights and democratization as a cross-cutting or important element in development work have without any doubt contributed to the fact that rights-based approaches have become almost exclusively related to the field of development. It must be emphasized, however, that such approaches could well become integral elements in other efforts of planned and institutional change, say in developed countries.

We see rights-based approaches primarily as a means of integrating human rights principles and aspirations into measures of planned and institutional change. An important caveat — and one that we seek to keep in focus throughout this chapter — is that rights-based approaches are not, and should not be, applied to all economic, social, political, and institutional change. Human rights principles are relevant in the field of development, and human rights should permeate development efforts, but there are certainly areas of the development universe where human rights may have a lesser role to play in determining what is done and not done.

This is then a crucial point of departure of this chapter: Rights-based approaches will imply a different design of development interventions, but not of all development interventions. There is a certain caution which needs to be asserted in making a rights-based approach a panacea for all development efforts.

The increased attention to a rights-based approach has taken place in an international human rights climate where the importance of economic, social, and cultural rights is being reconfirmed; where poverty is repeatedly being stated as a denial of human rights; and where there is a growing consensus that the current human rights challenge has gone beyond standard setting and has become one of implementation. These changes are matched, in part, by the development world through an acceptance of human rights as a legitimate concern for international assistance and a view that development assistance should remain poverty-focused in deed as well as in words. Development interventions should be human-centered and process oriented with concepts of empowerment, accountability, and participation as common currency.

In this chapter we examine the emergence of rights-based approaches to development and explore the aims, implications, and value of adopting the approach. The rationale of a rights-based approach is that human rights and development are interconnected and that it "adds value" to this relationship. But what exactly is the value added and what policy or institutional changes are implied? In addressing these questions, the chapter takes its point of departure in existing notions and practices of rights-based approaches and examines and clarifies the conceptual elements and modes of operationalization. It critically examines the inherent assumptions, strengths, and weaknesses in order to suggest ways to make a rights-based approach operational in development assistance.

Much uncertainty exists on the interpretation of what a rights-based approach may imply for donors and beneficiaries of development aid. This chapter is inspired by an objective of addressing this uncertainty. In seeking realistic ways of making human rights succeed in development assistance, we hope to clarify some of the prevailing questions.

The first section of this chapter traces origins of rights-based approaches and examines positions of relevant actors and agencies in order to show the variety of definitions that exists.

The second section examines the policies and practices of development agencies that define their work according to the principles of a rights-based approach. These principles are universality, indivisibility, accountability, participation, empowerment, and non-discrimination.

The third section asks what the underlying assumptions of rights-based approaches are. How are they justified? What are the strengths and weaknesses of these approaches? To what degree are the inherent assumptions and propositions sound? Based on this examination, an operational definition is proposed.

The final and concluding section of the chapter discusses the value-added dimensions of the rights-based approach and its limitations.

Background

At a conference in 2000, the High Commissioner for Human Rights stated that:

> Poverty eradication without empowerment is unsustainable. Social integration without minority rights is unimaginable. Gender equality without women's rights is illusory. Full employment without workers' rights may be no more than a promise of sweatshops, exploitation and slavery. The logic of human rights in development is inescapable.[1]

A rights-based approach to development shares this logic, or more specifically, would be the operational expression of it.

---

1   Mary Robinson, United Nations High Commissioner for Human Rights at International Conference, "Stopping the Economic Exploitation of Children: New Approaches to Fighting Poverty As a Means of Implementing Human Rights?" (Hattingen, Germany: February 22-24, 2000).

However, the exact nature of the logic is not clear. Indeed, it could be said that the role played by the interrelationship between human rights and development has been contested almost since the adoption of the Universal Declaration of Human Rights in 1948 (UDHR). Later, contestation erupted about the right to development, and disputes arose on the interrelationship between categories of rights, whether political and civil rights could be sacrificed for development or whether any development had to be foregone by a political system based on the respect of the rights. Discussion on the interrelationship not only became entangled in the politics of decolonisation but also quickly became a point of confrontation in the Cold War. The human rights regime was seen as questioning the sovereignty of states, and it was often asked if there was an underlying liberal-capitalist agenda being attached to the imposition of human rights in development.[2]

Discounting the purely political reasons for various blocs taking their respective positions, many challenged the justification of economic and social rights, and thus important linkages between human rights and development. Economic and social rights were disputed on the grounds that they were collective rights; that they confused goals and rights by entailing positive obligations that could not realistically be fulfilled; and that they identified no specific duty holder — in sum, they lacked the cogency and justiciability that were argued to be intrinsic to the nature of human rights.[3]

In fact, human rights and development remained two separate spheres institutionally and operationally well into the 1980s, and the recent rapprochement between them rests on a number of events or advances, politically, conceptually, and institutionally which have come together to create the circumstances that imbue the logic of a rights-based approach with its rationale.

While the drafters of the UDHR might have imagined a close interrelationship between economic, social, cultural, civil, and political rights, as well as between these rights and development, controversy during the drafting process codified these rights in two separate treaties and placed development in a different sphere altogether. The adoption in 1986 of the Declaration on the Right to Development can be seen as an attempt to realign development with human rights and emphasize the interrelationship of human rights as envisaged by the UDHR. In its preamble, the Declaration held that human rights and development were inter- dependent. It further stated that the right to development is "an inalienable right by virtue of which every human person and all peoples are entitled to participate in, contribute to, and enjoy economic, social, cultural and political development, in which all human rights and fundamental freedoms can be realised."[4] It went on to provide that "the human person is the central subject of development and should be an active participant and beneficiary to the right to development."[5] The main duty-holder of the right to develop-

---

2   Kevin Boyle, *Stock-taking on Human Rights: The World Conference on Human Rights* (Vienna: 1993), pp. 89 ff., i. In David Beetham (ed.), *Politics and Human Rights* (Oxford: Blackwell, 1995), pp. 79-95.
3   David Beetham, *Democracy and Human Rights* (Cambridge: Polity Press, 1999), p. 115.
4   Declaration on the Right to Development, adopted by the General Assembly Resolution 41/128, of December 4, 1986.
5   *Ibid.*

ment remained the state, but much more emphasis s placed on the obligations of the international community to facilitate development and effectively remove obstacles for the realization of the right to development.

A change in the international political climate was necessary before the issues raised by the right to development again came to the fore. With the demise of the Soviet Union, a new global order started to emerge based on principles of democratization, participation, and international cooperation. A new sense of international commitment could be discerned, together with a recognition of the need to strengthen the international community in a globalized world, where the challenges to be addressed stretched beyond the bounds of any single nation state.

In this new political environment, many of the old divisions were laid to rest, and human rights gained a new prominence in international politics.[6] Targets for development, first set forth during noteworthy conferences and summits of the 1990s,[7] were later adopted at the Millennium Assembly of the United Nations and elaborated in concrete terms in the Millennium Report. The Millennium Development Goals are often referred to as reflecting a rights-based approach, especially by UN organs. In human rights terms, however, the Vienna Declaration of 1993, establishing an agenda for the new world order, was more significant and underscored the indivisibility and equal priority of all rights — economic, social, cultural, civil, and political. Not least, it recognized that democracy, development, and human rights are interdependent and mutually reinforcing.[8]

With these political changes, the relationship between human rights and development started to move from being conceptual toward being intentional, in the sense that key actors within the development community started to integrate human rights concerns into their mandates and policies. Thus, the 1990s saw a host of supportive statements on the interdependence of development and human rights, especially in terms of policy declarations on the need for further integration, mainstreaming, collaboration, and analysis. In response to this new interest, an Independent Expert on the Right to Development was appointed in 1998 and started to define the scope and nature of the right to development. Efforts were intensified to clarify the content of economic and social rights.

If the post-Cold War political climate recharged the human rights agenda and confirmed the interdependence between human rights and development, it was the conceptual work around economic, social, and cultural rights that provided much of the normative elements needed to operationalize the relationship in terms of rights. The general comments of the Committee on Economic, Social, and Cultural Rights and documents such as the Maastricht Guidelines and Limburg Principles have done

---

6 Hans-Otto Sano, *Good Governance, Accountability and Human Rights,* in Hans-Otto Sano, Gudmundur Alfredsson, and Robin Clapp G. Alfredson (eds.), *Human Rights and Good Governance,* (The Hague: Martinus Nijhoff, 2002), pp. 123-146.
7 Notably, these were the *Rio Conference on Environment and Development* in 1993, the 1994 UN *International Conference in Cairo on Population and Development* in Cairo, the 1993 *World Conference on Human Rights* in Vienna, and the *Copenhagen Social Summit* in 1995.
8 General Assembly, Vienna Declaration, and Programme of Action, UN Doc. A/CONF.157/23 (July 12, 1993).

much to dilute the stark contrast between civil and political rights on the one hand, and economic and social rights on the other. The focus on economic and social rights also devolved the traditional attention from a strict state-centered human rights regime toward other duty-bearers and sparked the elaboration of new methods and means of accountability that went beyond strict legal procedures — a development that was important in operationalizing a rights-based approach.

Another trend in international relations emphasizing the role of human rights was the reform process of the UN that started in 1997, in which human rights were reconfirmed as a key priority of the UN. Accordingly, human rights became a cross-cutting issue for the four main fields[9] of the UN. The call of the Secretary-General on all entities of the UN to mainstream human rights into their activities represented a political endorsement and heightened interest in a rights-based approach. Through the 1990s, the relationship between human rights and development moved from an academic acknowledgement toward a growing willingness to operationalize these intentions.

A final set of influences in support of a rights-based approach to development was a movement from a growth-centered to a more human- and poverty-centered agenda of development. Already during the 1970s, the idea had emerged that development should be directed toward basic needs. Other concepts started to surface that highlighted the importance of gender and vulnerability in development, the value of participation and ownership for effective sustainability, and the "holistic nature" of poverty. Even more important was the introduction of the concept of good governance by the World Bank during the late 1980s. While initial definitions of the concept were mainly technical and apolitical, it implied a re-emergence of the state as a central actor within the development paradigm. These conceptual innovations not only highlighted a number of issues already central to human rights, but also led to the development of tools and practices that have influenced subsequent attempts to integrate human rights into development activities.

Defining a Rights-based Approach

The Office of the High Commissioner for Human Rights (OHCHR) has defined a rights-based approach in the following manner: "A rights-based approach to development is a conceptual framework for the process of human development that is normatively based on international human rights standards and operationally directed to promoting and protecting human rights . . . ."

Furthermore: "A rights-based approach to development includes the following elements:

- express linkage to rights
- accountability
- empowerment

---

9   Peace and security; economic and social affairs; development cooperation; and humanitarian affairs. See Secretary General's Report, *Renewing the United Nations: A Programme for Reform*. UN Doc. (A/51/ 950) (July 14, 1997).

- participation
- non-discrimination and attention to vulnerable groups."[10]

The definition adopted by OHCHR, which is also used by other UN members like the UNDP, can be compared to a definition used by Care International, which states:

> For CARE, a rights-based approach deliberately and explicitly focuses on people achieving the minimum conditions for living with dignity. It does so by exposing the roots of vulnerability and marginalization and expanding the range of responses. It empowers people to claim their rights and fulfil their responsibilities. A rights-based approach recognizes poor, displaced, and war-affected people as having inherent rights essential to livelihood security — rights that are validated by international law.[11]

Both of the definitions quoted relate a rights-based approach to a particular type of development: a focus on poverty, equity, or marginalized groups and a focus on rights-related empowerment and participation. For Care International, however, a rights-based approach is not tied narrowly to human rights. For OHCHR, there is a strong emphasis on non-discrimination and accountability.

The major distinction between these two definitions is, therefore, that the former may focus equally on duty-holders and on rights-claimants inasmuch as this definition emphasizes accountability, while the latter has a point of departure in rights-based empowerment — that is, in the claims of the rights-holders. Both of the definitions imply, however, that a rights-based approach presupposes a particular character of development — that is, one based on equity, poverty eradication, participation, and empowerment. Interpreted in this way, a rights-based approach becomes an integral element of a human development approach characterized by key concepts such as participation, empowerment, and support for vulnerable and marginal groups.[12]

In commenting on the relationship between a human development approach and a rights-based approach, Arjun Sengupta, the Independent Expert on the Right to Development appointed by the UN Commission on Human Rights argues that:

> The human rights approach to development added a further dimension to development thinking. While the human development approach aims at realizing individuals' freedom by making enhancement of their capabilities the goal of development policy, the human rights approach focuses on the claims that individuals have on the conduct of State and other agents to secure their capabilities and freedoms.[13]

---

10 Available at www.unhchr.ch/development/approaches.html.
11 CARE statement on "A Rights-Based Approach to Achieving HLS," ALMIS # 5250, November 2000, quoted in CARE, *Promoting Rights and Responsibilities* (June 2001), p. 11. Available at http://www.inter-action.org/files.cgi/2496_Analysis_of_RBA_Definitions1.pdf. (Accessed November 12, 2005.)
12 The human development approach became a strategy of organizations organizations such as UNDP and UNICEF during the late 1980s and early 1990s. Development with a human face, based on conceptions of human capability, poverty eradication, participation, environmental safe-guards, and gendered empowerment were characteristic traits.
13 Commission on Human Rights, Open-Ended Working Group on the Right to Development. *Fourth Report of the Independent Expert on the Right to Development,* Arjun Sengupta, submitted in accordance with the Committee Resolution 2001/9, UN Doc. E/CN.4/2002/WG18.2 (December 20, 2001).

Added to this perspective of claiming rights, however, the more recent thinking on rights-based development emphasizes the accountability of the duty-holders.

There are, therefore, three possible criteria defining a rights-based approach:

- A rights-based approach makes explicit reference to human rights achievement as an integral part of the objectives of development. This is what is expressed in the definition of OHCHR when "express linkage to human rights" is mentioned.[14] Inherent in this interpretation is that human rights achievement can be understood as one among several other objectives of development.

- A rights-based approach is a framework for the process of human development, operationally directed to promoting and protecting human rights. Thus, while goals other than rights-based goals can be involved in a rights-based approach, the latter must still be associated with a kind of development that reinforces human development and human rights; thus, dimensions of accountability of duty-holders will often be in focus in rights-based approaches.

- A rights-based approach empowers people to claim their rights. This criterion anchors a rights-based approach with empowerment of right-holders. Some actors such as Care International do not refer to human rights, but to rights in general.

As evident from the definitions above, these options are often mixed. What is characteristic of the definitions introduced above is the reference to substantive contents such as accountability, participation, empowerment, and anti-poverty — in short, the emphasis on a human development agenda combined with an emphasis on rights. Among these combined definitions between the normative and non-normative contents, however, it is not clear which principle is the prevailing one.

In the discussion below, we seek to clarify this balance by looking more closely into the assumptions of a rights-based approach.

The Scope of Rights-Based Development

One major question is the scope of rights-based development. How far does it extend in terms of reorganizing development interventions and support? To what degree should development agencies in general incorporate the notion?

In interpreting the right to development, the UN's Independent Expert on the Right to Development establishes a close linkage between a rights-based approach and the right to development. In his third report, the Independent Expert states:

---

14   ODI, the Overseas Development Institute, earlier defined a rights-based approach accordingly: "A rights-based approach to development sets the achievement of human rights as an objective of development policy" (1999). Compared to the formulation of OHCHR, the ODI formulation is more restrictive inasmuch as realization of human rights is set as the goal and objective of development policy. Interpreted in this way, human rights realization will define what development policy should be. The later formulation of OHCHR provides for a less rigorous way of implementing a rights-based approach.

Regarding the right to development as a human right implies two things, especially when that right refers to a process of development. First, the realization of each human right and of all of them together has to be carried out in a rights-based manner, as a participatory, accountable and transparent process with equity in decision-making and sharing of the fruits of the process while maintaining respect for civil and political rights. Secondly, the objectives of development should be expressed in terms of claims or entitlements of rights-holders which duty-bearers must protect and promote in accordance with international human rights standards of equity and justice.[15]

The assumption here that the objectives of development should be expressed in terms of claims or entitlements of rights-holders which duty-bearers must protect and promote, represents a quest for restructuring development processes, including the granting of development aid: Objectives of development have to be put in rights terms.

According to this understanding, however, the Independent Expert is promoting a very broad — and not, in our view, realistic — model that expects rights-based approaches to guide all development efforts. A similar rights-based approach was once suggested by André Frankovits and Patrick Earle, of the Human Rights Council of Australia, who argue that: "In effect, human rights and development are not distinct separate spheres. Development should in fact be seen as a subset of human rights."[16]

This position can be read as a grand scheme for the restructuring of development assistance according to human rights norms and instruments. Some human rights scholars tend to argue that the traditional development model has failed and that it has had a negative or detrimental impact on poor or marginalized populations. One question remains important, however: Can a rights-based framework remedy the structural or institutional ailments of the developing world? Or more specifically, when development policies have failed, is it because of a failure to include a rights framework, or is it because of political interference, corrupt state leaders and institutions, inadequate resources or capacity, or local class or political struggles?

Our view that a broad and all-encompassing approach is not realistic is partly based on an understanding of existing practices of development, where only a few cases of rights-based approaches prevail. More important, however, is our contention that a reorganization of development programs according to an all encompassing rights-based pattern must be based on a realistic assumption of real value-added in incorporating a human rights approach in all corners of development thinking. It cannot be based only on a normative interpretation.

---

15 Commission on Human Rights, Working Group on the Right to Development, *Report of the Independent Expert on the Right to Development*, Arjun Sengupta, pursuant to General Assembly Resolution 54/175 and Commission on Human Rights Resolution E/CN.4/Res/2000/5. UN Doc. E/CN.4/2000/WG.18/CRP/1 (2000), p. 8.
16 André Frankovits and Patrick Earle, *The Rights Way to Development: A Human Rights Approach to Development Assistance, Policy and Practice* (Maroubra: The Human Rights Council of Australia, Inc., 2001), p. 25.

Operational Strategies for the Application of Rights-Based Approaches

The Relationship Between Concepts and Operationalization

One critique of rights-based approaches concerns the alleged discrepancy between human rights principles and the reality of rights. Bas de Gaay Fortman states that while "the whole world appears to have a mouth full of human rights, in terms of implementation one might still speak of a crisis."[17] He argues that the basic weakness of human rights is that they are mainly proclaimed rather than implemented.[18]

Surely, that the reality does not correspond to the law does not necessarily remove the relevance of the law. Indeed, as Jack Donnelly has brilliantly argued, the paradox of rights is that the fewer you possess, the more important they become.[19]

Another, more serious aspect of the critique, is purported by Peter Uvin, arguing that rights-based approaches introduce little more than "rhetorical, feel good change"[20] or serve as "a fig leaf for the continuation of status quo,"[21] with little to offer in the way of operational practice. As always, it is refreshing when someone points out that the emperor has no clothes. While acknowledging the discrepancy between the conceptual and operational level of rights-based approaches, however, we posit that the discrepancy between the normative and the operational level stems not from conceptual sinister motives, but rather from the fact that rights-based approaches originate from legal principles, which are still in the process of being inscribed into practice.

Common Principles of Rights-Based Approaches?

A critique of rights-based approaches calls attention to the importance of their operational implications and questions whether they will change the reality of those in need. Hence, we ask: What does a rights-based approach have to offer current development paradigms? What kind of changes do rights-based organizations propose? How are program areas changed?

The ways in which organizations conceptualize a rights-based approach differ, as has been noted, and these differences become even more apparent when one examines how organizations operationalize the approach. Variations are unavoidable — and indeed necessary — for organizations operating with different mandates, programs, and implementation capabilities. For an approach where central values are said to be coherence, transparency, and an increased possibility for coordination, some consistency might, however, be warranted.

Despite these differences, it is possible to discern a number of common constituent elements or principles within the various applications of a rights-based

---

17 Bas de Gaay Fortman, "'Rights-Based Approaches': Any New Thing Under the Sun?" IDEA Newsletter (December 2000).
18 Ibid.
19 Jack Donnelly, Universal Human Rights in Theory and Practice (New York: Cornell University Press, 2002).
20 Peter Uvin, On High Moral Ground: The Incorporation of Human Rights by the Development Enterprise, p. 1. Available at http://fletcher.tufts.edu/praxis/archives/xvii/Uvin.pdf.
21 Ibid.

approach. While the terms may vary, most organizations emphasize principles such as universality, interdependence between rights, accountability, participation, non-discrimination, and empowerment.[22] A closer examination of these principles and how they have been interpreted and translated into practice follows.[23]

Universality

In human rights terms, universality relates to the foundational principle of the Universal Declaration, stating that "recognition of the inherent dignity and of the equal and inalienable rights of all members of the human family is the foundation of freedom, justice and peace in the world." A broad understanding of the principle could translate needs into rights held by "all people, everywhere, and at all times," simply by virtue of being human. It implies both an aspiration, namely that the enjoyment of rights should become universal (and thus, areas with an identified rights deficit should be targeted), and an obligation, namely that all individuals should be treated as holders of rights. In essence, then, by being a question of rights rather than charity, development transforms itself into a matter of justice.[24]

These principles were promoted by the UN Secretary General as one of the defining aspects of a rights-based approach:

> A rights-based approach to development describes situations not simply in terms of human needs, or of development requirements, but in terms of society's obligations to respond to the inalienable rights of individuals. It empowers people to demand justice as a right, not as a charity and gives communities the moral basis from which to claim international assistance where needed.[25]

Similar statements can be found by others who support a rights-based approach. UNDP notes that the vision of a rights-based approach is "to secure the freedom, well-being and dignity of all people everywhere."[26] UNICEF explicitly adopts universality as an overall guiding principle,[27] and both Oxfam and Sida express similar notions on the universal normative relevance and on the need to view development "beneficiaries" as rights-holders.[28]

Formally, the principle of universality within a rights-based approach has been argued to mean that all development programming should have the objective of

---

22   Craig G. Mokhiber, *Human Rights in Development: What, Why and How* (Geneva: UN OHCHR, 2000).

23   It is important to note that when we refer to "operationalize" or other terms relating to operationalization, we are primarily referring to intentions, guidelines, and action plans; we are not determining how or if these have been carried out in practice. In general, a number of organizations applying a rights-based approach have not moved beyond the intentional or piloting phase.

24   Stephen Marks, *The Human Rights Framework for Development: Five Approaches*. UNDP Global Forum on World Development, October 2000.

25   Annual Report of the Secretary-General on the Work of the Organization, UN Doc. A/53/1 (August 1998).

26   UNDP, *Poverty Reduction and Human Rights: A Practice Note* (June 2003).

27   UNICEF, *A Human Rights Approach to UNICEF Programming for Children and Women – What It Is, and Some Changes It Will Bring*, UNICEF Doc. CF/EXD/1998-04 (April 21, 1998). Available at http://www.coe-dmha.org/UNICEF/HPT_IntroReading01.htm.

28   Sida, *Democracy and Human Rights in Swedish Development Cooperation* (February 1999). Available at http://www.sweden.gov.se/content/1/c6/02/04/00/ab9c2080.pdf.

improving human rights. In real terms a universal application of human rights as the explicit goal of development may test the relevance of their application and many rights-based organizations take more implicit strategies for the promotion of human rights. In general, initiatives taken to promote the universality of human rights fall within three categories, ranging from the most to the least explicit: 1) promotion of a specific human right, 2) building the capacity of human rights-relevant institutions, and 3) promotion of human rights values or the creation of an enabling environment.

OHCHR argues for the first of these approaches, stating that "the explicit reference to rights as the objective of development and the establishment of express links to international, regional and national human rights instruments is a crucial element of a rights-based approach." This argument has been supported mainly by NGOs, such as Oxfam, but also by UNICEF, which define their programs in terms of the promotion of specific rights or classes of rights.

UNDP and Sida define the relationship mainly at the policy level and confine rights objectives to specific projects targeting primarily the two later categories.[29] These types of initiatives have been taken up generally by classical development organizations, thus broadening the agenda of what would be considered "development territory." UNDP continues to be concerned with classical good governance issues as well as with participation and empowerment in terms of creating an enabling environment for human rights, and its projects now also include support to parliaments, ombudsman, and national human rights institutions.[30] The approach taken is primarily an add-on approach, which does not necessarily explicitly target human rights within specific programs and projects.

Indivisibility

The principle of indivisibility of rights was strongly supported by the Vienna Declaration and by the Independent Expert on the Right to Development and has become an important element of a rights-based approach. In its positive form the principle denotes that a sustainable advancement of any right will depend on a similar advancement of all other rights. A negative reading of the principle stresses that no right should be pursued to the detriment of any others. The OHCHR defines the principle by stating:

> Rights-based approaches are comprehensive in their consideration of the full range of indivisible, interdependent and interrelated rights: civil, cultural, economic, political and social. This calls for a development framework with sectors that mirror internationally guaranteed rights, thus covering, for example, health, education, housing, justice administration, personal security and political participation."[31]

---

29   A third practice may be observed in organizations that adopt programs using the vocabulary of rights, but referring to what is arguably self-styled rights, a practice that may potentially undermine the carefully devised universal system.
30   UNDP, *Integrating Human Rights with Sustainable Human Development: A Policy Document* (New York: UNDP, 1998); UNDP, *A Human Rights-Based Approach to Development Programming in UNDP – Adding the Missing Link* (New York: UNDP, 2001).
31   Mokhiber, *supra*, note 22.

In general what the principle brings to development is a focus on the need for "holistic" programming or a comprehensive development agenda. Organizations operationalize a rights-based approach through a number of changes, including instituting:

- new areas of programming,
- new modes of analysis,
- increased coordination, and
- ground rules for development.

A comprehensive mode of development planning involves the adoption of new program areas focusing on non-economic aspects of poverty reduction. Most rights-based organizations stress the need for inter-sectoral strategies and approaches and the need to establish synergies among different program types. UNDP emphasizes that a rights-based approach requires particular attention to institution building, democratic support, and legal and policy reform. However, little attention is paid to how laws and social norms affect target groups of UNDP programming,[32] and changes are, in practice, related primarily to good governance programming. Sida emphasizes support for elections, media support, and judicial capacity-building programs as an immediate effect of the introduction of a rights-based approach.[33] UNICEF also emphasizes the need for holistic programming but stresses the corresponding need for integrated strategies combining advocacy, communication, and capacity and partnership building.[34] On the basis of their adoption of a rights-based approach, Oxfam has defined completely new program types, including a particular program on equitable participation in political, economic, and social policy- and decision-making.[35]

Holistic programming will call for new and more comprehensive situation analysis for program preparation. Additionally, acknowledging that few organizations can cover the full spectrum of rights, all organizations recognize that operationalizing comprehensive programs will require more coordination with other organizations. For UNDP, this is being done through the Common Country Assessment/UN Development Assistance Framework (CCA/UNDAF) procedures,[36] but otherwise, few organizations elaborate how this requirement is to be put into practice.

The final implication of the principle of indivisibility — that no program should act to the detriment of any human rights — has been explored in policies of only a few donors. UNDP, however, has developed a formal check list to avoid programming that may violate human rights. NORAD has also included this in its *Handbook on Human Rights Assessment*.[37] It seems surprising, however, that this dimension, which has been extensively considered within the humanitarian field, has not been explored more within rights-based development programming.

---

32   UNDP, *Poverty Reduction and Human Rights: A Practice Note* (June 2003).
33   Sida, *supra*, note 28.
34   Available at http://coe-dmha.org/Unicef/HPT_IntroReading01.htm.
35   Oxfam, *Strategic Plan 2001-2004* (Oxford: Oxfam International, 2001).
36   UNDP, *supra*, note 32.
37   NORAD, *Handbook in Human Rights Assessment* (February 2001).

Accountability

Accountability may be the principle where a rights-based approach distinguishes itself most clearly from other approaches to development. The principle is obviously a common requirement for all development activities. What is special about accountability within a rights-based framework, however, is that the principle is legalistic and focuses on how to transform rights-holders from being passive recipients of aid to being empowered claimants.

Once needs are transformed into rights, downward accountability is emphasized, along with accountability to donors.[38] Accountability within a rights-based framework focuses on organizational accountability and accountability between duty-bearer and rights-holder. This implies attention to new modes of account-ability such as laws, policies, institutions, administrative procedures, and other mechanisms of redress.[39]

The UN agencies mirror the definition of the OHCHR, and most other rights-based organizations also identify the same principles as central to increasing accountability. The operationalization of these principles, however, differs. Most initiatives group around three sets of activities:

- Analysis focusing on rights-holders and duty-bearers,
- Increasing the accountability of duty-holders, and
- Strengthening organizational procedures for accountability.

As noted, increasing accountability in programming to a large extent evolves around a focus on the relation between duty-bearers and rights-holders. As noted by Carolin Moser and Andy Norton, a potential limitation of a human rights perspective on accountability is the overriding focus on state-citizen relationships as the basis of obligations and corresponding rights.[40] The expansion of duty-holders to include the full range of relevant actors, such as individuals, states, local organizations and authorities, private companies, aid donors, and international institutions, is a necessary trait of a rights-based approach, but also one that points to the difficulty in keeping a strictly legally centered approach when exporting the rights-based ideals into a broader development agenda.

In general, various strategies are taken depending on the nature of the duty-bearer and the mandates of the rights-based organization. UNDP, thus, continues to work primarily with state accountability and applies what can be termed a capacity-development perspective. The focus of UNDP in this regard is not human rights, but rather the added value to development. UNDP states that "without a sound legal framework, without an independent and honest judiciary, economic and social development risks collapse."[41] In increasing the accountability of duty-holders, the

---

38 This should not be taken to imply that rights-based development does not require accountability toward donors.
39 *Ibid.*
40 Caroline Moser and Andy Norton, *To Claim Our Rights: Livelihood, Security and Sustainable Development* (London: Overseas Development Institute, 2001).
41 UNDP, *The Application of a Human Rights Approach to Development: What Is the Added Value?* Available at http://www.undp.org/governance/docshurist/rightsapproach.doc.

human rights framework offers a stronger and more stringent system for target setting and benchmarks.

Oxfam's strategy focuses less on capacity building of duty-holders than on global advocacy for human rights. They thus take the more confrontational role associated with traditional human rights work.[42] They also are more concerned with a related aspect of accountability –namely, strengthening the ability of individuals and civil society to claim and monitor rights. This dimension will be further examined in relation to the principle of empowerment below.

Lastly, a rights-based approach is generally acknowledged to require accountability not only to outcomes, but also to the processes of development. This naturally applies to all stakeholders, but also to the aid organization itself. OHCHR notes the need of rights-based organizations to pay "due attention to issues of accessibility, including to development processes, institutions, information and redress or complaints mechanisms."[43] While few organizations go as far, most organizations seek to enhance accountability by focusing on increased participation of beneficiaries and acknowledge the need for institutional accountability in terms of management based on organizational efficiency, openness, and accountability.

Participation, Non-Discrimination, and Empowerment

Participation, non-discrimination, and empowerment are distinct principles, but the consequences for rights-based organizations overlap somewhat. As these principles are not specific to a rights-based approach, it is important to identify their specific contributions to this approach.

Participation

In instrumental terms, participation enables people to make effective decisions on issues affecting their own lives. Rights-based approaches require "a high degree of participation, including from communities, civil society, minorities, indigenous peoples, women and others. Such participation must be 'active, free, and meaningful,' so that mere formal or 'ceremonial' contacts with beneficiaries are not sufficient."[44]

Participation should be seen as intrinsic to the process of development, and, understood as the broader aim of creating public participation, should itself be seen as one of the objectives of development. Initiatives to operationalize this principle fall within two categories: 1) increasing participation in programming and 2) increasing public participation through programming (see non-discrimination).

Increasing participation within programming relates primarily to a number of requirements to project cycle management. Aid organizations emphasize that participation must include all phases of programming, including formulation, implementation, and monitoring. The second aspect focuses especially on strength-

---

42   Oxfam, *Strategic Plan 2001-2004* (Oxford: Oxfam International, 2001).
43   Mokhiber, *supra*, note 22.
44   OHCHR, *What Is a Rights-Based Approach?* Available at http://www.unhchr.ch/development/approaches-04.html.

ening the involvement of media, interest groups, or civil society in public decision-making. Oxfam goes further and focuses also on international issues of participation, such as advocacy efforts on equitable access and the need for reform of the international decision-making bodies.

Non-Discrimination

Access to public decision-making by minorities or vulnerable groups is an important dimension of participation in development. Non-discrimination implies "[g]iving particular attention to discrimination, equality, equity and vulnerable groups. These groups include women, minorities, indigenous peoples and prisoners, but there is no universal checklist of who is most vulnerable in every given context."[45]

Discrimination goes beyond the economic sphere and emphasizes how laws, polices, or administrative practices may create or combat structural discrimination. A rights-based approach highlights the fact that a great deal of poverty originates from political, social, cultural, or institutional discriminatory practices — both overt and covert — at the international, national, and local levels. Operational implications relate primarily to methodological requirements and targeting the vulnerable.

The need to identify the vulnerable population in development programs is noted by all organizations examined in this chapter. UNDP notes that programs should account for those whom they reach as well as those whom they do not.[46] Targeting the vulnerable is generally seen as an issue of mainstreaming non-discrimination across all aspects of programming and creating mechanisms of inclusion and empowerment.

Empowerment

The last aspect of a rights-based approach is the emphasis of the principle of empowerment. The central premise of the principle is that development should not be understood simply as a process of improving people's incomes through economic growth, but also as a process of expanding the fundamental choices and freedoms of people. Empowerment emphasizes the need to target root causes of poverty, often related to non-economic or structural problems or, as in the above, simply to the absence of human rights. According to OHCHR,

> Rights-based approaches give preference to strategies for empowerment over charitable responses. They focus on beneficiaries as the owners of rights and the directors of development, and emphasize the human person as the centre of the development process. The goal is to give people the power, capacities, capabilities and access needed to change their own lives, improve their own communities and influence their own destinies.[47]

---

45 Mokhiber, *supra*, note 22.
46 UNDP, *supra*, note 32.
47 Mokhiber, *supra*, note 22.

The operationalization of empowerment in practice relates to the sum of the initiatives taken in relation to the principles above; however, the principle may be categorized by relating it primarily to two sets of initiatives — focusing on non-economic aspects of poverty, and enhancing people's ability to claim their rights.

This conception of empowerment is inspired by Amartya Sen's understanding of capability. Economic development represents only one of many ways to expand empowerment and human freedom.

Empowerment also implies people's capacity to claim and exercise their rights effectively. Sida focuses on a broad notion of fostering participation as the basis of empowering individuals and civil society.[48] UNDP elaborates that accountability, to be effective, needs to be demanded, and thus requires the empowerment of claimholders and the inclusion of civil society.

UNICEF underscores the need to pay attention to the root causes of poverty or vulnerability and promote empowerment, understood as the capacity of people to enjoy or claim their rights. For them this implies addressing the multiple causes of a given situation, including attention to the legislative frame and integrating strategies of advocacy and capacity building.[49]

Whereas UNDP often talks more generally about creating an "enabling environment," Oxfam works more directly with strengthening the ability of groups to demand social justice.[50] Oxfam adds an international perspective by also stressing the need to establish and implement "fair rules for the global economy,"[51] thus noting that in a globalized economy, many issues that affect local communities reach beyond national borders.

Principles, Assumptions, and Implications of a Rights-Based Approach

At two levels, it is necessary to explore more profoundly what the core dimensions of a rights-based approach are: First, it is necessary to examine how a rights-based approach relates to the right to development. Secondly, it is important to examine what the key principles and implications of the approach are when exposed in the development field.

Justifying a Rights-Based Approach in Development

The deliberations and strategizing of a rights-based approach have been based so far on concerns with current development practices, but many of the concerns raised are of a general and unfocused nature. A document by OHCHR refers to the "essentially pragmatic and empiricist approach of development professionals" and the inherent instrumentalist propositions of such an approach, which is then contrasted

48   Sida, *Democratic Governance: Four Reports on Democratic Governance in International development Cooperation Summary* (February 2003). Available at http://www.sida.se/shared/jsp/download.jsp?f=SIDA2950en_webb.pdf&a=2880.
49   UNICEF, *Human Rights for Children and Women: How UNICEF Helps Make Them a Reality* (New York: UNICEF, 1999).
50   Oxfam, *supra*, note 42.
51   *Ibid.*

with a normative-legal one.[52] Structural adjustment policies and donor condition-ality — that is, the imposition of policy benchmarks that the developing state should achieve as a condition of receiving loans and assistance — are often seen by human rights experts to be a dominant trait of past development policies. Such policies are believed to exacerbate already existing biases of an overriding economistic policy.[53]

It can, however, be argued that human rights agencies, in devising their respec-tive rights-based approaches, have been more concerned with the human rights prism than with a more thorough exploration of development thinking. Thus, the basic principles discussed in section four are characterized by general human rights concerns rather than by development concerns. This could mean that a better under-standing of the value added of a rights-based approach might be hampered by the fact that its basic tenets have not really been exposed to the development context. This seems particularly true as regards the insertion of key concepts like universality and indivisibility.

Figure 1, elaborated by Siddiq Osmani, illustrates a particular understanding of the origins and genealogy of RBA and its relationship to the right to development.[54] The diagram shows that a human rights approach to development derives from two sources — from development and from human rights activities. The human rights approach to development leads, in turn, to the implementation or realization of the right to development.

In our opinion, there are two principal objections to the figure as it stands, how-ever. First, the figure presupposes that the right to development has been formulated based on development experiences. This is the case only to a limited degree. The right to development hardly expresses any strong interpretation of learning from development work except as regards very general notions about the North-South relationship.

Figure 1. Human Rights-Based Approach to Development

Secondly, the figure can be interpreted to mean that a rights-based approach to development precedes the right to development in chronological terms. Such an in-terpretation would, however, be problematic inasmuch as the right to development and rights-based approaches have been interpreted on parallel tracks, so to speak.

---

52   Craig Mushier, *Human Rights in Development; What, Why, How* (Geneva: OHCHR, 2000). Available at http://www.vivatinternational.org/1%20POVERTY%20ERADICATION/human_rights _in_ devt.htm.
53   Frankovits and Earle, *supra*, note 16, p. 36. See also Patrick Van Weerelt, *The Application of a Human Rights Approach to Development: What Is the Added Value?* (New York: UNDP, 2000).
54   The figure was presented at the Nobel Symposium in Oslo, October 2003.

As an alternative, we have tried to use the model of Figure 1 as a source of inspiration for Figure 2. This latter figure sketches two parallel tracks that have occurred almost simultaneously. Development and human rights programs have engendered a common inspiration, namely the concept of a human rights-based approach to development. This approach is currently inspiring new practices of rights-based approaches among donors as well as among international NGOs and local NGOs.

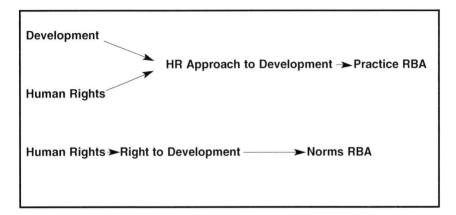

Figure 2. Practice and Norms, Rights-Based Approach to Development

A parallel process (as adopted, for example, by the Independent Expert of the Human Rights Commission[55]) is a normative one that is inspired by the right to development. OHCHR and UNDP have also been involved in a normative understanding of rights-based development.

The model stresses that there are normative as well as practical dimensions in justifying a rights-based approach. Implicit in the normative track is an assumption that RBA derives from discourses on the right to development.

One major challenge of the broader application of a rights-based approach is, therefore, to explore the linkages between normative and practical concerns of the development context — that is, to facilitate a strong dialogue between development experiences and human rights norms about development. The norms inherent in the Declaration on the Right to Development have to be incorporated in practical de-

---

55   Interestingly, the first report elaborated by the Independent Expert does not refer to a rights-based approach; see *UN Economic and Social Council, Commission on Human Rights* (1999). *Study on the Current State of Progress in the Implementation of the Right to Development,* submitted by Arjun K. Sengupta, Independent Expert, *Pursuant to Commission Resolution 1998/72 and General Assembly 53/155.* Only in later reports does the Independent Expert refer specifically to a rights-based approach. In the second report, it was stressed that "...the rights approach to development is not the same thing as realizing the right to development" (see UN Doc. E/CN.4/2000.WG.18/CRP.1 (September 2000), p. 4), while in the third report, it was stated that "...the realization of each human right and all of them together has to be carried out in a rights-based manner..." (see UN Doc. E/CN.4/2001/WG.18/2 [January 2001], p. 8). The tendency in the writings of the Independent Expert has been to strengthen the linkages between the right to development and rights-based approaches; see also Margot E. Salomon and Arjun Sengupta, *The Right to Development: Obligations of States and the Rights of Minorities and Indigenous Peoples* (London: Minority Rights Group International, 2003).

velopment efforts as part of a mainstreaming effort. It would, however, be premature to argue that this has already happened in development thinking and practices.

Four Constituent Elements of a Rights-Based Approach

The question of where the meeting points of normative and practical thinking are in the development context begs deeper theoretical work than is possible here. An examination of rights-based principles, however, reveals four obvious areas: in the development of values and application of norms of justice, in structures and institutions of power and governance, in the integration of the rule of law and legality in development, and in the analysis of poverty and entitlements.

These four points draw on the examination of normative principles above but seek to elucidate four constituent principles of a rights-based approach and their implications in the development field. In their implementation of a rights-based approach, NGOs tend to define their strategies not far from these principles.[56] Table 1 summarizes the principles and some of their major implications.

The first principle is that development efforts would benefit from being anchored in the normative or legal domain, typically international human rights law, but organizations like Care International should be careful to relate a rights-based approach only to international human rights law. The implication of this principle is that normative-legal entitlements become constituent elements of development policy.[57]

The second principle is well known and one of the most well argued in a rights-based framework. It serves analytical purposes, but its strongest implication may be to emphasize the accountability of duty-bearers and thus provide a means for linking human rights to governance development programs. Accountability in a rights-based sense defines an accountability of duty-bearers to human rights.

The third principle links the focus on justice and rights. The role of human rights in combating poverty has gained growing attention in the UN by the UNDP human development agenda, as well as through the growing focus on poverty by the OHCHR and UNESCO.

The last principle addresses how economic policies supported by development institutions may do human rights harm. For instance, structural adjustment policies have implied that public sector spending was cut, with adverse human rights implications. The implication here is that human rights establishes a bottom line, a set of minimum standards below which narrow economistic and political rationality

---

56   See, for instance, a checklist developed by Oxfam UK in use during 2003 to assess whether a rights-based approach is pursued:
- Do we focus on people's rights?
- Do we concentrate on worst violations and most vulnerable people?
- Do we support people to demand their rights?
- Do we strengthen accountability of governments for rights?
- Do we fight discrimination and promote equality?

57   OHCHR argues that human rights professionals generally work within a clearly defined normative legal policy framework. They thus tend to be highly skeptical of instrumentalist arguments. Craig Mokhiber, *Human Rights in Development; What, Why, How* (Geneva: OHCHR, 2000). Available at http://www.vivatinternational.org/1%20POVERTY%20ERADICATION/human_rights_in_devt.htm.

Table 1.

Principle 1	Principle 2	Principle 3	Principle 4
Development efforts based on clearly defined normative principles, including those of international human rights law, bring more just and sustainable development.	Rights-based development brings a clear division of responsibility based on a framework of rights-holders and duty-bearers.	Individual and group entitlements and rights are crucial in the creation of equity, non-discrimination, and well-being.	Human rights trump political and economic expediency.
Implication	**Implication**	**Implication**	**Implication**
Legal entitlements, including those of international law, must become constituent concerns of development policy.	There are clear gains in terms of good governance in applying a frame-work where accountability plays a crucial role.	Rights-based empowerment is an effective means for combating poverty and redressing prevailing unjust power and eco-nomic structures.	Do no human rights harm! Mainstream human rights in development.

cannot be allowed to move. Thus, the principle of "do no human rights harm" refers to the establishment of minimum conditions which have to be respected.

Conclusions

Interpretations of a rights-based approach have evolved conceptually before being operationally developed. Currently, UN agencies, donors, and NGOs operating at the international and local levels are involved in a process of operationalization. Such processes demand a clearer and more feasible conceptualization as well as an understanding of the value added of the approach compared with other approaches.

According to the analysis above, the implications of a rights-based approach are analytical and substantive. At the analytical level, a rights framework will imply a different analysis emphasizing not only a focus on rights and empowerment, but also a different focus on accountability and governance.

At the substantive level, a rights-based approach implies a focus on rights rather than needs, a focus on rights-based advocacy, capacity development in relation to rights implementation, and the "do not harm" principle. A rights-based approach has implications for bench-marking and monitoring — not least for performance assessment in relation to human rights respect, empowerment, accountability, and institutional capacity building — including institutional development to seek redress in cases of human rights violations. Non-discrimination and targeting of vulnerable groups should also be included in rights-based performance measurements, but the methods of non-discrimination are not yet well developed.

The analysis above indicates, too, what a rights-based approach is and what it is not. While part of the rights discourse tends to focus on participation, empowerment, and accountability — that is, themes that are recurrent also in the development field — the specific marks of a rights-based approach are three characteristics that may be performed in combination or separately:

- programs and projects are developed according to human rights law and principles;
- programs and projects have objectives of rights realization and rights empowerment; and
- programs and projects are defined with components of human rights accountability.

A rights-based framework may not have equal relevance in all spheres of development thinking. The extent to which rights-based approaches deal specifically with human rights issues or human rights-relevant institutions could serve as an important litmus test. In sum, four dimensions of potential contributions of a rights-based approach in development exist:

1) the foundation in universally accepted norms and legal standards, a fact with strong implications in terms of accountability and governance;

2) the force of legality, which strengthens sustainability;

3) the notion of justice forcefully inherent in human rights thinking, with strong implications for efforts of combating poverty and marginalization; and

4) the prospects of defining minimum standards in assessments of no harm done.

A rights-based approach includes normative as well as practical sources of inspiration and is applicable in four fields of development: 1) governance, 2) rule of law, legal change, and access to justice, 3) poverty, vulnerability, and discrimination, and 4) safeguard policies.

At the practical level, we think that a dialogue between development and human rights advocates may be more fruitful than confrontation as a tool to advance and consolidate a rights-based approach. Experiences are being gained now in the field. Learning from these experiences is important to conceptualize and consolidate a rights-based approach.

Part II. Duties and Responsibilities

4 | Obligations to Implement the Right to Development: Philosophical, Political, and Legal Rationales
Stephen P. Marks

The assumption of the Declaration on the Right to Development (1986) is that states have obligations with respect to this putative right. In fact, the Declaration enumerates four duties and responsibilities of states:

1. "The duty to formulate appropriate national development policies that aim at the constant improvement of the well-being of the entire population and of all individuals, on the basis of their active, free and meaningful participation in development and in the fair distribution of the benefits resulting therefrom;"[1]

2. "The primary responsibility for the creation of national and international conditions favourable to the realization of the right to development;"[2]

3. "The duty to co-operate with each other in ensuring development and eliminating obstacles to development;"[3] and

4. "The duty to take steps, individually and collectively, to formulate international development policies with a view to facilitating the full realization of the right to development."[4]

Furthermore, "should" appears 18 times in the text, usually defining what states should do, and the more imperative "shall" is used three times, twice defining duties of states[5] and once indicating how the Declaration shall be construed.[6] The claim that such duties and responsibilities are established in international law and relations as matters of accepted morality and law is problematical from the philosophical, political, and legal perspectives. This essay briefly explores each of these ways of understanding obligations in the context of the right to development.

Philosophical Rationale

Philosophers have addressed the idea that people have responsibility for the welfare of less fortunate people. Charity is a common obligation within most religious traditions. But the moral basis of an obligation of states to comply with the human

---

1   Declaration on the Right to Development, UN GAOR, 41st Sess., Supp. No. 53, at 183, UN Doc. A/RES/41/128 (1986), Article 2 (3).
2   *Id.*, article 3 (1).
3   *Id.*, article 3 (3).
4   *Id.*, article 4 (1).
5   Article 5 stipulates that "states shall take resolute steps to eliminate the massive and flagrant violations of the human rights" and Article 8 requires that "states shall ensure, *inter alia*, equality of opportunity for all in their access to basic resources, education, health services, food, housing, employment, and the fair distribution of income."
6   Article 9 (2).

right to development is not based on charity or beneficence. It is rather based on the logic of human rights, that is, a legitimate and enforceable claim by rights-holders against duty-bearers, explainable according to several philosophical approaches. I will offer a few, necessarily simplified, remarks about possible interpretations of obligations underlying the right to development from the perspective of natural law, contractarianism, consequentialism, and some of their contemporary variants, such as moral cosmopolitanism.

Under natural rights theory,[7] the moral basis for a duty toward other humans is their human nature and is independent of human constructs like borders and nationality — although in several leading natural rights theories, the political community does determine the extent of the duties. These theorists, from Thomas Aquinas and William Blackstone to Ronald Dworkin, consider that, within each society or political community, all humans are equally endowed with natural rights, and therefore have an equal entitlement to benefit from liberty and equality. The equal importance of each human life is, from this perspective, an objective truth with moral consequences. Dworkin refers to the principle of equal importance of each human life as "the special and indispensable virtue of sovereigns,"[8] meaning that the political community must treat all citizens equally.

An interesting preliminary reflection on the implication of natural law theory for the right to development is to take the proposition of classical naturalism that a human law in direct conflict with the natural right is not law.[9] This way of thinking might be applied to the right to development. The 1986 Declaration uses the natural law language of "an inalienable human right," the essence of which is that "every human person and all peoples are entitled to participate in, contribute to, and enjoy economic, social, cultural and political development." Internally, a law that allowed corrupt leaders to exploit resources for their own profit and against the people's right to development or that suspended human rights guaranteed by the constitution and international treaties — allegedly because the country had not gained a level of development to afford them — would be a "perversion of law," contrary to the "inalienable human right to development."

Externally, the right to development focuses as much on international society as it does on national social structures. Extending the reasoning of classical naturalism to international law, a similar argument could be applied, for example, to a particu-

---

7   The natural law tradition in legal theory considers certain rights to belong self-evidently to individuals as human beings and to be based on universally valid principles governing nature and society, the aim of which is the preservation of the natural and imprescriptible "rights of man," in the vocabulary of the 18th century. Finnis defines natural law theory as one that is "able to identify conditions and principles of practical right-mindedness, of good and proper order among men and in individual conduct." John Finnis, *Natural Law and Natural Rights* (Oxford: Clarendon Press, 1980), p. 18.

8   Ronald Dworkin, *Sovereign Virtue: The Theory and Practice of Equality* (Cambridge, MA: Harvard University Press, 2000), p. 6.

9   Aquinas famously said that "Since a tyrannical law is not in accord with reason, it is not a law absolutely speaking, but is instead a kind of perversion of law . . . For it has nothing of the character of law except to the extent that (a) it is a dictate of someone who is in charge of the subjects and that (b) it intends that the subjects obey the law in the right way, i.e., that they be good — not absolutely speaking, but in relation to that regime." Thomas Aquinas, "On the Law," *Summa Theologiae*, First part of the second part (i-ii) (Trans. Alfred J. Freddoso). Available at http://www.thomasinternational.org/projects/step/treatiseonlaw/delege092_1.htm.

larly predatory investment agreement that blatantly favored exorbitant returns on investment by a multinational corporation at the expense of the development of the host country. Such an agreement would have a direct impact on the enjoyment by every human person of this development and, accordingly, would not be valid as law.

The moral egalitarianism of liberal political philosophy tends to accept differences beyond rather than within state boundaries — not because the arbitrary division into geographical jurisdictions is just but because of the significance of the community to which one belongs, which to a large extent is coterminous with those national boundaries. It is within each state that the just distribution of opportunity or resources is to be settled, whether argued in terms of equality of resources[10] or equality of welfare.[11] The right to development includes the right to the "constant improvement of the well-being of the entire population and of all individuals,[12] which suggests equality of welfare. However, other provisions are much more in line with equality of resources and even equality of opportunity. Specifically, the 1986 Declaration calls on states to "ensure, *inter alia*, equality of opportunity for all in their access to basic resources, education, health services, food, housing, employment and the fair distribution of income." The frequent references in the Declaration to rights that are "inalienable" and "universal," to treatment that is "equal" and "fair," and to "the human person [as] the central subject of the development process" have a certain natural law resonance to them.

To reflect on the philosophical rationale for duties in the context of the right to development, we need to examine natural law theory that considers equal worth of human beings outside the confines of one's own political community. Such global approaches to moral egalitarianism are shared by proponents of "global liberalism" and "cosmopolitan liberalism" to be discussed below in the context of contractarian theories. Before doing so, it is worth looking at one more variant of natural law theory, namely, the substantive, neo-naturalist perspective. According to this view, certain basic goods, such as friendship, religion, play, knowledge, aesthetic experience, health, and life itself, are universal and thus the same moral principles guide human beings everywhere in the pursuit of those goods. Law provides authoritative rules with sanctions and adjudicative institutions to solve coordination and access problems in the enjoyment of those basic goods and thus contributes to the common good.[13]

The right to development could be conceived, from this perspective, as an effort at the coordination of access to these common goods on a global scale. Thus, an international norm establishing responsibility of an affluent state for the realization of development in a poorer country in a manner that ensures human rights would be based on the tenant that all human beings are endowed with the same natural rights to these basic goods. Under this argument, all humans have an equal natural right to benefit from the resources available in their respective countries and to a coordinated

---

10   Dworkin, *supra*, note 8, pp. 65-119.
11   *Id.*, pp. 11-64.
12   Declaration on the Right to Development, Preamble and Article 2 (3).
13   Finnis, *supra*, note 7, pp. 85-99.

effort internationally to share access to those basic goods. The 1986 Declaration affirms the "inalienable right" of peoples "to full sovereignty over all their natural wealth and resources."[14] Their "natural right" to development thus favors optimal social arrangements for participation in development and its benefits and a duty of those living in nations with greater economic advantages to act in ways that increase the potential for enjoyment of this right by the people in poorer countries. The abolition of slavery and the slave trade and the struggle for self-determination against colonialism are clear examples from history of a moral obligation to ensure the right to development of peoples. Natural law arguments have certainly been invoked to justify both of these movements, and their relevance to the right to development is evident.

Social contractarians[15] see law and the power of the state as a necessary protection from the brutality of the State of Nature (Hobbes) or from violent disputes over property in the State of Nature (Locke). Civil government provides the legislative, judicial, and enforcement powers to protect people from transgression of the Law of Nature. The Hobbesian and Lockean versions are not as relevant to the theoretical proposition that there are duties to realize what we call today the right to development as is Rousseau's version. For Rousseau, private property produces dependence, and social and economic inequality and laws, established under the *naturalized* social contract, protect those who have power through private property. The *normative* social contract remedies this factual situation by submitting individual wills to the collective or general will, which places the collective good above individual interests. The general will is directed toward the good of the individuals in society, who, in turn, are committed to the collective good through a democratic process. By the social contract, they constitute a political society and enact laws designed to ensure the freedom and equality with which they were naturally endowed.

This concept of a contract could be extended to international society to justify a sort of global social contract in which the members of the global community submit to the common will and reduce the corrupting influence of private property and accumulation of power by the few at the expense of the many. The concept of development compacts is akin to a global social contract in the sense that developing countries give up certain prerogatives to benefit from the advantages of international cooperation. Specifically, they agree to pursue development in ways that are participatory, equitable, transparent, accountable, and respectful of human rights in exchange for the benefits to be derived from a collective effort to advance the right to development and to gain the resources needed from international cooperation for such development. Developed countries provide better conditions of aid, trade, and debt relief in exchange, presumably, for the benefits they derive from seeing their resources go toward people-centered development that reduces potential internal and international instability and conflict. The global social contract also responds to a moral sense — noticeable in bilateral donor agencies, especially in countries like

---

14   Declaration on the Right to Development, Article 1 (2).
15   The doctrine of the social contract holds that individuals relinquish their freedom to appropriate property and use violence at will in exchange for the protection of society.

Norway, Denmark, and the UK — that justice requires poverty and oppression to be alleviated by those in a position to do so.

The most significant variant of the contractarian theory is John Rawls', *A Theory of Justice*,[16] as revised in *Political Liberalism*.[17] Rational judgments made behind the "veil of ignorance" of what principles would be fair in society result, theoretically, in the determination of principles of justice based on fairness. The first such principle of justice is that everyone should enjoy as much civil liberty as possible so long as these liberties are distributed equally among citizens. The second principle is that economic inequalities are allowed only when the least-advantaged member of society is better off than would be the case under alternative arrangements. The two principles are linked in that we cannot relinquish some civil liberties in order to gain an economic advantage but must ensure equal distribution of civil liberties before allowing economic advantages to emerge, subject, as mentioned above, to the improvement of the condition of the least well off. These principles of justice therefore constrain the social contract.

It is not difficult to extend the idea of justice as fairness to obligations related to the right to development. That civil liberties sequentially precede economic advantages is confirmed by the requirement of the right to development that development must not take place at the expense of civil and political rights.[18] The principle that economic inequalities cannot be allowed unless and until the least advantaged are better off than would otherwise be the case is affirmed by the obligation that development must benefit all and that "appropriate economic and social reforms should be carried out with a view to eradicating all social injustices."[19] Frequent references to poverty reduction and the realization of the Millennium Development Goals (MDGs) in the context of the right to development further reflect the concern for the least-advantaged members of society and, through MDG 8 on global partnerships, on the least-advantaged societies within the community of nations.

These speculations on the global application of justice as fairness, however, are outside of the Rawlsian model, which focuses on the relative deprivation of citizens within the domestic society. As Michael Blake points out in his valuable survey of theories of international justice,[20] for Rawls there is "no moral reason to regard the gap between wealthy and impoverished nations as morally problematic." Rawls assumes self-sufficient nation-states and focuses on the basic structures of the territorial state and the relationships among the citizens of that state. When he does address international politics, in *The Law of Peoples*,[21] he rejects the liberal principle of distributive justice because, unlike the national society, international society is made up of corporate entities, peoples that cannot be treated like individual moral agents.

16   John Rawls, *A Theory of Justice* (Cambridge, MA: Harvard University Press, 1971).
17   John Rawls, *Political Liberalism* (New York: Columbia University Press, 1993).
18   "States should take steps to eliminate obstacles to development resulting from failure to observe civil and political rights . . . ." Declaration on the Right to Development, Article 6 (3).
19   Declaration on the Right to Development, Article 8 (1).
20   Michael Blake, "International Justice," *The Stanford Encyclopedia of Philosophy* (Fall 2005 Edition), Edward N. Zalta (ed.). Available at http://plato.stanford.edu/archives/fall2005/entries/international-justice/.
21   John Rawls, *The Law of Peoples* (Cambridge, MA: Harvard University Press, 1999).

Further, international society lacks a basic structure similar to the nation-state. Blake criticizes Rawls' parallel between the autonomy of individuals with their state, on the one hand, and of states in their mutual relations, on the other. Rawls contends that in relations among states, there should be toleration of non-liberal states similar to the toleration of diverse beliefs of individuals within the liberal states. Blake's objection is that this results in tolerating illiberal states that do not allow individuals to enjoy human rights.[22] Rawls's answer seems to be that an outlaw state that violates universal human rights "is to be condemned and in grave cases may be subjected to forceful sanctions and even to intervention."[23] However, he uses "human rights" in a somewhat idiosyncratic way. While human rights "set a necessary, though not sufficient, standard for the decency of domestic political and social institutions,"[24] only Articles 3-8 of the Universal Declaration (civil and political rights) contain "human rights proper." Norms banning massive violations, such as apartheid and genocide are a "second class of rights," while economic, social, and cultural rights "presuppose specific kinds of institutions" and presumably are not "human rights proper."[25]

Distributive justice, for Rawls, does not apply to international relations, where the only duty to provide aid is limited to the minimum necessary to maintain basic political institutions, a functioning system of public law, and acceptable relations with other states but not to reduce gaps between the rich and poor nations or among people within their own countries. Blake criticized Rawls for seeming "to permit the forms of substantive oppression fundamentally in tension with liberalism."[26] This concern is curiously addressed by the 1986 Declaration insofar as it requires all states to respect all human rights in the context of development. I say "curiously" because the Declaration neither purports to be nor is based on a well-thought-out theory of justice but is rather a highly political document, replete with compromise language that was not necessarily intended to be coherent or consistent. Nevertheless, the right to development is based on a concept of international cooperation in which toleration of each state's "right and . . . duty to formulate appropriate national development policies" is constrained by the requirements of distributive justice ("fair distribution of the benefits resulting therefrom") and human rights ("promoting, encouraging and strengthening universal respect for and observance of all human rights and fundamental freedoms for all"). It would, therefore, be contrary to the principles of the right to development if international cooperation to promote development allowed "nonliberal states" to deny human rights. In this sense, the right to development responds to Blake's critique of Rawls.

Rawls includes among "familiar and traditional principles of justice among free and democratic peoples" eight principles, the last of which is "People have a duty to

---

22 Blake, *supra*, note 20, and "Reciprocity, Stability, and Intervention: The Ethics of Disequilibrium," in Chatterjee and Scheid (eds.), *Ethics and Foreign Intervention* (Cambridge, UK: Cambridge University Press, 2003).
23 Rawls, *supra*, note 21, p. 81.
24 *Id.*, p. 80. Elsewhere, he enumerates human rights as the rights to life (including "the means of subsistence), liberty, and iformal equality as expressed by the rules of natural justice." *Id.*, p. 65.
25 *Id.*, p. 80, note 23.
26 Blake, *supra*, note 20.

assist other peoples living under unfavorable conditions that prevent their having a just or decent political and social regime."[27] This duty applies to "burdened peoples," that is, "societies whose historical, social and economic circumstances make their achieving a well-ordered regime, whether liberal or decent, difficult if not impossible."[28] These societies "lack the political culture and traditions, the human capital and know-how, and, often, the material and technological resources needed to be well-ordered."[29] He stresses not only the political culture of a society but also "the religious, philosophical, and moral traditions, as well as the industriousness and cooperative talents of its members."[30]

While Rawls concedes that ". . . [w]ell-ordered peoples have a duty to assist burdened societies," he does not consider that this duty of assistance includes "a principle of distributive justice to regulate economic and social inequalities among societies."[31] It does, however, include "insisting on human rights." He is correct that "mere dispensing funds will not suffice to rectify basic political and social injustices . . . [whereas] an emphasis on human rights may work to change ineffective regimes and the conduct of the rulers who have been callous about the well-being of their own people."[32] While coercion is not appropriate for this duty of assistance, "certain kinds of advice" and making assistance conditional on such matters as respect for the rights of women, are appropriate. These elements of the Law of Peoples favor certain aspects of the right to development, but Rawls stops short of requiring distributive justice among peoples and explicitly rejects global egalitarianism. Some of his arguments are worth pondering in the context of the right to development.

First, Rawls does not reject the application of a global principle of distributive justice to "our world as it is with its extreme injustices, crippling poverty, and inequalities,"[33] as long as it applies temporarily to help the burdened societies achieve a working liberal or decent government such that they are "able to determine the path of their own future for themselves," in accordance with the "principle of transition."[34] This principle is not incompatible with the right to development principle that each state has "the right and the duty to formulate appropriate national development policies." However, for Rawls, as soon as they reach the "target and cutoff point" of having "just liberal or decent basic institutions," or the "political autonomy of free and equal liberal and decent peoples," the duty of others to assist ceases.[35] He shifts the target a page later to the "point at which a people's basic needs (estimated in primary goods) are fulfilled and a people can stand on its own."[36] His concern is with the just institutions of society and not the well-being of its people.

---

27 *Id.* P. 37.
28 Rawls, *supra*, note 21, p. 90.
29 *Id.*, p. 106.
30 *Id.*, p. 108.
31 *Id.*, Emphasis in original.
32 *Id.*, pp. 108-109.
33 *Id.*, p. 117.
34 *Id.*, p. 118.
35 *Id.*, p. 118.
36 *Id.*, p. 119.

Second, the right to development does not require countries in need of assistance or of more favorable conditions of trade and investment to meet the standard of cultural values and industriousness or of just institutions that Rawls seems to set. It does, however, call for "sustained action" on the part of developing countries, in exchange for "effective international co-operation . . . in providing these countries with appropriate means and facilities to foster their comprehensive development."[37] Development compacts, as proposed by Arjun K. Sengupta, would establish a duty to encourage and reward countries that demonstrate many of the virtues that Rawls considers determinative of wealth and poverty, as well as respect for human rights. If we can substitute the principles of equity, non-discrimination, accountability, transparency, and respect for human rights for the virtues listed by Rawls, there is a certain parallel between the Law of Peoples and the right to development. However, under the Law of Peoples, a poor but well-ordered society would have no claim to assistance, whereas, under the right to development, a poor society would not be entitled to assistance (that is, reduction of resource constraints) unless it was moving toward the well-ordered state, understood in terms of respect for human rights.

Third, there is clearly more to poverty than lack of certain virtues. At a deeper level, poverty and vastly unequal opportunities to make choices and to lead a life that one values involve processes that cannot be contained within the borders of each state. Investment and employment patterns of transnational corporations (TNCs), rules and practices of international trade, pricing of commodities, migration flows, international monetary policy, international banking, and numerous other structural dimensions of the international economy determine these opportunities as much if not more than the virtues Rawls speaks of. China and India have not suddenly discovered virtues of industriousness and efficiency; they are growing at rates of 8 and 9% and slowly reducing poverty because they have overcome obstacles to taking advantage of those structures. It can be argued that the right to development is based on an understanding of development that seeks distributive justice within and among nations. If that is so, a strong case can be made for a theory of international justice that entails obligations to contribute to such a process.

Utilitarianism assesses the rightness of decisions by their impact on the well-being of all affected individuals, or, as Jeremy Bentham expressed in his "fundamental axiom": "it is the greatest happiness of the greatest number that is the measure of right and wrong."[38] A utilitarian could explore whether and to what extent a duty to respond to development needs in other countries maximizes utility, although extending utilitarianism to various international patterns of exchange and processes of change is complex, as Sengupta's chapter in this book demonstrates. The basic question is whether there is a utilitarian advantage for the people in country A to support the development needs of the people in country B.

---

37   Declaration on the Right to Development, Article 4 (2).
38   Jeremy Bentham, *A Fragment on Government* (London: Payne, 1776). Available at http://socserv.mc-master.ca/econ/ugcm/ 3ll3/bentham/government.html. (McMaster University's Archive for the History of Economic Thought).

Consequentialist arguments may be more evident in supporting the idea of obligations in the right to development. In an essay that introduces human rights into the framework of consequential evaluation, Amartya Sen proposes a "rights-inclusive consequentialism" that has advantages over "rights-independent consequential evaluation" of utilitarianism and over libertarianism.[39] Turning to "human rights that individuals are supposed to have . . . because of their status as human beings," Sen acknowledges "the responsibilities that others have — irrespective of citizenship, nationality, and other denominations — to help this person to attain these freedoms. If others can help, then there is a responsibility that goes with it."[40] What is important for our purpose is that ". . . [s]ome of these obligations tend to be more fully specified than others" and that "even the fulfillment or violation of precisely specified obligations can go with imperfect obligations of others to help in a general way." This general duty to help, he continues, "through a consequential link, may be rather inexactly specified (telling us neither who must particularly take the initiative, nor how far he should go in doing this general duty), but this loosely formulated obligation — Immanuel Kant would call it an 'imperfect obligation' — to help may nevertheless be seriously considered by (and be influential with) responsible people."[41] The essential point from our perspective of the rationale for positing a duty to support the human right to development in other countries is this:

> It is important to see that in linking human rights to both perfect and imperfect obligations, there is no suggestion that the right-duty correspondence be denied. Indeed, the binary relation between rights and obligations can be quite important, and it is precisely this binary relation that separates out human rights from the general valuing of freedom (without a correlated obligation of others to help bring about a greater realization of human freedom). The question that remains is whether it is adequate for this binary relation to allow imperfect obligations to correspond to human rights, without demanding an exact specification of who will have to do what, as in the case of legal rights and specified perfect obligations.[42]

Sen correctly observes that ". . . [i]n the absence of such perfect obligations, demands for human rights are often seen just as loose talk."[43] He responds to this challenge with two questions: "Why insist on the absolute necessity of [a] co-specified perfect obligation for a putative right to qualify as a real right? Certainly, a perfect obligation would help a great deal toward the realization of rights, but why cannot there be unrealized rights, even rights that are hard to realize?"[44] He resists "the claim that any use of rights except with co-linked perfect obligations must lack cogency" and explains that ". . . [h]uman rights are seen as rights shared by all — irrespective of citizenship — and the benefits of which everyone *should* have. The

39 Amartya Sen, "Consequential Evaluation and Practical Reason," *The Journal of Philosophy*, Vol. XCVII, No. 9, September 2000, pp. 493-494.
40 *Id.*, p. 494.
41 *Id.*, p. 495.
42 *Id.*
43 *Id.*
44 *Id.*, p. 496.

claims are addressed generally — in Kant's language 'imperfectly' — to anyone who can help. Even though no particular person or agency has been charged with bringing about the fulfillment of the rights involved, they can still be very influential."[45]

This argument can be applied to the right to development. Indeed, the language of the Declaration on the Right to Development is a catalogue of imperfect obligations, which are nevertheless subject to specification as to what steps should be taken, when, with what forms of assistance, by whom, with what allocation of resources, with what pace of progressive realization, and through what means. As noted by Martin Scheinin in his chapter in this book, jurisprudence of human rights courts suggests a justiciable right to development, and therefore perfect obligations, at least in embryonic form. Sandra Liebenberg shows what steps South African has taken, and Yash Ghai indicates how the state's legal structure should be adapted to meet these obligations and, one could say, to move from imperfect to perfect obligations.

The general problem of whether and to what extent states have responsibilities has been addressed extensively in the literature by such authors as Stanley Hoffman,[46] Henry Shue,[47] and Thomas Pogge,[48] among others.

Shue argues that, without a minimum guarantee of subsistence, along with minimum protection of physical security, the realization of other human rights is not possible. He postulates three duties: "to avoid depriving, to protect from deprivation, [and] to aid the deprived."[49] He clarifies that the duty to aid becomes relevant only if the first two duties have been violated. Of special importance for the right to development is Shue's discussion of the duty to protect, which has two types: one being the duty to enforce the first duty (to avoid deprivation), and the second being the duty to design institutions that avoid the creation of strong incentives to violate the first duty. The requirement of adequate institutional protection leads him to condition sovereignty on the protection of basic rights and to justify intervention when the state fails to protect those rights. He argues that "the international community not only may but ought to step in."[50] Extended to the development field, he posits the "need for some institution to step into the breach when a national government fails" but laments that "at present no institution provides adequately for the subsistence rights of persons deprived, ignored, or ill-served by their own national government."[51] For this purpose, he favors philosophically "the adoption of transnational principles to nurture a sense of transnational responsibility."[52] He concludes on this

---

45   *Id.*, p. 497.
46   Stanley Hoffman, *Duties Beyond Borders: On the Limits and Possibilities of Ethical International Politics* (New York: Syracuse University Press, 1981). For reasons of space, this work will not be discussed in the present essay.
47   Henry Shue, *Basic Rights: Subsistence, Affluence and U.S. Foreign Policy*, 2nd ed. (Princeton, NJ: Princeton University Press, 1996).
48   Thomas Pogge, *World Poverty and Human Rights: Cosmopolitan Responsibilities and Reforms* (Cambridge, UK: Polity Press, 2002).
49   Shue, *supra*, note 47, p. 60.
50   *Id.*, p. 174.
51   *Id.*, p. 142.
52   *Id.*, p. 149.

point, "a government that does violate, or assist in violating the rights of people outside its own territory, is failing in its duties both to the victims of the deprivation and, as an agent with service duties, to its own population."[53]

Pogge addresses the same question from the perspective of moral cosmopolitanism, in both interactional and institutional variants. Cosmopolitanism considers the human person as the ultimate unit of moral concern, each human being of equal value for all, even those with the most remote affinity.[54] His version of moral cosmopolitanism is formulated in terms of "a rather minimal conception of human rights, one that rules out severe abuses, deprivations, and inequalities while still being compatible with a wide range of political, moral, and religious cultures."[55] He argues that those who "are influential and privileged participants in a transnational scheme of social institutions under which some persons are regularly, predictably, and avoidably denied secure access to the objects of their human rights . . . share responsibility for human rights fulfillment abroad."[56]

He makes a distinction between "interactional cosmopolitanism," according to which other individuals and collective agents are directly responsible for the fulfillment of human rights, and "institutional cosmopolitanism," where institutional schemes are responsible, while individuals have a shared indirect responsibility for the justice of any practice.[57] The two variants are complementary, although he assigns primary importance to the institutional. His institutional approach to distributive justice is "to choose or design the economic ground rules that regulate property, cooperation, and exchange and thereby condition production and distribution [with a view to achieving] an economic order under which each participant would be able to meet her basic social and economic needs."[58] "This," he concludes, "is what the assertion of social and economic human rights amounts to within the proposed institutional cosmopolitanism."[59] The words "right to development" could be substituted for "social and economic human rights" in the sense that the Declaration affirms that "All human beings have a responsibility for development, individually and collectively," although the right to development does not purport to rewrite "the economic ground rules."

Pogge's institutional cosmopolitanism includes a mechanism for making available to the global poor a small portion of the value of resources that states use or sell. This Global Resources Dividend (GRD)[60] has certain similarities with the Right to Development-Development Compact (RTD-DC), and Pogge's moral justification for responsibilities across borders appears to support the concept of an obligation to cooperate for the realization of the right to development.

---

53 *Id.*, p. 152.
54 Pogge, *supra*, note 48, p. 169.
55 *Id.*, p. 248, n. 270. He acknowledges that the absence of "a full list of well-defined human rightsí makes his conclusions íless precise and less definitive than one might have hoped." *Id.*, p. 177.
56 *Id.*, p. 227, n. 100.
57 *Id.*, p. 170.
58 *Id.*, p. 176.
59 *Id.*
60 *Id.*, pp. 196-215.

Thus, institutional cosmopolitanism provides the strongest moral arguments in support of the obligation of affluent countries to contribute to the institutional reforms and to provide resources that poor countries need to carry out their obligations to realize the right to development. It is another matter to provide the political rationale for affluent countries to accept this responsibility and for the developing countries to endorse the political implications of the moral obligation of political liberalism.

Political Rationale

Politically, the rationale for the right to development varies according to interests and relative power of the country concerned. Since the beginning of the drafting process in the 1970s to produce a normative instrument on the right to development, a dividing line has existed between those countries that never contemplated anything more than a vague moral commitment to support, in the context of the UN Commission on Human Rights, sound development policies, without acknowledging any legal obligations whatsoever, and those that saw the right to development as an agenda for the legally sanctioned transfer of resources from rich to poor countries.[61] Those divergent rationales have produced an unhealthy trend that persists today in the posture of damage control by some and unproductive provocation by others. In between, there are political rationales worth considering.

In the current political climate, governments that pay a relatively high percentage of their gross domestic product (GDP) in official development assistance (ODA), most developing countries, many international agencies, and most non-governmental organizations (NGOs) support the concept of the right to development without being explicit about the nature of the reciprocal responsibilities involved. A minority of skeptical donor countries (usually the US, Japan, and sometimes Australia, New Zealand, Canada, and Sweden) expresses opposition to any claim that the duties of donor countries are more than moral commitments to be carried out as each country sees fit and under no legal constraint.

A group of developing countries belonging to the Non-Aligned Movement (NAM) introduced language into UN documents about legal obligations to operationalize the right to development, presumably to reinforce the claim that donor countries have a duty to provide assistance, knowing that the countries in question will object. The most active members of the NAM in the Working Group on the Right to Development called themselves the "Like-Minded Group" (LMG) until 2004 and included Algeria, Bangladesh, Bhutan, China, Cuba, Egypt, India, Indonesia, Iran, Malaysia, Myanmar, Nepal, Pakistan, the Philippines, Sri Lanka, Sudan, and Vietnam. They tended to insert into resolutions and speeches on the right to development language about reducing inequities of international trade, the negative impacts of globalization, differential access to technology, the crushing debt burden, follow-up to the 2001 Durban Conference against Racism, and "the need

---

61 The explanations of votes underscore these divergences. See UN Doc. A/C.3/41/SR61 (1986),"quoted in Roland Rich, The Right to Development: A Right of Peoples?," in James Crawford (ed.), *The Rights of Peoples* (New York: Oxford University Press, 1988), p. 52.

for an international environment which is conducive to the realization of the right to development."[62]

This trend is manifested by the proposal of an international convention at the XIII Conference of NAM heads of state. They affirmed that "it is the duty of States, regardless of their political, economic and cultural systems, to promote and protect all human rights and fundamental freedoms of all peoples, in particular the right to development."[63] Further they "called on all States to undertake necessary policy formulation and institute measures required for the implementation of the right to development as a fundamental human right," calling on the UN to "continue to give priority to the operationalisation of this important right including, *inter alia*, elaboration of a Convention on the Right to Development."[64] When the UN Commission on Human Rights, at the behest of the NAM, called on the Sub-Commission on the Promotion and Protection of Human Rights to include in a concept paper a discussion of an "international legal standard of a binding nature," 47 countries voted in favor; the United States, together with Australia and Japan, cast negative votes; and Canada, Korea, and Sweden abstained.[65] When the Sub-Commission failed to produce this concept paper, the Commission noted this fact with concern and requested the Sub-Commission, "without further delay, to submit the concept document" at the 62nd session (2006) of the Commission.[66] The author of the report that was finally submitted side-stepped the issue of a binding legal instrument. After noting "strong differences of opinion among legal luminaries as to whether the right to development can be placed within a legally binding framework,"[67] she said, "In view of the ongoing discussions among duty bearers, partners and stakeholders, I am of the view that the successful identification of ways to infuse human rights values and principles into the development process would better serve the realization of the right"[68] and concluded that "the development of binding legal standards is premature at this time."[69] The Sub-Commission asked her to continue her work[70] but did not mention the "international legal standard of a binding nature," presumably having concluded, as had the author, that the political will was lacking to pursue the idea further, however important it was to the NAM.

---

62 Commission on Human Rights Resolution 2002/69, adopted on April 25, 2002, by a recorded vote of 38 votes to 0, with 15 abstentions.
63 Final Document of the XIII Conference of Heads of State or Government of the Non-Aligned Movement Kuala Lumpur, February 24ñ25, 2003, para. 336. Available at http://www.bernama.com/ cgi-bin/events/nam2003/speechnew_read.cgi?declare/dc2502_final.
64 *Id.*, para. 345.
65 The Commission on Human Rights adopted Resolution 2003/83 on August 25, 2003, by a vote of 47 in favor and 3 against, with 3 abstentions, requesting its Sub-Commission "to prepare a concept document establishing options for the implementation of the right to development and their feasibility, inter alia, an international legal standard of a binding nature, guidelines on the implementation of the right to development and principles for development partnership."
66 Commission on Human Rights Resolution 2005/4, adopted on April 12, 2005, by vote of 48 to 2, with 2 abstentions.
67 *Concept Document on the Right to Development.* Working paper submitted by Florizelle OíConnor, UN Doc. E/CN.4/Sub.2/2005/23, June 24, 2005, para. 14.
68 *Id.*, para. 18.
69 *Id.*, para. 69.
70 Sub-Commission on the Promotion and Protection of Human Rights, Resolution 2005/17. UN Doc. E/CN.4/2006/2 and E/CN.4/Sub.2/2005/44, October 17, 2005, p. 33.

While the 1986 Declaration does amplify developing world demands on the industrialized world for a transfer of resources, including several references to the nearly forgotten New International Economic Order (NIEO), donor countries regard the allocation of resources to development assistance and their trade and debt policy as a matter of the sovereign choice of their parliaments and governments rather than falling under binding international obligations.

Although the United States government has been the strongest opponent of consideration by the Commission on Human Rights of human rights-based obligations in the fields of aid, trade, and finance, President George W. Bush, in his March 22, 2002, speech to the UN Conference on Financing for Development in Monterrey, Mexico, said, "Developed nations have a duty not only to share our wealth, but also to encourage sources that produce wealth: economic freedom, political liberty, the rule of law, and human rights."[71] The policy that emerged from that affirmation of a duty is a fascinating paradox of the right to development debate. Indeed, in 2003, the US delegation explained to the Commission: "States . . . have no obligation to provide guarantees for implementation of any purported 'right to development.'"[72] In the same speech in Monterrey, President Bush proposed a $5 billion annual increase of ODA through a new Millennium Challenge Account (MCA), "devoted to projects in nations that govern justly, invest in their people, and encourage economic freedom." On January 23, 2004, President Bush signed the law creating the Millennium Challenge Corporation (MCC) to administer the MCA and the MCC Board began operation in February 2004.[73]

The paradox resides in the considerable similarity between the MCA and the Right to Development-Development Compact (RTD-DC): both refer to mutuality of obligations; both are based on transferring resources to reward countries that have sound development and human rights practices; both use the language of compact ("new compact for global development" in the MCA case and "development compacts" in the RTD case); both insist on investment in education and health; and both emphasize principles of accountability and transparency as part of good governance. While the parallels are appealing, in reality the MCA is more a vehicle to support growth and anti-corruption development policies that favor free markets, free trade, entrepreneurship, and economic freedoms, with only minimal attention to investing in people (that is, social expenditure on health, education, and related sectors) and almost none on human rights, except the right to property.[74]

---

71 Remarks by President George W. Bush at the International Conference on Financing for Development Monterrey, Mexico, March 22, 2002. Available at http://www.un.org/ffd/statements/usaE.htm (accessed December 20, 2002).
72 Commission on Human Rights, 59th Session, 2003, Statement by US government commenting on the Working Group on the Right to Development, on file with the author.
73 See http://www.mca.gov. See also "The Launching of the Millennium Challenge Account," Alan P. Larson, Under Secretary for Economic, Business, and Agricultural Affairs, Department of State, Foreign Press Center Briefing, Washington, DC, February 3, 2004. Available at http://fpc.state.gov/28839.htm.
74 The nature of MCA from the perspective of the right to development is examined in greater detail in Stephen Marks, "The Human Right to Development: Between Rhetoric and Reality," *Harvard Human Rights Journal*, Vol. 17 (Spring 2004), pp. 137-168.

Intense political controversy surrounds the question of whether and to what extent states have international obligations to respect, promote, and provide for the right to development. The political motivations are fairly clear. Developing countries that see the right to development as creating an entitlement to a transfer of resources in their favor — through aid, debt relief, terms of trade, and more equitable globalization — argue that the right to development creates binding obligations on industrialized countries and on international institutions. The countries that feel targeted strenuously oppose any concept of legal obligation, and the international institutions acknowledge a need to be attentive to General Assembly resolutions but are guided legally by their constitutions and the directors of their governing bodies.

Countries that spend considerable amounts of their taxpayers' money on development in line with the right to development do not welcome being told that they have a legal obligation to do so. Several delegations have mentioned "shared responsibilities," which avoids forcing the issue of legal vs. moral obligations. For some countries, that responsibility would mean a paradigm shift in development by systematically integrating human rights. For others, it would mean the responsibility to relieve debt and create more favorable terms of trade and investment for developing countries. The principle of shared responsibility means, at a minimum, that opportunities must exist to assess whether and to what extent each country's development policy — including its relations with donors, lenders and investors — is consistent with the shared objective of human development and human rights.

In sum, the political rationale for considering that there is an obligation to cooperate to realize the right to development is based on the balancing of the interests of these different groups of countries. Some wish to benefit from the reduction of resource constraints while others wish to see greater security and stability resulting from improved governance and well-being of the former group. In other words, the political rationale has to do with promoting competing economic interests between those countries that want access to increased aid, debt forgiveness, foreign investment and a level playing field in trade and those that want access to stable and cheap sources of labor, open markets, and natural resources.

Part of the calculation as to how these economic advantages can be realized is that improved governance, including respect for human rights, is a desirable and probably necessary condition for stability and equitable economic development. Developing countries should be willing to accept obligations to integrate human rights into their development policies and practices regardless of whether the richer countries provide incentives for such polices and practices. Instead, the former group (resource-poor countries) uses the right to development as a political basis to claim that the latter group (resource-rich countries) has an obligation to provide those incentives; and the latter group has its own political motivation for considering that the former group has an obligation to respect human rights as part of development. The difficulty is that neither group wants one-sided obligations — hence, the political rationale for development compacts.

Newly developed countries also have a political agenda to stress obligations of older developed countries. However, the case can be made for obligations upon them to contribute to "effective international co-operation" — for example, through South-South cooperation — to provide poorer developing countries "with appropriate means and facilities to foster their comprehensive development," as required by Article 4 of the 1986 Declaration. The right to development will not be taken seriously until each group accepts its obligations, whereas the politics are such that each group stresses the obligations of the other group. If and when the politics change, the legal rationale for reciprocal obligations will become more acceptable.

Legal Rationale

While the political discourse shows divergent approaches to the duties implied by the 1986 Declaration, it is argued by most of the authors represented in this volume that there is a legal basis for asserting that states do have such obligations. An impartial assessment requires a careful review of the international law applicable to the right to development, as regards both the duties of states toward one another and the duties of international institutions.

The arguments for a legal obligation stem not from the legal nature of the Declaration, which is a resolution expressing views of member states in an instrument that did not purport to create legally binding rights and obligations. They are based, rather, on the legal obligation to act jointly and separately for the realization of human rights and "economic and social progress and development," as stipulated in the UN Charter at Articles 55 and 56. For the states parties to the International Covenant on Economic, Social and Cultural Rights (ICESCR), the core legal argument is contained in Article 2 of the Covenant. It is in the logic of the right to development that the full realization of "all rights" cannot be successful if pursued piecemeal but only through a policy that is deliberately designed to achieve all the rights, progressively and in accordance with available resources. In that sense, the Covenant creates legal obligations to do essentially what the right to development calls for. These are the legal obligations of each of the 153 states parties (as of May 2006) not only to alter its internal policy but also to act through international cooperation toward the same end. Specifically, the duty, in Article 2, "to take steps, individually and through international assistance and cooperation" provides a legal basis for the reciprocal obligations mentioned above. The putative extension of this duty to cooperate for the right to development is expressed in Article 4(2) of the 1986 Declaration: "As a complement to the efforts of developing countries [to promote more rapid development], effective international cooperation is essential in providing these countries with appropriate means and facilities to foster their comprehensive development."

The obligation to cooperate as a legal obligation can have a restrictive and an extensive interpretation. According to the restrictive interpretation, an affluent state could argue that its legal obligation to engage in "effective international co-operation" in the realization of the right to development is fulfilled by three elements of its foreign policy. The first is its policy of foreign aid; the second is its participation in development institutions like the United Nations Development Program (UNDP) and the Organization for Economic Co-operation and Development (OECD), as well as in international financial institutions, like the World Bank and the regional development banks; and the third is its role in deliberations about development issues at the General Assembly, Economic and Social Council (ECOSOC), and international conferences and summits. Beyond that general involvement in the process of international cooperation, according to this restrictive interpretation, it has no other legal (or moral) obligations. Thus, under the restrictive interpretation, a country that provides aid at any level, even far below the 0.7% of GDP target; that participates in development institutions, even without doing much to promote innovative development policies; and that joins in deliberations on development at the UN, regardless of how it votes, would have no further obligations under the right to development. It has "cooperated" in development and could argue that the reference to be "effective" in Article 4 (2) of the Declaration is too vague to require more. This narrow approach does not give sufficient attention to the politically significant pronouncements of high-level conferences and legally significant interpretations of expert bodies.

A study on duties across borders by the International Council on Human Rights Policy[75] concludes that "the enormous and continuing increases in capacity of richer states, and other actors in richer societies, mean that very often they can provide assistance effectively . . . Their capacity also confers added responsibilities. This responsibility is set out in international human rights law, which states that richer societies have an obligation to assist poorer states, through international co-operation, with within their means, to achieve protection of [economic, social, and cultural] rights."[76] The authors consider that "richer states are not acting to remedy the effects of their policies when these damage the [economic, social and cultural] rights of people in other countries. They are failing to undo harm for which they are directly or indirectly responsible."[77] The Council's analysis of international responsibilities in the matter of economic, social, and cultural rights is also applicable to the right to development. Indeed, the externalities that make well-intentioned and right-to-development-based national development policies ineffective are, to a large extent, the result of rich states "not acting to remedy the effects of their policies."

A more extensive interpretation of the legal obligation to cooperate in development would add substance to the vague obligation to cooperate through the incorporation by reference of the most significant documents relating to the specifics of cooperation. According to this interpretation, the content of the obligation to cooperate would be provided by such documents as the General Comments drafted by the human rights treaty bodies, the declarations and programs of action of the international conferences and summits, resolutions that purport to contribute to the pro-

---

75   International Council on Human Rights Policy, *Duties sans Frontières: Human Rights and Global Social Justice* (Geneva, 2003).
76   *Id.*, p. 86.
77   *Id.*, p. 87.

gressive development of international law, and opinions expressed by leading experts and institutions.[78] The declarations and programs of action of international conferences and summits are not directly linked to a binding legal instrument in the way the general comments are. They, and the General Assembly Resolutions that endorse them, do nevertheless provide a considerable degree of guidance as to the specifics of the general legal obligation of international cooperation contained in the UN Charter and the International Covenants on Human Rights.

Another relevant interpretative document is the Maastricht Guidelines, which include the following regarding the obligations of states parties to the ICESCR:

> The obligations of States to protect economic, social, and cultural rights extend also to their participation in international organisations, where they act collectively. It is particularly important for States to use their influence to ensure that violations do not result from the programmes and policies of the organisations of which they are members.[79]

The Covenant, accordingly, requires that states act in international agencies and lending institutions, as well as during Security Council consideration of sanctions, in a way that does not cause economic, social, and cultural rights to suffer in any other country. This approach is consistent with Article 30 of the Universal Declaration on Human Rights, which excludes use of the Declaration by any state, group, or person "to engage in any activity or to perform any act aimed at the destruction of any of the rights and freedoms set forth herein." It is also consistent with Article 9 (2) of the 1986 Declaration, which excludes the interpretation of the Declaration in any way that would imply "that any State, group, or person has a right to engage in any activity or to perform any act aimed at the violation of the rights set forth in the Universal Declaration of Human Rights and in the International Covenants on Human Rights." Trade, monetary, and development policies that violate rights guaranteed by the ICESCR would be suspect, but the use of the terms "aimed at the violation" — thus implying intentionality — would make it extremely rare that any activity or act would be contrary to this provision.

It is, therefore, possible to speak of "obligations," even of legal obligations, falling on those states that have ratified the ICESCR. These obligations do not fall only on developed countries but apply to developing countries as well. Although many resource-poor countries tend not to welcome being reminded of it, under the extensive interpretation they have a legal obligation to pursue development policy based on meaningful participation, equitable sharing, and full realization of human rights, all of which are explicitly contained in the 1986 Declaration. Thus the Declaration articulates in terms acceptable to virtually every country a set of obligations that derive their legal force from existing treaty obligations. Whether this particular articu-

---

78 This is the approach taken by the Committee on Economic, Social, and Cultural Rights in its General Comment No. 3 on the nature of states parties obligations (Article 2, para. 1 of the Covenant), adopted by on December 14, 1990, UN Doc. document E/1991/23, para. 14.
79 *The Maastricht Guidelines on Violations of Economic, Social, and Cultural Rights,* adopted at a meeting of experts convened by the International Commission of Jurists on January 22-26, 1997, Guideline 19.

lation of duties, including international cooperation aimed at the full realization of the Declaration, will acquire a legally binding character through a new treaty or the emergence of a customary norm is uncertain. The conclusion of the Sub-Commission member entrusted with the concept document "that the development of binding legal standards is premature at this time"[80] illustrates the perils of the treaty route, although her failure to make a proper assessment of the potential of legally binding instruments is not the end of the story. Similarly, the frequent reference to the obligations of the right to development in high-level diplomatic settings does not provide a definitive answer to the question of a customary norm.

The UN summits tend to make one allusion to the right to development, often as a reluctant political compromise, and then deal with the key issues and mechanisms without any further reference to the right to development. For example, world leaders agreed in September 2000 at the United Nations Millennium Summit on a set of goals and targets for combating poverty, hunger, disease, illiteracy, environmental degradation, and discrimination against women, which eventually became the MDGs. The Summit Declaration included the commitment "to making the right to development a reality for everyone and to freeing the entire human race from want."[81] In his report on the implementation of the MDGs, however, the UN Secretary-General quoted the above sentence on the right to development in the section on poverty eradication but not in the section on human rights.[82] Nor did he provide any indication of whether or how the right to development could have a role in the MDGs. At the same time, development and UN agencies have devoted considerable attention to the relations between the MDGs and human rights. UNDP's Human Development Report 2003, which was devoted to the MDGs, affirmed that the MDGs contribute to the right to development. In particular, the report not only affirmed that "achieving the Goals will advance human rights" but also recognized "that the targets expressed in the Goals are not just development aspirations but also claimable rights."[83] The analysis uses the language of obligations: "Viewing the Goals in this way means that taking action to achieve them is an obligation, not a form of charity. This approach creates a framework for holding various actors accountable, including governments, citizens, corporations, and international organisations. Human rights carry counterpart obligations on the part of others — not just to refrain from violating them, but also to protect and promote their realization." Finally the report affirms that "The Millennium Development Goals more explicitly define what all countries agree can be demanded — benchmarks against which such commitments must be measured."

In 2004, the UN Commission on Human Rights established a high-level task force on the implementation of the right to development, within the framework of the Working Group pm the Right to Development, and gave it a mandate at its first

---

80 *Supra*, note 69.
81 General Assembly Resolution 55/2. United Nations Millennium Declaration, adopted on September 8, 2000, para. 11.
82 Implementation of the United Nations Millennium Declaration, Report of the Secretary-General, UN Doc. A/57/270, July 31, 2002, paras. 38 and 82-89.
83 UNDP, *Human Development Report* 2003, p. 28.

session to consider "obstacles and challenges to the implementation of the Millennium Development Goals in relation to the right to development" and to identify specifically social impact assessments and best practices in the implementation of the right to development.[84] At its second session, in 2005, the mandate of the task force was "to consider Millennium Development Goal 8, on global partnership for development, and to suggest criteria for its periodic evaluation with the aim of improving the effectiveness of global partnerships with regard to the realization of the right to development." The task force completed this mandate at its November 2005 session and its report[85] was approved by consensus by the Working Group in February 2006.[86] If the Human Rights Council approves the Working Group's recommendation, the task force will apply the 15 criteria it developed on a pilot basis, to selected partnerships "with a view to operationalizing and progressively developing these criteria, and thus contributing to mainstreaming the right to development in the policies and operational activities of relevant actors at the national, regional and international levels, including multilateral financial, trade, and development institutions."[87]

Philip Alston takes the argument for mainstreaming human rights in the MDGs a step further by noting that these goals "have been endorsed in an endless array of policy documents adopted not only at the international level but in the policies and programs of the national governments to whom they are of the greatest relevance."[88] In assessing whether the MDGs involve obligations under customary international law, he applies the two tests for a human rights claim having that character — (i) the right is indispensable to a meaningful notion of human dignity (upon which human rights are based) and (ii) the satisfaction of the right is demonstrably within the reach of the government in question assuming reasonable support from the international community" — and concludes that "many of the MDGs have the virtue of satisfying these criteria without giving rise to great controversy" and therefore "that at least some of the MDGs reflect norms of customary international law."[89] He has reservations regarding MDG 8 (global partnerships for development) because, with respect to that goal, "developed country governments would be expected to resist strongly any suggestion that there are specific obligations

---

84   *Report of the High-Level Task Force on the Implementation of the Right to Development* (Geneva, December 13-17, 2004), UN Doc. E/CN.4/2005/WG.18/2, January 24, 2005, para 3. The first session was extensively analyzed by Margot E. Salomon in "Towards a Just Institutional Order: A Commentary on the First Session of the UN Task Force on the Right to Development," *Netherlands Quarterly of Human Rights*, Vol. 23, No. 3 (2005); and "The Significance of the Task Force on the Right to Development," Special Report, Human Rights and Development, Roberto Danino and Joseph K. Ingram (eds.), *Development Outreach*, The World Bank, Vol. 8, No. 2 (scheduled for summer 2006).
85   *Report of the High-Level Task Force on the Implementation of the Right to Development on Its Second Meeting* (Geneva: November 14-18, 2005), UN Doc. E/CN.4/2005/WG.18/TF/3, December 8, 2005.
86   *Report of the Working Group on the Right to Development on Its Seventh Session* (Geneva, January 9-13, 2006), UN Doc. E/CN.4/2006/26, February 22, 2006, para. 35.
87   *Id.*, para. 77.
88   Philip Alston, "Ships Passing in the Night: The Current State of the Human Rights and Development Debate Seen Through the Lens of the Millennium Development Goals," *Human Rights Quarterly*, Vol. 27 (2005), p. 774. This article is based on a paper prepared by Alston as a contribution to the work of the Millennium Project Task Force on Poverty and Economic Development entitled "A Human Rights Perspective on the Millennium Development Goals."
89   *Id.*

enshrined in customary international law."[90] He points out that the persistent rejection by developed countries of a more general legal duty to provide aid "and the failure of even the most generous of donors to locate their assistance within the context of such an obligation, would present a major obstacle to any analysis seeking to demonstrate that such an obligation has already become part of customary law."[91]

Nevertheless, Alston acknowledges "that the emergence of a growing international consensus around the MDGs provides a strong argument in favor of revisiting . . . in the years ahead" the development compacts as proposed by Sengupta in his capacity as Independent Expert on the Right to Development.[92] Further, he considers that "[a]t some point, the reiteration of such commitments [to mobilize resources to ensure that countries committed to the MDGs have the additional resources necessary] . . . will provide a strong argument that some such obligation has crystallized into customary law."[93] This line of argument is directly relevant to the right to development not only in the context of the proposed development compacts but more generally as part of the idea that an inchoate duty of the undifferentiated international community can evolve into a specific obligation to reduce resource constraints on countries that adhere to the principles of the right to development.

The philosophical and political arguments discussed above thus also have a legal rationale — namely, the emerging customary norm according to which developing countries must apply these principles and developed countries must reduce economic constraints over which they have control, where the developing country has made its best efforts to meet the MDGs or other development goals, and is unable to do so because of those constraints.

Conclusion

The claimed obligations in the Declaration on the Right to Development, as reaffirmed, *inter alia*, by the Vienna Declaration and Program of Action, the Monterrey Consensus, and the Millennium Declaration state moral positions that are consistent with several philosophical theories on duties in international affairs, including global liberalism, contractarianism, consequentialism, and institutional cosmopolitanism. There is no doubt that they are also — and perhaps essentially — political affirmations of these obligations. However, the basis of all law is politics. The sustained effort to establish law through the politics of the Commission on Human Rights (and its successor Council), the General Assembly, and international summits and conferences has succeeded in two ways. First, the 1986 Declaration provided a normative basis for incremental confirmations and enactments of legal obligations. Thus, the jurisprudence of human rights courts and commissions cited by Scheinin and some of the interpretations of law by the treaty bodies cited by Salomon in their chapters emerge from the inchoate political will of states to affirm the right to development. Second, the Declaration provided the normative basis for the eventual recognition of

---

90   *Id.*, p. 775.
91   *Id.*, p. 777.
92   *Id.*
93   *Id.*, p. 778.

a legal right to development. The proposal of NAM and the mandate given to the Sub-Commission to examine the feasibility of "an international legal standard of a binding nature"[94] have little likelihood of success under the current political climate. Whether the development of a binding legal instrument stands a better chance is the Human Rights Council is impossible to gauge. The preconditions for serious consideration of a binding legal instrument are that the affirmation of legal duties of the Declaration be depoliticized and that implementation of obligations be tested on a project or bilateral program basis.

The commitment of the Millennium Summit "to making the right to development a reality for everyone and to freeing the entire human race from want" is not trivial. The existence of a legal obligation does not ipso facto transform a philosophical precept or a political platform into behavior conforming to the norm. Sen is correct to note that "human rights may well be reflected in legislation, and may also inspire legislation, but this is a further fact, rather than a defining characteristic of human rights themselves."[95] Thus the "reality" of the right to development and the obligations it implies depends more on "social ethics and public reasoning" than on a formal legally binding instrument.

Whether states conform to the four duties and responsibilities and the score of "shoulds" and "shalls" mentioned at the beginning of this essay is determined by complex webs of decision-making and balancing of interests and influence. Law and morality will constrain the forces that act against the principles of the right to development — many of which are identified and analyzed in other essays in this volume — only to the extent that power relations tilt in favor of putative beneficiaries of the right to development, namely, the vast majority of the population of world who enjoy neither the fruits of development nor respect for their human rights. The individuals, civil society organizations, governments, and international institutions that act resolutely on their behalf contribute to tilting that balance. The cumulative effect of the political, legal, and philosophical rationales that they use is to move the right to development incrementally from a political instrument of a group of states to a more fully enforceable legal right of the community of nations.

---

94 See *supra*, note 65.
95 See Amartya Sen, "Human Rights and Development," in this book.

5 | The Right to Development and Its Corresponding Obligations
David Beetham

"And he said, Now, this schoolroom is a Nation. And in this nation there are fifty millions of money. Isn't this a prosperous nation? Girl number twenty, isn't this a prosperous nation, and a'n't you in a thriving state?" . . .

"I said I didn't know. I thought I couldn't know whether it was a prosperous nation or not, and whether I was in a thriving state or not, unless I knew who had got the money, and whether any of it was mine. But that had nothing to do with it. It was not in the figures at all. . . ."

"That was a great mistake of yours," observed Louisa.

– Charles Dickens, *Hard Times*

Definition of the Right to Development

This chapter is concerned with the duties, obligations, or responsibilities that are entailed by the right to development. Critical to this discussion is a clear conception of what that right involves and how it should be defined. As I am no expert on the subject of development, my primary qualification for addressing this issue must be whatever advantage exists in approaching the subject with a fresh pair of eyes. I hope that this confession will serve to explain, if not excuse, a certain skepticism on my part, not about the right to development itself, but about the dangers of conceptual inflation, or "terminological creep," to which the right seems to me intrinsically prone, especially under the pressure to achieve a political consensus among different state parties. My preference is to apply Occam's Razor to narrow the definition of the right to a minimum core meaning, which is clearly distinct from other human rights, rather than inclusive of them all, or the sum of the interrelationships among them.

In light of this approach, I find some merit in concentrating on the original idea of a nation's or people's right to economic development, however much this may require further explication in its relation to individual human rights. In my understanding, the right to development was first formulated by representatives from developing countries, particularly though not exclusively from francophone Africa, and was intimately linked to two demands: first, for a new international order, which would be more favorable to the economic development of less developed countries, and, second, for the full control by peoples over their own natural wealth and resources.[1] Both demands find a place in the 1986 UN Declaration on the Right to Development (Articles 1 and 3), although their impact is somewhat blunted by the comprehensive list of other articles.[2]

The right to development was originally asserted as a claim against the developed countries, in the context of what was perceived as a perpetuation of colonialism

---

1   Laurent Meillan, "Le Droit au Développement et les Nations Unies: Quelques Réflexions," *Droit en Quart Monde*, No. 34 (January 2003), p. 14.
2   Ian Brownlie and Guy S. Goodwin-Gill (eds.) *Basic Documents on Human Rights*, 4th Edition (Oxford: Oxford University Press, 2002), pp. 845-851.

through economic domination and exploitation. In its more strident formulations, the collective right to development was defined as a right specific to the Third World, and was counterposed to the individual human rights championed by the developed countries. A typical example is the statement of the foreign minister of Senegal, Doudou Thiam, in an economic conference of the group of 77 in 1967: "Il s'agit de dénoncer le vieux pacte colonial, dont la situation actuelle n'est encore que le prolongement. De lui substituer un droit nouveau. De même que l'on a proclamé dans les Nations développées pour les individus le droit à l'instruction, à la santé, au travail, nous devons proclamer, ici, hautement, pour les Nations du tiers-monde le droit au développement."3

This antithesis between a collective right to development and the human rights of the individual has subsequently been firmly rejected, and rightly so. It appears that the link between a nation's or people's right to economic development and individual human rights is now firmly established through two key propositions:

> 1) Without economic development, the resource constraints that limit the realization of human rights for a country's people cannot be overcome. This proposition applies as much to civil and political rights (provision of police forces, courts, legal aid, and so forth) as to economic, social, and cultural rights. This proposition is phrased carefully, so as to avoid the claim that economic development is a *necessary condition* for realizing individual human rights. As the Limburg principles on economic, social, and cultural rights insist, for example, lack of resources should never be used by states as an excuse for not progressing with a human rights program: "the obligation of progressive achievement exists independently of the increase in resources; it requires effective use of resources available."4 Yet it would be difficult to contest the proposition that a condition of economic underdevelopment and societal impoverishment constitutes a severe limitation on the range of human rights that can be effectively realized. In a recent article, Professor Sengupta steers a careful course through these divergent currents. "The resource constraint," he writes, "may not be quite binding if the implementation of any one human right is considered in isolation. But it may be quite severely binding for any programme trying to implement all the rights." And he asserts again later: "A reduction in income poverty is almost always associated with growth. . . . With regard to the non-income variables . . . it is possible at a given moment to raise these values by reallocating the resources within a given level of income. But this cannot be sustainable, even in the medium term, without an increase in the availability of resources."5

---

3   Meillan, *supra*, note 1. [Eds. translation: "Our task is to denounce the old colonial compact and to replace it with a new right. In the same way that developed countries proclaimed individual rights to education, health and work, we must claim here, loud and clear, that the nations of the Third World have the right to development."]
4   Limburg Principles on the Implementation of the International Covenant on Economic, Social and Cultural Rights, *Human Rights Quarterly*, 9, (1987), pp. 122-135, para. 23.
5   Arjun K. Sengupta, "On the Theory and Practice of the Right to Development," *Human Rights Quarterly*, Vol. 24 (2002), pp. 887-888.

Although an increase in resources may be realized through assistance from international donors, the only secure way to a sustainable and continuing increase in resources for a country, and to expanded economic opportunities for its citizens, is through its own economic development. Indeed, a progressive overcoming of a condition of one-sided economic dependency is what the right to development is surely about.

2) The second proposition about the relation between economic development and individual human rights qualifies the first. Not any and every process of economic development will serve to protect and enhance the human rights of a country's population, but only one that is directed toward the more equitable distribution of economic opportunities and resources. Being in a thriving nation, to use Dickens' terminology, means nothing to those who are not themselves thriving. Dickens' irony was directed not only at the socially divisive consequences of industrial "development," but even more at the schoolroom teachings of political economy that legitimized them. It has taken the experience of similarly extreme liberal economic doctrines by a much later generation to revive the realization that economic development as such can be accompanied by intensified inequalities and social exclusions of all kinds.[6]

In this context, the right to development signifies the right to a form of economic development which serves to expand the human rights of a country's people, and, through doing so, enhances their own capacity to contribute to society's further development. For the individual, it signifies the right to share in society's economic development. This second proposition, then, posits a reciprocal relation between economic development and the realization of individual human rights, not just a causal link in one direction.

My summary, then, of what I take to be the key components of the right to development in the human rights literature (both texts and commentaries) is the following: the right to development, as a nation's or people's right to economic development, is something distinct from the different individual rights of the international human rights covenants, but also intimately connected with them, both as a crucial means to, and as a product of, their progressive realization.

Inflationary Tendencies in the Concept

To elucidate and justify this relatively narrow interpretation of the right to development, one might consider inflationary tendencies found in the literature, which extend the concept well beyond this core meaning, with a corresponding danger of losing clarity of focus. Two tendencies in particular contribute to this inflation. The first trades on an ambiguity in the term "development," as between an economic process at the societal level, and the personal development of the individual. Both meanings are of course well established in scientific discourse and everyday usage

---

6 For example, UNDP, *Human Development Report 1996* (New York: Oxford University Press, 1996); Amartya K. Sen, *Development as Freedom* (Oxford: Oxford University Press, 1999).

alike; and it could well be said that the all round development of the individual constitutes the aim of any human rights agenda. However, because a term in common
usage has many different meanings does not justify including them all in the corresponding human right. To make the personal development of the individual into a
separate human right, say, as the sum of all other human rights, is to lose an important critical focus in the right to development. Note that I am making a clear distinction here between an individual's right to share in society's economic development
(which is implicit in what has already been said above) and a separate "right to personal development."

One thing that encourages the inclusion of the latter is a certain unease about the
status of collective rights in a human rights canon that has the dignity of the individual as its focus and rationale.[7] Yet, if we unpack the idea of a collective right, we
find that it has two essential components. The first is that it is a right that can only
be asserted and exercised collectively, by and on behalf of a *determinate group* of
people (as opposed to an indeterminate group, in such terms as freedom of association, assembly, and so forth). Such are the rights of peoples to self-determination, of
indigenous peoples to live as a distinct people, and of national minorities to protect
their own distinctive language and culture — so, too, is it a nation's or people's right
to economic development. The second is that the right in question counts as a
"right" only because of the value that it has to the *individuals* in the group, and because, correspondingly, a violation of the right is damaging to the individual members of the group and to their individual well-being or dignity.

A collective right, in other words, necessarily has both a collective and an individual dimension. It is worth adding at this point that, when I use the term "nation"
or "people" as subjects of the right to development, I am giving the terms no more
weight than simply "those people sharing a common state and subject to its legal jurisdiction." Radical theorists of globalization and radical cosmopolitans alike would
argue that only individuals can be proper subjects of a right to economic development, though for different reasons: the former, because in their view the state has, as
a matter of fact, lost all power to determine its own economic policy; the latter, more
normatively, because neither the state nor the nation can have any special moral significance in a scheme of global justice.[8] For neither set of theorists could people
grouped as a nation have any significance as subjects of a right to development.

To counter such views does not entail believing that the division of the human
race into separate states is the best of all conceivable arrangements. It is enough to
acknowledge 1) that, as the world is arranged, states have a deeply embedded existence; 2) that they are still a prime locus, alongside the international level, for the
creation of binding policies and regulations that matter for their citizens' well-being;
and 3) that, as a result, members of a state have some special rights and responsibilities in relation to one another, which they do not have toward non-members, and

---

7   Meillan, *supra* note 11.
8   See, for example, Brian Barry, "Statism and Nationalism: a Cosmopolitan Critique," in Ian Shapiro
and Lea Brilmayer (eds.), *Global Justice: Nomos XLI* (New York: New York University Press, 1999),
pp. 12-66.

which give people grouped as a "nation" or "people" a normative as well as practical significance. These considerations do not entail assigning any deep metaphysical or primordial significance to the idea of national identity, and they hold sufficiently, regardless of the arbitrariness of any particular state boundaries.

If one inflationary tendency, then, in the right to development, lies in its extension to embrace an individual right to personal development, a second derives from the development studies literature and its conception of societal development as a multifaceted process. So the preamble to the 1986 UN Declaration declares that "development is a comprehensive economic, social cultural and political process," a phrase which is repeated in Article 1 of the Declaration itself. Indeed, that article continues expansively: development so understood is a condition "in which all human rights and fundamental freedoms can be fully realized."[9] Development at the societal level is indeed a multifaceted process, but it does not follow that all these facets should be included equally in the "right to development." Again, there seems to be a high price to be paid in a loss of focus by extending the right beyond the original conception of a right to *economic* development. Narrowing the concept may well be controversial, but two considerations for doing so seem to be compelling:

> 1) The centrality of resource constraints as an obstacle to realizing human rights, and of economic development in overcoming or at least mitigating these constraints, is critical. It is this centrality that defines both the distinctiveness of the right to development from the sum of individual rights and also its connection to them. When one reads the depressing litany from across the developing world of increases in infant mortality, in lost schooling, in the loss of food security, in the incidence of preventable disease, and so on, it is hard not to conclude that a condition of economic underdevelopment or distorted development lies at their root. To be sure, other factors are involved, and many of them are listed in the articles of the UN Declaration. Yet the issue of economic development is surely both paramount and general.

> 2) The more the right to development is expanded to include all possible aspects of development, the more difficult it becomes to specify what would count as a violation or infringement of the right, since almost anything might count as such, and the responsibility for not fulfilling it becomes correspondingly diffuse and unidentifiable. The UN Committee on Economic, Social and Cultural Rights has labored long and hard in trying to specify, for each right of the Covenant, "an absolute minimum entitlement in the absence of which a state party is to be considered to be in violation of its obligations."[10] It has recognized the need to do so for the rights to be taken seriously and for the responsibility for protecting them to be both clearly assignable and realizable. A broad and multifaceted conception of the right to development moves us in the opposite direction and makes assigning

---

9   Ian Brownlie and Guy S. Goodwin-Gill, *supra*, note 2, pp. 848-849.
10   Philip Alston, "Out of the Abyss: The Challenge Confronting the New UN Committee on Economic, Social and Cultural Rights," *Human Rights Quarterly* 9, 332-381 (1987), p. 353.

the responsibilities that correspond to the right impossible because they are virtually unlimited. By the same token, almost any government anywhere could claim that they were contributing to the right to development in some aspect or another. In sum, a wide definition of the right to development provides a convenient excuse for the evasion of responsibility.

Since the subject of this chapter is about defining obligations, the second consideration above is especially relevant to my purpose. If we can concentrate on *economic* development, then it at least becomes possible to specify what would count as a violation or infringement of the right to development. It would occur where 1) a government's policies or institutions are such as to damage the economic development of its people, or to encourage a markedly unequal form of that development, or 2) policies or institutions at the international level are such as to damage a country's economic development or to encourage a markedly unequal form of that development.

This is a large enough agenda to be sure. Yet at least it has the merit of identifying potential responsible agents and the kinds of responsibility that might be relevant for securing a right to development. This brings me to the main subject of the chapter.

Obligations Not to Damage or Harm

The previous section argued for a concept of the right to development, which would enable us to specify clearly what would count in principle as a violation or infringement of the right and who the responsible agents might be. These agents are governments, and their corresponding obligation is not to initiate or support policies or institutional arrangements, whether domestic or international, which systematically damage any country's economic development or encourage a markedly unequal form of that development. These are not the only obligations governments have; as with all human rights, they also have positive duties to "aid and protect."[11] However, the merit of specifying what would count as a violation or infringement of a country's right to economic development is that it concentrates attention on what everyone would agree to be a compelling obligation — not to cause damage or harm. Certainly, as with all public policy, there is room for disagreement about what exactly causes any particular damage or harm and whether such damage might be justifiable if it could be shown to be necessary to some much greater good. But it would be difficult to contest the principle that the first duty of governments, as of citizens also, is not to cause damage or harm. Since the application of this principle in relation to the right to development raises different issues at the domestic and international levels, I shall treat each separately, beginning with the international level, since it increasingly conditions the room for maneuver of domestic economic policy.

The language of responsibility in international development policy and literature is almost always couched in terms of positive duties — to give aid, assistance, and so

---

11   Henry Shue, *Basic Rights* (Princeton, NJ: Princeton University Press, 1980), p. 53.

forth, especially to the less developed countries. Article 4.2 of the UN Declaration points out that "sustained action is required to promote more rapid development of developing countries. As a complement to the efforts of developing countries, effective international cooperation is essential in providing those countries with appropriate means and facilities to foster their comprehensive development."[12] Such positive assistance is of course essential, and it remains a scandal that so few countries manage to attain even the modest UN goal of 0.7 percent of GDP devoted to this purpose. Yet the very language and policies of development assistance or "cooperation" tend to reinforce a relationship of one-sided dependency between the developed and developing worlds, and convey an image of benevolence on the part of developed countries that obscures the fact that they also pursue or support international policies that inflict considerable damage on developing countries. The idea of a violation or infringement of the right to development focuses our attention on this damage and on the failure in a primary obligation not to cause damage or harm. There are a number of significant reasons for considering the matter this way:

> 1) There is universal agreement on the obligation not to damage or harm others, whatever the relationship (or lack of it) in which we stand to them. This consideration is argued forcefully by Thomas Pogge in his latest book, *World Poverty and Human Rights*: "Our starting point . . . (is the) deeply entrenched view that any moral duty not to wrong another person, or not to harm him unduly, is much weightier than any corresponding duty to protect him against like wrongs from other sources."[13] Actually, I think Pogge overstates the case and does so because he wants to carry the argument over poverty to those who subscribe to the liberal tenet that the only general duties we owe to others are duties not to harm, not duties to aid. As I have argued elsewhere, I believe that this liberal distinction is ultimately arbitrary, since both sets of duties find their justification in the same underlying principle, namely, the supreme value that we attach to individual well-being and autonomy and the equal worth of all human beings.[14] Given, however, that so many people believe that the duty not to harm is indeed much weightier, demonstrating that the relations between developed and developing countries breach this duty constitutes a powerful and potentially far-reaching argument. As Pogge says elsewhere, "we are not bystanders who find ourselves confronted with foreign deprivations whose origins are wholly unconnected to ourselves."[15]

> 2) Providing evidence of damage to development or infringements of the right to development sets the practice of development assistance in a different moral light. Some theorists of international justice would argue that the damage inflicted turns the duty to give aid from a "duty of benevolence" to a much more compelling "duty of justice,"

---

12   Brownlie and Goodwin-Gill, *supra*, note 2, p. 850.
13   Thomas W. Pogge, *World Poverty and Human Rights* (Cambridge: Polity Press, 2002), p. 132.
14   David Beetham, *Democracy and Human Rights* (Cambridge: Polity Press, 1999), pp. 125-129.
15   Thomas W. Pogge, (ed.), *Global Justice* (Oxford: Blackwell, 2001), p. 14.

since it serves as a form of compensation for damage inflicted.[16] I think this move is mistaken, since it implies that, if the source of harm or damage were to be removed, the duty to provide aid would be much less morally compelling. Yet considerations of justice would still apply, regardless of any damage caused, whether we derive such considerations from the extension of Rawlsian principles of justice to the international sphere (as in the pathbreaking work of 1979 by Charles Beitz)[17] or, as I myself would prefer, from the injustice entailed by the failure to realize basic human rights in a world of abundance. However, even though the duties to provide development assistance are morally compelling anyway, there is no doubt that the assistance itself appears in a very different moral light if the "donors" are also implicated in policies which damage that same development. Who can fail to be shocked by calculations that show that the cost to Southern producers from Northern subsidy and protectionist regimes is many times greater than the value of the same governments' combined development assistance? Furthermore, those calculations do not include the value of all the other economic transfers from developing to developed countries.

3) Considering the matter from this point of view links the discussion on the right to development firmly with the burgeoning critical literature on the arrangements of the international economic system and the institutions and policies that sustain them — the so-called global economic architecture. The argument here is that significant features of these arrangements and the rules governing them — on trade, finance, investment, the environment — systematically disadvantage the poorest countries and damage their economic development, further intensifying global inequalities. This happens because the structure of the international economic institutions accords much greater decisional power to the governments of the developed countries, to the extent that they should be considered largely responsible for the global economic arrangements which these institutions endorse.

Two objections to this last argument are worth considering before I review the empirical evidence in support of it. The first objection is that all countries, even the least developed ones, gain more than they lose from their membership in the international economic order and are therefore better off than they would be outside it in some form of "autarchy." Even if such a proposition could be proved, it is simply beside the point. The issue is not whether economic relations between countries, taken as a whole or in principle, are a good or bad thing. It is whether those features that are particularly damaging to developing countries could be other than they are, and therefore subject to a change of policy by those with the power to effect it. Loose talk

---

16   See, for example, A. Dobson, *Justice and the Environment* (Oxford: Oxford University Press, 1998), and J. Lichtenberg, "National Boundaries and Moral Boundaries, a Cosmopolitan View," in P. G. Brown and H. Shue (eds.), *Boundaries: National Autonomy and its Limits* (Totowa, NJ: Rowman, 1981), pp. 79-100.
17   Charles Beitz, *Political Theory and International Relations* (Princeton, NJ: Princeton University Press, 1979).

about "globalization" may convey the impression that the pattern of international economic relations is an unstoppable force of nature, but actually it is structured and sustained by political decision, including decisions about what *not* to regulate, as well as what to regulate, and how to do so.[18]

A second objection is that, since developing countries are members of the international organizations in question and take part in their proceedings, they thereby demonstrate consent to the decisions that flow from them. And consent legitimates the outcomes, whatever their balance of advantages and disadvantages may be. This objection, however, is no more tenable than the first. It is notorious that in many of the relevant organizations (for example, IMF, World Bank) formal voting power is massively weighted in favor of the developed countries. And even where it is not (for example, WTO) their decisional power is still disproportionate because of huge inequalities in the resources available for research and preparation of negotiating positions, and in the relative costs to the respective parties of not reaching agreement, or of opting out altogether. Although consent obtained under conditions of inequality may convey the appearance of legitimacy, it does not meet the normative criteria established by the tradition of liberal political philosophy, which requires an original equality between the contracting parties if the outcomes are to be considered at all fair or just.[19] The recent refusal of developing countries to reach agreement at Cancun shows how prejudicial to them was the trade deal on offer, but it also exposed for all to see the inequity of the relations among the respective parties.

What, then, is the state of the evidence about the damage that is caused to the economic development of developing countries by significant and avoidable features of international economic arrangements? Here, I shall confine myself to brief summaries in three key areas — trade, finance, and the environment. What is significant is the convergence of evidence and argument on these issues between those who might be termed "insiders," such as George Soros[20] and Joseph Stiglitz,[21] with more longstanding opponents of current international economic arrangements, such as Naomi Klein[22] or George Monbiot.[23]

Trade

- Developed countries use their bargaining power to open up Third World markets to their goods, while maintaining tariffs and subsidies that damage developing countries' producers, especially in agriculture and textiles.

- Northern governments underwrite and enforce international contracts which distort development needs (for example, arms and construction) or

18 Paul Q. Hirst and Grahame Thompson, *Globalization in Question: The International Economy and the Possibilities of Governance* (Cambridge: Polity Press, 1996), Chapter 1.
19 John Rawls, *A Theory of Justice* (Oxford: Oxford University, 1971).
20 George Soros, *On Globalization* (Oxford: Public Affairs, 2002).
21 Joseph Stiglitz, *Globalization and its Discontents* (London: Allen Lane, 2002); and Joseph Stiglitz, *The Roaring Nineties: Seeds of Destruction* (London: Allen Lane, 2003).
22 Naomi Klein, *Fences and Windows* (London: Flamingo, 2002).
23 Geroge Monbiot, *The Age of Consent* (London: Flamingo, 2003).

saddle countries with excessive long-term payments (for example, power generation and other public utilities).

■ Technology patents, including patents on naturally occurring foods and drugs, enable Northern companies to extract large and continuing transfers from developing countries.

■ Transfer pricing enables multinational companies to avoid taxation in all jurisdictions, but it has a particularly heavy impact on countries with limited state budgets.

According to Soros,[24] "Trade liberalization all too often fails to live up to its promise. . . . Western countries pushed trade liberalization for the products they exported, but at the same time continued to protect those sectors in which competition from developing countries might have threatened their economies." Stiglitz comments that "(t)he critics are right in claiming that the WTO is biased in favor of the rich countries and multinational corporations."[25]

Finance

■ The high cost of credit for home-grown firms in developing countries increases the difficulties that they face in competing with international companies.

■ Capital market liberalization has impeded economic growth and made countries vulnerable to speculative flows, which can create or exacerbate financial crises.

■ IMF policies for countries in financial crisis have been contractionary and damaging to the public sector, burdening countries with long-term pay ments at inflated rates of interest while exacerbating the contagion effects of crisis on other countries.

Soros observes that ". . . financial markets are inherently unstable and the playing field is inherently uneven . . . Emerging market economies are suffering from capital outflows and higher borrowing costs,"[26] while Stieglitz purports that ". . . if IMF policies had simply failed to accomplish the full potential of development, that would have been bad enough. But the failures in many places have set back the development agenda."[27]

The Environment

■ Global warming, largely caused by developed countries and responsible for an intensification and frequency of extreme events such as drought and flooding, impacts particularly severely on developing countries and on populations at the margin of subsistence.

■ Demand from Northern consumers leads to rapid depletion of non-renewable natural resources in developing countries (oil, minerals,

---

24   George Soros, *On Globalization* (Oxford: Public Affairs, 2002), p. 33.
25   Joseph Stiglitz, *Globalization and its Discontents* (London: Allen Lane, 2002), p. 60.
26   Soros, *supra*, note 19, p. 123.
27   Stiglitz, *supra*, note 20, p. 76.

hardwood, fish stocks, and so forth), often causing local environmental pollution and damaging traditional livelihoods.

■ The lower capacity for effective environmental regulation in developing countries is widely exploited by Northern companies and colluded in by their governments.

Lonergan posits that ". . . until there is recognition that those countries which have not caused these problems are indeed the ones that are going to suffer most, the outlook, I think, for many countries . . . is very bleak."[28]

What is being claimed here is not that the consequences of countries' increased insertion into the global economy are all negative. It is rather that those features that are particularly damaging for the economies of developing countries could be made less detrimental through a change in policy or regulation, and that the governments of developed countries must take the major share of responsibility for their persistence. International economic relations in the 1990s, concludes Joseph Stiglitz in his latest book, were "built by brute force, by dictating inappropriate conditions in the midst of crisis, by bullying, by imposing unfair trade treaties or by pursuing hypocritical trade policies — all of which are part of the hegemonic legacy that the US established in the 1990s but seem to have become worse in the next administration."[29]

National Priorities and International Obligations

The right to development of developing countries, then, is seriously infringed by international arrangements that have been initiated or sustained by the governments of developed countries, in breach of a basic obligation not to cause harm or damage to others. This happens because, as Pogge observes, "our representatives in international negotiations do not consider the interests of the global poor as part of their mandate. They are exclusively devoted to shaping each such agreement in the best interests of the people and corporations of their own country."[30] Many people would argue that they are right to do so. We share a common citizenship and many other characteristics with our fellow nationals, they argue, and are linked to them by bonds of mutual recognition and mutual responsibility. It is therefore right that both we and the governments that represent us should give priority to the needs and interests of fellow nationals over those of other nations, with whom we do not stand in any special relationship.

This common-sense viewpoint has formed the subject of lively philosophical debate between so-called "cosmopolitans" and "communitarians," the former contending that the principles of justice require that "everyone should count for one" regardless of where they live, and the latter contending, in turn, that principles of justice can apply only within bounded political communities, in which there exist strong ties of mutual recognition and an acknowledged reciprocity of obligations.[31]

---

28 Stephen Lonergan, "UN early warning and assessment centre, Nairobi," quoted in *The Guardian*, August 11, 2003, p. 8.
29 Joseph Stiglitz, *The Roaring Nineties: Seeds of Destruction* (London: Allen Lane, 2003).
30 Pogge, *supra*, note 12, p. 20.
31 Shapiro, I. and Brilmayer, L. (eds.), *Global Justice: Nomos XLI* (New York: New York University Press, 1999).

Neither position, however, if taken to an extreme, looks remotely plausible. We cannot ignore or eliminate the special responsibilities that we recognize and owe to our fellow nationals, yet neither can we make these the limits of our moral concern or obligation in an increasingly interconnected and interdependent world. As Samuel Scheffler has observed, we confront here "two ideas — the idea of special responsibilities and the idea of global justice — which are evidently in tension with each other . . . yet each of these ideas is rooted in values that occupy a central place in the moral outlook of many people."[32] How we might reconcile this tension, or which idea we should give priority to when they conflict, Scheffler does not consider. Yet it is one of the central questions to which any theory of human rights and their corresponding obligations has to provide a convincing answer.

What we are looking for, then, is a clear principle that will enable us to determine when, and under what circumstances, those who live in developed countries (and the governments that represent us) would be justified, indeed required, to give priority to international obligations over special responsibilities to fellow nationals, given that we must acknowledge the force of both. Two ideas may help us here. One is advanced in the recent writings of Peter Singer, who has relaxed the heroic stringency of his earlier work to accommodate the moral limitations of ordinary mortals, though his basic starting point is the same — a version of the marginal utility principle. Since the gap between living standards in the developed and developing countries is so enormous, he argues, and since relatively small sums which would only add to the marginal superfluities of the well-off would transform the lives of the impoverished, it must be justified, indeed morally required, for transfers to be made from the former to the latter, since no significant damage would be done to their basic interests or the fulfillment of their special duties to family, friends, and others by doing so. And such transfers should be set at the point which, if generalized, would enable the minimum needs of everyone for "enough to eat, clean water to drink, shelter from the elements and basic health care" to be met.[33]

This is a clear and persuasive idea in principle, except to those who acknowledge no positive duties to aid whatsoever. It serves to identify the nature of the transfers at issue, from the marginal disposable income of those whose living requirements and special responsibilities are already met and the limits of such transfers — the point where the most basic human rights are satisfied for all. It represents, we could say, a minimal, rather than a maximal, conception of international justice. Singer weakens his argument for those who take special responsibilities to co-nationals seriously with his contention that such transfers *between* countries should take priority over transfers *within* countries.[34] He provides no evidence that these are in competition with one another; rather, both are in competition with a relatively small amount of marginal expenditure of the large numbers of the well-off. Indeed, what evidence

---

32   Samuel Scheffler, "The Conflict between Justice and Responsibility," in Shapiro and Brilmayer, *supra*, note 28, pp. 86-115 (1999), p. 102.
33   Peter Singer, *One World: the Ethics of Globalization* (New Haven: Yale University Press, 2002), Chapter 5.
34   *Ibid.*, pp. 174-175.

there is indicates that those countries which come closest to achieving UN targets for development assistance (the Nordic ones) are also the ones that operate the most redistributive policies domestically. In other words, the principles of national and international justice are mutually reinforcing in practice, rather than conflictual.[35]

Singer is primarily concerned with the issue of aid and with specifying positive duties of assistance, both by individuals and governments, to those in greatest need. Yet the right to development, as I have conceived it, looks at the obverse side of the coin, at the damage done to societies' economic development by the arrangements of the international economic order. Here a second idea seems particularly relevant for deciding between the respective claims of international justice and the special responsibilities due to co-nationals. It is advanced by Thomas Pogge in Chapter Five of his latest book, where he discusses "the bounds of nationalism." In this chapter he sets out a hierarchy of obligations, with "negative duties not to wrong (unduly harm) others" at the top. When it is a question of other kinds of duty, he argues, such as the duties to aid and protect, then "it is morally more important to attend to the needs of our compatriots than to give like assistance to foreigners." When we come to negative duties, however, the distinction between compatriots and foreigners (or between those to whom we are specially connected and third parties) becomes arbitrary, and avoiding harm to third parties must "trump" any duties to aid and protect, even those with whom we stand in a special relationship.[36]

The relevance of this principle to infringements of the right to development should be evident. Yet there are two problems with the principle as it stands, neither of which Pogge addresses. The first is a classic conceptual conundrum, to the effect that not to provide protection where we have the clear responsibility and capacity to do so is equivalent to harming, so Pogge's basic distinctions will not withstand close examination. A more practical objection is that, if governments of the developed countries were to reverse most of the policies mentioned in the previous section as being particularly damaging to developing countries, it would harm some of their own nationals and their businesses in the process. The point at issue, therefore, is not so much to distinguish among different kinds of obligation as it is how to assess the relative harms involved, to nationals and non-nationals respectively, in maintaining current policies or changing them.

By this criterion, one may thus conclude that Western nationals would experience less harm in both numbers and degree as a result of changing the policies in question than developing countries would from maintaining them. The damage to those from developed countries would be incurred by those most able to sustain it; when this is not the case, however, the governments involved have the resources to provide forms of transitional assistance that are not so externally damaging as current subsidies and protectionism. In other words, we have here the obverse of Singer's marginal utility principle; we could call it the "relative sustainability of harms" principle. And here

35   Charles Jones, *Global Justice: Defending Cosmopolitanism* (Oxford: Oxford University Press, 1999), Chapter 6.
36   Thomas Pogge, *supra*, note 12, pp. 132-133.

the concept of the right to development could be invoked to give support to this principle: Whereas the harms incurred clearly damage the economic development of developing countries, the same could not be said of the harms that would be incurred by already developed countries from a change in the relevant policies.

We thus have two robust principles for determining where the claims of international justice should override any special responsibilities owed to co-nationals and where international obligations should override domestic ones, whether on the part of citizens or their governments. One is the marginal utility principle, which endorses an overriding positive obligation to provide assistance to satisfy basic human rights from the discretionary expenditure of the well-off. The second is what I have called the "relative sustainability of harms" principle, which requires the elimination of international policies that damage the economic development of developing countries as an obligation that is prior to avoiding harms that might occur to nationals of already developed countries by doing so. The strong support that it provides for this second principle, in my estimation, gives the idea of the right to development its special distinctiveness and normative force within the human rights agenda.

The fact that governments in the main do not acknowledge these principles or act according to them does not render them invalid or utopian. Yet, in confronting the world as it is, those campaigning for changes in the international economic order and for greater protection for human rights should be clear about their grounds for doing so and should be able to answer deep-seated objections, one of the most pervasive of which is that governments are expected to give priority to the interests of their own nationals. Few individuals will come out publicly and say that they are against human rights, but many will challenge the corresponding obligations which are necessary if these rights are actually to be realized. Being clear about the justification for these obligations is a necessary starting point for any effective response.

At the same time, we need to understand why governments and their publics do not give these obligations the weight that they merit. Two kinds of reasons are usually advanced. One points to the moral limitations of the average citizen of the developed countries. Our moral sensibilities, it is argued, change more slowly than the world around us, and the pace of globalization has outstripped the capacity of nation-centered moralities to adapt to an expanded universe of interdependency.[37] A less generous version identifies a malign effect of neo-liberal economics, which has been to legitimate self-interest-maximizing behavior throughout public life. One consequence has been a perceived resistance to increases in taxation, with development assistance budgets declining proportionately as a result; or, where governments have increased them (as recently in the UK) they have done so only "by stealth." Yet the level of support for international NGOs suggests that public attitudes are more complex in reality, and that open and serious public debate about official aid budgets would be beneficial. Opinion surveys quoted by Peter Singer show that, although most US citizens think that the percentage of the federal budget spent on official aid is between 10 and 20 times higher than it actually is, they nevertheless believe that

---

37   Lichtenberg, *supra*, note 15, pp. 94-95.

it should be reduced. The figure that they find appropriate to "cut" it to, however, is more than five times what is actually being spent — a sum that is, in any case, a small fraction of the projected annual *increase* in the US military budget for 2003 and successive years.[38]

This brings us to a second kind of explanation, which is more relevant to Western governments' failure to end the damage done to developing countries by international economic arrangements. This is, not surprisingly, that these governments are in hock to their own producer and financial interests, on whose monetary support they rely to meet the costs of their own re-election, and who are consequently given priority and preferential access in the formation of government policy. Although this relationship finds its most extreme manifestation with the current U.S. administration, it is evident to a greater or lesser extent in all the developed countries. It demonstrates a close link between the failure to meet their international obligations abroad and the distortions to which the democratic process is subject at home.[39]

Prospects for changing this balance of moral and political forces may seem distant, but they are not hopeless. Recent years have witnessed the development of an increasingly vocal international public opinion, in which progressive forces in both developing and developed countries have combined to campaign for changes to the international economic order, with some modest successes to their credit. The emergence of a new bloc of developing countries at Cancun, under the leadership of Brazil, China, and India, may signal a turning point as significant as the development of trade unionism in the industrial era. A clearly focused "right to development" could provide a unifying rubric for the different agendas of this movement and would have a much more critical purchase than simplistic slogans of anti-globalization.

Infringements of the Right to Development by Domestic Governments

The focus thus far has been on the damage to economic development caused by international economic arrangements. An earlier section, however, identified the other source of infringements to the right to development as coming from the policies and institutions of a country's own government. Some commentators find it convenient to lay the onus for the poor economic development of developing countries on their own governments' corruption and other deficiencies, which divert attention from the responsibility of the rest of the world. Yet there is no doubting that domestic governments share some of the responsibility for economic under-development and that authoritarian regimes that are major human rights violators are among the most damaging in this respect as well.

It is at this point that the agendas for economic development and democratization converge. Other contributors to this book have written eloquently about this connection,[40] to which I will add a few remarks.

---

38 Singer, *supra*, note 33, pp. 182-185.
39 Greg Palast, *The Best Democracy Money Can Buy* (London: Robinson, 2003).
40 Sen, *supra*, note 6, Chapter 6.

First, electoral democracy on its own is insufficient either to diminish the scale of corruption or to prevent "elite capture" of the democratic process. Indeed, the costs of electoral campaigning can serve to consolidate both. With rare exceptions, the kind of economic development indicated by the "right to development" requires both strong institutions of public accountability and the emergence of political parties committed to an at least modestly redistributive and socially empowering agenda.[41]

Second, Western governments must take some of the blame for the emergence of authoritarian regimes in developing countries. In the past they have either actively encouraged or colluded in the establishment of many of them. In the present, they maintain international arrangements which allow such regimes to plunder their countries' resources and saddle their peoples with debt burdens stretching into the distant future. Here, the right of peoples to "full sovereignty over all their natural wealth and resources," pronounced in Article 1 of the UN Declaration, has proved to be something of a two-edged sword. Conceived initially to protect against neo-colonial exploitation, it overlooks the possibility that the product of such resources might be appropriated by their own ruling elites. Indeed, there is increasing evidence that the possession of substantial natural resources, especially mineral resources, diminishes the prospects for economic development, by maximizing elite discretion over the process of rent distribution, and that such resources provide a fertile soil for "coups, civil wars, oppression and corruption."[42]

At this point, it is important to insist that the rights encompassed by the right to development belong to peoples rather than to governments and that there are circumstances in which, as with any human right, they may have to be asserted on behalf of people against their own governments.[43] At what point a people may need external assistance or intervention to help protect their rights, and what form this intervention should take, are among the most pressing — and also divisive — issues in international politics today. One reason for their divisiveness is that, as this chapter has argued, we inhabit two different worlds simultaneously, each with its own distinct morality. On the one hand is the world of sovereign nation states, with the claims of nationhood, self-determination, and the normative primacy of co-nationals. On the other hand is the emerging supra-national order, with the claims of human rights, transnational justice, and universal equality. The language of the UN Declaration reflects both these worlds. Thus it emphasizes sovereignty, self-determination, and the rights of nations to their own resources and to freedom from foreign interference. At the same time, it insists on responsibilities and obligations that transcend national boundaries and that require institutions that can work only by limiting national sovereignty. How we negotiate the tensions between these two worlds and their respective moralities is the key to establishing a coherent right to development and its corresponding obligations.

---

41   David Beetham, *Democracy and Human Rights* (Cambridge: Polity Press, 1999), Chaper 5.
42   Pogge, *supra*, note 12, pp. 163-164.
43   Allan Rosas, "The Right to Development," in Asbjørn Eide, Catarina Krause and Allan Rosas (eds.), *Economic, Social and Cultural Rights* (Dordrecht: Martinus Nijhoff, 1995), pp. 247-255.

Conclusion

To make a human right realizable or effective requires not only identifying who the appropriate agents are who have an obligation for upholding the right, but also specifying what would count as an infringement of the right in question so that the scope of that obligation can be determined. I have argued that to do this for the right to development requires narrowing its definitional scope to "a nation's or people's right to economic development." An infringement or violation of this right can be said to occur "when a government initiates or supports policies or institutional arrangements, whether domestic or international, which systematically damage any country's economic development, or encourage a markedly unequal form of that development." The obligation not to act in this way ties in with a widespread conviction that we should not cause damage or harm to others. In the central part of the chapter, I examine the damage that is caused to the economic development of developing countries by current international economic arrangements, and I identify principles that will help determine when governments should give priority to international obligations over the interests of their nationals, where these conflict. Tensions between international and national moralities are explored further in the context of regimes that damage their own countries' economic development and the problems of how to address them. I conclude that, given a narrowing of definitional focus and an effective resolution of the tension between universalist and nation-centric normative demands, the right to development can serve as a coherent reference point for campaigns to reform international institutions and policies.

International Human Rights Obligations
in Context: Structural Obstacles and the
Demands of Global Justice
Margot E. Salomon

Widespread deprivation of economic, social, and cultural human rights today is largely a consequence of a global system that structurally disadvantages half the world's population.[1] In the area of international law aimed at the protection and promotion of human rights, we are witnessing a trend towards responding to this massive failure of the international community of states to allow for minimum essential levels of human rights to be secured globally, a shift that requires revisiting the ways in which responsibility is determined. Drawing on the right to development and on the authoritative interpretations of several UN human rights treaty-bodies,[2] the first part of this chapter will focus on the evolving normative human rights framework as applied to the structural determinants of global injustice, manifested in the form of world poverty. The latter part of this chapter will consider the attribution of responsibility to collective state conduct for violations of socio-economic rights. It argues that the design of the asymmetrical global order, disproportionately benefiting some at the expense of others, is a satisfactory indicator of causality and therefore legal responsibility. Secondly, that the responsibility of powerful states acting together can be ascertained based on whether they could have foreseen and averted the deleterious effects of their decisions. It proposes that the power and control exercised by multilateral economic institutions over a state's ability to lift itself out of poverty informs the parameters of the human rights obligation of international cooperation, and lastly, that the primary obligation of the international community now must be to remedy this human catastrophe, requiring effect be given both to negative as well as positive external obligations. The aim is to draw out developments in international human rights law regarding the contemporary scope of state obligations, as informed by the dictates of an economically interdependent world. The quest for global justice in international law is a search for legal obligations that are anchored in global institutional arrangements that are fair to impoverished nations and peoples.

---

1   "The core message . . . is that many of the world's poorest countries and regions face structural impediments that have made it very difficult to achieve sustained economic growth. Thus it is not an accident that they are the poorest." *UNDP Human Development Report 2003: Millennium Development Goals* (Oxford: Oxford University Press, 2003), Chapter 3; "At the global level, the present system of governance is based on rules and policies that generate unbalanced and often unfair outcomes. Global governance needs to be reformed . . . ." *A Fair Globalization: Report of the World Commission on the Social Dimension of Globalization* (Geneva: ILO, 2004), Annex 1: Guide to Proposals and Recommen-dations, p. 143. Referring to the ILO World Commission report, Joseph Stiglitz remarks: " . . . the emerging consensus [is] that globalization — despite its positive potential — has not only failed to live up to that potential, but has actually contributed to social distress." *The Guardian (UK)*, March 12, 2004.
2   These Committees are mandated to examine the progress made by States parties in meeting their obligations under the human rights treaties: see, ECOSOC Res. 1985/17 (Committee on Economic, Social and Cultural Rights — CESCR); Convention on the Rights of the Child Art. 43(1) (Committee on the Rights of the Child). Convention on the Rights of the Child (1989), entered into force September 2, 1990, GA Res. A/RES/44/25, annex 44, UN GAOR Supp. (No. 49), p. 167, UN Doc. A/44/49 (1989).4 UN Millennium Declaration, Arts. 2 and 6, UN Doc. A/55/2 (2000).

Global Structural Obstacles and the International Law of Human Rights

International human rights law today is informed by a search for global justice, ". . . on the international struggle, on the promises not kept by the rich countries."[3] Representative world conferences over the past decade have repeatedly articulated their commitment to collective responsibility in order to free the world's people from want, to uphold the principles of human dignity and equality upon which the human rights canon is premised, and to achieve this through respect for the basic principles of social justice and equity at the global level.[4] Through the widespread recognition of the interwoven and interdependent nature of present-day economies, a global consensus has been reached that national development efforts in which human rights can be realized require an international enabling environment.[5] According to the targets and indicators related to the Millennium Development Goal (MDG) 8,[6] which calls for a global partnership for development, this would include an open, multilateral, trading and financial system that is equitable, rules-based, predictable, and non-discriminatory;[7] enhanced debt relief for heavily indebted poor countries; and cancellation of external debt for developing countries.[8] This would also require fulfilling the commitment of donor countries, reflected in the Monterrey Consensus and reaffirmed in the 2002 Declaration and Plan of Implementation of the World Summit on Sustainable Development, to meet the target of providing 0.7 percent of their national wealth in official development assistance.[9] The Member States of the United Nations have committed themselves to

---

3   Center for Human Rights and Global Justice, *Human Rights Perspectives on the Millennium Development Goals*, Conference Report (New York University: November 2003), p. 12. Available at www.nyuhr.org.
4   UN Millennium Declaration, Arts. 2 and 6, UN Doc. A/55/2 (2000).
5   See the Monterrey Consensus, para. 6, for one of many examples. Final Outcome of the International Conference on Financing for Development, UN Doc. A/CONF.198/A1 (2002).
6   The MDGs reflect a globally endorsed strategy for poverty reduction and sustainable human development in a range of key areas such as hunger, education, and gender equality, as well as environmental sustainability.
7   Millennium Development Goal 8: To Develop a Global Partnership for Development. Available at www.unmillenniumproject.org. This goal is meant to address, *inter alia*, the current trade-distorting barriers, tariffs, and subsidies that play such a key role in keeping Africa impoverished, as elsewhere in the developing world. In the words of the UN Secretary-General Kofi Annan, what is required is the "elimination of the [trade] system's egregious biases against developing countries . . . [and] a deal on agriculture that will help the poor." Noting further, "[n]o single issue more gravely imperils the multilateral trading system, from which you [the world's business leaders] benefit so much." Secretary-General's speech to the World Economic Forum, Davos, Switzerland, February 2004, SG/04/223. For a critique of Goal 8 from a human rights perspective, see Margot E. Salomon, "Addressing Structural Obstacles and Advancing Accountability for Human Rights: A Contribution of the Right to Development to MDG 8," *Briefing Note to the UN High-Level Task Force on the Implementation of the Right to Development* (November 2005). Available at www.ohchr.org/english/issues/development/taskforce.htm.
8   Following on from the G8 decision at the summit in July 2005, the World Bank and IMF annual meeting, September 24-25, 2005, concluded that 18 countries stand to have their debts cancelled by the end of 2005. While this could free up money to invest towards meeting the MDGs, existing IFI imposed economic conditionality limiting countries' spending on social goods could counter these objectives. On the decision to cancel multilateral debt, see IMF Press Release, No. 05/210 (September 24, 2005); "World Bank, IMF Strike Debt Deal, Shift Sights to WTO," *Bridges Weekly Trade News Digest* (September 28, 2005).
9   Monterrey Consensus, *supra* n. 5, at para. 6; Declaration and Plan of Implementation, UN World Summit on Sustainable Development, para. 85(a), UN Doc. A/CONF.199/20 (2002). Despite US objection, the continued support for the 0.7 percent GNI target was reaffirmed by the General Assembly at its 2005 Summit, 2005 World Summit Outcome, UN Doc. A/60/L.1, (September 15, 2005), para. 23(b).

". . . free[ing] our fellow men, women and children from the abject and dehuman-izing conditions of extreme poverty, to which more than a billion of them are cur-rently subjected [and] to making the right to development a reality for everyone and to freeing the entire human race from want."[10] Yet despite global rhetorical con-sensus, and some incremental advances,[11] the international community of states is failing to move expeditiously towards setting this key commitment in motion.[12]

World poverty reflects a transgression of international human rights norms and its remedying engages the international human rights legal regime. Today, the con-dition of poverty is understood as reflecting, at a minimum, a denial of human rights,[13] and is characterized not solely in terms of lack of income but also in terms of qualitative deprivations, such as lack of power, choice, and capability.[14] Interna-tional law aimed at the protection and promotion of human rights is underpinned by the proposition that rights create corresponding duties. It is indeed this binary re-lation that distinguishes human rights from the general valuing of freedom that ex-ists without a correlated obligation to help bring about that freedom.[15] Signifying

10   Millennium Declaration, *supra* n. 4, at Art. 11.
11   The European Union members of the G8 donor states meeting in July 2005 at Gleneagles saw an-nouncements by France and the UK of timetables to reach 0.7 percent ODA/GNI by 2012 and 2013 re-spectively and reaffirmed the recent EU agreement to reach 0.7 percent ODA/GNI by 2015 with an interim target of 0.56 percent ODA/GNI by 2010 — a doubling of EU ODA between 2004 and 2010. "G8 Finance Ministers' Conclusions on Development." Press Release, UK Government (June 11, 2005).
12   In 2003 Pogge estimated that far from meeting the 0.7 percent GNI target, developed countries ag-gregate official development assistance had fallen to 0.22 percent. This includes the contribution of Norway, Sweden, Denmark, Luxembourg, and the Netherlands who have come close to or gone beyond meeting the target. Thomas Pogge, *The First UN Millennium Development Goal* (2003), p. 16. Paper pre-sented at the Oslo Lecture in Moral Philosophy, University of Oslo (September 2003). Available at www.etikk.no/globaljustice. Notably, the development literature provides that aid should not only be in-creased but also made more effective through stronger governance, increased ownership at the national level, and through better aid practices, for example, by untying aid and improving donor coordination. See *UNDP Human Development Report 2003: Millennium Development Goals, A Compact among Nations to End World Poverty, supra* n. 1, at Chapter 8.
13   CESCR, Statement on Poverty and the International Covenant on Economic, Social and Cultural Rights (25th session, 2001) UN Doc. E/C.12/2001/10, para. 1. Whether we should speak of the mani-festations of world poverty as a denial of human rights or as a violation of human rights is a topic of on-going consideration. Unlike the terms "denial" or "non-fulfillment," a "violation" suggests the existence of an identifiable perpetrator, or, responsibility for an act which may not be directly imputable to a state, but for which the state remains responsible. See *Velasquez Rodriguez v Honduras*, Inter-American Court of Human Rights (Ser. C) No. 4, Judgement of July 29,1988, para. 172. Similarly, Alston points out that "in legal terms the maxim [that extreme poverty is a human rights violation] is only true to the extent that a government or other relevant actor has failed to take measures which would have been feasible ("to the maximum extent of available resources" etc., as the language of [Art. 2(1) of] the ICESCR puts it) and which could have had the effect of avoiding or mitigating the plight in which an individual living in poverty finds him or herself." Philip Alston, "Ships Passing in the Night: The Current State of the Human Rights and Development Debate Seen Through the Lens of the Millennium Development Goals," *Human Rights Quarterly* 27 (2005), p. 786.
14   Drawing on the seminal work of Nobel Prize-winning economist Amartya Sen, the Committee on Economic, Social and Cultural Rights has defined poverty as " . . . a human condition characterized by sustained or chronic deprivation of the resources, capabilities, choices, security and power necessary for the enjoyment of an adequate standard of living and other civil, cultural, economic, political and social rights . . ." CESCR Statement on Poverty, *supra* n. 13, at para. 8. Sen distinguishes between income poverty and capability poverty, arguing that development is not the acquisition of more goods and serv-ices but the enhanced freedom — that is the capability — to lead the kind of life one values. Poverty is the deprivation of these basic capabilities. Amartya Sen, *Development as Freedom* (Oxford: Oxford University Press, 1999), Chapter 4.
15   Amartya Sen, "Consequential Evaluation and Practical Reason," *The Journal of Philosophy* 9 (2000), p. 478. See also Arjun Sengupta, *First Report of the Independent Expert on the Right to Development* (General Assembly, 55th session 2000) UN Doc. A/55/306, para. 8 and *Fourth Report of the Independent Expert on the Right to Development* (Working Group on the Right to Development, 3rd session 2002) UN Doc. E/CN.4/2002/WG.18/2, paras. 15, 31, 35; and Stephen P. Marks, *The Human Rights Framework for Development: Seven Approaches* (2004), pp. 18-20. Available at www.hsph.harvard.edu/fxbcenter.

the violation of human rights on a massive scale is the fact that 46 percent of the world's people, concentrated in developing countries, live below the World Bank's $2-a-day poverty line[16] and have an aggregate global income of 1.2 percent;[17] 1.2 billion people globally (one in every five) try to survive on $1 a day.[18] Add to this that the global order favors a small number of (wealthy) countries that hold sway over a global institutional system that entrenches this division and undermines equal claims in sharing the benefits of cooperative efforts.[19] How then is international human rights law evolving to respond to these realities of global injustice?

In response to deprivations inadequately addressed by the current global institutional system, ensuring human rights today might increasingly be understood as having two quite clearly defined legal dimensions: that of the obligations of each state (when acting nationally and extraterritorially) and that of the collective obligations of the international community of states. The latter, which forms the focus of this article, pertains to the aggregate obligations of the international community to secure a system that is globally just. In the context of international development and the alleviation of world poverty, the term "international community" might be used narrowly, applying to those states in positions of power and influence over the international economic order.[20]

Collective Duties of International Cooperation and the Right to Development

The Declaration on the Right to Development (DRD), adopted in 1986 by the United Nations General Assembly,[21] emerged in large part as a response to the call by developing countries for an international order in which international cooperation would reduce the perceived unfairness of the prevailing economic system.[22] The Declaration gave legal expression to the notion that the ability of states to develop and to fulfil their human rights obligations domestically are constrained by the actions and structural arrangements of the international community. The DRD is informed by the purposes of the United Nations as defined in its Charter,[23] notably,

---

16   Moreover, the figure of $2 a day has been criticized as being wholly without value as a measure by which to assess the scale of world poverty. A more accurately derived figure, it has been argued, would reflect a substantially higher degree of world poverty and less favorable trends in what is already modest improvement as presented by the World Bank. Thomas Pogge and Sanjay Reddy, *How Not to Count the Poor* (2003). Available at www.columbia.edu/~sr793/techpapers.html. A less technical summary is provided in Thomas Pogge, *supra* n. 12, pp. 5-12.
17   Thomas Pogge, *World Poverty and Human Rights* (Cambridge: Polity Press, 2002), p. 2.
18   UNDP *Human Development Report 2003: Millennium Development Goals, A Compact Among Nations to End Human Poverty, supra* n. 1, at Overview 5.
19   "We judge that the problems we have identified are not due to globalization as such but to deficiencies in its governance . . . There is concern about the unfairness of key global rules on trade and finance and their asymmetric effects on rich and poor countries." *A Fair Globalization, supra* n. 1, p. xi.
20   As opposed, for example, to standard-setting within the UN which has the "international community" constituting all UN member states.
21   Declaration on the Right to Development, GA Res. A/RES/41/128, December 4, 1986, annex, 41 UN GAOR Supp. (No. 53) 186, UN Doc. A/RES/41/53 (1986).
22   Borne of the debates around the need for a New International Economic Order (NIEO) of the 1970s. See the General Assembly Resolutions on the Declaration and Programme of Action on the Establishment of a New International Economic Order, GA Res. 3201 (S-VI) and GA Res. 3202 (S-VI) of May 1, 1974 and on the Charter on the Economic Rights and Duties of States, GA Res. 3281 (XXIX) of December 12, 1974.
23   Charter of the United Nations, entered into force October 24, 1945, 59 Stat. 1031, TS 993, 3 Bevans 1193.

to achieve international cooperation in solving international problems of an economic and social nature and to promote respect for human rights, as well as by the
articulation in the Universal Declaration of Human Rights (UDHR) of a universal
entitlement to a human rights-based international order. Thus, the DRD builds on
Charter-based collective duties of cooperation in the creation of a just international
order and the elimination of global inequity so that human rights might be realized.[24]

With the adoption of the Declaration, the General Assembly recognized the right
to development as an inalienable human right.[25] The DRD is significant in that,
conceptually, it provided a normative basis for the emerging awareness that "development" was more than economic growth and moreover, that growth was not an end
in itself.[26] As the intergovernmental UN Working Group on the Right to
Development concluded recently, ". . . the implementation of the right to development requires growth with equity. Development has to be grounded in economic
policies that foster growth with social justice."[27] The Working Group agreed that
only "a rights-based approach to economic growth and development contributes to
the realization of the right to development."[28] Accordingly, respect for human rights
must determine the strategies for growth as well as guide its distribution domestically
and internationally.

By clearly defining development as a human right, the DRD recognizes people as
right-holders, as active subjects in their development. Article 2(1) of the DRD states
that "[t]he human person is the central subject of development and should be the active participant and beneficiary of the right to development." It recognizes states
acting at the national level,[29] as well as cooperating at the international level[30] as
duty-bearers. At this latter level, states are understood to be agents with duties that
require cooperative action geared towards the creation of equitable international conditions favorable to advancing human dignity and freedom through the enjoyment
of rights.

---

24 DRD Preambular paragraphs 1 and 3 refer explicitly to the UN Charter Article 1(3) and the
Universal Declaration of Human Rights Article 28, respectively. Article 1(3) states: "The Purposes of the
United Nations are . . . To achieve international co-operation in solving international problems of an economic, social, cultural, or humanitarian character, and in promoting and encouraging respect for human
rights and for fundamental freedoms for all without distinction as to race, sex, language, or religion" and
is closely linked to the purposes elaborated in Charter Articles 55 and 56 which address International
Economic and Social Cooperation. Article 28 UDHR states: "Everyone is entitled to a social and international order in which the rights and freedoms set forth in this Declaration can be fully realized." GA
Res. 217A (III), adopted December 10, 1948, UN GAOR, 3rd Session Resolutions, pt.1, p. 71, UN Doc.
A/810 (1948).
25 DRD, Art. 1(1).
26 The right to development requires " . . . equality of opportunity for all in their access to basic resources, education, health services, food, housing, employment and the fair distribution of income,
[e]ffective measures . . . undertaken to ensure that women have an active role in the development process
. . . [and] appropriate economic and social reforms . . . carried out with a view to eradicating all social injustices." DRD, Art. 8(1).
27 Report of the Working Group on the Right to Development, (6th session, 2005), UN Doc.
E/CN.4/2005/25, para. 42.
28 Ibid., para. 46.
29 DRD Arts. 2(3), 3(1), 5, 6(3), 8(1), 8(2), 10.
30 DRD Arts. 2(3) 3, 4, 5, 6, 7, 8, 10.

Integral to its logic is a recognition that the implementation of the right to development domestically may be undermined by global disadvantage that developing countries face in their dual role as duty-bearers and claimants of the right to development. The debates and negotiations that took place during the drafting and adoption of the Declaration left no doubt that what the proponents of the right to development demanded was an international economic and social order based on equity and justice; an approach that continues to inform its interpretation today.[31] While the DRD reflects the general apprehension of relieving developing states acting domestically of their traditional primary responsibility for the realization of human rights,[32] the right to development invites a complementary claim by developing states against the international community for the effective implementation of the right. The right to development exists as a result of and in relation to the international community and can only be achieved through the shared effort of that community.[33]

In an interdependent world, sustained (rights-based) economic growth in any one country is largely dependent on the states and other actors of the international economy that influence trade, finance, and capital flows. The language of the DRD recognizes that states acting at the national level have the "duty" to formulate national development policies, devised in a participatory manner and aimed at improving the situation of the entire population through the equitable distribution of its benefits. However, the article also provides that these states possess this same "right."[34] This "right" of states can be understood as exercisable against the international community in its ability to constrain developing states from implementing policies that further the realization of human rights.[35] Similarly, "equality of opportunity" is recognized in the DRD as a "prerogative both of nations and the individuals who make up nations."[36]

The right to development as proclaimed by the community of states is, as such, conditioned by international cooperation in the creation of an international environment conducive to the elimination of poverty and to the realization of human rights. The recent complementary principle of a shared responsibility recognizes that the ability of a developing state to formulate and execute human rights policies for its people cannot be disassociated from the influence and cooperative role of certain

---

31 Report of the Intergovernmental Working Group on the Right to Development, (5th session, 1982) UN Doc. E/CN.4/1983/11. See also Arjun Sengupta, "On the Theory and Practice of the Right to Development." *Human Rights Quarterly* 4 (2002), pp. 849-850; Margot E. Salomon, "Towards a Just Institutional Order: A Commentary on the First Session of the UN Task Force on the Right to Development," *Netherlands Quarterly of Human Rights* 3 (2005), p. 409.
32 DRD, Preambular para. 15.
33 Hector Gros Espiell, "Community-Oriented Rights: Introduction." in Mohamed Bedjaoui (ed.), *International Law: Achievements and Prospects* (Leiden: Martinus Nijhoff Publishers, 1991), p. 1170. See also, Stephen P. Marks, "Emerging Human Rights: A New Generation for the 1980's?" *Rutgers Law Review* 33 (1981), pp. 435-452.
34 Art. 2(3).
35 Anne Orford, "Globalization and the Right to Development," in Philip Alston (ed.), *Peoples' Rights* (Oxford: Oxford University Press, 2001), p. 137.
36 DRD, Preambular para. 16; Art. 8(1).

members of the international community of states acting collectively.[37] The right to development is a human right that is largely exercised by a state on behalf of its people; but in the final analysis its fulfillment means that each individual person becomes capable of living a life free from poverty — the life she or he has chosen, in short, a life in larger freedom.[38]

Collective Obligations of International Cooperation and the Position of Treaty-Bodies

States have accepted the obligation of international cooperation in relation to a range of human rights by becoming parties to such instruments as the International Covenant on Economic, Social and Cultural Rights (ICESCR)[39] and the Convention on the Rights of the Child (CRC). The ICESCR, like all international human rights treaties, applies to persons found in territories under a State parties' jurisdiction. In addition, each State party is required, by Article 2(1), to take steps through international assistance and cooperation with a view to realizing the Covenant rights.[40] The CRC provides for similar requirements in relation to the economic, social, and cultural rights found among its provisions[41] and articulates the particular need of developing countries for international cooperation.[42] Yet, unlike the Declaration on the Right to Development, the ICESCR, and the CRC, while based also on the obligation of international cooperation, are geared towards viola-

---

37 The Millennium Declaration entrenches the principle of a shared responsibility and links it to the principles of equity and social justice — principles reflected in the duty of international assistance and co-operation as codified in international human rights law. The Millennium Declaration states: "We recognize that, in addition to our separate responsibilities to our individual societies, we have a collective responsibility to uphold the principles of human dignity, equality and equity at the global level." (Values and Principles, para. 2); "Solidarity. Global challenges must be managed in a way that distributes the costs and burdens fairly in accordance with basic principles of equity and social justice. Those who suffer or who benefit least deserve help from those who benefit most (Values and Principles, para. 6); "Shared responsibility. Responsibility for managing worldwide economic and social development, as well as threats to international peace and security, must be shared among the nations of the world and should be exercised multilaterally. As the most universal and most representative organization in the world, the United Nations must play the central role." (Values and Principles, para. 6), *supra* n. 4. The General Assembly reaffirmed these values and principles at its 2005 World Summit: "We reaffirm that our common fundamental values, including freedom, equality, solidarity, tolerance, respect for all human rights, respect for nature and shared responsibility, are essential to international relations." 2005 World Summit Outcome, *supra* n. 9 at Values and Principles, para. 4.
38 See Sen on the conceptualization of development as freedom, *supra* n. 14. See also Margot E. Salomon and Arjun Sengupta, *The Right to Development: Obligations of States and the Rights of Minorities and Indigenous Peoples* (London: Minority Rights Group International, 2003). Available at www.minorityrights.org.
39 International Covenant on Economic, Social and Cultural Rights (1966), entered into force January 3, 1976, GA Res. A/RES/2200A (XXI), 993 UNTS 3.
40 ICESCR Art. 2(1): "Each State party to the present Covenant undertakes to take steps, individually and through international assistance and co-operation, especially economic and technical, to the maximum of its available resources, with a view to achieving progressively the full realization of the rights recognized in the present Covenant by all appropriate means, including particularly the adoption of legislative measures." ICESCR Article 11 on the right of everyone to an adequate standard of living, including adequate food, clothing, and housing reaffirms "the essential importance of international cooperation" in ensuring the realization of this right (Art. 11(1)). Regarding the fundamental right to be free from hunger, Article 11(2) imposes an obligation on States parties to take measures "individually and through international cooperation." See, also, Articles 22 and 23.
41 CRC, Art. 4: "States Parties shall undertake all appropriate legislative, administrative, and other measures for the implementation of the rights recognized in the present Convention. With regard to economic, social and cultural rights, States Parties shall undertake such measures to the maximum extent of their available resources and, where needed, within the framework of international cooperation."
42 CRC, Preambular para. 12, Arts. 23(4), 24(4), 28(3).

tions against individuals and do not have as their underlying purpose the remedying of global structural disadvantages.

Nevertheless, the Committee on Economic, Social and Cultural Rights (CESCR) today emphasizes the structural deficiencies of the international order and has begun to consider how States parties, and states generally, should address them. The Committee has begun to interpret the obligation of international assistance and co-operation in light of contemporary human rights violations which are linked — be it by omission or commission — to the global institutional order. We see a similar trend in the work of the Committee on the Rights of the Child exemplified by its position in 2003 that the "implementation of the Convention [on the Rights of the Child] is a cooperative exercise of *the states of the world*."[43] Such a reference to the "states of the world" is all the more significant for a claim to a collective global obligation since all but two states (Somalia and the United States) have ratified the CRC.

In its general comment on *The Nature of States Parties Obligations under the Covenant*, the CESCR, citing Articles 55 and 56 of the UN Charter[44] affirms that "international cooperation for development and thus for the realization of economic, social and cultural rights is an obligation of all States" and notes "in particular the importance of the Declaration on the Right to Development. . . ."[45] The Committee on the Rights of the Child also draws attention to the pledge undertaken by UN Member States in accordance with UN Charter Articles 55 and 56 in meeting obligations of international cooperation under the Convention on the Rights of the Child.[46] In clarifying the content of obligations, the CESCR observed that the extent of states parties' resources (financial and otherwise) — to be considered in fulfilling the obligation to take steps to "the maximum of its available resources" included not only resources existing within the State party, but also those available from the international community.[47] In 2003, the Committee on the Rights of the Child concluded that in order for a state to be able to demonstrate that it has implemented the economic, social, and cultural rights found in the Convention to the maximum extent of its available resources, it must show that, where necessary, it has sought international cooperation to undertake all possible measures towards the

---

43   Committee on the Rights of the Child, General Comment No. 5, General Measures of Implementation of the Convention on the Rights of the Child (Arts. 4, 42 and 44, para. 6), (34th session, 2003) UN Doc. CRC/GC/2003/5 (2003), para. 60. Emphasis added.

44   UN Charter Art. 55: "With a view to the creation of conditions of stability and well-being which are necessary for peaceful and friendly relations among nations based on respect for the principle of equal rights and self-determination of peoples, the United Nations shall promote: a. higher standards of living, full employment, and conditions of economic and social progress and development; b. solutions of international economic, social, health, and related problems; and international cultural and educational cooperation; and c. universal respect for, and observance of, human rights and fundamental freedoms for all without distinction as to race, sex, language, or religion." Art. 56: "All Members pledge themselves to take joint and separate action in co-operation with the Organization for the achievement of the purposes set forth in Article 55."

45   CESCR, General Comment No. 3, The Nature of States Parties' Obligations (Art. 2.1) (5th session, 1990) UN Doc. HRI/GEN/1/Rev.7 (2004), para. 14.

46   CRC, General Comment No. 5, General Measures of Implementation, *supra* n. 43, at para. 60.

47   CESCR, General Comment No. 3, The Nature of States Parties Obligations, *supra* n. 45, at para 13. Notably assistance need not only be financial in nature, see CESCR, General Comment No. 2, International Technical Assistance Measures (Art. 22), (4th session, 1990) UN Doc. E/1990/23, annex III p. 86 (1990); Draft Report of the Committee on Economic, Social and Cultural Rights to ECOSOC, UN Doc. E/C.12/2003/CRP.1.

realization of the rights of the child, paying special attention to the most disadvantaged groups.[48] Since there is an obligation under these multilateral human rights treaties for states to seek international assistance and cooperation when necessary in order to fulfill the rights as provided, the implication is that there is an equal obligation upon those states in a position to assist.[49] This would reasonably entail an obligation to countenance the request — that is, to discuss, consider, and respond satisfactorily.

In elaborating the obligations derived from the Covenant,[50] the Committee would seem to be extending the scope of Article 2(1) in several significant respects. First, while the Committee's mandate is limited to the consideration of Covenant rights, it refers to international cooperation for "development" as a corresponding obligation. While it specifically links development to the realization of economic, social, and cultural rights, the mention of development implies recognition of the need for a broader approach to the realization of the Covenant rights as set out in the DRD. In the same sentence, the Committee noted that, pursuant to the UN Charter as elsewhere, international cooperation for development imposes an obligation on all states. The Committee thus chose not to limit its comment to the obligations imposed on States parties but to refer explicitly to the obligations of all states under the Charter, a point reaffirmed in subsequent statements.[51] The Committee notes in particular the importance of the Declaration on the Right to Development, an instrument that was designed on the basis of cooperation among the international community of states.

In its general comment on the right to health, the CESCR provided that "for millions of people throughout the world, the full enjoyment of the right to health still remains a distant goal . . ." and recognized the ". . . formidable structural and other obstacles resulting from international and other factors beyond the control of [developing] states that impede the full realization of Article 12 in many States parties."[52] In its specific consideration of international obligations in relation to the right to health, the Committee again refers to Article 56 of the UN Charter, as well as the Covenant commitments to take joint and separate action in the achievement of the right, referring to " . . . the existing gross inequality in the health status of people, particularly between developed and developing countries . . . which is . . . unaccept-

---

48   CRC, General Comment No. 5, General Measures of Implementation, *supra* n. 43, at paras. 8-9; to provide but two from among many recent examples, see CRC Concluding Observations: Equatorial Guinea, (37th session, 2004) UN Doc. CRC/C/15/Add.245, paras. 14 and 53; CRC Concluding Observations: Brazil, (37th session, 2004) UN Doc. CRC/C/15/Add.241, paras. 19, 21, 23, 36, 48(e), 50 (i), 58(d).
49   The Committee remarks that it is "particularly incumbent upon those states and other actors in a position to assist to provide "international assistance and cooperation ..." CESCR, General Comment No.14, The Right to the Highest Attainable Standard of Health (Article 12), (22nd session, 2000) UN Doc. E/C.12/2000/4 (2000), para. 45; see also CESCR Statement on Poverty, *supra* n. 13, at para. 16.
50   The pronouncements by the UN human rights treaty monitoring bodies are authoritative, non-binding interpretations and elaborations of the treaties they are mandated to oversee.
51   Under the section on International Cooperation and Assistance, the Committee remarks that: "The Charter of the United Nations commits all nations to the development of an equitable and just international order that encourages peace, solidarity, social progress and better standards of life for all nations large and small." CESCR, Statement on Human Rights and Intellectual Property (27th session, 2001) UN Doc. E/C.12/2001/15 (2001), para. 14.
52   CESCR General Comment No. 14, The Right to Health, *supra* n. 49, at para. 5

able and is therefore *a common concern to all countries.*[53] An interpretation sensitive to the structural impediments to the exercise of economic, social, and cultural rights is also seen in the Committee's reference to the member states of international financial institutions, notably the World Bank, International Monetary Fund (IMF), and regional development banks,[54] and to the international financial institutions themselves and their ability to have an impact on the right to health through their lending policies, credit agreements, and structural adjustment programs.[55] Similar references are made with regard to the right to food[56] and the right to water.[57] The Committee on the Rights of the Child, in its general comment on the Implementation of the CRC, also refers to the need for international financial institutions and the World Trade Organization to pursue international cooperation and economic development aimed primarily at the full implementation of the Convention.[58]

In 1998, when the CESCR discussed the issue of globalization in the context of realizing economic, social, and cultural rights, it emphasized that "international organizations, as well as the Governments that have created and manage them, have a strong and continuous responsibility . . . ."[59] The Committee further directed its calls to the World Bank and IMF to give explicit recognition to economic, social, and cultural rights, and to the World Trade Organization to devise methods that would facilitate a more systematic consideration of the impact upon human rights of particular trade and investment policies.[60] In its *Statement to the Third Ministerial Conference of the World Trade Organization* in 1999,[61] the Committee considered trade liberalization as a means of contributing to human well-being (defined in terms of human rights law) and not as an end in itself.[62] In 2001, the Committee provided the view that actors other than states, including international organizations, "carry obligations, which must be subject to scrutiny." Then departing quite considerably from a traditional understanding as to the duty-bearers in international law, went on to remark that ". . . all actors [must be] held to account for their obligations under

---

53 *Ibid.*, para. 38, emphasis added.
54 *Ibid.*, para. 39.
55 *Ibid.*, para. 64
56 CESCR, General Comment No. 12, The Right to Adequate Food (Art. 11), (20th session, 1999) UN Doc. E/C.12/1999/5 (1999), para. 41.
57 CESCR, General Comment No. 15, The Right to Water (Arts. 11 and 12), (29th session, 2002) UN Doc. E/C.12/2002/11 (2002), para. 60.
58 CRC, General Comment No. 5, General Measures of Implementation, *supra* n. 43, at para. 64.
59 CESCR, Decision on Globalization and its Impact on the Enjoyment of Economic, Social and Cultural Rights (18th session, 1998) UN Doc. E/1999/22, para. 5.
60 *Ibid.*, para. 7. At its first session, the UN High-Level Task Force on the Implementation of the Right to Development addressed the need for the WTO to undertake human rights impact assessments (Report of the High-Level Task Force on the Implementation of the Right to Development, (1st session, 2004), UN Doc. E/CN.4/2005/WG.18.2, paras. 41 and 51), a point subsequently endorsed by the Working Group on the Right to Development, *supra* n. 27, at paras. 52-53 and 54(e).
61 CESCR, Statement to the Third Ministerial Conference of the World Trade Organization (21st session, 1999) UN Doc. E/C.12/1999/9 (1999).
62 *Ibid.*, para. 6. Emphasis on the instrumental role of growth is not new to the Committee. In 1990, it similarly described the importance of having international agencies contribute "... not only to economic growth or other broadly defined objectives, but also to enhanced enjoyment of human rights." CESCR, General Comment No. 2, International Technical Assistance Measures, *supra* n. 47, at para. 6. The UNDP's most recent human development report makes the same important point: " . . . greater opennessto trade, like economic growth, is not an end in itself: it is a means to expanding human capabilities . . . ." *International Cooperation at a Crossroads: Aid, Trade and Security in an Unequal World*, UNDP, *Human Development Report* (Oxford: Oxford University Press, 2005), Chapter 4, p. 113.

international human rights law." [63] In 2002 the Committee issued a joint statement with the Special Rapporteurs mandated by the UN Commission on Human Rights on *The Millennium Development Goals and Economic, Social and Cultural Rights*,[64] in which it emphasized the importance and added-value of integrating human rights into the Millennium Development Goals,[65] a set of goals, targets, and indicators that reflect a globally endorsed strategy for poverty reduction and sustainable human development.[66]

The Committee's concern with global inequality is at the forefront of its gen-eral comment on the right to water, where it notes that "the Committee has been confronted continually with the widespread denial of the right to water in developing countries. Over one billion persons lack access to a basic water supply, while several billion do not have access to adequate sanitation . . . the continuing contamination, depletion and unequal distribution of water is exacerbating existing poverty. . . ."[67] The Committee had earlier addressed the collective corresponding duties of the international community of states to protect human rights generally and Covenant rights in particular in its 2001 *Statement on Poverty and the International Covenant on Economic, Social and Cultural Rights*. Affirming that poverty is both a human rights issue and constitutive of a denial of human rights,[68] and in light of the indivisible and interdependent nature of all human rights,[69] the Committee ties the eradication of poverty to the implementation of the human rights normative framework, including the right to development.[70] Referring to poverty as a global phenomenon,[71] the Committee identified the international community of states as duty-bearers, substantiated by its determination that core obligations necessary to meet the minimum essential levels of Covenant rights give rise not only to national responsibilities of all states but also to ". . . international responsibilities for developed states . . . ."[72] Notably, the Committee has taken the view that meeting core obligations in relation to economic, social and cultural rights are not subject to progressive realization but rather are to be given immediate effect,[73] and are guaranteed under customary international law thereby binding all states and other legal persons.[74] The

---

63 CESCR, Statement on Human Rights and Intellectual Property, *supra* n. 51, at para. 10 (Accountability).

64 The Millennium Development Goals and Economic, Social and Cultural Rights, A Joint Statement by the UN Committee on Economic, Social and Cultural Rights and the UN Commission on Human Rights' Special Rapporteurs on Economic, Social and Cultural Rights, November 29, 2002.

65 *Ibid.*, para. 9. On the importance of integrating human rights into the MDGs see, Philip Alston, *supra* n. 13; Margot E. Salomon, *supra* n. 7; Report of the High-Level Task Force, *supra* n. 60.

66 The Committee on the Rights of the Child also interprets international cooperation to include meeting the internationally agreed targets for international development assistance of 0.7 percent of gross national income which form the basis of the MDGs. See CRC, General Comment No. 5, General Measures of Implementation, *supra* n. 43, at para. 61. The CRC has also remarked on the obligation to move quickly in meeting the goal, CRC Concluding Observations: Germany (35th session, 2004), UN Doc. CRC/C/15/Add.226, para. 21.

67 CESCR, General Comment No. 15, The Right to Water, *supra* n. 57, at para. 1.

68 CESCR, Statement on Poverty, *supra* n. 13, at para. 1.

69 *Ibid.*, para 8.

70 *Ibid.*, para. 10.

71 *Ibid.*, see especially para. 18.

72 *Ibid.*, para. 16.

73 CESCR, General Comment No. 15, The Right to Water, *supra* n. 57, at para. 37.

74 CESCR Concluding Observations: Israel (30th session, 2003) UN Doc. E/C.12/1/Add.9, para. 31.

Committee on the Rights of the Child links the Millennium Declaration "pledge" to cooperate internationally in the elimination of poverty to the universally applicable "pledge" under Articles 55 and 56 of the UN Charter to act jointly to achieve virtually identical objectives.[75]

The international responsibilities of developed states apply also to structural obstacles that inhibit developing states from providing sustainable anti-poverty strategies. The CESCR clearly links the removal of these global structural obstacles to the collective responsibility of the relevant states of the international community because effective poverty reduction strategies by developing states "lie beyond their control in the contemporary international order."[76] The centrality of the role of the international community in fulfilling human rights today is reinforced by the explicit reference in this regard to both Article 28 of the UDHR, which refers to the entitlement of all to a just social and international order in which human rights can be realized,[77] and to the Declaration on the Right to Development, Article 3(3), which holds that "States have the duty to cooperate with each other in ensuring development and eliminating obstacles to development. . . ."[78]

These examples suggest an emerging trend in the jurisprudential work of the Committee on Economic, Social and Cultural Rights and of the Committee on the Rights of the Child as to the critical impact of the global financial and trade structures and the decisions taken under their auspices on the exercise of human rights. The positions of the Committees underscore the expectation that human rights will be integral to international decision-making where those decisions may impact on them, and whether explicit or implied, to the collective nature of corresponding obligations.

A notable development towards strengthening the obligations that states have to secure the human rights of people outside of their domestic constituency can be found in the General Comment to Article 2 on *The Nature of the General Legal Obligations Imposed on States Parties to the Covenant* adopted in 2004 by the Human Rights Committee (HRC)[79] under the International Covenant on Civil and Political Rights (ICCPR).[80] The HRC unequivocally interpreted the term "within their territory and [to all persons] subject to their jurisdiction" to apply to "anyone within the *power or effective control* of that State Party, even if not situated within the territory of the State Party."[81] Consistent with its earlier pronouncements, the Committee then explicitly held that a State parties' "jurisdiction" is determined by the exercise of power or effective control of it or its agents, including when "acting outside of its

---

75   CRC, General Comment No. 5, General Measures of Implementation, *supra* n. 43, at para. 61
76   CESCR, Statement on Poverty, *supra* n. 13 see, especially, at para. 21.
77   Similarly see, CESCR Statement on Human Rights and Intellectual Property, *supra* n. 51, at para. 14.
78   *Ibid.*, para. 21 and *supra* n. 17.
79   Human Rights Committee, General Comment No. 31, The Nature of Legal Obligations Imposed on States Parties to the Covenant (Art. 2), (80th session, 2004) UN Doc.CCPR/C/21/Rev.1/Add.13 (2004).
80   General Assembly Res. 2200A (XXI), 21 UN GAOR Supp. (No. 16), p. 52, UN Doc. A/6316 (1966), 999 UNTS 171, entered into force March 23, 1976.
81   HRC, General Comment No. 31, The Nature of General Legal Obligations, *supra* n. 79, at para. 10.

territory"[82] and subsequently restates the obligation under Article 2 as requiring that States parties respect and ensure the Covenant rights "for all persons in their territory and *all persons under their control.*"[83] According to the HRC, the principle of power or effective control applies "regardless of the circumstances in which such power or effective control was obtained,"[84] and whether it was with the acquiescence of the Government on whose territory the violation was committed or in opposition to it.[85]

In considering the extraterritorial obligations of individual states under the ICESCR, the CESCR has also concluded that a State parties' obligations under the Covenant apply "to all territories and populations under its effective control."[86] The Committee expressed its view that the Covenant "applies to all areas where [the State party] maintains geographical, functional or personal jurisdiction."[87] The International Court of Justice (ICJ) has endorsed the CESCR's position that a State party is bound by the provisions of the ICESCR in "the exercise of powers available to it."[88] In the same Advisory Opinion, the ICJ similarly considered the jurisdiction of States parties under the Convention on the Rights of the Child to extend beyond the borders of the state in question.[89] While the Court did not mention obligations of international cooperation under the ICESCR or under the CRC, it was not relevant to the subject under its consideration. An earlier pronouncement by Judge Weeramantry, however, declared that "the recognition by States of the right to health [under Article 12 of the ICESCR] is . . . that they recognize the right of 'everyone' and not merely of their own subjects. Consequently each state is under an obligation

---

82   *Ibid.* Emphasis added. See also HRC Concluding Observations: USA (53rd session, 1995) UN Doc. CCPR/C/79/Add.50, para. 284; HRC Concluding Observations: Israel (63rd session, 1998) UN Doc. CCPR/C/79/Add.93, para 10; HRC Concluding Observations: Israel, (78th session, 2003) UN Doc. CCPR/CO/78/ISR, para. 11; HRC Concluding Observations: Belgium (81st session, 2004) UN Doc. CCPR/CO/81/BEL, para. 6. In the early case of *Lopez Burgos v Uruguay*, the HRC affirms in some detail the extraterritorial application of Article 2(1) although this particular case dealt with the treatment by Uruguay of a Uruguayan national abroad, *Delia Saldías de Lopez v Uruguay*, Communication No. 52/1979 (1981), paras. 12.1-12.3; see similarly, *Celiberti de Casariego v Uruguay* Communication No. 56/1979 (1981), paras. 10.1-10.3. The European Court of Human Rights (ECHR) in the Bankovic case adopted a restrictive view of Article 1 of the European Convention on Human Rights, however applied effective control as the decisive criterion in reaching its conclusion on the extraterritorial application of the ECHR. Case of *Bankovic, Stojanovic, Stoimenovski, Joksimovic and Sukovic v Belgium, the Czech Republic, Denmark, France, Germany, Greece, Hungary, Iceland, Italy, Luxembourg, the Netherlands, Norway, Poland, Portugal, Spain, Turkey and the United Kingdom* (Appl. No. 52207/99), ECHR, admissibility decision of December 12, 2001, para. 75. See also case of *Issa and Others v Turkey* (Appl. No. 31821/96), ECHR judgement of November 16, 2004, para. 74.
83   HRC, General Comment No. 31, The Nature of General Legal Obligations, *supra* n. 79, para. 12. Emphasis added.
84   *Ibid.*, para. 10; HRC Concluding Observations: Belgium (2004), *supra* n. 82, para. 6.
85   *Lopez Burgos v Uruguay, supra* n. 82 , at para. 12.3; *Celiberti de Casariego v Uruguay, supra* n. 82, at para. 10.3.
86   CESCR Concluding Observations: Israel (19th session, 1998) UN Doc. E/C.12/1/Add. 27, para. 8; CESCR Concluding Observations: Israel (2003), *supra* n. 74, at para. 31.
87   CESCR Concluding Observations: Israel (1998), *supra* n. 86, at para. 6; See, also Magdelena Sepúlveda, *The Nature of the Obligations under the International Covenant on Economic, Social and Cultural Rights,* (Antwerp: Intersentia, 2003), pp. 272-277.
88   In this instance, the Court observed that the Occupied Palestinian Territories have been subject to Israel's territorial jurisdiction as the Occupying power. However, citing CESCR's concluding observations of 2003 on Israel, it notes that it is by exercising control there that Israel's obligations extend to "all territories and populations under its effective control." ICJ, *Legal Consequences of the Construction of the Wall in the Occupied Palestinian Territory*, Adv. Op., (2004) para. 112. Available at www.icj-cij.org.
89   *Ibid.*, para. 113.

to respect the right to health of all members of the international community."[90] Virtually all the Covenant rights (not just the right to health) are framed as rights belonging to "everyone," such as the right of everyone to be free from hunger[91] and the right of everyone to an adequate standard of living.[92]

The view of the HRC that extraterritorial jurisdiction under the ICCPR is determined by the exercise of effective control was similarly endorsed by the ICJ when it noted that ". . . while the jurisdiction of States is primarily territorial, it may sometimes be exercised outside of the national territory. Considering the object and purpose of the International Covenant on Civil and Political Rights, it would seem natural that, even when such is the case, States parties to the Covenant should be bound to comply with its provisions. The constant practice of the Human Rights Committee is consistent with this . . . In conclusion, the Court considers that the ICCPR is applicable in respect of acts done by a State in the exercise of its jurisdiction outside its own territory."[93]

This interpretation is consistent with the established position of the Committee that enjoyment of the Covenant rights is not limited to citizens of the State party,[94] although read together with its interpretation of Article 2(1) more generally, it adds a new dimension to the traditional subjects of this category (the traditional subjects being migrants, refugees, stateless persons). The implication is that the fulfillment of Covenant rights by each State party relates not only to non-citizens within *its* territory, but may impose obligations with regard to persons who are not nationals of its country and domiciled in another country. In sum, on the basis of the ICCPR, a State party has certain obligations to the people of other countries; that is, there exist extraterritorial human rights obligations, and they are determined by the exercise of power or effective control.

For our purposes, it is the widescale deprivation of socio-economic rights that drives the search to make international law relevant to the form and exercise of state power today. To these ends, we favor the interpretation of the legal obligations under the ICCPR that emphasizes power or effective control as determinants of jurisdiction. There is a consensus that all human rights are interdependent and interre-

---

90   Judge Weeramantry (diss. op.), ICJ, *Legality of the Use by a State of Nuclear Weapons in Armed Conflict*, ICJ Rep (1996), p. 144.
This pronouncement is relevant in the context of intellectual property. The current intellectual property regime under the WTO's Agreement on Trade-Related Aspects of Intellectual Property Rights (TRIPS) and bilateral and regional trade deals (TRIPS Plus) is criticized for favoring the interests of technology holders over the wider public interest. It leaves developing countries limited space to determine national policies that would contribute to poverty reduction, allow access to essential medicines, and provide for food security. See *The Report of the Commission on Intellectual Property Rights: Integrating Intellectual Property Rights and Development Policy* (UK: 2002); *International Cooperation at a Crossroads, supra* n. 62 at Chapter 4, p. 135.
91   ICESCR Art. 11(2), which reiterates the need for states parties to take cooperative measures in the realization of this right.
92   ICESCR Art. 11(1), which also reiterates the essential importance of international cooperation in the realization of this right.
93   ICJ, *Legal Consequences of the Construction of the Wall in the Occupied Palestinian Territory, supra* n. 88, at paras. 109 and 111.
94   HRC, General Comment No. 15, The Position of Aliens under the Covenant (27th session, 1986), UN Doc. HRI/GEN/1/Rev.7 (2004); HRC, General Comment No. 23, The Rights of Minorities (Art. 27) (50th session, 1994) UN Doc. HRI/GEN/1/Rev.7 (2004).

lated,[95] and that poverty is characterized by the inability of people to enjoy their civil, political, and economic, social, and cultural rights,[96] a point emphasized in the Declaration on the Right to Development.[97] The role of states acting internationally as multilateral donors where they exercise power in relation to civil and political rights in the domestic context can have an indirect effect on the ability of a recipient state to secure the economic, social, and cultural rights of its people. An example is in relation to the role of parliaments and civil society in developing countries in the preparation of the donor-required poverty reduction strategy papers (PRSPs).[98] The PRSPs have considerable influence on the realization of the minimum essential levels of economic, social, and cultural rights,[99] in particular for people most likely to be affected in times of national economic hardship. When this issue was raised during an Evidence Session of the United Kingdom's International Development Committee on the World Bank and IMF, information was provided to the effect that these World Bank/IMF processes were not designed to involve parliaments in recipient countries, nor were funds properly allocated to further capacity-building that would allow for effective civil society partici-pation.[100] Bilateral and multilateral donors have themselves recognized the negative impact they are having on democratic governance in recipient countries.[101]

Second, the legal principle that power or control are determinants of responsi-bility as endorsed by the HRC opens the way for developing countries to request and expect that donors do not exercise their power in such a way as to place them in breach of their binding international human rights obligations, including with re-

---

95   UN World Conference on Human Rights, Vienna Declaration and Programme of Action (1993), UN Doc. A/CONF.157/23, part. 1, Art. 5.

96   CESCR Statement on Poverty, *supra* n. 13, at para. 8. Similarly, the importance of addressing poverty reduction from the perspective of the interdependence of all human rights is widely recognized within the human rights community. See Paul Hunt, Manfred Nowak, and Siddiq Osmani, *Draft Guidelines: A Human Rights Approach to Poverty Reduction Strategies* (Geneva: UN Office of the High Commissioner for Human Rights, 2002).

97   DRD, Preambular para. 4, Preambular para. 10 Arts. 6(2), 6(3), and 9.

98   Poverty reduction strategy papers (PRSP) plan a country's macroeconomic, structural, and social policies and programs to promote economic growth and poverty reduction. Established by the World Bank and International Monetary Fund and promoted as "country-owned," there is considerable skepti-cism as to whether any heterodox economic policies that do not reflect the favored neo-liberal model would be able to inform a PRSP. A World Bank/IMF accepted PRSP is required not only for loans from the World Bank and IMF but also as a condition for debt relief measures under the HIPC (Heavily Indebted Poor Countries) debt initiative, increasingly for support from bilateral donors, and it informs the decisions of private investors.

99   The nature of obligations under the ICESCR impose a minimum core obligation to ensure the sat-isfaction of, at the very least, minimum essential levels of each right. CESCR, General Comment No. 3, The Nature of States Parties Obligations, *supra* n. 45, at para. 10; CESCR Statement on Poverty, *supra* n. 13, at paras. 15-18.

100 The UK's International Development Committee is appointed by the House of Commons to ex-amine the expenditure, administration, and policy of the Department for International Development. At its Evidence Session, November 9, 2004, on The Annual Autumn Meeting of the IMF and World Bank, representatives of the NGOs Action Aid and the Bretton Woods Project, from which these views were drawn, were among the witnesses invited to give evidence. Transcripts available at www.parliament.uk/parliamentary_committees/international_development.cfm.

101 Questions remain about the amount of genuine autonomy enjoyed by countries, given the greater financial power and technical capacity of donors in some aid dependent countries," *Partnerships for Poverty Reduction: Rethinking Conditionality* (Department for International Development: UK Policy Paper, March 2005), para. 5.17. The World Bank and IMF remarked likewise, see para. 6.1. See also the recent studies by Action Aid undertaken in 13 countries, "Global Democracy Endangered, Says New Report." Press Release, Action Aid International, (September 15, 2005).

gard to the right of its citizens to take part in the conduct of public affairs, which "covers all aspects of public administration, and the formulation and implementation of policy at international, national, regional and local levels"[102] and by "exerting influence through public debate and dialogue with their representatives or through their capacity to organize themselves."[103] This need to use human rights as a shield has been noted in relation to obligations under ICESCR.[104]

A third reason the extraterritorial scope of human rights treaties may be valuable as a means of addressing obligations in relation to global deprivation is in clarifying the scope and significance of international assistance and cooperation under treaties that deal with economic, social, and cultural rights, to which we will now turn.

The Demands of Global Justice: International Obligations Revisited

Many of the specific parameters pertaining to the duty of international cooperation are not yet clearly drawn. However, a perceptible shift is taking place in which the international law of human rights is seeking to inform its scope and content. This shift can be seen in the attention being given by the UN to operationalize the right to development[105] and to the role of international law in the alleviation of poverty and the realization of human rights throughout the world. The CESCR, and to a lesser degree the CRC, are interpreting their respective instruments with increasing sensitivity to injustices of the global order; while the HRC, within the scope of its civil and political rights mandate, is reaffirming and refining the contours of extra-territorial jurisdiction under the ICCPR providing insight into the scope of external human rights obligations generally.

The emerging jurisprudential and doctrinal trend seems to support a general distinction between extraterritorial obligations (that is, the negative effects of a states' policies and activities on the people in another country) and obligations of international cooperation more broadly (that is, responsibilities of states in their collective capacities — for example, as members of international organizations and in relation to the global order as a whole).[106]

---

102 HRC, General Comment No. 25, The Right to Participate in Public Affairs, Voting Rights and the Right of Equal Access to Public Services (Art. 25), (57th session, 1996), UN Doc. CCPR/C/21/Rev.1/Add.7, para. 5.
103 *Ibid.*, para. 8.
104 Paul Hunt, "Relations Between the UN Committee on Economic, Social and Cultural Rights and International Financial Institutions" in Willem van Genugten, Paul Hunt and Susan Mathews (eds.), *World Bank, IMF and Human Rights* (Nijmegen: Wolf Legal Publishers, 2003), pp. 145-150.
105 Currently, several UN bodies are seized by the matter. The Commission on Human Rights established a High-Level Task Force on the Implementation of the Right to Development (CHR Res. 2004/7); in 2003 the Sub-Commission on the Promotion and Protection of Human Rights was mandated by the Commission on Human Rights to undertake a two-year study on various elements related to furthering the right to development, and in February 2004 the OHCHR, also as mandated by the Commission, convened a High-Level Seminar on the Right to Development focused on global partnerships for development (CHR Res. 2003/83 paras. 2 and 5).
106 This doctrinal distinction is emerging quite consistently. See Rolf Künnemann, *Report to ICESCR on the Effect of German Policies on Social Human Rights in the South* (The Foodfirst Information and Action Network, 2001, available at www.fian.org); Sigrun I. Skogly and Mark Gibney, "Transnational Human Rights Obligations," *Human Rights Quarterly* 24 (2002), p. 781; *Duties sans Frontières: Human Rights and Global Social Justice* (Geneva: International Council on Human Rights Policy, 2003); Margot E. Salomon,

note continues on following page

In an era of international economic interdependence, actions and decisions within the global order cannot always be easily disaggregated and attributed to a particular state for purposes of state responsibility. However, responsibility need not be limited to the establishment of a *direct causal* relationship between people suffering from poverty and the acts or omissions of specific states. World poverty is also attributed to the existing global system, elements of which *by design* cause and/or fail to remedy this widespread deprivation. In giving meaning to these obligations, we face the problem that states acting internationally are not merely assisting too little but are also preventing development too much through their failure to refrain from actions and arrangements that contribute to world poverty. Their failure to remedy the causes of ongoing breaches through reform of the system perpetuates this deprivation.

The challenge we face is to define the obligations of the "undifferentiated international community" required to address the structural impediments to the realization of fundamental human rights.[107] This is a somewhat distinct exercise from determining the responsibilities of differentiated duty-bearers where causality might be easier to demonstrate, such as when states are acting domestically or extraterritorially. Moreover, despite some recent progress by Northern governments in publicly recognizing their mutual responsibility to address poverty elsewhere,[108] overall there is little readiness to embrace a notion that there exist *obligations* of international cooperation in this regard, not least for fear of being locked into resource transfers or of suggesting a diminished set of responsibilities belonging to developing states at the domestic level for fulfilling economic and social rights.[109]

Due Diligence and the Undifferentiated International Community

While the responsibility for human rights falls to the state as duty-bearer, violations do not presuppose that the state is the perpetrator of human rights abuses, nor that the state or its agents are directly responsible for breaches.[110] State responsibility

---

note continued from preceding page
International Cooperation and the Global Responsibility for Human Rights (Oxford: Oxford University Press, forthcoming, 2006). These are not wholly discreet areas and as Künnemann has pointed out " . . . well-defined cooperation of states . . . is necessary to ensure . . . extraterritorial obligations . . . ." Rolf Künnemann, "Extraterritorial Application of the International Covenant on Economic, Social and Cultural Rights," in Fons Coomans and Menno T. Kamminga (eds.) *Extraterritorial Application of Human Rights Treaties* (Antwerp, Intersentia, 2004), p. 201, p. 227.
107   In considering the "internationalization of responsibility," Alston makes the point that while it can be argued that there exists an obligation of international cooperation based on repeated commitments by the international community of states; he concludes that it is "at best, a generic one which attaches to the undifferentiated international community." Philip Alston, *supra* n. 13, p. 777.
108   See, notably, the EU statement to the 2004 Working Group on the Right to Development: "The EU is of the view that another issue that merits consideration following the [UN High-Level Seminar on the Right to Development] is that of accountability of all involved, based on human rights principles. That means accountability of multilateral donors, including the World Bank and International Monetary Fund, bilateral donors and recipient governments. All should ensure that they are adopting a human rights approach." Statement on behalf of the European Union, Working Group on the Right to Development (5th session, 2004), agenda item 4(a): Consideration of the ideas and proposals raised at the High-Level Seminar.
109   At the meeting of the Task Force on the Right to Development (December 2004), Sweden, a country that remains among the most progressive on the notion of shared responsibility for development, remarked that: " Our position is no secret, there is no legal obligation of international cooperation we do it out of a sense of international solidarity . . . we have a moral obligation ...." Notes on file with author.
110   *Velasquez Rodriguez v Honduras supra* n. 13, at para. 172.

also exists where the perpetrator cannot be identified.[111] Further, under international human rights law, acts or omissions that have the *effect* of impairing the enjoyment or exercise of rights are as stringent a determinant of state responsibility as intent.[112] What might this tell us about the attribution of responsibility under international human rights law for the 500,000 women a year who die in pregnancy and childbirth while these deaths are 100 times more likely to occur in sub-Saharan Africa than in high income countries,[113] and for the 30,000 children, coming almost exclusively from developing countries, who die each day of preventable diseases?[114]

It is widely accepted that a state's failure in meeting its positive obligations to exercise due diligence in preventing and adequately responding to human rights violations determines whether its responsibility is triggered and not only whether the act that caused the violation was shown to have been committed by its agents and is thereby directly imputable to it.[115] Applying the familiar due diligence standard to the international community in its relationship to world poverty, we would ask whether it ought to have acted differently and thus is it wholly or partly at fault for the current state of affairs; could the agents acting together have *foreseen* that their conduct and decisions would lead to these events occurring; and could they have reasonably averted the harm[116] without substantial costs to themselves?[117] There is no shortage of authoritative literature detailing particular global policies and their debilitating impact on people in poor countries, which is matched by widespread awareness as to what needs to be done to address them, as reflected in the multitude of international commitments and calls to address trade protectionist measures, to eliminate external debt including odious debt incurred by previous undemocratic regimes, to increase aid, and to reform global governance.[118] Hunger concentrated in developing countries is not a result of there being not enough food to eat but rather of certain people just not having enough to eat — this raises serious questions

---

111   *Ibid.*
112   See Art. 1(1) International Convention on the Elimination of All Forms of Racial Discrimination entered into force 4 January 1969, GA Res. A/RES/2106 (XX), 660 UNTS 195; Art. 1(1) Convention on the Elimination of All Forms of Discrimination Against Women (1979), entered into force September 3, 1981, GA Res. A/RES/34/180, 1249 UNTS 20378.
113   UNDP, *Human Development Report 2003: Millennium Development Goals, supra* n. 1, at Overview, 8.
114   *Ibid.*
115   HRC, General Comment No. 31, The Nature of Legal Obligations, *supra* n. 79, at para. 8. In *Osman v UK* (Application No. 87/1997/871/1083), ECHR judgement of October 28, 1998, para. 116, responsibility hinged on the fact that the authorities knew or ought to have known of the existence of the immediate risk to life of a person and failed to take measures which, judged reasonably, might have been expected to avoid said risk; see also *Mastromatteo v Italy* (Application No. 37703/97), ECHR, judgement of October 24, 2002, para. 68; *Velasquez Rodriguez v Honduras, supra* n. 13, at paras. 172, 174.
116   *Ibid.*
117   See Thomas Pogge, *What is Global Justice?*, Lecture in Moral Philosophy (University of Oslo, September 2003). Available at www.etikk.no/globaljustice.
118   Recent studies calling for the democratization of the WTO, IMF, and World Bank include: *Final Report and Recommendations Derived from the Multi-Stakeholder Consultations Organized by the New Rules for Global Finance Coalition* (November 2004-September 2005); *On Addressing Systemic Issues, Section F, Monterrey Consensus Document, Financing For Development/New Rules for Global Finance* (2005); *International Cooperation at a Crossroads, supra* n. 62; *Investing in Development: A Practical Plan to Achieve the Millennium Development Goals* (UNDP, 2005); *Our Common Interest, Report of the Commission for Africa* (2005), available at www.commissionforafrica.org; *EU Heroes and Villains: Which Countries are Living up to their Promises on Aid, Trade, and Debt?*, Joint NGO Briefing Paper, Action Aid, Eurodad and Oxfam (2005); *A Fair Globalization, supra* n. 1.

of distribution, access, and accountability.[119] In light of these facts, it is suggested that the standard of due diligence has an important role to play in determining parameters for the disaggregated appraisal of collective state conduct in order to move beyond a limited attribution of responsibility only to undifferentiated state players of the global institutional order. Its effective application at the international level would seek to render imperfect duties — a duty that does not clearly belong to any particular agent (by belonging to many agents) — perfect.[120]

Power or Effective Control and the Parameters of International Cooperation

As noted earlier, the exercise of "power or effective control" determines the extraterritorial scope of human rights treaty obligations.[121] The nature of these obligations may be helpful in clarifying the parameters of international assistance and cooperation in relation to economic, social, and cultural rights, which remain somewhat nebulous. We might use the World Bank and IMF as examples. While to greater or lesser degrees the World Bank and IMF are reflecting on the place of human rights within their mandates,[122] neither intergovernmental institution is prepared to declare that it is in any way bound by international human rights law.[123] However, increasingly power or control are determinants of responsibility under international human rights law, as such, the responsibilities of the international financial institutions (to provide just one example of a global institutional power) may also be determined according to that doctrine. Their position as duty-bearers under international human rights law would be brought about as a result of their *power* to impact on the exercise of human rights and their *control* in effecting the fulfillment of human rights, including via their control over other agents who are meant to deliver human rights, notably the member governments of developing countries. To take it one step further, it is not just their power or control, but the power or con-

---

119 In developing countries, more than 850 million people, 300 million of whom are children, go to bed hungry every night. Of these 300 million children, 90 percent are suffering long-term malnourishment and 6 million children die annually of malnourishment. More than 40 percent of Africans do not even have the ability to obtain sufficient food on a day-to-day basis. All the while, the international trading system is rigged in favor of the rich countries. See *Fast Facts: The Faces of Poverty* (New York: UN Millennium Project, 2005); *International Cooperation at a Crossroads, supra* n. 62, at Chapter 1.
120 On the undertaking of *ex ante* human rights impact assessments in the areas of international trade as part of meeting the due diligence standard, see Margot E. Salomon, *supra* n. 31, at p. 423.
121 HRC, General Comment No. 31, The Nature of Legal Obligations, *supra* n. 79; *Ilascu and Others v Moldova and the Russian Federation,* (Application No. 48787/99), ECHR judgement of July 8, 2004, para. 314; on the ICJ's endorsement of the tenet "control entails responsibility" see Richard Lawson, "Life after Bankovic: On the Extraterritoriality of the European Convention on Human Rights" in Coomans and Kamminga (eds.), *supra* n. 106, p. 86, n. 14.
122 Joseph K. Ingram, World Bank Representative to the UN and the WTO, *Speech to the High Level Seminar on the Right to Development* (February 2004); Klaus Enders, International Monetary Fund, *Challenges to Developing Countries If They Are to Benefit From the Current Phase of Globalization,* Speech at the High Level Seminar on the Right to Development (personal capacity) (February 2004). Representatives of the World Bank and IMF attended and contributed to the drafting of the Conclusions and Recommendations of the UN High Level Task Force on the Right to Development, December 2004 and November 2005. The Task Force was a collaborative effort by human rights experts and representatives of trade and development institutions to explore ways of bridging the various perspectives and experiences, with a view to making constructive suggestions aimed at the implementation of the right to development.
123 See, François Gianviti, "Economic, Social and Cultural Rights and the International Monetary Fund," in Philip Alston (ed.), *Non-State Actors and Human Rights* (Oxford: Oxford University Press, 2005), p. 113.

trol differential relative to the developing state — as per their organizational capacity, their mandates to grant debt relief, provide loans and set their conditions, to grant credit, and determine national economic policies — that implicates them.[124] If we accept the convincing legal premise that an agent cannot be responsible for a violation unless it had some "factually possible and meaningful way" of preventing the violation,[125] that is, "agents and agencies can only be obligated to act in ways for which they have an adequate set of capabilities,"[126] then conversely, we must accept the reasoning that possession of the capability to ensure that minimum levels of human rights are not violated in fulfilling a given mandate imposes the responsibility upon an agent to act.

Judge Loucaides of the European Court of Human Rights made a similar point in the context of state responsibility under the European Convention on Human Rights. He linked accountability to "a failure to discharge [its] positive obligations in respect of *any* person *if it was in a position to exercise its authority directly or even indirectly* over that person or over the territory where that person is engaged with regard to the acts complained of."[127] Notably, Loucaides remarked that authority may take the form of effective influence through political, financial, military or other substantial support . . . ."[128] The "financial influence" exercised by international financial institutions is perhaps not dissimilar to the "functional jurisdiction" referred to by the CESCR as among the various types of jurisdiction that create international legal responsibilities for the protection of human rights.[129] This premise sits comfortably with the position that the principle of jurisdiction extends also to *de facto* effective control.[130]

International Obligations to Remedy and to Prevent Human Rights Violations

Obligations of international cooperation are understood to have both negative dimensions (obligations of abstention) and positive dimensions (obligations of action). The CESCR has explained that positive obligations of states acting internationally include obligations to "facilitate" and "provide" for the realization of Covenant rights, while it is reticent to assert an international obligation of states to "fulfill" Covenant rights in other countries.[131] However, the negative/positive distinction

---

124 See, Paul Hunt, *supra* n. 104, p. 148. Similarly, FIAN asks, "[i]f the influence of institutions such as the World Bank or the WTO on national politics has reached such a level, the question to answer is whether these institutions should also take over responsibilities for the observance of human rights standards." Rolf Künnemann (2001), *supra* n. 106.
125 See, Martin Scheinen, "Extraterritorial Effect of the International Covenant on Civil and Political Rights," in Coomans and Kamminga (eds.), *supra* n. 106, p. 75.
126 Onora O'Neill, "Global Justice: Whose Obligations?" in Deen K. Chatterjee (ed.), *The Ethics of Assistance: Morality and the Distant Needy* (Cambridge: Cambridge University Press, 2004), p. 250.
127 Judge Loucaides, (part. diss. op.), *Ilascu and Others v Moldova and the Russian Federation, supra* n. 121, p. 139. Emphasis added.
128 *Ibid.*; See also *Assanidze v Georgia*, (Application No. 71503/01), ECHR judgement of April 8, 2004.
129 CESCR Concluding Observations: Israel (1998), *supra* n. 86, at para. 6.
130 UN Committee Against Torture, Concluding Observations: United Kingdom, (33rd session, 2004) UN Doc. CAT/C/CR/33/3, para. 4(ii)(b).
131 With regard to international cooperation in the realization of economic, social, and cultural rights, the CESCR considers States parties to have international obligations to respect the enjoyment of rights in

note continues on following page

may be somewhat more fluid when applied to human rights deprivations resulting from the structures of the global order that contribute to the violation of human rights through a failure of its creators, controllers, and primary beneficiaries to provide a feasible alternative[132] and their failure to exercise due diligence, which could reasonably avoid the continuance of widespread world poverty.

The obligations of states to respect and observe human rights owed to people everywhere might impose negative obligations in so far as they are required to abstain from any act that would violate the human rights of people anywhere in the world. However, if basic rights have already been violated in a global context, and, for example, people are starving, then the obligation imposed is also positive — that is, every agent, to a greater or lesser degree, is under an obligation to take action to remedy that violation and to prevent its continuation. And while in part the primary obligation is to *stop* imposing the global order, and in this sense it is negative,[133] reform requires action, so in that sense there is a positive obligation. The duties corresponding to the right to development provide a further example. The scope of the duty of states acting at the international level in the realization of the right to development provides for both a negative duty to ensure that they abstain from actions that inhibit the right to development and a positive duty based on shared responsibility to ensure an international enabling environment within which the right to development can be realized. Thus, under the conditions of interdependence and international cooperation within the global order, negative and positive obligations cannot be fully separated.

While all states are to contribute to the common objective of eradicating world poverty, the responsibility of a state for the creation of a just institutional order is in accordance largely with its weight and capacity in the world economy.[134] The content of this principle of common but differentiated responsibilities in the context of international cooperation for human rights is informed by the contribution that a

---

note continued from preceding page

other countries (CESCR General Comment No. 14, The Right to Health, *supra* n. 49, at para. 39) and to protect the rights of people in other countries (para. 39). Depending on the availability of resources, this could include an obligation to facilitate, for example, access to goods and services in other countries (para. 39). According to the Committee, international obligations would also include an obligation to provide aid. (para. 39; CESCR General Comment No. 12, The Right to Food, *supra* n. 56, at para. 36; CESCR General Comment No. 15, The Right to Water, *supra* n. 57, at paras. 30-36).

132 While the then World Bank President James Wolfensohn noted that poverty in the 47 countries of sub-Saharan Africa is increasing (James D. Wolfensohn, *Conference on Human Rights and Development: Towards Mutual Reinforcement*, Ethical Globalization Initiative and the Center for Human Rights and Global Justice (New York University: March 2004). Pogge makes the significant point that that even if world poverty was in decline, it does not follow that the global order is not harming the poor, since world poverty might be going down despite the global order and not because of it. And, even if the global institutional order were having a poverty-reducing affect, it might still be harming the global poor severely. Moreover, as he explains, the basis for relieving the international community of its duties to address world poverty is not to be determined by a "diachronic comparison with an earlier time, but on a counterfactual comparison with its feasible institutional alternatives." Thomas Pogge, *supra* n. 12, pp. 19-20.

133 Thomas Pogge, "Priorities of Global Justice," in Thomas Pogge (ed.), *Global Justice* (Oxford: Blackwell Publishers, 2001), p. 22; Thomas Pogge, "The International Significance of Human Rights," *Journal of Ethics* 4 (2000), p. 45.

134 See, for example, the Final Act of the United Nations Conference on Trade and Development VII (1987) as cited in Analytical Compilation of Comments and Views on the Implementation and Further Enhancement of the Declaration on the Right to Development, UN. Doc. E/CN.4/AC.39/1989/1, p. 22.

state has made to the emergence of the problem;[135] because it wields relative power at the international level that is manifested as influence over the direction of finance, trade, and development (effective control); because it is in a position to assist,[136] and because the state benefits most from the existing distribution of global wealth and resources.

In our search for global justice and giving meaning to contemporary international obligations, we might summarize the above-mentioned points as follows: the due diligence standard and the "duty to prevent" applied at the international level can play a role in attaching international legal responsibilities for poverty to often undifferentiated duty-bearers; the power to have an effect on poverty, and the capability to act to prevent or redress it, contributes to determining duty-bearers and the *existence* of world poverty informs the parameters of the obligation of international cooperation delineating a requirement to *remedy* related violations of economic, social, and cultural rights and to *prevent* further violations.

Conclusion

In determining responsibilities of the international community of states we need to release ourselves from the instinct to identify a detailed causal chain from state behavior to world poverty. First, the global institutional system, as currently designed, allows for the perpetuation of poverty or, at a minimum, has failed sufficiently to relieve poverty and the situation is worsening.[137] Second, the multiplicity of actors can make it extremely difficult to track and attribute individual state responsibility. Third, as a result of this key characteristic of the structure of the global system, every actor within that system is implicated, with obligations determined through the system of weighted responsibility described earlier. Clearly, effective action to address world poverty is largely beyond the capability of any one state in an interdependent world. Consequently, the obligation of each state to contribute to this objective through international cooperation — with its rights and obligations dosed accordingly[138] — is strengthened.

Human rights norms and principles do not exist in isolation; they form an integral part of the international order. Influenced by the forces of economic globalization, international human rights law is evolving to provide a framework for a system of global justice, one in which we will not condone a situation whereby 93 percent of people in developing countries in need of anti-retroviral therapy do not have access to it,[139] and where 1.4 million children die every year because they lack access

---

135 See, New Delhi Declaration of Principles of International Law Relating to Sustainable Development, 70th Conference of the International Law Association, Res. 3/2002, para. 3.

136 CESCR, Statement on Poverty, *supra* n. 13.

137 The UNDP concludes in its most recent Human Development Report that within the existing rules-based multilateral system "costs and benefits have been unevenly distributed across and within countries, perpetuating a pattern of globalization that builds prosperity for some amid mass poverty and deepening inequality for others." *International Cooperation at a Crossroads, supra* n. 62, Chapter 4, p. 113.

138 See, Georges Abi-Saab, "The Legal Formulation of the Right to Development." in *The Right to Development at the International Level*, René Jean Dupuy (ed.), Workshop of the Hague Academy of International Law (1979), Hague Academy of International Law (1980), pp. 170–171.

139 *The State of the World's Children 2005: Summary* (New York: UNICEF, 2004), p. 16.

to safe drinking water and adequate sanitation.[140] The Declaration on the Right to Development — which not only permits addressing structural disadvantage but demands it[141] — epitomizes this evolution. The observable shift toward duties under international law to advance global justice relies primarily on the legal regime for the protection and promotion of human rights and its growing impact on the form and exercise of state power today.[142] If it continues, this trend will result in an international community of states much more responsive to the rights and aspirations of the people who today find themselves tyrannized by an unjust global order.

---

140 *Ibid.*, p. 15.
141 Insightful remark by Paul Hunt, *The Nobel Symposium on the Right to Development and Human Rights in Development* (Oslo: Norwegian Centre for Human Rights, October 2003). Notes on file with author.
142 Not to the exclusion of non-state power.

7 | Development and the Human Rights Responsibilities of Non-State Actors

Bård A. Andreassen

In a world of interconnected threats and opportunities, it is in each country's self-interests that all of these challenges are addressed effectively. Hence, the cause of larger freedom can only be advanced by broad, deep, and sustained global cooperation among states. The world needs strong and capable States, effective partnership with civil society and the private sector, and agile and effective regional and global intergovernmental institutions to mobilize and coordinate collective action.

Report of Kofi Annan, UN Secretary-General
In Larger Freedom, September 2005

The Salience of Non-State Actors

In political theory, human rights are moral and legal entitlements of protection that people have against political and societal threats. These are threats against people's rights to decent living, freedom, and agency that arise from political, economic, and social exchange and interaction. Throughout modern history, absolutist or unabridged state power, and the consequential abuses of state authority, have been a major source of such threats.

The doctrine of modern human rights arose on the ruins of Nazi barbarism after 1945. Its vision was to tame, regulate, and civilize state power. The international system of human rights that evolved in the following decades was a slowly, yet carefully and patiently, negotiated package of legal norms and standards for decent governance and state behavior, and for the protection of basic values in human life.

On the basis of the historical experiences from which it emerged, the modern human rights system is unabashedly focused on the state, specifically on legal protection from state abuse and as a way of regulating the state-citizen relationship. Traditionally, defining the state-citizen relationship had been the privilege of the state. Protection against state abuse was also the main focus of the post-1945 United Nations-based international human rights regime, designed to protect universal values beyond national legislative systems.

These tenets of the modern human rights system are still highly pertinent and necessary. Contrary to what some have suggested, the state is not at all "dead" and continues to be a source of abuse. However, dramatic changes brought about by economic globalization and advances in communication technology have rendered a state-centered focus obsolete and have led human rights scholars to call for a "reimagining" of our conception of the nature of human rights and the relationship between different actors within the human rights regime.[1] The global community is

---

1 Philip Alston, "The Not-a-Cat Syndrome: Can the International Human Rights Regime Accommodate Non-State Actors," in Philip Alston (ed.), *Non-State Actors and Human Rights* (Oxford: Oxford University Press, 2005), p. 4.

moving from a monocentric world clustered around states, to a polycentric world with different actors, state and non-state. This shift affects the way human rights and freedoms of individuals and groups are implemented, including the right to development.

This chapter addresses the growing importance of actors outside the state, the so-called non-state actors, in the context of the human rights system.[2] Although a wide number of actors can be labeled under the rubric of non-state, the actors of main interest here are international corporate actors or the so-called transnational companies (TNCs). Over the past fifteen years, transnational companies have increasingly taken advantage of accelerating economic globalization and conditions in countries with huge problems of corruption, internal violent conflict, and serious human rights abuses. This has led to a concern among human rights watchdog organizations and gradually the international human rights law community about the legal principles that could be invoked to establish human rights responsibilities of corporate businesses, as well as the positive and negative impact of business on human rights in the countries and communities where they operate.[3]

Of particular interest is the nature and scope of the human rights responsibilities of transnational companies and "other business entities" in a development context. The reference to "other business entities" implies that human rights responsibilities in principle apply to any corporate entity, while interest here is primarily with entities that operate internationally in the global economy. Due to space limitations, I will only briefly refer to responsibilities of non-governmental organizations (NGOs) and other non-state actors outside of the business field.

TNCs and other businesses are central actors in development. Development discourse has only recently manifested concern, however, with the ethics of corporate behavior and specifically with the human rights impact of TNCs in the global economy as "agents of development." In light of the discussion of the right to development by Professor Sengupta in his chapter in the this book, and of the rights-based approach to development by several other chapters, I will examine the conceptual and practical dimensions of the right to development discourse as an entry point for defining the relationship between human rights and corporate actors, in particular the TNCs. Are TNCs responsible under international human rights law for respecting and contributing to the implementation of the right to development? What human rights standards, if any, apply to TNCs? What are or should be the content and scope of such responsibilities?

---

2   *Id.* Alston makes a valid point about the "questionable utility" of the terminology of non-state actors. This terminology underlines the state-centrism of the human rights system, where the UN as an "editorial rule" since 1945 has required that the state is referred to with a capital (upper-case) "S" (with a striking parallel in any biblical reference to "God" (also with an upper-case format), while today "the world is a much more poly-centric place than it was in 1945 and that she who see the world essentially through the prism of the 'State' will be seeing a rather distorted image as we enter the twenty-first century."

3   It should be noted that there is, as of yet, no systematic international data collection and recording for the human rights impact of corporate business, although there is a growing literature based on descriptive cases. There is obviously a lacuna in systematic data collection in the field, although The Business and Human Rights Resource Centre (http://www.business-humanrights.org/Home) is making an impressive attempt to fill this gap.

Research on corporate social responsibility has blossomed over the past decade, including studies on the role of companies involved in human rights breaches. Much of this interest can be attributed to the combined effects of the end of the Cold War, accelerated globalization with rapidly increasing foreign investment and transnational trade, and the digital revolution.[4] Studies focus heavily on corruption and bribes but also on violations of the right to organize, the right to collective bargaining, and other trade union rights, as well as on gender discrimination, unlawful child labor, and other abuses of rights of women and children.

With reference to the another main category of non-state actors, the UN Independent Expert on the Right to Development stated that the obligation to facilitate human rights realization "falls not only on States nationally and internationally, but on international institutions, on the civil society, and on any body in the civil society in a position to help. NGOs are one constituent of civil society that can and has often played a very effective role in the implementation of human rights."[5] The issue arising is whether an obligation to facilitate human rights realization also falls upon TNCs, assuming that they are in a "position to help." The focus of this chapter, therefore, is to examine the nature and scope of human rights responsibilities for commercial actors. Other interesting dimensions of this topic such as the causes and risk factors that may lead businesses to breach human rights, experiences with "constructing" corporate cultures and practices compatible with human rights ethics, and assessments of how human rights concerns of TNCs may be converted into an asset for improved competitiveness will not be systematically discussed.

Counter Arguments

Various arguments are made to absolve non-state actors of any responsibility for human rights, even of the minimal obligation to "do no harm." One argument is based on the non-ratification by companies of human rights treaties, which can only be ratified by states. Accordingly, only states have obligations under international law and non-state actors are by definition not subject to this body of law and cannot have legal responsibilities, the argument goes. Today, however, international human rights law assumes that non-state actors indeed have legal personality, that is, they are regarded by law as a "person" with legal status. Emberland, for instance, in a recent study of litigation before the European Court of Human Rights, examines how human rights law provides wide-ranging protection of business entities such as "companies in addition to not-for-profit organizations and natural persons."[6] The matter discussed further below is whether these rights and protection also imply responsibilities and duties.

4   Simon F. Reich, "Global Versus National Norms: Are Codes of Conduct Converging Across Regions" *Working Paper 2005.3* (University of Pittsburgh: Ford Institute for Security). Available at http://www.fordinstitute.pitt.edu/pub-workingpapers.html#. Accessed February 25, 2006.
5   "Third Report of the Independent Expert on the Right to Development," UN Doc. E/CN.4/2001/WG. 18/2, para. 25.
6   Marius Emberland, *The Human Rights of Companies: Exploring the Structure of ECHR Protection.* (Oxford: Oxford University Press, 2006), p.3. The "overall conclusion" of the study is that the European Court of Human Rights is "sympathetic to corporate complaints, at least as far as the treaty text and its interpretative modes permit it to be so, and as long as conflicting interests do not suggest a tempered response." *Id.*, p. 205.

Second is the *stay away/trickle down* argument, according to which private parties, such as TNCs or other large business entities, should avoid being involved in "politics and human rights." They should focus on commercial matters, such as investment and production and the functioning of markets. Their activities in developing countries will over time "trickle down" and improve income opportunities and the welfare of the lower classes and the poor. This classical economist argument — still widespread in international financial institutions and among TNCs — avoids the question of responsibilities in cases where there is no documented positive "trickle down" and does not address the rules of conduct for production and corporate activities prior to the perceived trickle-down effects.

Third is the *failure of attribution* argument stating that human rights violations are not perpetrated by private firms but by governments, and, hence, it is impractical and perhaps impossible to trace responsibility for human rights abuses to private actors. For example, the US government responded to the UN Draft Norms on the Responsibilities of Transnational Corporations and Other Business Enterprises with Regards to Human Rights,[7] as follows: "while it is true that private entities have been alleged to have been complicit in or even aided, human rights abuses committed by governments, the fundamental cause of such abuses has been the action or inaction of the government, not the private entity."[8]

These arguments do not adequately explain why these powerful actors (in some cases, controlling more economic resources than national economies) should not be responsible under international law if their actions are contrary to internationally recognized human rights norms. There is an ongoing debate about how international human rights law can address this issue. One aspect of this debate concerns filling the so-called gaps in the understanding of the nature and scope of human rights responsibilities of non-state actors. Another aspect is the effort to establish a framework that acknowledges rights and responsibilities of these actors while respecting the principles on which the human rights regime is based. Alston argues that a human rights regime that does not address situations where powerful private non-state actors (business or others) are involved in human rights violations and does not make these actors accountable one way or the other will loose credibility and render itself irrelevant.[9]

It is also worth noting that prominent transnational companies are adopting codes of conduct that make social responsibilities and at least some human rights part of their corporate objectives.[10] These codes are voluntary agreements that reflect a double agenda. One trend has been "human rights entrepreneurialism," that is, ef-

---

7   Norms on the Responsibilities of Transnational Corporations and Other Business Enterprises with Regard to Human Rights, UN doc. E/CN.4/Sub.2/2003/12/Rev.2, August 26, 2003. As these Norms have not been adopted by the Human Rights Commission, they are commonly referred to as *draft* norms. Hereinafter I use "draft Norms" and "Norms" interchangeably to refer to this document.
8   United States Mission to International Organizations, Geneva, Switzerland, "Re: Note verbal from the OHCHR of August 3, 2004" (GVA 2537), September 30, 2004.
9   *Supra*, note 1, p. 19.
10   Ralph G. Steinhardt, "Corporate Responsibility and the International Law of Human Rights: The New *Lex Mercatoria*" in Alston (ed.), *supra*, note 1, p.178f.

forts to compete for sales through public commitment to human rights.[11] This is an instrumental approach, which is principally different from seeing human rights respect as an intrinsic value and goal for any, including commercial, behavior. Another trend in this new corporate strategy of market adaptation conducive to respect for human rights is changing corporate cultures and behavior. From a normative human rights angle, therefore, this mixture of instrumental concerns and a genuine shift in norms and values may have a mutually reinforcing and overall positive effect on human rights conditions and protection.

Among existing voluntary codes of conduct, the most widely used is the UN Global Compact. It was launched in July 2000 and now counts some 3,000 participants, including over 2,500 businesses in 90 countries around the world, as well as additional labor and civil society participants.[12] The Global Compact guidelines mainly focus on respecting (and to some extent promoting) human rights. They are formulated to inhibit firms from abusing human rights (the "no-harm" principle) and aim to support labor standards and enhance anti-corruption practices. Another global voluntary mechanism, the SA 8000, which was organized by Social Accountability International, has "certified" nearly 800 firms in about 50 countries.[13]

In spite of the relatively limited scope of these measures and gaps in our knowledge about their human rights impact, they point to a new trend (most of these "certifications" have taken place over the past five years), reflecting potential changes in corporate cultures, or at least an alternative to the "stay away/trickle down" model discussed above. They represent more than another type of entrepreneurialism where companies seek new ways to compete.

Non-State Actors, Obligations, and the Right to Development

The new interest in human rights responsibilities of non-state actors has been triggered by current processes of globalization. Globalization represents increasing cross-border economic and financial transaction and interaction; it also represents exchanges of symbolic and communication messages, ideas, and values, including human rights ethics and law. Globalization manifests a deepened international interconnectedness and interdependence of states and societies, as well as colossal growth and acceleration in financial flows, economic production, and trade in markets that extend beyond national borders.

Globalization accelerated rapidly in the 1980s and 1990s and was strengthened by political choices expanding economic liberalization, deregulation, and privatization. It facilitated and was reinforced by the increasing power of TNCs and other non-state actors — not the least of which was international media networking and the expansion of neo-liberal ideology and models (in politics as well as economics).

---

11   *Id.*, p. 180.
12   See www.globalcompact.org (accessed April 15, 2006).
13   Social Accountability International is an international non-governmental organization working to improve workplaces and communities by developing and implementing socially responsible standards. See www.sa-intl.org. (Accessed January 5, 2006.)

TNCs contributed to economic growth, resulting in both higher income for significant segments of the population and widening social inequities, particularly in some countries in East and South East Asia. August Reinisch said about this process, "the loss of state control over TNCs, and the promotion of liberalization, privatization, and deregulation by International Financial Institutions (IFIs), contributed to a situation where human rights, particularly social and labor rights, but also the environment and other social goods . . . (have become) . . . increasingly *threatened* by non-state actors."[14] Mary Robinson remarked that this development led to a need for "a legal regime [to] help to underpin the values of ethical globalization," implying that the voluntary Global Compact spearheaded by the UN was not enough.[15]

The call for legal human rights standards to tackle these new threats represents both a reaction against expanded globalization and a reliance on some of the means globalization makes possible.[16] Consumer boycotts, for example, require a widespread and effective use of information made possible by global media and the Internet. Globalization has contributed to the international spread of ethical standards and inspired a discourse on the ethical responsibilities of globalized corporate entities. Although not the only focus of corporate ethics, human rights norms became gradually a central component of the conceptual framework of this discourse as international non-governmental organizations, including Amnesty International, began using human rights norms as standards for international campaigns against the "harmful effects" of TNCs on local populations and environments.

From a different angle, also influenced by neo-liberal policies, the development community began focusing on the role of the private sector in such areas as infrastructure, pharmaceuticals, employment, and economic growth. The social and economic power of transnational corporations required looking afresh at the role of business in society. While not new in historical terms, the importance of the issue had escalated. Already in the 1970s, the responsibility of corporate actors had been debated, and in 1976, the Organization for Economic Co-operation and Development (OECD) issued its first Guidelines for Multinational Enterprises to promote responsible business conduct consistent with applicable laws. In 1977, the International Labor Organization (ILO) adopted the Tripartite Declaration of Principles concerning Multinational Enterprises, which incorporated relevant ILO conventions and recommendations. These instruments, however, were not sufficient to tackle the challenges of globalization in the late 1990s.[17]

The concept of corporate social responsibility, as revived in the 1990s and gradually brought into the development agenda, included not only labor conditions but also occupational health and safety, concern for the environment, anti-corruption,

---

14   August Reinisch, "The Changing International Legal Framework for Dealing with Non-State Actors" in Alston (ed.), *supra*, note 1, p. 77, emphasis added.
15   Mary Robinson, Second Global Ethic Lecture, University of Tübingen, Germany, January 21, 2002, reprinted in "Globalization Has to Take Human Rights into Account," *Irish Times*, January 22, 2002.
16   Reinisch, *supra*, note 14, p. 77.
17   These guidelines were substantially updated and revised in June 2000 by OECD. The Declaration was subsequently amended in 1987, 1995, and 2000 to incorporate legal instruments that had been passed after its original adoption.

community development support, human rights responsibilities, and corporate ethics. The term corporate social responsibility (CSR) was used to capture these issues, and tools for measuring CSR were developed through codes of conduct, reputation management, self-reporting of social and environmental impact, and dialogues with stakeholders (mostly limited to Western countries). The debate, however, focused mostly on how business interests could produce "less harm" to local communities and the environment in developing countries. It focused very little, if at all, on how companies could respect human rights norms or whether they had responsibilities to promote or advance human rights principles and hence to be partners in human rights-based development.

It was recognized that the private business sector could advance development and benefit the poor by subcontracting with local small businesses. However, development institutions were skeptical about assuming that just working with private sector actors would benefit poor people. In spite of the potential for transnational business to contribute to development, TNCs were, on the contrary, seen to be implicated in human rights abuses. Corporate irresponsibility resulting in the contamination of land, water, and air deprived people of their rights to a safe, sustainable environment, their ability to maintain their livelihoods, and their ability to attain the highest standard of health. Environmental degradation has affected peoples' health in both developed and developing countries.

Discussion and debate about the right to development has not devoted much attention to non-state actors and corporate social responsibilities, in spite of the role of the business sector in economic development. This discourse, in line with mainstream human rights law, has remained basically state-centric. In spite of the new interest noted above, the subject has been largely neglected in key international development institutions like the United Nations Development Programme (UNDP) and the World Bank. In the UNDP *Human Development Report 2005 — International Cooperation at a Crossroads: Aid, Trade and Security in an Unequal World* (a subject particularly relevant to TNCs), there is hardly any mention of non-state actors and TNCs in development contexts, let alone the corporate responsibility and accountability of such actors.[18]

Giving some attention to the issue, the World Bank-sponsored *World Development Report 2005 — A Better Investment Climate for Everyone* mentions leveraging the concerns firms have for their reputation as a strategy for producing positive international spill-over effects of international transactions and cooperation, in addition to cooperation for environmental protection and combating corruption.[19] According to the report, international cooperation on matters related to the "investment climate" that respect human rights principles may include codes of conduct setting rules to avoid corruption, ensure environmental protection, and promote international labor standards.

18   United Nations Development Programme, *Human Development Report 2005 — International Cooperation at a Crossroads: Aid, Trade and Security in an Unequal World* (New York: UNDP, 2005).
19   World Bank, *World Development Report 2005 — A Better Investment Climate for Everyone* (Oxford: Oxford University Press), p. 184.

The current proliferation of codes of conduct and similar arrangements may create confusion about which standards should apply and give the impression that these codes are mainly of concern to firms that have a clear interest in enhancing or maintaining their international reputations but have less impact on others. This point may be supported by figures demonstrating that out of approximately 65,000 TNCs around the world, about 4,000 produce reports on their social and environmental performance. But companies reporting are mainly those with high public profiles and trade name, indicating that the motive for reporting is largely market/public relations determined.[20]

How does this relate to the right to development discourse? The Declaration on the Right to Development asserts that the state has the primary responsibility for the creation of national and international conditions favorable for the realization of the right to development (Article 3). The Declaration applies a conventional state-centered human rights instrument language. However, the use of the term primary indicates that there are "secondary" or other "lower order" responsibilities for the implementation of the right to development. In other words, there is scope for further specifications of human right responsibilities of non-state actors, both as perfect (specified) or imperfect (unspecified), in the Kantian sense of the terms, and as obligations of conduct and obligations of result in legal terms. The role of non-state actors is suggested by the reference in the Preamble of the Universal Declaration on Human Rights to a "common standard of achievement for all peoples and all nations, to the extent that every individual and every organ of society . . . shall strive by teaching and education to promote respect for these rights and freedoms . . . to secure their universal effective recognition and observance . . . ."

Hence, taking the vision of human rights as articulated by the Universal Declaration seriously, these "organs of society" include institutions outside the orbit of the state, such as commercial and other non-state actors. The right to development discourse should face this conceptual and practical challenge, given the significance of these actors as agents of globalization and development with impact on human rights.

Indirect and Direct Human Rights Responsibilities of Non-State Actors

Human rights responsibilities of non-state actors result from either the *indirect* or *direct* application of human rights law in holding them accountable. International law imposes *direct obligations* on non-state actors to respect international law by

---

20 Jem Bendell, "Making Business Work for Development: Rethinking Corporate Responsibility" in *id21 Insights* No. 54 (March 2005), Institute for Development Studies, University of Essex. (Also available at http://www.id21.org/insights/insights54/insights-iss54-art00.html.) These figures, however, do not tell much about the quality and impact of these reports. An assessment of the corporate responsibility reporting by the 100 largest Norwegian firms concluded recently that there is scope for major improvement in this reporting, both as regards legally mandated reporting by the boards of directors, and voluntary reporting in the annual reports and in separate non-financial reports. See also Audun Ruud, Janka Jelstad, Karoline Ehrenclou, and Irja Vormedal, *Corporate Responsibility Reporting in Norway: An Assessment of the 100 Largest Firms,* Report No. 9/05 (Program for Research and Documentation for a Sustainable Development, Centre for Development and the Environment, University of Oslo).

virtue of their having legal personality under international human rights law. Alternatively, they are subjected to *indirect obligations* deriving from the direct obligations of the state where they are registered or where they do business to enforce their human rights treaty obligations. Indirect responsibility follows from the principle that states are obliged to ensure that national law effectively enforces international law vis-à-vis non-state actors. In cases where the country of operation is not willing to enforce respective national legislation, or such legislation does not exist, the home country may take legal redress towards a company operating abroad. This action represents, in other words, legal extraterritoriality, making companies directly responsible for upholding at least some human rights principles. Much of the controversy in this field concerns how far international human rights law goes at present in making private entities such as TNCs directly responsible for human rights abuses.

Indirect Responsibilities of Non-State Actors: State Responsibilities for Non-State Activities

In this chapter, we have emphasized that the main logic of international human rights law is that the state is responsible for protecting people against human rights abuses. But this may also be interpreted as implying that states are responsible for the effects of non-state behavior as well. For instance, the UN Convention on the Rights of the Child considers parents or guardians as having the primary responsibility to bring up a child but emphasizes that, while states should assist parents, they are also legally obliged by the treaty to ensure that the child is protected in the private sphere.

States, in other words, have an indirect human rights liability for non-state actors, and the legal premise for this liability is that states are not only obliged to respect human rights but also to protect and enforce them effectively. If the state fails to protect individuals from harm by institutions and actors that may fall under the label "any organ of society," it is not fulfilling its obligation to protect and enforce people's human rights.

This means that even if the state is responsible for all harm caused by private actors by protecting individuals from harm, non-state actors are not devoid of

duties to respect human rights. Rather, we may assume that there is a certain degree of *duality of obligations* or complementarity: the state is the primary duty-bearer, but the private parties have responsibility to respect the rights of other private parties. This point is reflected in Article 29 of the Universal Declaration stating that everyone's rights should be exercised with "due recognition and respect for the rights and freedoms of others."

However, this duality of obligations of the state and non-state actors is expressed in far too general terms in the provisions of human rights treaties to be of practical value in determining precisely the nature of direct state responsibility for private actors' harmful activities. More specific criteria are required, such as the due diligence test used in the UN Declaration on the Elimination of Violence against Women.[21]

---

21   Declaration on the Elimination of Violence against Women, adopted by the UN General Assembly in Resolution A/48/104 on December 20, 1993.

According to that text, states should ". . . exercise due diligence to prevent, investigate and, in accordance with national legislation, punish acts of violence against women, whether those acts are perpetrated by the State or by private persons."[22] This due diligence test is part of a general obligation of the state to take effective steps "by all appropriate means and without delay" to prevent or respond to a potential or actual violations by a private actor as well as by the State and, in cases of abuses, to provide compensation, that is "just and effective remedies" for the harm that a victim has suffered.[23]

Such due diligence tests represent a monitoring mechanism and are occasionally relied upon by human rights supervisory bodies to address the actions of private actors. General Recommendation 19 of the UN Committee on the Elimination of Discrimination against Women states that under "general international law and specific human rights covenants, States may also be responsible for private acts if they fail to act with due diligence to prevent violations of rights or to investigate or punish acts of violence, and for providing compensation."[24] The High Commis-sioner for Human Rights prepared, in consultation with individual experts and key intergovernmental organizations, [NGOs], agencies, and programs, a set of principles and guidelines on human trafficking, which include the principle that "states have a responsibility under international law to act with due diligence to prevent trafficking, to investigate and pursue traffickers."[25] Although the requirement of due diligence is *de lege ferenda* (a matter of what the law ought to be, rather than being existing positive law), it has achieved growing support, indicating that a rule of international customary law is emerging that may be applicable to all international human rights treaties and relate to all categories of non-state actors — including TNCs. We may argue, therefore, that the mechanism of due diligence tests offers opportunities to expand the principle of indirect state obligations further to these "agents of globalization."

An important question regarding indirect state obligations is whether and to what extent states have responsibilities and obligations to take action on TNCs activities abroad. In some national legal systems the "home" states of a business entity has a duty to ensure that its jurisdiction is followed by extraterritorial business activities, and in accordance with human rights principles.[26] The trend, however, is to create voluntary guidelines and oversight systems, and expect that firms carry out voluntary reporting about their own corporate behavior.[27]

---

22   *Id.*, Article 4 (c).
23   *Id.*, Article 4 (d).
24   General recommendations made by the Committee on the Elimination of Discrimination against Women, General Recommendation No. 19 (11th session, 1992), para. 9. Available at http://www.un.org/womenwatch/daw/cedaw/recommendations/recomm.htm.
25   Recommended Principles and Guidelines on Human Rights and Human Trafficking: Report of the United Nations High Commissioner for Human Rights to the Economic and Social Council, UN Doc. E/2002/68/Add.1, May 20, 2002, principle 1.
26   An example of this is the 1977 US Foreign Corrupt Practices Act (FCPA), which halted the practice of bribery as a means of obtaining foreign business. On the US Foreign Corrupt Practices Act (1977), see http://www.usdoj.gov/criminal/fraud/fcpa.html.
27   In March 2000, the UK Foreign Office and the US Department of State brought together leading companies from the extractive industries and initiated a "dialogue on human rights and security"

note continues on following page

Direct Obligations of Non-State Actors

The issue of direct obligations of non-state actors is more controversial and legally less well-settled in human rights law than the indirect obligations discussed above. The issue is whether international human rights law imposes obligations directly on non-state actors to respect human rights and to ensure that human rights abuses do not occur as a result of its operations.

The concept of individual responsibility for grave international crimes was affirmed in the Nuremberg Judgments in the following, frequently cited, terms: "[that] international law imposes duties and liabilities upon individuals as well as upon States has long been recognized . . . Crimes against international law are committed by men, not by abstract entities, and only by punishing individuals who commit such crimes can the provisions of international law be enforced."[28] This doctrine of individual responsibility in cases of grave international crimes has been reinforced by the Statutes of the International Criminal Court (ICC), adopted in the diplomatic conference in Rome in 1998.[29] It is also well established that some (specified) non-state actors are bound by international humanitarian law. Rebel movements, for example, are obliged to comply with the Geneva Conventions (according to common Article 3) while the Additional Protocols of 1977 refer to the obligation of insurgent forces to protect prisoners and respect prohibitions such as those on attacking civilians, taking hostages, carrying out terrorist acts, or using starvation as a method of combat.

We have already quoted the Preamble of the Universal Declaration that refers to the responsibilities of "every individual and every organ of society" to contribute to the promotion of respect for human rights and freedoms. Although the legally binding nature of the Declaration is contested (even if it is common to consider components of it a part of customary international human rights law), these words support an argument to impose on non-state actors some responsibilities under human rights law. This interpretation of general human rights law and of international criminal law referred to above suggests the potential strengthening of direct accountability of non-state actors, and there appears to be a slowly evolving international political will to develop human rights law in this direction, as evidenced by a number of international initiatives addressing direct responsibility of TNCs.

---

note continued from preceding page
addressing the role and responsibilities of transnational corporations. This initiative has later been joined by the Dutch and Norwegian governments and a number of companies and non-governmental organizations. In December 2000, a set of Voluntary Principles, urging but not obliging companies to report on human rights abuses in their countries of operation were issued. It states, that "Companies should record and report any credible allegations of human rights abuses by public security in their areas of operation to appropriate host government authorities. Where appropriate, Companies should urge investigation and that action be taken to prevent any recurrence." See http://www.voluntaryprinciples.org/ timeline/ index.htm.
28 Judgment of the Nuremberg Tribunal, International Military Tribunal, Nuremberg (1946), 41 *American Journal of International Law* 172 (1947).
29 The Statute was adopted on July 17, 1998, by the United Nations Diplomatic Conference of Plenipotentiaries on the Establishment of an International Criminal Court. The Rome Statutes entered into force on July 1, 2002. Cf. A/CONF/183./9 of July 17, 1998.

International Initiatives for Strengthening Direct Accountability

As mentioned above, the earliest international initiatives on the responsibilities of commercial non-state actors were the OECD Guidelines for Multilateral Enterprises of 1976 and the ILO Tripartite Declaration of Principles concerning Multinational Enterprises and Social Policy Reform of 1977. In 1999, the United Nations Global Compact was proposed and was officially launched in 2000. Currently, the most debated initiative is the draft Norms and responsibilities of transnational corporations and other business enterprises with regard to human rights.[30] Below, some key points of each of these initiatives are highlighted.

The OECD Guidelines for Multilateral Enterprises were adopted on June 21, 1976, by the OECD members (with the exception of Turkey) as a countermeasure to the extensive and growing protection of the rights of investors.[31] The Guidelines were revised in June 2000 and contain recommendations to private enterprises in the 30 OECD member states and 8 adhering non-member states (Argentina, Brazil, Chile, Estonia, Israel, Latvia, Lithuania, and Slovenia). The major multinational enterprises responsible for most of the world's foreign investment are incorporated in these countries. The revised guidelines cover ethical standards on employment and industrial relations, the environment, bribery, consumer interest, and competition. In the "general policy" section, the Guidelines require enterprises to take into account established policies in the countries in which they operate and to consider the views of other stakeholders. In this regard, enterprises should "respect the human rights of those affected by their activities consistent with the host government's international obligations and commitments."

Thus, the Guidelines demand more than respect for national labor standards and employment conditions: corporate entities should also measure their activities against the international human rights obligations of the host country. The revised Guidelines strengthened the monitoring and conflict resolution mechanisms by setting up a National Contact Point (NPC) in each member state. These NPCs, usually located in one or several government ministries, are undertaking promotional activities in their respective countries, and receive complaints in specific instances. They also cooperate in annual meetings of all NCPs where individual reports are discussed, information is exchanged, and conceptual issues addressed. From 2000 to 2005, more that 100 "specific incidences" (that is, cases of complaints of breaches of the guidelines submitted by local "stakeholders," NGOs, and others) had been received and were being dealt with by the NPCs.[32]

Importantly, the European Commission has resolved that EU businesses ought to adhere to and follow the OECD Guidelines: "the OECD Guidelines for Multinational enterprises are the most comprehensive, internationally endorsed set of rules

---

30   *Supra*, note 7.
31   Joachim Karl, "The OECD Guidelines for Multinational Enterprises," in Michael K. Addo (ed.) *Human Rights Standards and the Responsibility of Transnational Corporations* (The Hague: Kluwer International, 1999), p. 89.
32   OECD, *Guidelines for Multinational Enterprises: 2005 Annual Meeting of the National Contact Points Report by the Chair* (Paris: Investment Division, OECD). Available at www.oecd.org/investment.

governing the activities of multinationals. In promoting CSR in developing countries, EU businesses should demonstrate and publicize their world-wide adherence to
them."[33] Adherence to the "internationally endorsed" codes of conduct is aimed at
leveling the competitiveness of European firms with, in particular US businesses.
Adopting European guidelines with more specific and demanding requirements
could, on the other hand, reduce competitiveness of European firms and, hence, undermine the effectiveness of these voluntary guidelines. For the firms applying them,
the Guidelines are voluntary, but for the states adhering to them, it may be argued
that they are "committed to promoting them," which suggests a genuine duty to see
that they are respected.[34]

The second international initiative is the ILO Tripartite Declaration of Principles
concerning Multinational Enterprises and Social Policy Reform of 1977, adopted in
context of the debate on a New International Economic Order in the 1970s.[35] The
aim of the Declaration was "to encourage the positive contribution which multinational enterprises can make to economic and social progress and to minimize and resolve the difficulties to which their various operations may give rise." In the General
Policy section of the Declaration, which remains voluntary in nature, all concerned
parties are urged to respect the sovereign rights of States, obey the national laws and
regulations, and to give due consideration to local practices and respect relevant international standards. In particular, they "should respect the Universal Declaration
of Human Rights and the corresponding International Covenants adopted by the
UN and the ILO with special regard to instruments protecting freedom of expression
and association as essential freedoms to "sustained progress." In doing this, all concerned parties (mainly multinational enterprises) should honor states' national legislation and international legal obligations.

The 1977 ILO Declaration is the centerpiece of the ILO corporate responsibility
agenda and covers multinational enterprises as well as domestic businesses. It refers
to a long list of binding ILO conventions, including the most central ones on
freedom of association, the right to organize and bargain collectively, the abolition of
forced labor, and the right to equality of opportunity and treatment. But it remains
a non-binding instrument that is essentially promotional in nature. The importance
of the Declaration, however, in addition to bringing pressure on transnational corporations to respect human rights, is that it demonstrates how labor rights are essential parts of human rights, and offers, as an ILO instrument, references to all key
labor conventions and recommendations. It also emphasizes that neglect of these
standards represents a "threat to sustainable and social development" everywhere. It

---

33 Commission of the European Communities, *Communication from the European Commission Concerning Corporate Social Responsibility: A Business Contribution to Sustainable Development*, Com (2002) 346 final, Brussels, July 2, 2002.
34 Report of the Sub-Commission on the Promotion and Protection of Human Rights, UN Doc. E/CN.4/2005/91, p. 7.
35 After the adoption of the Declaration by the Governing Body on November 16, 1977, a large number of new Conventions and Recommendations have been adopted by the International Labour Conference, and included as addendum to the Declaration though periodical revisions, notably in 1987, 1995, and 1998. See also for the full text of the Tripartite Declaration of Principles concerning Multinational Enterprises and Social Policy. Available at http://www.ilo.org/public/english/standards/norm/sources mne.htm.

refers, therefore, to widely recognized lex lata (existing law) instruments with a well-established monitoring and supervisory system.

In January 1999, UN Secretary-General Kofi Annan launched the UN Global Compact at the World Economic Forum in Davos, calling on private companies to commit themselves to respect nine core principles in relation to human rights, labor rights, and the environment. Since the launch, the initiative has been joined by hundreds of private companies throughout the world. The NGO CorpWatch launched the "Citizens Compact on the United Nations and Corporations" in Davos in January 2000, setting out a number of principles, including the following: "The United Nations does not endorse or promote products or brand names of any private corporation, and will avoid the appearance of such endorsements."[36] In fact, the UN has established strict rules regarding the use of the UN logo. Although the Citizens Compact has been discontinued, CorpWatch and other NGOs have criticized the UN Global Compact for allowing TNCs to improve their public image without any real changes in their overall corporate social, environmental, or human rights behavior.

This is an issue that requires more systematic empirical analysis. The Global Compact is a voluntary and self-regulatory mechanism, although it does introduce human rights law into the policies of private companies and calls on them to report in accordance with the Global Compact Guidelines for Communication for Progress (COP), which was updated in January 2003.[37] Participants are supposed to communicate with their stakeholders on an annual basis about progress in implementing the Global Compact principles through their annual financial reports, sustainability reports, and other means, such as public reports and websites. As Steinhart emphasizes, the Compact has no "policing" clout other than a minimal requirements for annual self-reporting. At the same token, it may initiate "human rights entrepreneurialism" where firms try to distinguish themselves from competitors in the market by Compact-related codes of ethical behavior.[38] This instrumental motivation of the CSR agenda may still, as a side effect, help to improve corporate behavior conducive to human rights.

All of these initiatives refer to "human rights responsibilities" in general terms, but still lack a precise notion of the content and operational requirements of responsibilities. There are significant gaps in defining what practical responsibilities that multinational businesses as non-state actors have, or should have. This issue has been addressed by the UN Sub-Commission on the Protection and Promotion of Human Rights, which, in 1997, set up a Working Group on the Working Methods and Activities of Transnational Corporations. In resolution 1997/11, the Senegalese member of the Sub-Commission, El Hadji Guissé, was asked to produce a working document on the subject of human rights and transnational corporations.[39]

---

36 The principles are available at http://www.corpwatch.org/article.php?id=992 (visited April 17, 2006).
37   Global Compact Guidelines for "Communication on Progress," available at http://www.globalcompact.org/CommunicatingProgress/cop_guidelinaes.pdf. (Accessed April 17, 2006.)
38   Supra, note 10, p. 206.
39 For a review of the details of the drafting process, see David Weissbrodt and Muria Kruger, "Human Rights Responsibilities of Business as non-State Actors" in Philip Alston (ed.), 2005, supra, note 1.

Following from the discussions of Guissé's report, the Sub-Commission established a three-year Working Group that started drafting a code of conduct for transnational corporations in 1999, based on an initial draft prepared by Sub-Commission member, Professor David Weissbrodt. Revised drafts were discussed in the Sub-Commission sessions in 2000, 2001, and 2002. The 2002 revised draft was discussed in consultation with non-governmental organizations in March 2003, leading to further revisions and submission of a final set of draft Norms, unanimously approved by the Sub-Commission in its resolution 2003/16, in July/August 2003.[40]

The drafting process brought some clarification on the scope and nature of non-state actor's responsibilities. According to the document, non-state actors including "transnational and other businesses" have both direct and indirect obligations for human rights respect and protection, and, as Weissbrodt subsequently concluded, ". . . the Norms draw upon the existing web of international obligations which already apply, either directly or indirectly, to business and pull them together into one document which clearly and directly states the human rights standards applicable to business."[41]

During the drafting process, much consideration was given to the compulsory or voluntary nature of the Norms. As adopted in 2003, the Norms are not merely a voluntary CSR initiative.[42] They require a number of implementation provisions and allow NGOs and "others" to submit information and reports about a firm's compliance with the Norms as soon as a firm has adhered to the Norms, and, of course, depending on the adoption of the draft Norms by the Human Rights Council (the former Human Rights Commission). Yet, the initial position of the Commission in discussing the document may have represented a setback to efforts to give legal significance to the Norms, since it recommended that the Economic and Social Council should "Affirm that [the document containing the draft Norms] has not been requested by the Commission and, as a draft proposal, has no legal standing, and that the Sub-Commission should not perform any monitoring function in this regard."[43]

On the other hand, in the same decision the Commission also asked the Office of the High Commissioner for Human Rights to compile a report identifying ways to strengthen standards on business' human rights responsibilities, taking into account the draft Norms. In its report, released in March 2005, the High Commissioner comprehensively analyzes existing initiatives and sets out arguments presented for and against the draft Norms, and finds that although most companies do not favor the Norms, some are exploring how to use them through the Business Leaders Initiative on Human Rights.[44] In April 2005, the Commission created the position of Special Representative on the issue of human rights and transnational

---

40   *Supra*, note 7.
41   *Id.*, p. 328.
42   *Id.*, p. 338.
43   Commission on Human Rights Decision 2004/116, adopted on April 20, 2004.
44   See http://www.blihr.org/.

corporations and other business enterprises,[45] and Secretary-General Kofi Annan appointed John Ruggie to this position in July 2005, a particularly well-qualified choice since he was Special Adviser on the Global Compact and is Professor of International Affairs at Harvard University's Kennedy School of Government and Director of its Center for Business and Government. He submitted his interim report in February 2006.[46] While acknowledging useful elements in the Norms, Ruggie considers that "the Norms exercise became engulfed by its own doctrinal excesses" and contains "exaggerated legal claims and conceptual ambiguities," which "created confusion and doubt even among many mainstream international lawyers and other impartial observers."[47] His principal objections concern the claimed legal authority of the Norms as more than voluntary and yet declaratory of existing law, on the one hand, and the allocation of human rights responsibilities between states and firms, on the other.[48] He concludes that "the divisive debate over the Norms obscures rather than illuminates promising areas of consensus and cooperation among business, civil society, governments, and international institutions with respect to human rights."[49]

Indeed, the draft Norms were not drafted as a binding treaty. They refer, however, to binding provisions, and assume that any corporate entity is bound by the exiting laws of a country, including the international legal instruments that the home or host country has ratified. They are, in other words, soft law standards but refer to core human rights conventions that should be upheld by TNCs and other businesses in countries that give support to the Norms. At any rate, the Norms strengthen the legal position that international provisions incorporated in domestic law, and refer to obligations that are binding on non-state actors, including TNCs and other businesses. Main norms supported by the Norms are the right to equal opportunity and equal treatment, the right to security of persons, the rights of workers, and a general provision for respecting national sovereignty and human rights. They contain references to civil and political as well as economic and social rights; refer explicitly to the right to development as a right companies should respect and promote, and attempt to formulate voluntarily accepted direct obligation to protect, respect, secure, and promote a broad specter of human rights; and suggest self-reporting by businesses that may be subject to external scrutiny and verification.

The scope of non-state actors' human rights responsibilities are, according to the Norms, wide-reaching, and claim that they apply to transnational corporations and other business enterprises "regardless of the international or domestic nature of its activities."[50] TNCs and other businesses have "the obligation to promote, secure the

---

45 Human Rights and Transnational Corporations and Other Business Enterprises, Commission on Human Rights Resolution 2005/59, adopted on April 20, 2005. The decision to create the position was endorsed by the Economic and Social Council in its decision 2006/273, adopted on July 25, 2005.
46 Interim report of the Special Representative of the Secretary-General on the issue of human rights and transnational corporations and other business enterprises, UN Doc. E/CN.4/2006/97, February 22, 2006.
47 *Id.*, para. 59.
48 *Id.*, paras. 59-69.
49 *Id.*, para. 69.
50 Draft Norms, *supra*, note 7, article 21.

fulfillment of, ensure respect of, and protect human rights recognized in international as well as national law, including the rights and interests of indigenous peoples and other vulnerable groups." The legal nature of these responsibilities, however, remains utterly controversial and legally unsettled.

Hence, the draft Norms have been met with stout objections and strong support.[51] The main arguments against them have been that they represent a shift away from voluntary adherence to ethical and human rights standards for corporate entities, that the tone of the draft is unduly negative towards business, and that the implementation provisions are burdensome and unworkable. Against the argument that only states have and should have obligations under international human rights law, supporters of the Norms emphasize that rather than challenging state responsibilities, they complement them by establishing a balance between the primary obligations of states and secondary responsibilities of non-state actors to respect, protect, and promote human rights. They emphasize that the Norms do not duplicate other initiatives of human rights and corporate responsibilities. On the contrary, they set a common set of standard for all businesses and provide needed requirements for evaluating current and future performances. Not least, the Norms may give opportunities to address human rights in countries where the state is unwilling or unable to secure rights protection.

The Norms are still in the process of being discussed and may be subject to further revisions and adjustments. Until December 2006, they were being tested out in a "'road-testing" process by businesses that participate in the Business Leaders' Initiative on Human Rights. These firms are, on their part, committed to examine what is "essential," "expected," and "desirable" behavior for all companies.[52]

Trends and Outstanding Issues

These international initiatives indicate a trend of international law towards regulating companies directly through soft law mechanisms. With the increasing incorporation of human rights treaties into domestic law, the practice of using human rights in case law and national jurisdiction evolves and makes human rights norms directly applicable to non-state actors. Assuming that law emerges in response to new demands of protection against societal threats in national or global society, one conclusion from the above analysis is that non-state actors as agents of development have moral responsibilities to respect human rights, following principles expressed in the UDHR Preamble and elsewhere. Gradual, but clear trends in international law to make non-state actors morally and legally responsible for selected human rights are evolving, particularly rights of the child and certain labor standards, based on the obligations to respect and protect from abuse and harm.

The ethical and human rights accountability of TNCs are also related to trade and investment. In a report submitted to the Sub-Commission on Human Rights,

---

51   See the points raised by Ruggie. See also supra note 46 above, and a wider range of perspectives in the report by the UN High Commissioner for Human Rights to the Human Rights Commission, UN Doc. E/CN.4/2005/91, February 15, 2005.
52   *Id.*, para. 22.

Trade and Investment, the High Commissioner for Human Rights recommended that the promotion and protection of human rights be included among the objectives of investment agreements and argues that the "right and duty" of states to regulate investments policies with the aim of promoting and protecting human rights should be ensured.[53] It suggests that as investors' rights are strengthened through investment agreements, their obligations towards individuals and communities should be strengthened as well. At the global level, demands are being made that the World Trade Organization should be accountable to human rights norms.

In spite of some advances in conceptual clarification and the development of practical guidelines and compacts that have been reported above, demanding issues still require further clarification. For instance, when companies are linked together as contractors and sub-contractors, where does responsibility for human rights harms rest? What is a company's *sphere of influence* on human rights, and what is meant by complicity in human rights abuses in complex economic transactions where several companies are involved? Another issue is the *scope of responsibility*. Should TNCs actively take responsibility for human rights by promoting or protecting them? And even more demanding, should firms support the economic and other conditions for human rights by investing in community development projects, such as infrastructure, health, or education?

On such questions, much more clarification is needed. The current bottom line is that states have a primary responsibility for securing and guaranteeing international conventions. Insisting on human rights responsibilities of non-state actors does not abridge the responsibilities of states. Commercial non-state actors, for their part, have duties to abide by national law, including applicable provisions of the country's obligations under international law. In addition, firms have opportunities to include human rights standards in their own operations — for instance, by including human rights clauses in contracts and developing company cultures of ethical governance that respect basic human rights. And as noted, some legal systems require that firms when operating abroad are fully bound by their home country's legislation – for example, the US Alien Tort Claims Act giving US courts authority to hear civil cases by foreign citizens for injuries caused by US firms abroad.[54]

International norm-setting processes, for instance the UN Global Compact, have given businesses better tools for formulating ethical policies and practices. Economic actors and particularly big transnational corporations have, as the Preamble to the draft Norms emphasizes, great potential and capacity to foster economic well-being, development, technological improvement, and wealth. They also have the capacity to harm human rights by their operations, employment practices, and interaction with governments. To address these questions as human rights issues requires that conceptual gaps of corporate responsibility be filled.

---

53 Human rights, trade and investment. Report of the High Commissioner for Human Rights, UN Doc. E/CN.4/Sub.2/2003/9, July 2, 2003, paras. 31-35.
54 *Id.* para. 17. However, in spite of the possibility of making a remedy under the Aliens Tort Claims Act, in practice it has remained a legal tool with limited impact. See also *supra* note 46, para.15 and in particular para. 62.

Indirect responsibilities follow from the duty to uphold human rights that states have under human rights law giving firms, at a minimum level, legal duties to respect the human right provisions that the state is bound to fulfill. Every state in the contemporary world has ratified at least one and usually several human rights treaties, and all UN member states have responsibilities under the Universal Declaration of Human Rights, which reaffirms, in large part, norms that are binding in customary international law. The right to a fair hearing in criminal matters and other aspects of the rule of law are typically the realm of domestic law, but current initiatives of CSR suggest a list of rule of law matters that are regulated by human rights law under widely ratified treaties over matter directly relevant to business entities and their activities.[55] The mechanism of indirect responsibility is a fruitful approach for the clarification of TNCs human rights responsibilities. Such norms are particularly useful for firms operating in states unable or unwilling to take human rights seriously, and therefore have little concern for the human rights impact of TNCs operating under their jurisdiction.

Voluntarism and the Obligation of Corporations Under International Human Rights Law

Are voluntary agreements by non-state actors to respect codes of conduct a better way of changing a company's behavior than legal regulations and mechanisms? Voluntarism enhances commitment and reflects a concern for ethical engagement. In instrumental terms, voluntary compliance may be effective because it makes commercial sense to comply with international norms to the extent that the company's public image is a factor in the marketing of its products and in attracting investors.

On the other hand, in spite of a positive trend, voluntarism has little adherence at a global scale, and the results are equally modest. Chinese companies, rapidly expanding in international trade and investment, are generally absent from any voluntary CRS mechanism. And TNCs continue to take commercial advantage of repressive regimes, or move their operations to countries with weak protection of workers rights, child protection, or anti-corruption laws. The vast power vested in non-state actors makes their operations crucial for whether people can enjoy basic human rights; not just the right to work, a decent wage, freedom to organize and the right to bargain collectively but also the right to secure non-discrimination on grounds specified by human rights law, and the right to health, education, and a decent livelihood.

---

55   The Office of the High Commissioner for Human Rights, in its comments on the draft Norms, suggested the following list as being relevant to business: " the prohibition of discrimination, the right to life, liberty, and security of the person, freedom from torture, the right to privacy, freedom of opinion and expression, the right to seek, receive, and impart information, freedom of association, the right to organize, the prohibition of bonded or forced labour, the prohibition of forms of child labour, the right to health, the right to an adequate standard of living and the right to education. Similarly, the rights of certain groups of people particularly affected by the activities of business are relevant — such as the rights of women, children, employees, indigenous peoples, and migrant workers and their families." Report of the United Nations High Commissioner on Human Rights on the responsibilities of transnational corporations and related business enterprises with regard to human rights, UN doc. E/CN.4/2005/91, February 19, 2005, para. 42.E/CN.4/2005/91, p. 15.

Therefore, in spite of important difficulties in documenting and measuring human rights abuses of TNCs, their considerable power justifies efforts to develop better legal mechanisms to ensure cooperation of non-state actors in respecting human rights and contributing to their protection.

The effectiveness of international standards depends on the enforcement efficiency of domestic legal and non-legal institutions and the functioning of international monitoring bodies. The effectiveness of human rights law is based on domestic legal jurisprudence. In addition to effective legal institutions, the growth of corporate cultures of accountability and compliance with human rights norms require strong civil societies, including free media, to create awareness and publicly articulate accountability. International human rights law may help to harmonize rules in cases of weak national regulations, bring coherence to standards and establish references for national law by setting benchmarks, and by establishing minimum thresholds for what is internationally impermissible. But what is at stake is national and local implementation enforced by one of the key attributes of the human rights system, that is, its capability of public oversight and monitoring of corporate behavior conducive to human rights principles.

The Way Forward: Non-State Actors, Responsibilities, and Development

This chapter has discussed the importance of addressing human rights responsibilities of non-state actors. The state-centric structure of international human rights law should not prohibit a dynamic development of the responsibilities of "other organs of society" to respect human rights, although many conceptual issues need to be resolved further before the human rights norms of TNCs and other businesses can become part of the human rights standard vocabulary.

Transnational corporations are "agents of development" but for too long their operations have not been part of the human rights and development agenda. There is, however, an emerging legal discourse for dealing with non-state actors. TNCs and other businesses have great potentials for supporting human rights, including enhancing the economic conditions for human rights promotion. But they also have a large potential for undermining the foundation of sustainable development by environmental degradation and human rights abuses.

One conclusion from this analysis is that the application of human rights law to develop human rights responsibilities of non-state actors is evolving gradually and step by step. TNCs human rights responsibilities are still predominantly a matter of soft law and voluntarism, although national case law that refers to human rights provisions and instruments demonstrates the potential relevance of international human rights law for the definition and specification of non-state actors' human rights responsibilities. The reference to the right to development in the draft Norms remains, however, unexplored.

In the foreseeable future, the state will remain the key agent of human rights enforcement. But in contemporary globalization the state, as a key actor in development and the prime duty-holding party for rights assurance under international law,
has a duty to ensure that powerful economic actors exhibit corporate behavior that
does not abuse fundamental rights and freedoms as enshrined in international law.
Perhaps more urgently than ever, states have a responsibility to find new ways — voluntary or enforceable by law — to control the potentially exploitative and harmful
power of national and international economic actors. At the end of the day, this implies upholding the human rights vision of protecting people's welfare, freedom, and
agency from new social and economic threats caused by contemporary globalization.

To be ensured, modern human rights require more than good judicial process and
remedies. They also require civic engagement, public openness, the free flow of information, and civic and social movements and organizations that can engage in
"shaming and blaming" campaigns — for instance, consumer boycotts — that pressure individual firms that violate human rights. Such responses to human rights
problems, outside institutions and mechanisms of the legal system, are important additional means to hold TNCs and other non-state actors accountable to human
rights principles and may help make legal as well as voluntary mechanisms more robust.

Hence, voluntary guidelines need to be supplemented by public engagement.
Voluntary reporting, at the same time, should be subject to critical and independent
examination by non-governmental organizations and watch dog institutions. As a
fairly new agenda of human rights enhancement, widespread corporate human rights
responsibility practices of TNCs are only likely to evolve step by step —
provided a continued civic and political commitment can be sustained. It is fair to
conclude that some progress has been made in identifying indirect obligations of
TNCs, but much more conceptual clarification (and norm-making) is needed about
their explicit legal duties. The human rights community should continue to collab-
orate with the international business community in advancing this agenda. Yet even
if voluntary codes of conduct are contributing to the human rights agenda, still
better legal responses may be needed to confront challenges and societal threats to
people's welfare and freedom caused by powerful business entities in the era of
globalization.

Part III. National Realities and Challenges

8 | Redesigning the State for "Right Development"
Yash Ghai[1]

Introduction

This chapter deals with the relevance of the right to development for the design of institutions at the national level. The right to development has had remarkably little impact on constitutional lawyers, political scientists, or human rights activisits. It has remained, with negative consequences, where it germinated, within the provenance of diplomats and international lawyers. It has become the focus of contention between diplomats of the North and the South, generating more heat than light. The North suspects, perhaps correctly, that the South wants to use the right to development to extract resources from the North and has no intention of implementing the domestic obligations expressed in the right to development. The South may think that the lukewarm, if not outright negative, attitude on the part of the west, toward the right to development is a manifestation of bad intentions — the North's determination to preserve the present unequal economic and political order and the libertarian resistance to the social justice agenda of the right to development.

Much of the debate has concentrated on the legal status and "bindingness" of the Declaration on the Right to Development[2] ("the Declaration") and has generated very erudite and arcane arguments on the nature of human rights, rights holders, and duty bearers. There has been relatively little exploration of the many dimensions of the right to development or its overall orientation. Even academics who have studied the topic have been trapped in the polemics of the North-South controversy. The reports of the Independent Expert have attempted a way out of this stalemate, but his proposals so far are largely anchored in the dynamics of international relations.[3]

In order to explore and exploit the potential of the right to development, it is necessary to locate it within the domain of national politics and constitutions. It is surprising that almost no attempt has been made at this approach. Those parts of the reports of the Independent Expert that aim at analytical clarity and elaboration can indeed provide the start of the effort to locate it within the obligations and structure of the state. I believe that significant further intellectual developments of the concept and implications of the right to development can occur only when the right to development is related to the domestic obligations of the state and to the design of its institutions. I also believe that real gains for the people from the right to development will take place only when it is implemented in the laws and institutions of in-

1   The author acknowledges gratefully the Distinguished Researcher Award from the University, which has facilitated the preparation of this chapter, and editorial assistance from Jill Cottrell.
2   Declaration on the Right to Development, GA Res. A/RES/41/128, December 4, 1986, annex, 41 UN GAOR Supp. (No. 53) 186, UN Doc. A/RES/41/53 (1986), (hereafter, "the Declaration").
3   See Arjun Sengupta's chapter in this book.

dividual states — for the impact of assistance from the North, however generous, will limited as well as problematic.

Moreover, the domestic engagement of the right to development will enrich the study and practice of human rights, which are largely mired in studies of judicial and international enforcement of rights. In practice, lawyers analyze rights in an exceedingly narrow framework, focussing on violations of rights and the judicial response to them but paying little attention to the design of the state and its dynamics that have major impacts on the respect for or protection of human rights. In addition, the Declaration's emphasis on interdependence and indivisibility of human rights will encourage governments, legislatures, judiciaries, and even private organizations to view rights in a holistic way, balancing one kind of rights against another. It is also my belief, however, that a national-oriented analysis of the right to development and modalities for its implementation will alert us to the dynamics of the right to development and political difficulties inherent in it.

It is with the aim of broadening the approach to the right to development that I have chosen to explore the Declaration as the agenda for designing state constitutions. Numerous interesting developments in the making and substance of constitutional reforms in recent years show a significant departure from approaches and ideas of only a few years ago. One can classify post-Second World War constitutions of countries in the South by different generations and aspirations (postcolonial state sovereignty, nation-building, and democracy; one party regime; military rule; and ethnic democracy).[4] Each of these reflected a different mode of making or changing constitutions.

Contemporary efforts at constitution making bear at least some resemblance to the right to development.[5] The concern with designing institutions that manifest the sovereignty of the people, protect individual and collective rights, and lay the foundations of social and economic development reflects the right to development in many respects. In one sense these recent experiments in constitutions show at least one approach to giving effect to the holistic aspirations of the right to development, in the holistic structures of the state. What is obvious from these recent constitutions is that they have as their mission no less than the total transformation of the colonial and post-colonial state, to a significant extent based on the primacy of human rights. It is equally clear that this goal cannot be accomplished simply by elaborating and strengthening the machinery for the enforcement of rights or engaging in negotiations with "donors" (often more accurately described as lenders); institutions and procedures that are "rights friendly" also must be created.

---

4   Yash Ghai, "A Journey Around Constitutions: Reflections on Contemporary Constitutions," 2005 *South African Law Journal* (forthcoming).
5   See, for example, Vivien Hart, Democratic Constitution Making (Washington: USIP, 2003; available on the USIP website at http://www.usip.org/pubs/specialreports/sr107.pdf (visited January 6 2006); Julius Ivonhbere, *Towards a New Constitutionalism in Africa*, CCD Occasional Paper No. 4 (London: Centre for Democracy and Development, 2000); and various contributions in Goran Hyden and Denis Venter (eds.), *Constitution-Making and Democratisation in Africa* (Pretoria: African Institute of South Africa, 2001). For country studies, see, for example, for South Africa, Hassen Ebrahim, *Soul of a Nation* (Oxford: University Press, 1998), and for Eritrea, Bereket Habte Selassie, *The Making of the Eritrean Constitution: The Dialectic of Process and Substance* (Asmara: The Red Sea Press, Inc., 2003).

The critical aspects of the right to development which are relevant to constitutions and constitution making are the principle of self-determination, the definition of development, the indivisibility and integration of rights, the imperative of social justice, and a constant emphasis on popular participation. Equally critical is the message that it is at the level of the state and through the obligations of the state, which are derived from the Declaration, that the right to development will be achieved. My analysis, while urging the designing of the constitution on the basis of the logic and coherence of the right to development, offers limited optimism, for the logic of such a constitution runs contrary to the interests of ruling elites (and their foreign partners) that have embedded themselves in colonial economic and bureaucratic structures.

This chapter examines the domestic implications of the right to development as they have been manifested in the new constitutions of several countries. Through looking at participatory ways of making and adopting constitutions and through analyzing their contents, it also shows how these constitutions differ from their predecessors and how they connect to the right to development. I argue that a more imaginative and considered use of the right to development can assist in the search for people-oriented governance and development, and in this way, I hope, demonstrate aspects of the right to development so far insufficiently explored. My intention is for this to serve as a tentative guide to the practical elaboration of the principles of the right to development (as for example, the modalities of participation).

This chapter also looks at the difficulties of orienting the state toward greater human rights and social justice and the ways in which constitutions may raise people's expectations (and even empower them) without changing the fundamental realities of their predicament, thus uncovering dynamics which marginalize human and peoples' rights. After a general discussion of the relevance of the Declaration to the process and contents of the constitution, demonstrated by various national provisions, the chapter turns to a study of the constitution-making process in Kenya between 2000 and 2005 for reflections on these contemporary debates.

Importance of Constitutions

Emphasis is often placed on the role of the international community and cooperation between states. The state, however, remains the entity primarily responsible for what takes place at the national level. States have a duty to take steps, individually and collectively, to formulate international development policies with a view to facilitating the full realization of the right to development.[6] They have to take "resolute steps to eliminate the massive and flagrant violations of the human rights of people and human beings[7] and have to remove violations of human rights, described as "obstacles to development."[8] Article 8 is the most explicit of all in acknowledging the role of the state: "States should undertake, at the national level, all the necessary measures for the realisation of the right to development . . . ." It also enjoins states

---

6 See the Declaration, *supra* note 2, article 4.
7 *Ibid.*, Aticle 5.
8 *Ibid.*, Aticle 6(3).

to encourage popular participation in all spheres as an important factor in development and in the full realization of all human rights. Article 10, reiterating the obligation of states to "ensure the full exercise and progressive enhancement of the right
to development," prescribes the "formulation, adoption and implementation of
policy, legislative and other measures at the national and international levels."

The right to development is so comprehensive and requires such a major re-ori-
entation and structuring of the state, however, that the very constitution of the state
must be modified in order to fully implement it. It is not sufficient merely to revise
or strengthen the bill of rights. In order to fully incorporate the right to development
into the structure of the state, one should analyze obstacles to the exercise or protection of human rights (such as the centralization or abuse of power, misallocation of
resources, or lack of democracy and accountability) and design institutions and procedures that place primacy on human rights. New institutions may be necessary to
fully implement the right to development (for example, to facilitate the participation
of the people in the affairs of state), and the parameters for balancing different kinds
of interests would have to be established. One of these balances is between individual
rights and collective rights. Collective rights (not directly acknowledged in the
Declaration), which may relate to the rights of minorities, with respect to culture or
participation, are best dealt with in the constitution. A new constitution may also be
necessary for the full exercise of the right to self-determination, which the
Declaration refers to as one of the foundations of the right to development. The constitution would have to be made with the full participation of the people.

Fortunately, there seems to be considerable support for the proposition that constitutions of many countries are outdated and need to be reviewed to accord sufficient attention to the primacy of human rights and a greater degree of
democratization and participation (Giovanni Sartori has estimated that, "of the 170
or so written documents called constitutions in today's world, more than half have
been written since 1974").[9] Some of these constitutions were drafted as part of waves
of democratization that have swept the globe — the end of military rule in Latin
America, the replacement of one-party regimes in Africa, the collapse of communism
in Eastern Europe, and the broadening of public participation in Asia. What they
have in common is a greater commitment to democracy: fair elections, separation of
powers, judicial review of laws and policies (through constitutional or ordinary
courts), and bills of civil and political rights.

Constitutions of Eastern Europe part company with constitutions of other regions in their forthright entrenchment of relatively free market economies, parsi-
mony about social justice and social rights, and restrictive role for the state. The
emphasis is on the traditional, even conservative, type of political process, mediated
by the electoral process, for which the constitution provides a framework, leaving

---

9 Giovanni Sartori, *Comparative Constitutional Engineering: An Inquiry into Structures, Incentives and
Outcomes* (Basingstoke: Macmillan, 1994), p. 197. I have examined the purposes and dynamics of con-
temporary constitutions in my article, "A Journey Around Constitutions: Reflections on Contemporary
Constitutions," *op. cit.*

choices of values and policies to governments and parliaments.[10] Other constitutions favoring a more active role for the state in the energetic pursuit of human rights and social justice set up an ambitious agenda for social and economic reform.[11] Some constitutions even take social justice or poverty as their leitmotif, providing coherence for their provisions. The expansion of the state is, however, to be accompanied by greater accountability mechanisms, a role for civil society, and insulation of the exercise of sensitive sectors of public powers (such as the conduct of elections, auditing functions, prosecutorial responsibilities, and appointment and tenure of judges) from executive or partisan political pressures.[12]

Considerable evidence suggests that constitutions are now taken more seriously than before. As constitutions are generally negotiated instruments or have been adopted after significant public participation, many communities or groups have a vested interest in their implementation. Civil society organizations use constitutions, litigation, and lobbying to achieve objectives of legality or integrity. Other constitutions are adopted as part of an international process, directed toward the rehabilitation of states previously mired in conflict, and there are serious pressures for adherence to the constitution. Constitutions today not only rely on legitimacy, public knowledge, and support, but they also provide mechanisms for their own implementation or observance, such as judicial review (particularly constitutional courts), periodic assessments of the functioning of the constitution, human rights commission, independent electoral commission, and improved budgetary and au-

---

10   Elster, Offe and Preuss, *Institutional Design in Post-Communist Societies: Rebuilding the Ship at Sea* (Cambridge; New York: Cambridge University Press, 1998),
11   One of the earliest examples of a post-Second World War constitution aiming at a social revolution is the Indian Constitution (1950). The preamble states as its goals: social justice, liberty, equality, and fraternity. Article 38 says, "The State shall strive to promote the welfare of the people by securing and protecting as effectively as it may a social order in which justice, social, economic and political, shall inform all the institutions of the national life." The constitution commits the state to the elimination of all discrimination against members of lower castes and imposes positive obligations of affirmative action (Art 46). To promote participation, it requires the establishment of village panchayats (councils) as instruments of self-government (Art. 140) and of workers in industries (Art. 143A). Thailand's constitution (1997) requires the state to ensure "fair distribution of incomes" (Art. 83), provide "social security and fair wages" (Art. 86), assist "the elderly, the indigent, the disabled or the handicapped, and the underprivileged" for good life and self-reliance (Art. 80), and, more generally, the promotion of public participation in policy making and plans for economic, social, and political development, the scrutiny of the government (Art. 76) and through decentralization for "self-determination" (Art. 78). The South African constitution (1996) avoids grand statements of this kind; instead, its principles are woven into the binding provisions of the constitution. For example, it defines equality as "full and equal enjoyment of all rights and freedom," thus transforming affirmative action, seen elsewhere as exceptions to equality into the pre-requisite of equality (Art. 9). It explicates the purpose of human rights as upholding the dignity of the human person (Art.10). The guarantee of the protection of property makes special provision for land, which may be redistributed, subject to certain conditions, in order to redress past injustices, particularly the appropriation of African land (Art. 23). The constitution has also set a trend in the guarantee of social and economic rights – culture and language (Arts. 30 and 31), education (Art. 29), and housing, food, water, and health (Art. 27). Participation is to be secured through a significant degree of decentralization as well as access to official information (Art. 32). Intervention by the Constitutional Court has compelled the government to take these rights seriously.
12   In Chapter 9, entitled, "State Institutions Supporting Constitutional Democracy," the Constitution of South Africa establishes offices of the public prosecutor, Human Rights Commission, Gender Commission, Commission for the Protection and Promotion of Culture and Language, Auditor General and the Electoral Commission. The constitution states that these institutions are "independent, and subject only to the Constitution and the law, and they must be impartial and must exercise their powers and perform their functions without fear, favour or prejudice" (Art. 181). The Constitutions of Uganda (1995) and Thailand (Art. 297), in addition to some of the above institutions, also establish independent commissions against corruption.

diting procedures. There are therefore considerable advantages to linking constitutional reform to the right to development.

The Process of Constitution Making

The Declaration says little about constitutions and even less about constitution making, but one can easily discern implications for both. The Declaration's constant reiteration of the importance of self-determination and participation provides sufficient clues. The concept of self-determination refers here principally to the decision of a people to determine their political status and to pursue their economic, social, and cultural development, rather than as authority for secession. The "determination" is that of the people, not elitist cabals: There is nothing more fundamental in this "determination" than the basic rules by which a people regulate their public space, define national values and aspirations, and establish the mandate and competence of state authorities — in other words, the constitution. The emphasis on participation reinforces this understanding of "determination."

Participation is seen in the Declaration as an essential aspect of development. The preamble says that development must be based on the "active, free and meaningful participation" of the "entire population and of all individuals." Several articles require public participation (for example, Article 8.2 requires states to "encourage popular participation in all spheres as an important factor in development and in the full realisation of all human rights"). Participation is central to its concept of development: "The human person is the central subject of development and should be the active participant and beneficiary of the right to development" (Art. 2.1). Development is about individuals taking responsibility, separately and collectively, for their own development; they also have duties to the community. Other international instruments seek to guarantee participation rights, most prominently the International Covenant on Civil and Political Rights, but these are somewhat narrowly conceived and are limited to the right to vote, to contest elections, and to have access to public service.[13] None of them places participation at the center of human rights and development as the Declaration does.

The value of popular participation in constitution making has been recognized in several countries that have promoted such participation in their recent constitution-making exercises, particularly in Africa. It is now customary for constitutions to locate sovereignty in the people, and it is natural that they should determine how it should be delegated and exercised. There are more pragmatic reasons for encouraging popular participation, however. Unlike perhaps older, classical constitutions, constitutions today do not necessarily reflect existing national polities or power relationships, consolidating the victory and dominance of a particular class or ethnic group. Instead, they are instruments to enhance national unity and territorial integrity,

---

13   See Henry Steiner "Political Participation as a Human Right," 1 *Harvard Human Rights Yearbook* p. 77 (1988), Thomas Franck, "The Emerging Right to Democratic Governance," 86 *American Journal of International Law*, p. 46 (1992); Gregory Fox, "The right to political partitipaction in international law" in Gregory Fox and Brad Roth (eds.), *Democratic Governance and International Law* (Cambridge, UK; New York: Cambridge University Press, 2000), pp. 48-90; and Yash Ghai, *Minorities and Public Participation* (London: Minority Rights Group, 2002 revised edition).

defining or sharpening a national ideology and developing a collective agenda for social and political change — negotiated rather than imposed.

If these are the contemporary functions of constitutions, then the process for making them is crucial to developing a national consensus. Popular input is likely to define the agenda of reform, and the constitution is more likely to reflect the people's concerns and aspirations — not merely those of elites, who are largely urban based. Many constitutions in recent years have been made in the aftermath of civil conflicts, and an important task of the process is to promote reconciliation among the communities previously engaged in conflict. Additionally, a good process enhances people's understanding of the nature of public power and the role of constitutionalism. An effective process can be an essential component of political development, inculcating elements of a democratic political culture, tolerance, and pluralism. It can be empowering for those hitherto marginalized by politics and economy. It can increase society's capacity to handle differences and conflicts, by encouraging habits of listening to others and searching together for common ground. Engagement with the process will facilitate people's understanding of the terms of the constitution and increase their capacity to mobilize its protective provisions. Underlying these goals is the objective of legitimacy, which is achieved in substantial measure when citizens have been involved in the process and are able to feel and claim ownership of the product. An inclusive process in which all communities and key social groups and interests are able to participate is critical for these objectives.

This undoubtedly overly romantic picture of a participatory process has ardent supporters.[14] Detractors, however, as well as some of those who support such an approach, suggest concerns that are worth noting. A participatory process should avoid the perils of spontaneity and populism. It must address the issue of whether the people are sufficiently prepared, both psychologically and intellectually, to engage in the process; how to solicit views of the public and special and organized groups; and how to analyze, assess, balance, and incorporate of these views. The engagement cannot be "one off" but must be continuous and include fresh opportunities to comment on the draft and meaningful forms of participation afterwards. Transparency and integrity throughout the process are essential to win and sustain people's trust and confidence, and to guard against the dangers of manipulation. Constitution making can easily become just another form of politics, driven by narrow and short-term interests and ultimately generating bitterness instead of goodwill. A high degree of participation may raise expectations that cannot be, or are not, satisfied; the emphasis on culture, which often results from participation, may lead to constitutions that are looking to an era long gone, with little connection to national or international social or economic realities — in effect, widening the gap between the constitution and society. A proper assessment of the impact of popular participation

---

14   Two major international projects (one by the United States Institute of Peace and the other by International Institute for Democracy and Electoral Assistance (IDEA) on the study of constitution making are premised on the value of public participation: see their respective websites: USIP Project on Constitution-Making, Peacebuilding, and National Reconciliation. Available at http://www.usip.org/ruleoflaw/projects.html#project3 and http://www.idea.int/conflict/ cbp/. (Accessed January 6, 2006).

cannot be made if the concept of "people" is not disaggregated, nor without some moderation of romanticism about the "people." There is no such thing as the people; there are religious groups, ethnic groups, the disabled, women, youth, forest people, pastoralists, sometimes "indigenous peoples," farmers, peasants, capitalists and workers, lawyers, doctors, auctioneers, as well as practising, failed, or aspiring politicians, all pursuing their respective agendas. They bring different levels of understanding and skills to the process. Sometimes the composition or procedures of constituting bodies favors one or another of these groups. Unless one believes in the invisible hand of the political marketplace, not all of these groups can be counted on to produce a "good" constitution — certainly not the politicians. A participatory process can also be manipulated by warlords, ethnic entrepreneurs, or religious bigots, who can turn it into a source of fundamentalism and intolerance — and deep societal divisions based on ethnicity, linguistic, and religious differences.

These considerations suggest that it is critical to plan carefully for the scope and modalities of participation. Civic education programs should be created to engage people through narratives that have meaning for them, even if they are not cast in language of constitutionalism; to define the relationship between the popular roles and those of experts; and above all, to expose them to the methods of decision-making and the adoption of the constitution.

Substantive Orientation of the Constitution

Since constitution making can be difficult, complex, expensive, and sometimes divisive, rarely does a country embark upon the making of a new constitution without very good reason. Governments, political parties, ethnic or religious groups, or others are reluctant to start or engage in the process unless the goals and procedures of review suit them and are predetermined. Considerable negotiations and compromises, therefore, precede the formal establishment of the process.

A prior agreement on goals has many advantages. Identifying priorities helps to give direction to the process and assists in balancing different aims and interests. For example, national unity and identity may require both effective state institutions and forms of self-government for regions and communities, to ensure balance between individual and community rights. Increasingly, goals are defined by reference to local traditions as well as culture (for example, Islam) and international norms (such as democracy, national unity, human rights, social justice, and gender equity).

If the original goals are too numerous, specific, and detailed, they may clash with ideas generated in the review process itself or convey a feeling that key interest groups have already made up their minds. It is important that the process leave room for ideas and recommendations to emerge from consultations with the people, particularly certain sectors of society, such as those from rural areas, or marginalized women, or minorities, who may have little influence on the initial choosing of goals.

The Declaration provides a particularly clear orientation for a constitution. The goal of the Declaration is development, which is defined in the second paragraph of the Preamble as a "comprehensive economic, social, cultural and political process, which aims at the constant improvement of the well-being of the entire population and of all individuals on the basis of their active, free and meaningful participation in development and in the fair distribution of benefits resulting therefrom."[15] Human rights are the key to this view of development, and the Declaration identifies the denial of human rights as a "serious" obstacle to development. It requires that the approach to human rights be holistic, meaning that economic, social, and cultural rights must be given as much importance as civil and political. All human rights and fundamental freedoms are "indivisible and interdependent," and "equal attention and urgent consideration should be given to the implementation, promotion and protection of civil, political, economic, social and cultural rights." The promotion and protection of certain human rights and fundamental freedoms cannot justify the denial of other human rights and fundamental freedoms.

The agenda for reform includes taking all measures necessary for this development, particularly taking account of factors that lead to the denial of rights like poverty, corruption, and unequal distribution of resources. Since human rights and fundamental freedoms of all kinds are at the core of development, measures for their protection and enjoyment constitute the agenda for reform. A more specific agenda is set out in Article 8, under which states are required to take all necessary measures for the realization of the right to development. The state is to "ensure, *inter alia*, equality of opportunity for all in their access to basic resources, education, health services, food, housing, employment and the fair distribution of income." "Effective measures" that ensure an active role in the development process for women should also be undertaken. More broadly, Article 8.1 states that "appropriate economic and social reforms should be carried out with a view to eradicating all social injustices."

The aspect of human rights considered most immediately relevant to a constitution is participation in the electoral process — and thus, the requirement of a democratic order (whose specifics are left to the state concerned). Also included, however, are pre-requisites of democracy, such as the freedom of expression and the right of assembly and procession or marches. The freedom of conscience and belief, as well as the right to the use of one's language and the enjoyment of culture emphasize pluralism, which is an essential part of democracy. There is little explicit mention of transparency or accountability or the separation of powers, however (although the independence of the judiciary is an explicit requirement of due process and the protection of legal procedures and safeguards). Some regional instruments that require democracy permit a broader meaning of that concept, but these rights are directed at the restrictions of the powers of the state (although state's obligations demand an active role for the state in ensuring people's civil and political rights). The emphasis on protection and enforcement has focused attention on remedies, largely through the judicial process, and the courts have in recent decades elaborated principles and rules for the interpretation of rights and the lawful restrictions on rights. Otherwise, neither the formulation of rights nor the jurisprudence of courts has clear implications for the design of the state.

---

15   Preamble, para. 10; see also Articles 1 and 6.

In this respect, also, the Declaration goes beyond the other human rights instruments. By making human rights the principal basis of development, the Declaration makes the respect for rights the touchstone of the constitution, requiring all its provisions to conform to and facilitate human rights. Mention has already been made of the importance of participation in the making of constitutions, but under the Declaration participation also applies, even more strongly, to the conduct of state affairs, formulation of state policies, and the implementation of social justice, and therefore critical parts of the ongoing processes of the state. This has very clear implications for the design of state institutions, their representative character, modes of decision-making, and even accountability. In particular, the imperative of participation leads to the devolution of powers down to local and even village levels.

This imperative also leads to the recognition of a constitutional role for civic society organizations as a vehicle for popular participation. Political parties, highly manipulative and geared primarily toward gaining state power, generally discourage genuine participation when fearful of accountability. The importance placed by the Declaration on social, economic, and cultural rights also has a major relevance for the purposes of the state and defines an expansive role for it. Affirmative action mandated by the Declaration in order to increase women's participation in development can take many forms, including some forms of representation in the legislature and other state or private institutions. Additionally, the fair distribution of income and access to resources and opportunities require fundamental changes to the structure of the state, still marked by colonial features in numerous countries. In short, the Declaration seeks to make central what previously has been marginal. As we draw out some of the major implications of the Declaration in its theoretical and practical manifestations, it becomes clear that it is a truly revolutionary document, whose implications were perhaps not understood, and certainly not intended, by its proponents.

Some idea of the impact of human rights on constitutions can be obtained by examining the links between rights and poverty, links which are now well understood.[16] The essential purpose of human rights, a life lived in dignity, is rendered impossible by poverty. The daily struggles of the poor constantly humiliate them and remind them of their helplessness in the face of the state and economy. They constantly experience massive violations of their rights to health, education, shelter, and physical and moral security. The second link between rights and poverty is that the framework of human rights is essential to alleviate poverty. This framework alerts us to the real purpose of development, which is the achievement of all aspects of human development — the protection of entitlements to work, health, literacy, participation, a life in freedom, association, and solidarity. It reminds us of the obligations incumbent upon public authorities to secure policies and institutions in which these entitlements can be realized through the efforts of individuals, families, and communities. The framework also emphasizes the moral and legal duties of the

---

16 This and a few following paragraphs are adapted from my contribution to the report of the Commonwealth Human Rights Initiative, *Human Rights and Poverty Eradication: A Talisman for the Commonwealth* (New Delhi: CHRI, 2001), pp. 29-30.

global society to ensure a moral, political, and economic order in which all persons can live in dignity. It is based on the fundamental principle of equality of all human beings. It provides a balance between the different aspirations and interests of individuals and communities, and a way of reconciling them, thus preventing the lurches to extremes of economic or social policies or ideologies implicit in so much of the practices and justifications of globalization.

Human rights provide targets, benchmarks, and indicators for evaluation of social, economic, and political policies and the modalities of their implementation. It is becoming increasingly clear that development policies and allocation of resources that are not based on the framework of human rights are unlikely to advance human welfare or enhance social stability. Most analyses of contemporary ills and problems advocate as remedies democratization, equality, participation, and empowerment, as is evident from the resolutions of international conferences on women, children, population, and social development.[17]

As another example, through links between corruption and poverty, we can draw further inferences for constitutional engineering. Corruption threatens the very existence of the state as a viable community with collective goals and institutions. Corruption produces mafias, just as mafias fuel corruption and other illegal practices. In extreme cases, the writ of the state does not run in all its jurisdiction, as that jurisdiction is usurped by illegal organizations. Key politicians and business people become involved in commercial deals that may prevent policies to help the poor. Corruption depletes public revenues, which are siphoned off for private accumulation. It also weakens the capacity for revenue collection. Much of the money obtained through corruption flows out of the local economy and is deposited in foreign banks.

A great deal of the money acquired through corrupt means also feeds into and contaminates the political process. It undermines democracy, enhances corporations' influence over public affairs, and diminishes the value and integrity of the vote. In many places, corruption is tied to ethnicity and fuels the politics and practices of patronage (examples abound, including Kenya, India, Malaysia, and Papua New Guinea).[18] Typically, the result is an erosion of moral standards, to the point that the exposure of corruption has no effect on corrupt practices or the reputation of those involved in it. Under such circumstances, people readily experience a sense of hopelessness and cynicism. Corruption destroys trust between citizens and state and threatens the legitimacy of public power.

In all these ways, corruption negates the rights of the poor, depriving them of their right to participation and denying them access to economic and social welfare. Eliminating corruption and promoting good governance are crucial to developing an environment conducive to social, political, and economic development. A constitution must address corruption, as many constitutions are beginning to do.

---

17 Yash Ghai, *Human Rights and Social Development: Towards Democratisation and Social Justice* (Geneva: UNRISD, 2001), p. 45.
18 For a study of the impact of corruption on the operation of the Papua New Guinea Constitution, see Yash Ghai, "Securing a Liberal Democratic Order Through a Constitution: The Case of Papua New Guinea" 28 *Development and Change* (1997), pp. 303–330.

The Decomposition of the Post-Colonial State?

Thus, as argued above, the right to development requires a transformation of the post-colonial state, which is still rooted in the administrative structures and methods of colonialism, into a democratic and participatory state. Those administrative structures, however, are frequently captured and used by local elites who are more corrupt, and less inspired by any professional pride, than the colonial public service. The constitutional experience of many developing countries, particularly in Africa, shows the ineffectiveness of constitutional norms and the restrictions on power in the face of corrupt politicians and bureaucrats. A constitution which merely sets up the legislative and executive organs of the state and endows them with power is unlikely to bring about a fundamental change in policies and behavior.

A constitution must restructure state organs, provide for the vertical and horizontal dispersal of power, establish effective rules and institutions for accountability and integrity, and ensure real possibilities of the exercise and enforcement of rights. Above all, crucial to the transformation of politics is the empowerment of the people and their constant engagement in the affairs of the state. For these purposes both the process of devising a new constitutional order as well as its structures and contents are critical. But can the transformation be achieved? An examination of the constitution review process in Kenya, which had many of the hallmarks necessary to bring about a transformation, points to crucial answers to this question.[19]

The Kenyan Struggle to Achieve the Right to Development Through a Constitution

The demand for a new constitution in Kenya came from numerous social, political, religious, and professional groups, in a true sense representing a people's movement (although propelled by largely self-appointed leaders). It led to the vitalization of civil society and imbued religious and social organizations with a zeal for constitutional reform. Many initiatives were taken by civil society groups to mobilize the people and give some institutional form to the movement by providing platforms for national debates and fashioning alliances and consensus. Political rallies, suppressed under draconian laws or administrative caprice during the long years of a one-party rule, were revived, giving a sharp edge to protest and offering forums and discourses outside state institutions and laws, thereby delegitimizing them.

The state, however, had in fact little legitimacy. The demand for reform came because people attributed the ills of society and their own suffering to a perverted constitution which had disempowered them and facilitated the most capricious exercises of state authority. The background to the constitutional review lies in the last 40 years of Kenya's history. The Independence Constitution of 1963, bitterly negotiated and designed to promote democracy, human rights (including specially the rights of minorities), devolution of powers, and checks and balances, was amended over a period of only a few years, marking a return to the colonial state.

---

19 I was the chairperson of the Constitution of Kenya Review Commission as well as the Kenya National Constitutional Conference for the period of November 2000-June 2004.

These amendments dismantled freedoms and multi-party democracy, replaced the system for devolution of powers by a highly centralized administration, and modified the parliamentary system by grafting on a powerful and centralized presidential system, which was fuelled by patronage politics. The resources of the state (and to some extent of the private sector) were plundered by threats and corruption. Instead of protecting the public, the police became their oppressors. Many social groups and communities suffered discrimination and were marginalized, while others suffered privations because they were seen to be opposed to the government. Those who criticized the government were routinely detained or victimized by the abuse of legal process — and were in due course silenced.[20]

The institutions of the government and economy decayed under the shadow of a powerful president and his inner circle. There was no effective separation of powers. Parliament became ineffective. The principle of judicial independence was subverted and the courts subordinated to the executive. There were few institutions for accountability, such as an ombudsman, and those that did exist, such as the auditor-general, were rendered toothless. Public service or other state agencies were not readily accessible; merit as the criterion for appointment or promotion was replaced by political or ethnic connections, or monetary payments. The country experienced a sharp decline in its economy and a breakdown of its infrastructure; decreasing levels of production and export; an upsurge in illegal acquisition of huge tracts of land, often unutilised; and massive unemployment. People increasingly lost access to the basic necessities of life, while a few lived in unimaginable affluence. Guarantees of the security of person or business disappeared. Consequently, there was a massive retreat from public life, a lack of openness and trust, and pervasive fear, which drove many into exile.

The Reform Agenda

The agenda of reform was strongly influenced by this experience. Spurning the president's offer to appoint a group of foreign experts to write a new constitution, people wanted to control the process themselves to ensure that the outcome would reflect their own values and aspirations (which included participatory democracy, human rights, social justice, and basic needs). They achieved both of these objectives after a lengthy struggle and after elements of civil society had begun its own unofficial process of review.[21] Kenya had a highly participatory process (colloquially referred to as a "people-driven" process, symbolized by "Wanjiku," a woman's name — although used originally by President Moi in a derisory way to show the incompetence of the people). The law prescribed the accountability to the people of all or-

---

20   The background to the independence Constitution and the way it was gutted in later years are discussed in Y. P. Ghai and J. P. W. B. McAuslan, *Public Law and Political Change in Kenya: A Study of the Legal Framework of Government from Colonial Times to the Present* (Nairobi: Oxford University Press, 1970; reprinted with a new Introduction by Ghai, 2001).
21   The legal framework for the process was the Constitution of Kenya Review Act (hereafter "Review Act"), which incorporated the broad consensus on process and goals negotiated over several years through national conferences. The best account of the early stages of the reform movement is Willy Mutunga, *Constitution Making from the Middle: Civil Society and Transition Policies in Kenya, 1992-1997* (Harare and Nairobi: Mwengo and Sareat, 1999).

gans of review and required that the process be inclusive, accommodating the diversity of the people, "including socio-economic status, race, ethnicity, gender, religious faith, age, occupation, learning, persons with disabilities and the disadvantaged." People had to be provided "with an opportunity to actively, freely and meaningfully participate in generating and debating proposals to alter the Constitution." The final outcome must "faithfully" reflect the wishes of the people of Kenya.

The early stages of the process were managed by an organ that was intended to be independent, the Constitution of Kenya Review Commission (CKRC), appointed by Parliament so as to represent regions, gender, and social interests through members versed in the law or public affairs. For many months, the CKRC provided civic education to the people so that they could understand the process and its objectives as well as constitutional options to implement them. In cooperation with NGOs and other relevant groups, the CKRC prepared materials on Kenya's constitutional history and political system, incorporating concepts and ideas from other places. The Commission held many public meetings throughout the country and made extensive use of the media to reach all regions. Assisted by a lengthy questionnaire prepared by the CKRC, the people then submitted their recommendations. The public response, as well as that of numerous professional and social organizations, was overwhelming. The Commission then undertook a careful and detailed analysis of the recommendations before preparing its report and the draft constitution.

The draft constitution built on principles advanced by the people (and prescribed in the Review Act) and on detailed recommendations received by the Commission. Written in Swahili and English, and circulated and discussed widely throughout the country, the draft was generally received enthusiastically by the people. It was then submitted to the National Constitutional Conference (NCC), the most representative body ever assembled in Kenya (with 629 members, comprising all MPs, three representatives of each district, political parties, religious communities, women, professional associations, the disabled, NGOs, and other interests), whose responsibility was to debate and adopt the draft (with modifications if necessary). The NCC was required to make its decisions by consensus if possible; otherwise, decisions would be determined by the votes of two-thirds of its members. The NCC referred to a referendum "contentious" issues that did not receive the two-thirds vote. While the preceding stage of the process had produced considerable national consensus, the proceedings of the NCC turned out to be very fractious.

Politicians (particularly the previous opposition, now newly elected to power), who had hitherto largely ignored the process, became concerned about fundamental changes in values and structures of authority, especially the democratization of the political process. They also disagreed on the restructuring of the executive and the relationship between the center and provinces — in essence, it was a fight about the spoils of power. The national consensus developed previously through debates and public consultations seemed to unravel. The NCC nevertheless managed to adopt the draft constitution (in a somewhat modified form) by the requisite majority, despite bitter opposition from the president's faction in the cabinet.

Substantive Proposals

Before turning to an analysis of this story, it is necessary to describe the principal approach and provisions of the CKRC's draft, which survived, in its essentials, the decisions of the NCC. They represented the critical components of a constitution oriented to the right to development.

A shorter (and more accessible) form of the Commission's report[22] identified the principal points made by the people, and states them as follows:

- Give us the chance to live a decent life: with the fundamental needs of food, water, clothing, shelter, security and basic education met by our own efforts and the assistance of government

- We want a fair system of access to land for the future and justice for the wrongs of the past

- Let us have more control over the decisions which affect our lives, bring government closer to us — and let us understand better the decisions we can't make ourselves but affect us deeply

- We don't want power concentrated in the hands of one person

- We want our MPs to work hard, respect us and our views — and the power to kick them out if they don't

- We want to be able to choose leaders who have the qualities of intelligence, integrity and sensitivity which make them worthy of leading

- We want an end to corruption

- We want police who respect the citizens — and who can be respected by them

- We want women to have equal rights and gender equity

- We want children to have a future worth looking forward to — including orphans and street children

- We want respect and decent treatment for the disabled

- We want all communities to be respected and free to observe their cultures and beliefs

- We assert our rights to hold all sections of our government accountable — and we want honest and accessible institutions to ensure this accountability.[23]

These principles became the Commission's inspiration.[24] Fortunately, they were consistent with the goals of review prescribed in the Review Act: national unity,

---

22   The CKRC produced an enormous – indeed an excessive – amount of documentation. But the document that best captures the mood of the process and provides a concise summary of the process and the CKRC's recommendation is entitled, *The People's Choice: The Report of the Constitution of Kenya Review Commission – Short Version* (Nairobi: The Commission, September 18, 2002), hereafter the "*Short Version.*"
23   *Ibid.*, p. 8.
24   Referring to its travels around the country, the Commission wrote, "They knew, of course, that statistics showed that about 60% of Kenyans live below a poverty line [of US$1 a day]. They saw with their own eyes what this means and found the experience a humbling one. For they found people struggling with the lack of almost everything needed for a decent life, yet working hard, and asking not for 'handouts' but for the means to help themselves. They found people who, having so little, were most hospitable

note continues on following page

recognition of diversity, human rights, equality, basic needs, devolution and participation, democracy, governance, and the rule of law. It was clear that these objectives could not be achieved simply by improving the electoral system and having a stronger and a more comprehensive bill of rights. Unless the institutions of power — the executive, legislature, judiciary, and public service — were designed and structured to be "participation, human rights and democracy friendly," the bill of rights would remain a piece of paper (as was the experience with the old constitution).

The ambitious agenda of reform that emerged from consultations required that the state be equipped with power. Power without defined goals and acceptable procedures — and appropriate and effective accountability — however, could subvert the very purposes of the review and the aspirations of the people. It was necessary to examine every institution and procedure for their tendency to uphold or undermine fundamental constitutional principles and their disposition to fulfill their constitutional mandates.

Popular Participation

At the outset, it was obvious that the people would have to be empowered through the process. They had been forced into passive submission and docility as a result of years of authoritarianism, and without empowerment (and knowledge), they would be unable to mobilize the participatory and protective provisions of the constitution. After overcoming initial reluctance, they engaged enthusiastically and fully and gave a searing critique of existing institutions, policies, and personnel — to the considerable embarrassment of the government and their MPs.[25]

Participation, as a continuous process of engagement, in different capacities along with the affairs of the state, became an important concern of the Commission in the drafting of the constitution. They encouraged participation beyond a vote every five years, which Kenyans had already exercised regularly (in more or less free elections) for some years without any great advantage to themselves. Many people, therefore,

---

note continued from preceding page

to the Commission teams, and prepared to raise their eyes from the daily struggle to participate with enthusiasm in the process of review. And they found a nation which the existing system of government, and constitution, have grievously let down."

"For that 60% of the people, the dominant concern is what the Review Act calls 'basic needs'. The most basic of all is for food and water. From farmers, there were calls for irrigation so they could grow more crops – or grow crops at all. In many places there is no piped water, and women have to walk long distances each day to collect water in buckets. In many communities there is no form of health facility, not so much as a clinic – or there is a building with no nurse (a doctor within reach is a mere dream) and no drugs. There may be a school – but schools fees and other charges mean that many people cannot afford to send their children to it. Literacy and school attendance rates, instead of going up, have actually declined, and people who went to school many years ago complain that their grandchildren cannot go, even to primary school. A key to the improvement of the quality of life in many communities would be a road worth the name. But in many places roads, even in the dry season, are so bad that there is no way of getting crops to market, children to school, sick people to hospital – there were communities where people said the roads are so bad they can't even use a wheelbarrow to take sick people to a clinic. For many there is inadequate housing – either in a physical sense, or in the sense that they lack security because they are squatters, or because they have not received title deeds to land to which they are entitled" (*Short Version*, p. 8).

25 In the *Short Version*, the Commission says that the process is "more than merely agreeing on the terms of the new constitution. It is about self-discovery and identity. It is to give voice to the people and to affirm their sovereignty. It is to give them an opportunity to reflect on our national and constitutional history. It is also an audit on our state and government, the first truly popular assessment of the record of present and past administrations" (pp. 6 and 7).

sought the power to remove their MPs for failure to serve their constituents (a proposal that found favor with the Commission and appeared in the draft constitution). To resolve the conflict between a minister's constituency interests and national responsibilities, many suggested, and the Commission recommended, that ministers be drawn from outside the legislature.

Several other proposals encouraged public participation: Parliament was to promote participation in the legislative process by holding public hearings through committees; facilitate the submission of legislative proposals by non-members to the National Assembly; recognize the role of nongovernmental organizations as consultative or advisory bodies; encourage participation in state institutions or processes, including access to courts on public interest issues; recognize certain forms of community authority (for example, collective ownership and management of land, dispute settlement at local levels and increase participation through democratized political parties. The establishment of lower-level tiers of authority and strengthened rights of expression and association, as well as access to official information, would also facilitate public participation. The public had to be involved in the process whereby the government discharges its international obligations, particularly in respect of the implementation and observance of human rights treaties.

Representation

In institutional terms, it was essential to increase the representativeness, and therefore the responsiveness, of institutions of the state, which had effectively excluded women, social and ethnic minorities, and the disabled. An electoral system that guaranteed their representation became a major preoccupation of numerous organizations and think tanks and took up a great deal of the Commission's time. It opted for the mixed member proportional system (MMP), under which parties would have to rank members of these communities high up in their list of non-constituency candidates, which would secure not only their representation but also overall proportionality (although the NCC did not favor this approach, preferring to specifically set aside seats for them). The executive authorities were to be structured to increase participation and accountability (under which test the Kenyan presidency would have to go, as many Kenyans told us).

A collegial parliamentary system seemed better adapted to participation than the presidential, especially in a multi-ethnic country, with the president playing both a ceremonial role and that of the guardian of the constitutional order and legality. Such a system would establish a productive tension between different branches of the executive. Indirectly, it would also strengthen Parliament, as the prime minister would be dependent on (as well as be able to count on the support of) Parliament. Throughout Kenya's history as an independent state, Parliament has been subordinate to the executive, and several problems of accountability derived from this factor. As the new constitution was considered, it was recognized that a better balance between the legislature and executive was necessary. The Commission hoped to achieve this through the adoption of the cabinet system (with government ultimately responsible to the legislature), the appointment of ministers from outside Parliament, and the creation of a stronger committee system. The Commission also wanted to provide greater resources for Parliament, including control over its own calendar, taking away the executive's power to prorogue or dissolve the legislature, and giving Parliament the power to veto appointments to various state offices.

Participation as well as effectiveness required that legislative and executive powers be devolved to sub-national levels — perhaps the most widely expressed recommendation. The Commission recommended that power flow upwards rather than downwards, from the villages to the national capital, and it was at the village level that it saw the exercise of direct democracy and self-government. A system of devolution inevitably required some federal features, including divisions of powers and responsibilities and a second chamber that would represent regional interests at the center and forms of representation at local levels.

The Judiciary

It was widely recognized that the judiciary, even at the highest levels, was both corrupt and incompetent. Judges colluded with the executive to give decisions favorable to it; prosecution of persons out of favor was a common occurrence; and judges took massive bribes in private litigation. Prosecutions against members and friends of the regime were hardly ever instituted, however heinous the offence. Demands were made for the dismissal of all judges and for the constitution to provide for a new judicial system in which the judges would be appointed by an independent judicial service commission. Judges would have the security of tenure, but the judicial service commission would investigate complaints of misconduct. So serious and widespread were the complaints against judges that the CKRC commissioned a high-level committee of Commonwealth judges to advise it on provisions for the judiciary. The committee found the allegations justified and recommended that judges be invited to resign, failing which, inquiries should be held against individual judges for their removal.[26] The CKRC included this recommendation in its draft. These changes in the judiciary were to be accompanied by reforms of the legal system: an independent attorney-general, independent prosecutorial process, liberal rules of access to courts, and a new office, called the public defender, which would provide legal assistance and representation to those unable to afford legal services.

Accountability

A major theme of the draft was public accountability, to be secured in ways already mentioned, but also through a strong regime to control corruption and other forms of misconduct, especially in public office. All public office holders (including legislators and ministers) were to abide by a code of conduct (whose details were

---

26   *The Kenya Judiciary in the New Constitution: Report of the Advisory Panel of Eminent Commonwealth Judicial Experts* (Nairobi: CKRC, May 2002). The Panel said that almost everyone who addressed them (this included leaders of the legal profession, NGOs, senior business people, and judges, who met the Panel surreptitiously) that the judiciary practiced two principal forms of corruption: taking bribes and taking orders from the government. "The Panel was shocked and dismayed by the widespread allegations of corruption in the Kenya Judiciary. While many of Kenya's judges continue to fulfil their judicial office faithfully to their judicial oath, public confidence in the independence and impartiality of the Judiciary has virtually collapsed" (p. 17).

specified in a schedule); the implementation and supervision of the code would be the responsibility of an independent commission. A commission on human rights and administrative justice would investigate complaints of maladministration (the bill of rights includes a new right, that to "administrative justice") and violations of human rights. The draft required new legislation to give the people the right to information held by the government: it requires the government to disseminate information of public interest and concern to the people (a provision directed in part at the culture of government secrecy and the frequent refusal of the government to publish reports of commissions of inquiries).

Beyond Institutional Reform

These reforms dealt with state power and institutions. The draft constitution also wanted to grant a significant role to organizations outside the state structures. A very critical factor was the democratization of political parties. Parties in Kenya have tended to be either ethnic associations or, more frequently, personal fiefdoms. They have not facilitated public participation or debate; they have seldom decided on policies; and they rarely have a role outside elections. The draft contained wide-ranging rules on the registration and supervision of political parties in order to increase their role in a democratic society, encourage them to expand the presence of women and other disadvantaged groups, and make these parties more responsible. In return, they would be entitled to state funding.

The greater recognition of Kenya's ethnic diversity would also create an opportunity for communities to pursue their goals through instituting a variety of measures, including encouraging the expression of their culture and languages, adopting laws about the family, and in some instances, recognizing communal ownership and management of land and other resources.

A second element in this strategy was to insulate the exercise of certain sensitive state powers and functions from direct political control and manipulation, including such functions as the conduct of elections, the audit of government accounts, the integrity of the budgetary process, the protection of the environment, management of public land, central banking, and receiving and dealing with complaints. These functions were to be vested in independent commissions and officers, and their independence and resources were to be constitutionally guaranteed.

The scope of the draft constitution goes beyond institutional factors. It mandates that state power be exercised for specified purposes, and it establishes a broad agenda for reform (reflecting to a significant degree distrust of politicians). First, it contains a chapter on National Goals, Values and Principles, which include social justice and basic needs, gender and inter-generational equity, public participation, democracy and transparency of government affairs, and promotion of civil society. Second, the draft contains a strong bill of rights, which aims to secure some balance between individual and group rights and protects the cultural and linguistic rights of minorities. It imposes obligations on the state for affirmative action. It also establishes mechanisms of enforcement. Third, various chapters start off with goals specific to their subject: devolution, land, and environmental policies, for example.

Finally, knowing the far-reaching nature of its approach and the provisions of the draft, the CKRC gave considerable thought to its implementation. It sets out in detail legislative and administrative measures that must be taken (and who must take them) over a period of five years following the adoption of the constitution. An independent commission would be appointed for this period to facilitate and oversee this timetable. Parliament would provide the public with periodic progress reports.

The CKRC was aware that this was a very ambitious constitution, seeking to bring fundamental changes in goals, structures, and the mode of exercising power. Its mandate, to review the existing constitution in light of the goals set out in the Review Act and the views of the people, could have led to less ambitious recommendations, by merely remedying the defects of that constitution. It became clear early on, however, that the constitution was perceived to have such major faults that a new constitution would be necessary.

The Path to Adoption

In order to prepare for the consideration of a totally new system, the CKRC then undertook a massive program to disseminate its report and recommendations and provide critics with opportunities to articulate their reservations. These steps were critical to generate public understanding and support for these proposals, for it seemed likely that politicians would not like some provisions (particularly those dealing with structures and procedures for exercise of state power). The NCC endorsed the approach of the draft and most of its provisions, adding some of its own, particularly on culture. Most of the opposition was orchestrated by politicians, either together as a social and economic class or as factions, assessing their prospects of access to power. MPs disqualified from being appointed ministers or potentially recalled by their constituents for failure to discharge their responsibilities were among those most adversely affected by the draft, and these elements disappeared at the NCC.

The CKRC draft, although widely welcomed and endorsed by the Kenyan people, became a source of contention and acrimony. In its final stages, the NCC was increasingly split along ethnic lines and was marked by bitter controversy among the key factions of the government. Politicians appeared to others to act in a most irresponsible manner, concerned only with their narrow interests. Religious groups, influenced by political factions of similar ethnicity, argued (the ostensible issue being the constitutional recognition of Kadhi courts). Civil society and NGOs failed to play the constructive role that was expected of them, although they had done so in earlier stages of the process. Women alone maintained a relatively united front, at least on gender issues.

Controversies that fragmented the NCC became even more bitter and fractious after the adoption of the draft constitution. The minister for justice and constitutional affairs, who had led the boycott of the NCC by the presidential faction in a provocative walk out, hijacked the review process. It was a complete turn about by him and President Mwai Kibaki, who, when in opposition, had campaigned for a severe diminution of presidential powers. Confident of a parliamentary majority, they gave carte blanche to the National Assembly to change the decisions of the NCC (thus upsetting the carefully negotiated terms of the political settlement of the 1990s on the mode of replacement of the old constitution).

The president's main aim was to retain the powerful presidency and the centralization of power in the national government. The revised draft that the president's supporters introduced also took away the proposal to set up a second chamber, which parliamentarians of all hues saw as a diminution of their own powers. The post-NCC discussions and decisions became an affair only for political parties, completely excluding other sectors of society.

The Review Act provided for the actual enactment of the constitution by the National Assembly, but its powers were restricted solely to a yes (by two-thirds) or a no vote. The government refused to follow this procedure and initiated moves to subvert the constitution, implicating the judiciary, the CKRC, and various social and religious groups. Some sort of consensus among political groups would seem to emerge (to capture the process in the common interests of politicians) and then collapse, repeatedly. Several provisions of the draft constitution critical to the right to development project were eliminated in the so-called consensus-building process (confined to political parties). The most important of these changes were the reversion to an executive presidency, with little accountability to the public, and less to parliament than even in the current constitution, and the reversion to a high degree of concentration of power in the central government. The manner in which the president and his faction highjacked and subverted the process was also greatly resented by the people. So when the new document was put to the people in a referendum on the 21 November 2005, it was roundly defeated, only one province out of 8 voting in favour. The defeat of president's draft means that the process has to be resumed in a form yet to be determined (as of December 2005).

Understanding the Obstacles

The values and goals explicit and implicit in the right to development have wide appeal to the people of the less developed parts of the world. The terms of reference of constitution review bodies as well as recommendations made by the people are concerned primarily with social justice, basic needs, affirmative action, participation, and integrity. At the raw edge of the economy, they do not extol markets or globalization or the user-payer principle; instead, they want equity. Excluded from all decision-making, they want local forms of self-government. Exploited by politicians and bureaucrats, they want integrity and efficiency in public life. Above all, they want a life of dignity and recognition of their personal worth and their respective cultures. Constitution makers realize that a document that does not respond to these concerns of the people may suffer from a legitimacy deficit. But constitution makers who themselves do not favor these goals generally place them as aspirations, in the chapter on general principles or directives of state policy, lacking legal effect. The substantive provisions — the allocation of power and the mode of its exercise — may bear little relationship to the principles. South Africa, on the whole, avoids grand statements; instead, the constitution weaves these goals into the substantive provisions. The Kenya draft does both: it has a rather long set of principles, but many of them are the subject of separate chapters or sections with binding effect.

These provisions are easy to envisage and formulate. A number of constitutions contain such provisions, and in some cases their implications have been elaborated in judicial decisions. Kenyans looked for inspiration, not so much for ideas as for text, to India, South Africa, and Spain, among other countries. It is when principles are transformed into binding provisions that they can become the source of controversy. This was the experience in Kenya, where the draft provided a large measure of executive and legislative accountability, extensive sharing of power, public participation, and economic and social rights. Nothing demonstrated the clash between the people and their representatives better than the struggle to retain or remove these provisions, which was fought out, first in the NCC and later in the National Assembly.

The goals and values explicit in the draft generally went unchallenged, but institutional structures raised numerous questions; in other words, the controversy was about who would exercise power and how, rather than for what purposes power would be exercised. Perhaps the politicians realised that once they were in power, there would be no effective controls on how power is exercised. What the politicians seemed to have grasped was that the rules governing access to power and the institutions for the exercise of power were likely to be more immediately operative than the values inscribed in the constitution.

The nature and degree of public participation undoubtedly had a profound impact on the process. Their participation enlarged the agenda of reform and turned an elite affair into a national enterprise. It facilitated efforts to redefine politics and political process (and indeed substituted for ordinary politics). For nearly the first time since independence, the people had engaged in "rational" and discursive politics and focused on issues other than ethnicity. Their involvement promoted conversations not only between the people and the commission, but also among the people themselves. It produced firm articulation of the interests of groups based on non-ethnic affiliations (for example, trade unions versus employers, rural versus urban, tradition versus modernity, and pastoral versus settled communities) Discourse among the people made them aware of the histories, contributions, anxieties, and aspirations of others, deepening understandings that are so critical to developing national identity and unity, along with a sense of justice. This approach facilitated the CKRC task of balancing different interests. In turn, it also gave considerable legitimacy to the process, (which frustrated the efforts of the faction around President Kibaki to dilute the draft).

To make participation effective, it was necessary to visit all parties of the country and hold many meetings with the people. This procedure highlighted a paradox: many countries with a poorly developed culture of democracy (for example, Uganda, Ethiopia, and Thailand) often have had the most participatory processes that have engaged all segments of the population. This becomes necessary due to the absence of effective intermediary institutions, such as political parties, trade unions, NGOs, and social groups.

Unfortunately, such a process does not usually lead to institutionalization, so participation may fail to produce long-term change or established social forces. Once the formal structures and procedures of the process are dismantled, the situation can easily turn to "politics" as usual, with people being marginalized once again. This happened with reform attempts in the 1980s, when political parties hijacked the process and moved it to parliament (well illustrated in Mutunga's study).[27] This time, however, it appears that it has not been as easy for politicians to hijack the process, both because participation itself vested the process with great legitimacy and because the last word lay with the people in the referendum.

The above reflections show the need for structured participation and for an agency with responsibility to turn people's views into legal text. These were initially the responsibility of the CKRC, whose draft was originally regarded as a successful reflection of people's views. Where Kenyans were not in agreement, it produced a reasonable balancing and a measure of consensus. The document was relatively coherent; above all, it provided a basis on which the NCC could debate the issues. If the NCC had started from scratch, consensus of any kind would have been infinitely more difficult. The NCC was conceived of as a negotiating body. It was a microcosm of the nation, with multiple bases of representation that brought to it opposing interests elected directly by their constituencies and organizations: failed, current, and aspiring politicians; women versus elderly men from the districts; local politicians versus national politicians; internationalists and parochialists; and the religious and the more secular. Considering the scale of the divergences, delegates, guided by the CKRC draft, were generally able to resolve differences, and indeed, showed great consideration for other groups, particularly women, minorities, and the disabled.

The greatest difficulties attended issues of political power because they were based on politicians' personal ambitions rather than on principles. Most parliamentarians perceived their role as politicians operating at the national level, concerned about preserving the centrality and monopolies of national level institutions. They showed remarkably little concern for policy issues, although these were a dominant feature of the draft. They were not very concerned about the role, authority, and procedures of the National Assembly, either, which the draft sought to strengthen. Political parties failed to provide leadership or cohesion and advanced few proposals. The Kenya African National Union (KANU), allegedly the most trans-tribal party of all parties, did not even try to present a united position. To some extent, parliamentarians were united by their interests as a class, which coalesced around ministerial ambitions, parliamentary privileges, and the absence of accountability to their constituencies. For similar reasons, they opposed independent commissions that took specific responsibilities away from politicians.

---

27 The legal framework for the process was the Constitution of Kenya Review Act (hereafter "Review Act"), which incorporated the broad consensus on process and goals negotiated over several years through national conferences.

Despite these strong bonds, major political factions remained divided by personal agendas. A principal effect of politicians' involvement was to ethnicize a process that had, up to then, remained surprisingly free of ethnic politics and had focused on issues that transcended ethnic concerns. This was manifested most dramatically during night meetings involving politicians representing their own ethnic groups in order to bolster their own positions. The process was also similarly affected by the manner in which caucusing was conducted, which generally took place in regional (that is, ethnic) tents, thereby contributing to the fragmenting of civil society and other non-political groups. The ethnic factor also undermined the ability of political parties to provide leadership and cohesion to the NCC. Curiously, ethnic issues as such (for example, land distribution, patronage style of administration, affirmative action, or linguistic identity) played only a minor role in the debates. Politicians succeeded in casting the matter in terms of their own ethnic group's access to power (one group, for example, opposed dual nationality because it believed that there were more Kenyans overseas who belonged to a rival ethnic group!).

It was clear in the submissions to the CKRC that most communities had realized that their own economic and social positions were unaffected merely through the domination of government by the members of their community. Yet at the NCC, every delegate was in a sense a "leader" and had aspirations and expectations of office or other advantages if their "community" controlled the government. They were therefore particularly susceptible to "ethnic" appeals or lobbying. The closing and decisive stages of the NCC were characterized by ferocious debates rooted in ethnic (and derivatively, religious) divisions.

The last point shows that the blessings of a participatory process are mixed. It also demonstrates that constitution making is a highly political process. It can of course be a political process in a positive sense — that of deliberation and principled negotiations, agreeing and committing to national goals and integration, defining the moral responsibility of leadership, and laying the foundations of freedom and social justice. This is indeed the way in which many stakeholders and participants perceive the process. The other sense of "political" that dominated the Kenyan process was crass, concerned with maximizing the advantages to a particular group, motivated by the desire to aggrandise power, driven by a degree of ruthlessness, and based not on consensus but on coercion or corruption.

The somewhat undignified conclusion to the work of the NCC reawakened the controversy stirred by President Moi in the 1980s, when he advocated the preparation of a draft by a team of experts and derided the capacity of "Wanjiku" to participate in such an exercise. The government of his successor, then strongly committed to a people-driven process, now proposed the premature dissolution of the NCC and its replacement by a team of experts, which would produce the draft for consideration by the National Assembly.

Although President Kibaki's close associates preferred this approach because they realized that they enjoyed little support in the NCC, it won support within some sectors that were by then somewhat disillusioned by the fractious, often unruly, proceedings of the NCC. Delegates squandered some of the legitimacy that the NCC had begun with, by demanding what seemed to the public to be large allowances for attendance and expenses. In televised broadcasts they were shown as rowdy and intolerant of opposing views and not particularly well versed in constitutional issues. There was some playing to the gallery, inspired by the presence of television cameras, which intensified the tendency toward intransigence and extremism. Delegates paid little regard to professional advice and insisted on actually doing the drafting rather than making decisions. Because they distrusted politicians, they incorporated into the draft many matters that should have been left to future governments and parliaments and included details that would have been better dealt with by statute. These inclusions greatly increased the length and complexity of the document and introduced inconsistencies and a few unworkable provisions that opened the draft to public and professional criticism — and the delegitimizing of the NCC.

Hence, the careful balancing of the CKRC draft was to some extent upset by the decisions of delegates, and attempts to fashion a new consensus were sabotaged by politicians. The CKRC was not able to play the role of the honest broker and promote compromises because several of its members had aligned themselves with one of the two major protagonists. These commissioners, many of whom had little legal expertise, had allowed themselves to be used by politicians from the very beginning of the process. The CKRC was, justifiably, perceived to be neither independent nor expert — two qualities that were critical to success in a participatory process. Experts could have provided a basis for consensus by searching for common ground and could have introduced greater coherence and technical improvements in the draft. The problem of developing a consensus if multiple interests are represented remains an issue for exploration and may suggest other approaches to a constitution.

These difficulties were compounded by the bifurcation in the procedure for adopting the constitution. Due to political compromises in the 1990s between President Moi, who wanted a restricted and closed process, and the opposition, who agitated for a participatory process and a constituent assembly, the Review Act provided that the draft must be adopted by the NCC by a vote of two-thirds of its members and then enacted by the National Assembly. The dynamics of the process were such that those who enjoyed popular support wanted to minimize the role of the Assembly, and those who considered that they had a parliamentary majority aimed to expand the role of the Assembly. The Kibaki faction that had walked out of the NCC did so because of its strategy to remove key decisions to the Assembly against the scheme and provisions of the Review Act. The government, in fact, hijacked the participatory process, emasculated the more radical provisions of the draft, and restored a centralized, presidential system. So far, in a contest between politicians and civil society, politicians have shown themselves to be less trustworthy than the latter (to a large extent because politicians control the resources of the state and its institutions, which are central to control and accumulation, as well as the inadequate democratization of society). Politicians are also more adroit at manipulating the ethnic factor.

Conclusions

Two comments are immediately relevant. The first is that the procedure for adopting and enacting the constitution that vests the final decision in a representative body can, paradoxically detract from the participation of the people. The second is that participation cannot be used to ensure legitimacy for the process if the people feel that they have been marginalized, or even worse, that they have become the victims of a fraud. This much is evident from the defeat of the Kibaki draft in the referendum. But in principle it is doubtful if a referendum, which would otherwise give the people the final say, is desirable in a divided society, as it might reflect and reinforce the divisions.

I do not mean to suggest that the Kenya process is typical of a participatory process, even though it might have lessons for other countries (and certainly for its own future efforts at constitution making). The importance of the context cannot be overrated. But Kenya does illustrate the extremely political nature of constitution making, however much the process may have been designed to ensure a measure of rationality and the participation of the people. Politicians will always claim a special purchase on the process, and will generally succeed. It is also necessary to ponder on the strategies of getting better results from participation and on the kinds of contribution that people can best qualified to make.

These are not easy questions, as the purpose of the process may transcend the immediate task at hand — getting a new constitution. A new constitution needs fertile ground in which to flourish, and participation can provide that fertility. Even if no constitution or suitable constitution is adopted, however, the process may succeed if it creates a consciousness and empowerment that changes the relationship between the state and civil society, generates ideas and defines aspirations, and lays the foundation for future reform. The tension between politicians and other groups can at times be productive, regardless of immediate outcomes. Another issue that is also critical is the implementation of a progressive constitution. The contemporary world is a graveyard of excellent constitutions. Few constitution-making processes or constitutions provide adequate framework for enforcement, but unfortunately, this issue cannot be explored here.

Regarding the right to development, we can conclude that its vision is inspiring and that it is not difficult to turn that vision into a legal text, but resistance to that vision and text is quite likely to come from vested interests. Opponents of the Kenya draft were in large part motivated to maintain their purchase on the state (the principal means of wealth accumulation). Their primary concern was therefore with the structure of the state and the possibilities of plundering its resources, along with minimizing effective mechanisms of accountability. In other countries with more developed market economies and class formations, a right to development constitution would be resisted for its emphasis on social justice and redistribution, ceilings on land holding, the strict regime of environmental protection, and similar approaches. In Kenya itself, groups (local and foreign business communities and foreign states as well) would also have resisted the implementation of many of its provisions geared toward social justice. In this case, the opportunity to incorporate into the constitution the vision that the right to development inspires was squandered. But the earnest way in which ordinary Kenyans engaged in the referendum campaign and their determination to enact the constitution as approved by the national constitutional conference gives room for optimism. The participatory process had empowered them and they had developed a vision of Kenya which they were not willing to give up on. Perhaps the very hijacking of the people's draft reinforced their resolve to continue the fight for a just constitution, and their right to development.

9 | Making a Difference: Human Rights and Development — Reflecting on the South African Experience

Sandra Liebenberg

Human rights lawyers, like other progressives, too often frame the issue dichotomously: Law either makes all the difference or no difference at all.[1]

Introduction

> We therefore, through our freely elected representatives, adopt this Constitution as the supreme law of the Republic so as to — Heal the divisions of the past and establish a society based on democratic values, social justice and fundamental human rights . . . Improve the quality of life of all citizens and free the potential of each person.[2]

Even a cursory reading of the 1996 South African Constitution reveals the ambitious role it envisages for the law in contributing to far-reaching socioeconomic transformation in South Africa. In the words of Justice Kriegler of the Constitutional Court:

> We do not operate under a constitution in which the avowed purpose of the drafters was to place limitations on governmental control. Our constitution aims at establishing freedom and equality in a grossly disparate society.[3]

Nowhere is this more evident than in the inclusion in the Bill of Rights of a full range of justiciable socio-economic and cultural rights alongside traditional civil rights and liberties, as well as rights designed to ensure transparency and accountability in the exercise of public power.[4]

This integrated approach to human rights was informed by the experience of South Africa's colonial and apartheid history. Black communities were not only deprived of their political and civil rights, but also systematically dispossessed of land and housing and deprived of access to a range of social services, such as education, health care, food, water, and social security.[5] Confining the Bill of Rights in South Africa's first democratic constitution to civil and political rights and the protection

---

1   R. L. Abel, *Politics by Other Means: Law in the Struggle against Apartheid*, 1980–1994 (New York: Routledge, 1995), p. 549.

2   Preamble to the Constitution of the Republic of South Africa (Act 108 of 1996), (hereafter, "the Constitution").

3   *Du Plessis v. De Klerk*, 1996 (5) BCLR 658 (CC) at para. 147.

4   The latter rights include the right of access to information (s. 32) and the right to administrative justice (s. 33).

5   The Truth and Reconciliation Commission process has been criticized for its failure to deal with the systemic social and economic injustices perpetrated against the black population by both the state and private sector under apartheid. See the discussion in S. Terreblanche, *A History of Inequality in South Africa 1652–2002* (Scottsville: University of Natal Press & KMM Review Publishing, 2002), pp. 124-132.

of private property rights would have entrenched existing inequalities and frustrated the reconstruction and development of the society.[6] Thus, it was hoped that socio-economic rights would facilitate the new government's avowed commitment to people-centered development.[7] Perhaps more significantly, however, it was envisaged that the inclusion of socio-economic rights in the Bill of Rights would help empower disadvantaged groups, particularly those living in poverty, to protect and advance their fundamental interests in the process of development.[8] In this way the South African Constitution came to embrace a holistic and interdependent concept of human rights.[9]

Another innovative feature of the Bill of Rights is its express application of the rights not only to relations between the citizen and the state, but to private persons and entities.[10] Thus human rights norms are applicable in all spheres where disparate power relations have the potential to undermine human rights. This concern is particularly pressing in the South African context given the apartheid era's legacy of social and economic inequality.[11]

---

6   Petition to the Constitutional Assembly by the Ad Hoc Committee for the Campaign for Social and Economic Rights, July 1995. Extracts from this influential petition are reproduced in S. Liebenberg and K. Pillay, *Socio-Economic Rights in South Africa: A Resource Book* (Cape Town: Community Law Centre, UWC, 2002), p. 19.

7   The Reconstruction and Development Programme (RDP) Base Document was adopted by the ANC shortly before the April 1994 election as its basic policy framework for overcoming the legacies of apartheid. The RDP White Paper was adopted in September 1994, which aimed at creating "a people-centered society which measures progress by the extent to which it has succeeded in securing for each citizen liberty, prosperity and happiness." RDP White Paper 4, section 1.1.1. See discussion on the RDP by H. Marais, *South Africa: Limits to Change – the Political Economy of Transformation* (Kenwyn: University of Cape Town Press, and London and New York: Zed Books Ltd., 1998), Chapter 8

8   In their Petition to the Constitutional Assembly (*supra*, note 6), a broad range of civil society organizations asserted their belief that "[t]he most disadvantaged sectors of our society should be granted every available means to protect and progressively realise these individual and collective human rights in South Africa." They called on the Constitutional Assembly to "[e]nsure that the most disadvantaged members of our society may progressively realise their basic human rights through the highest law of our land – the South African Constitution."

9   "Interdependence" embraces the notion that human rights should be treated holistically in order to ensure human survival and development. Craig Scott writes: "The term interdependence attempts to capture the idea that values seen as directly related to the full development of personhood cannot be protected and nurtured in isolation." "The Interdependence and Permeability of Human Rights Norms: Towards a Partial Fusion of the International Covenants on Human Rights," *Osgoode Hall Law Journal* 27/ 769 (1989), p. 886. South Africa has also ratified a host of international human rights treaties, including the International Covenant on Civil and Political Rights (1966), the Convention on the Elimination of All Forms of Racial Discrimination (1966), the Convention on the Elimination of All Forms of Discrimination against Women (1979), the Convention on the Rights of the Child (1989), the African Charter on Human and Peoples' Rights (1981), the African Charter on the Rights and Welfare of the Child (1990), the Protocol to the African Charter on Human and Peoples' Rights on the Establishment of an African Court on Human and Peoples' Rights (1988), and the Protocol to the African Charter on Human and Peoples' Rights on the Rights of Women in Africa (2003) Curiously, although South Africa signed the International Covenant on Economic, Social and Cultural Rights (1966) [ICESC] in 1994, it has to date failed to ratify this major human rights treaty.

10   Section 8 (1) provides that the Bill of Rights applies "to all law," encompassing both statutory and common law. Section 8 (2) states that "[a] provision of the Bill of Rights binds a natural or a juristic person if, and to the extent that, it is applicable taking into account the nature of the right and the nature of any duty imposed by the right."

11   As the late Mahomed DP wrote in *Du Plessis v. De Klerk*, 1996 (5) BCLR 658 (CC) (dealing with the application provisions in the interim (1993) Constitution):

> Black persons were previously denied the right to own land in 87% of the country. An interpretation of the Constitution which continued to protect the right of private persons substantially to perpetuate such unfairness by entering into contracts or making dispositions subject to the condition that such land is not sold to or occupied by Blacks would have been for me a very distressing conclusion. These and scores of other examples leave me no doubt that those responsible for the enactment

note continues on following page

The right to development has been conceptualized as the right to a particular process of development in which all human rights can be fully realized. It thus encompasses both a process that is consistent with human rights norms, and the achievement of the goal of full realization of human rights. One of its primary values lies in promoting an integrated vision of human rights, which includes both civil and political rights as well as economic, social, and cultural rights. The significance of this concept lies in ensuring that the interests of disadvantaged groups are not marginalized in the development processes.

This chapter reflects on aspects of the South African experience of a rights-based approach to development which, as I have highlighted, is constitutionally mandated. It will do so by examining the evolving jurisprudence of the Constitutional Court, the work of the South African Human Rights Commission, the integration of human rights principles in legislation, policies, and budgetary processes, and their influence on citizen participation and mobilization. The focus will be on socio-economic rights, given the relative novelty of their constitutional protection as fully justiciable rights, and the dearth of scholarship on the role that they can play in facilitating the redress of economic deprivation and inequality within the processes of development.[12] Any discussion of the right to development or human rights in development must consider how socio-economic rights can be realized in practice and integrated in the work of institutions and organizations concerned with the protection and promotion of human rights. This chapter will discuss illustrative case studies of the influence of human rights on developmental processes in South Africa without purporting to be a comprehensive analysis of the subject.

In this undertaking I am conscious of the tendency of human rights lawyers to claim too much for the law and legal institutions, which are constrained as much by their own institutional limitations[13] as by the political and economic context in which they operate. Nevertheless, the South African experience thus far suggests that integrated, justiciable human rights guarantees can provide the poor and marginalized with opportunities to assert their needs and interests in developmental processes.[14]

---

continued from preceding page

of the Constitution never intended to permit the privatisation of Apartheid or to allow the unfair gains of Apartheid or the privileges it bestowed on the few, or the offensive attitudes it generated amongst any to be fossilized and protected by courts rendered impotent by the language of the Constitution. (para. 85).

12   Socio-economic rights have traditionally been marginalized within human rights discourses. Even when they are affirmed rhetorically, they still do not enjoy the same level of protection as civil and political rights. For example, they are not subject to individual complaints procedures (for example, the ICESCR) or are excluded from domestic constitutions (for example, the U.S. and Canada), or subject to weaker forms of judicial protection (for example, Directive Principles of State Policy in the Indian, Irish, and Namibian Constitutions). See further in this regard: S. Liebenberg (2001), "The Protection of Economic and Social Rights in Domestic Legal Systems," in A. Eide, C. Krause, and A. Rosas (eds.), *Economic, Social and Cultural Rights: A Textbook* (Dordrecht/Boston/London: Martinus Nijhoff Publishers, second revised edition, 2001), p. 55.

13   In the *TAC* case, note 35, below, the Court was explicit about its institutional constraints in rejecting the attempts of the amici curiae to persuade it to interpret the socio-economic rights provisions in sections 26 and 27 of the Constitution to incorporate a minimum core obligation (see paras. 37-38).

14   According to Article 2(1) of the UN Declaration on the Rights to Development (1986): "The human person is the central subject of development and should be the active participant and beneficiary of the right to development."

The Social and Economic Context

The President of the Constitutional Court, Judge Chaskalson, graphically described the socio-economic conditions in South Africa in the *Soobramoney* case:

> We live in a society in which there are great disparities in wealth. Millions of people are living in deplorable conditions and in great poverty. There is a high level of unemployment, inadequate social security, and many do not have access to clean water, or to adequate health services. These conditions already existed when the Constitution was adopted and a commitment to address them, and to transform our society into one in which there will be human dignity, freedom and equality, lies at the heart of our new constitutional order. For as long as these conditions continue to exist that aspiration will have a hollow ring.[15]

It is estimated that 18 million people in South Africa, representing 45 percent of the population, live below the poverty line, according to an absolute measure of poverty, pegged at an income per adult of R353 per month. Of these, 10 million people live in "ultra-poor" households earning less than R193 per month, per adult.[16] Poverty in South Africa has strong racial, gender, age, and spatial (rural/provincial) dimensions.[17] South Africa has a high rate of structural unemployment[18] and is ranked as one of the most unequal societies in the world in terms of income inequalities.[19] Land distribution can play a major role in human development, particularly in rural areas where "it can contribute to sustainable livelihoods, food, security and an asset base for rural households."[20] However, the pace of land reform has been slow.[21] The situation of poverty is aggravated by the AIDS pandemic, which is taking a severe toll on the social and economic fabric of society.[22]

---

15 *Soobramoney v Minister of Health, KwaZulu-Natal*, 1997 (12) BCLR1696 (CC), para. 8.
16 United Nations Development Programme (UNDP) (principal author: V. Taylor), *South Africa: Transformation for Human Development* (2000), p. 55. The World Bank uses a relative measure of poverty in terms of which the poorest 40% of households are classified as poor, and the poorest 20% as "ultra poor." According to this definition, 53% of the South African population are poor, and 29% are ultra-poor: World Bank, *Key Indicators of Poverty in South Africa* (1995), p. 8. According to another study, although South Africa is an upper-middle-income country in per capita terms, most households experience either outright poverty or vulnerability to poverty: J. May (ed.), *Poverty and Inequality in South Africa*, Report prepared for the Office of the Executive Deputy President and the Inter-Ministerial Committee for Poverty and Inequality, (Durban: Praxis Publishing, 1998), p. 1.15
17 UNDP, *Ibid.*, pp. 55-56.
18 The official employment statistics (as of September 2005) put the official national rate of unemployment at 27.7 %. According to the expanded definition, the unemployment rate rises to 38.9%. The expanded definition includes discouraged work seekers (those who said they were unemployed but had not taken active steps to find work in the four weeks prior to the interview). Statistics SA, Statistical release P0210, Labour Force Survey September 2005 (September 2005) (available at www.statssa.gov.za). Unemployment statistics obscure significant aspects of the nature of employment in South Africa. This includes the related phenomena of the 'working poor' earning very low wages, the decline in formal sector employment, and the growth of non-standard forms of employment characterised by low wages, minimal benefits, and no security. See J. Theron, "Employment is not what it used to be: The nature and impact of the restructuring of work in South Africa" in E. Webster and K. Von Holdt (eds.), *Beyond the Apartheid Workplace* (Scottsville: University of KwaZulu-Natal Press, 2005).
19 By 1996, the poorest quintile of the population received 1.5% of total income, compared to 65% received by the richest quintile, according to UNDP, *supra*, note 16, p. 64.
20 *Ibid.*, p. 59.
21 See E. Lahiff and S. Rugege, "A Critical Assessment of Land Redistribution Policy in the Light of the Grootboom Judgment," *Law, Democracy and Development* 6 (2002), p. 279.
22 The HIV prevalence for 2005 for persons between the age group 15–49 is at 15.6%: O. Shisana et al., *South African National HIV Prevalence, HIV Incidence, Behaviour and Communications Survey*, 2005

note continues on following page

In 1996 the government adopted a macro-economic strategy entitled Growth, Employment and Redistribution (GEAR), which attracted substantial criticism from civil society movements in South Africa.[23] Critics claim that the strategy represented a retreat from the people-orientated development policy of The Reconstruction and Development Programme (RDP). Instead, faith was placed in the "trickle down" effects of economic growth, including job creation. This growth was to be achieved by creating an optimal climate for private investment through placing strict limits on state spending and economic intervention.[24] It has been argued that the GEAR strategy failed to meet many of its targets, particularly in the sphere of substantially reducing unemployment.[25]

Nevertheless, the democratic government has made progress in socio-economic development through improving basic service delivery.[26] There are also recent indications that the government is ameliorating some of the targets of its GEAR policy and envisaging a more active role for the state in redistribution.[27]

---

note continued from preceding page

(Cape Town: HSCR Press, 2005). According to an official study by Statistics South Africa, there was a 57% increase in deaths in South Africa from 1997 to 2002. This provides indirect evidence of the impact of the HIV epidemic on mortality levels in South Africa: Statistics South Africa, *Mortality and Causes of Death in South Africa, 1997–2003: Findings from Death Notification* (Statistics South Africa, 2005). (Available at http://www.statssa.gov.za/publications/). The Department of Health describes the pandemic as "the most important challenge facing South Africa since the birth of our new democracy." It "has claimed millions of lives, inflicting pain and grief, causing fear and uncertainty, and threatening the economy." *HIV/AIDS & STD Strategic Plan for South Africa 2000–2005*, cited in the TAC case, para. 1.

23 The Congress of South African Trade Unions (COSATU), a major trade union federation in South Africa, criticized the process of adoption of the policy for being non-participatory and lacking in transparency. *Accelerating Transformation: COSATU's Engagement with Policy and Legislative Processes during South Africa's First Term of Democratic Governance* (2000), p. 83.

24 COSATU has been one of the most vocal critics of the GEAR policy, particularly the emphasis on private sector-led growth, the adoption of rigid deficit and debt reduction targets, the reduction of corporate tax, and the restructuring of the state linked to the drive to reduce state spending. See *Accelerating Transformation* for a critique of the GEAR approach as well as the principles underlying an alternative approach (*supra*, note 23, pp. 83-90). One scholar has described the relationship between the RDP and GEAR as follows:

> Like motherhood and apple pie, GEAR's stated objective defied criticism. It would achieve, claimed the government, growth with job creation and redistribution, superficially reconciling it to the RDP. But rather than determine how the RDP could be achieved without unleashing unmanageable fiscal laxity and monetary instability, GEAR predicated the RDP on fiscal and monetary stringency. H. Marais, *supra*, note 7, p. 161.

According to Prof. Terreblanche, "The possibilities that, even if higher growth rates were attained, this would be 'jobless growth', or that, even if the higher rates were sustained over time they would not in fact 'trickle down' to the poor, were not even considered." Terreblanche, *supra*, note 5, pp. 116-117.

COSATU was joined by civil society organizations, such as the South African National NGO Coalition (SANGOCO) and the South African Council of Churches (SACC) in The People's Budget Initiative to develop alternative macroeconomic and budgetary policies to promote an active state role in social development.

25 Terreblanche, *supra*, note 5, p. 117, and pp. 117-121. See also COSATU, *supra*, note 23, pp. 90-95.

26 See E. Pieterse and M. van Donk, "Incomplete Ruptures: The Political Economy of Realising Socio-economic Rights in South Africa," in *Law, Democracy and Development* 6 (2002), pp. 193, 202, 220-225 (Annexure A). Highlights include the provision of free health care for pregnant women and children under 6 years old; the Primary School Feeding Scheme; the extension of the social security net; and the adoption in 2000 of a policy of free basic municipal services to all households.

27 In July 2005, President Mbeki launched the South African government's Accelerated and Shared Growth Initiative for SA (Asgi-SA). Its primary aim is to halve unemployment and poverty by 2014 and assist the government in its meeting the Millennium Development Goals. This initiative sets out a range of strategies to achieve an average growth rate of around 5% between 2004 and 2014. See A *Catalyst for Accelerated and Shared Growth – South Africa (ASGISA)*: Summary Background document. (Available at http://www.info.gov.za/speeches/briefings/asgibackground.pdf).

The Role of the Courts in Enforcing Socio-Economic Rights

It is within the above historical and social context that the Constitutional Court is faced with the challenge of giving meaning and effect to the rights entrenched in the Bill of Rights.

The state is required to "respect, protect, promote, and fulfil the rights in the Bill of Rights."[28] The duties imposed by all the rights in the Bill of Rights are enforceable by the courts.[29]

The Constitutional Court has handed down a number of landmark judgments in the realm of civil and political rights. For example, it has declared the death penalty unconstitutional;[30] it has consistently declared that laws that discriminate against gay people are unconstitutional;[31] it has upheld the rights of prisoners to vote;[32] and it has held the African customary law rule of male primogeniture (restricting intestate inheritance to a male who is related to the deceased) to be a violation of the rights to gender equality.[33]

The major provisions on socio-economic rights are contained within sections 26 and 27 of the Constitution. These rights expressly impose a positive duty on the state to take "reasonable legislative and other measures, within its available resources, to achieve the progressive realization" of the relevant rights.[34]

---

28   Section 7(2) of the Constitution requires the state "to respect, protect, promote and fulfil" the rights in the Bill of Rights. This framework of analysis has also been adopted by a number of human rights treaty bodies, such as the UN Committee on Economic, Social and Cultural Rights and the African Commission on Human Peoples' Rights (for example, *The Social and Economic Rights Action Center and the Center for Economic and Social Rights v. Nigeria*, Comm. No. 155/96, October, 2001).

29   Section 38. The Constitutional Court is the highest court in all constitutional matters (s. 167(3)(a)). When deciding a constitutional matter within its power, a court "must declare that any law or conduct that is inconsistent with the Constitution is invalid to the extent of its inconsistency" and "may make any order that is just and equitable." (172(1) & (2)).

30   *S. v. Makwanyane*, 1995 (6) BCLR 665 (CC).

31   For example: *National Coalition for Gay and Lesbian Equality v. Minister of Justice*, 1998 (12) BCLR 1517 (CC); *National Coalition for Gay and Lesbian Equality and Other v. Minister of Home Affairs and Others* 2000 (1) BCLR 38 (CC); *Du Toit and Another v. Minister of Welfare and Population Development and Others* (*Lesbian and Gay Equality Project as amicus curiae*) 2002 (10) BCLR 1006 (CC); *Satchwell v. President of the Republic of South Africa and Another* 2002 (9) BCLR 986 (CC); and *Minister of Home Affairs and Another v. Fourie and Another* 2006 (3) BCLR 355 (CC).

32   *Minister of Home Affairs v. National Institute for Crime Prevention (NICRO) and Others* 2004 (5) BCLR 445 (CC).

33   B*he v. Magistrate, Khayelitsha; Shibi v. Sithole; SA Human Rights Commission v. President of RSA* 2005 (1) BCLR 1 (CC).

34   Section 26 (Housing) reads as follows:
(1) Everyone has the right to have access to adequate housing.
(2) The state must take reasonable legislative and other measures, within its available resources, to achieve the progressive realisation of this right.
(3) No-one may be evicted from their home, or have their home demolished, without an order of court made after considering all the relevant circumstances. No legislation may permit arbitrary evictions.
Section 27 (Health care, food water and social security) reads as follows:
(1) Everyone has the right to have access to –
(a) health care services, including reproductive health care;
(b) sufficient food and water; and
(c) social security, including, if they are unable to support themselves and their dependants, appropriate social assistance.
(2) The state must take reasonable legislative and other measures, within its available resources, to achieve the progressive realisation of each of these rights.
(3) No one may be refused emergency medical treatment.

note continues on following page

To date, the Constitutional Court has decided eight major cases directly relating to socio-economic rights.[35] A number of significant socio-economic rights cases have also been decided in the High Courts and the Supreme Court of Appeal. This chapter will focus on two of the leading cases that established the foundations of the Constitutional Court's jurisprudence on socio-economic rights — Grootboom and TAC.[36]

The Grootboom Case

Grootboom concerned a group of adults and children who had moved onto private land from an informal settlement owing to the "appalling conditions" in which they lived.[37] They were evicted from the private land. Following the eviction, they camped on a sports field in the area, but they could not erect adequate shelters as most of their building materials had been destroyed during the eviction. Accordingly, they found themselves in a precarious position where they had neither security of tenure, nor adequate shelter from the elements.

They applied to the Cape High Court on an urgent basis for an order against all three spheres of government to be provided with temporary shelter or housing until they obtained permanent accommodation.[38] The High Court upheld the claim on the basis of the right of children to shelter set forth in section 28(1)(c). On appeal, the Constitutional Court declared that the state's housing program did not comply with section 26(2) (the right of everyone to have access to adequate housing).[39]

In interpreting section 26, the Constitutional Court declined to read in an implied obligation on the state to ensure that disadvantaged groups have access to es-

---

note continued from preceding page

Section 28(1)(c) gives every child (a person under the age of 18 years) a right to basic nutrition, shelter, basic health care services, and social services. The right to education is protected in s. 29, and prisoners' socio-economic rights in s. 35(2)(e). Religious and cultural rights are protected in sections 15, 30, and 31. The Bill of Rights includes a property clause that incorporates both the defensive function of protecting existing property rights as well as placing a positive duty on the state to take legislative and other measures that enable people to gain access to land on an equitable basis, to promote tenure security, and to provide restitution of property or equitable redress to a person or community dispossessed of property after June 19, 1913, as a result of past racially discriminatory laws or practices. For an insightful analysis of South Africa's constitutional property jurisprudence, see A. J. van der Walt, *Constitutional Property Law* (Cape Town: Juta & Co., 2005).

35   *Soobramoney, supra* note 15; *Government of the Republic of South Africa and Others v. Grootboom and Others* 2000 (11) BCLR 1169 (CC) [hereafter, "Grootboom"]; *Minister of Health v. Treatment Action Campaign and Others* 2002 (10) BCLR 1033 (CC) [hereafter, "TAC"]; *Minister of Public Works and Others v. Kyalami Ridge Environmental Association and Others* 2001 (7) BCLR 652 (CC); *Khosa v. Minister of Social Development; Mahlaule v. Minister of Social Development* 2004 (6) BCLR 569 (CC) [hereafter, the "Khosa" case]; *Port-Elizabeth Municipality v. Various Occupiers* 2004 (12) BCLR 1268 (CC) [hereafter, the "PE Municipality" case]; *Jaftha v. Schoeman and Others; Van Rooyen v. Stoltz and Others* 2005 (1) BCLR 78 (CC); *President of RSA and Another v. Modderklip Boerdery (Pty) Ltd and Others* 2005 (8) BCLR 786 (CC).

36   For a comprehensive analysis of South Africa's jurisprudence on socio-economic rights, see S. Liebenberg, "South Africa," in M. Langford (ed.), *Socio-Economic Rights Jurisprudence: Emerging Trends in Comparative and International Law* (Cambridge: Cambridge University Press, forthcoming, 2006).

37   In the words of Judge Yacoob in the Constitutional Court judgment: "The root cause of their problems is the intolerable conditions under which they were living while waiting in the queue for their turn to be allocated low-cost housing." *Grootboom, supra,* note 35, para. 3.

38   *Grootboom v. Oostenberg Municipality and Others,* 2000 (3) BCLR 277 (C).

39   It held that there was no violation of the right of children to shelter in terms of s. 28(1)(c). For an analysis of the Court's reasoning on this aspect, see: J. Sloth-Nielsen, "The Child's Right to Social Services, the Right to Social Security, and Primary Prevention of Child Abuse: Some Conclusions in the Aftermath of Grootboom," *South African Journal on Human Rights* 17 (2001): p. 232.

sential levels of socio-economic rights.[40] Instead the Court held that the relevant inquiry in respect of the positive duties imposed by section 26 is whether the legislative and other measures taken by the state to realize the rights are "reasonable." The Court wrote:

> A court considering reasonableness will not enquire whether other more desirable or favourable measures could have been adopted, or whether public money could have been better spent. The question would be whether the measures that have been adopted are reasonable. It is necessary to recognise that a wide range of possible measures could be adopted by the state to meet its obligations. Many of these would meet the requirement of reasonableness. Once it is shown that the measures do so, this requirement is met.[41]

The Court then proceeded to outline its criteria for assessing whether the government's conduct was reasonable. These include the adoption of a comprehensive, co-ordinated, and workable program capable of realizing the rights.[42] Additionally, the program must be reasonable both in its conception and implementation,[43] it must be balanced and flexible and make appropriate provision for short-, medium-, and long-term needs.[44] The reasonableness of the government's programs will be evaluated in their social, economic, and historical context. Account will also be taken of the capacity of institutions responsible for implementing the program,[45] as well as the resource constraints of the state.[46] The Court furthermore held that the needs of the poor, given their particular vulnerability, should receive special attention.[47] In relation to the duty of "progressive realisation," the Court said that the state must take steps to achieve the goal of effectively meeting the basic needs of all in our society:

---

40   This approach was argued for by the *amici curiae*, the South African Human Rights Commission and the Community Law Centre (UWC). See Heads of Argument on Behalf of the Amici Curiae, September 10, 2003. (Available at http://www.communitylawcentre.org.za/ser/docs_2002/Grootboom_Heads_of_Arguments.doc). They derived support for this argument from the following views of the UN Committee on Economic, Social and Cultural Rights:
   The Committee is of the view that a minimum core obligation to ensure the satisfaction of, at the very least, minimum essential levels of each of the rights is incumbent upon every State party...In order for a State party to be able to attribute its failure to meet at least its minimum core obligations to a lack of available resources it must demonstrate that every effort has been made to use all resources that are at its disposition in an effort to satisfy, as a matter of priority, those minimum obligations." General Comment No. 3 (Fifth session, 1990) The Nature of States' Parties Obligations: Art. 2(1) of the Covenant on Economic, Social and Cultural Rights, UN doc. E/1991/23, para. 10.
For a critique of the Court's failure to endorse minimum core obligations, see D. Bilchitz, "Towards a Reasonable Approach to the Minimum Core: Laying the Foundations for Future Socio-Economic Rights Jurisprudence," *South African Journal on Human Rights* 19 (2003); S. Liebenberg, "South Africa's Evolving Jurisprudence on Socio-Economic Rights: An Effective Tool in Challenging Poverty," *Law, Democracy and Development* 6 (2002), p. 159.
41   *Grootboom, supra,* note 35, para. 41.
42   *Ibid.,* paras. 38-39.
43   *Ibid.,* para. 42.
44   *Ibid.,* para. 43.
45   *Ibid.,* para. 43.
46   According to the Court, "[t]here is a balance between goals and means. The measures must be calculated to attain the goal expeditiously and effectively but the availability of resources is an important factor in determining what is reasonable." *Ibid.,* para. 46.
47   *Ibid.,* para. 36.

It means that accessibility should be progressively facilitated: legal, administrative, operational and financial hurdles should be examined and, where possible, lowered over time.[48]

It is also significant that the Court endorsed the views of the UN Committee on Economic, Social and Cultural Rights to the effect that "retrogressive measures" are prima facie incompatible with the duty of progressive realization and require special justification.[49]

The state had placed evidence before the Court of its comprehensive national housing legislation,[50] policies and programs. The Court conceded that what had been done represented "a major achievement"[51] and "a systemic approach to a pressing housing need."[52] The Court wrote:

> Large sums of money have been spent and a significant number of houses have been built. Considerable thought, energy, resources and expertise have been and continue to be devoted to the process of effective housing delivery. It is a programme that is aimed at achieving the progressive realisation of the right of access to adequate housing.[53]

Nonetheless the Court held that the housing program had failed to meet the constitutional test of reasonableness in that it focused exclusively on meeting housing needs in the medium- to long term but did not include measures to provide short-term, temporary relief to those in desperate need.[54] It held that "[t]hey are not to be ignored in the interests of an overall programme focussed on medium and long-term objectives."[55] The Court justified this criterion of reasonableness on the basis that the measures adopted, though statistically successful and capable of achieving an overall advance in the realization of the right, "cannot leave out of account the degree and extent of the denial of the right they endeavour to realise." In the words of the Court: "Those whose needs are most urgent and whose ability to enjoy all rights therefore is most in peril, must not be ignored by the measures aimed at achieving the realisation of the right."[56]

The Court interpreted the right of access to adequate housing purposively, noting that this right is entrenched "because we value human beings and want to ensure that they are afforded their basic necessities."[57] A society "must seek to ensure that the basic necessities of life are provided to all if it is to be a society based on human dignity, freedom and equality."[58]

The Court thus declared that the state housing program did not comply with section 26(2) of the Constitution ". . . in that it failed to make reasonable provision

---

48 *Ibid.*, para. 45.
49 *Ibid.*, See General Comment No. 3 (1990), para. 9.
50 In particular, the Housing Act, 107 of 1997.
51 *Grootboom, supra* note 35, para. 53.
52 *Ibid.*, para. 54.
53 *Ibid.*, para. 53 (footnotes omitted).
54 *Ibid.*, paras. 64 and 68.
55 *Ibid.*, para. 66.
56 *Ibid.*, para. 44.
57 *Ibid.*
58 *Ibid.* Human dignity, freedom, and equality are the founding values of the South African Constitution: s. 1(a) and s. 7(1).

within its available resources for people in the Cape Metropolitan area with no access to land, no roof over their heads, and who are living in intolerable conditions or crisis situations."[59]

The Grootboom judgment was the first judgment to interpret the scope of the positive duties on the state to realize socio-economic rights and also elaborated on the role of the courts in enforcing socio-economic rights.[60]

The TAC Case

The TAC (Treatment Action Campaign) case involved a challenge to the limited nature of the measures introduced by the state to prevent mother-to-child transmission (MTCT) of HIV. The Treatment Action Campaign is a dynamic civil society organization that mobilizes a range of social sectors (communities affected by AIDS, church groups, the trade union movement, and other NGOs) in a campaign for adequate medical treatment for persons living with HIV/AIDS.[61] The TAC argued that the state violated the right of access to health care services in section 27 of the Constitution through its policy that prohibited the administration of the antiretroviral drug, Nevirapine, at public hospitals and clinics outside a limited number of research and training sites. This drug was of proven efficacy in reducing intrapartum mother-to-child transmission of HIV. Secondly, it argued that the state had failed to produce and implement a comprehensive national program for the prevention of MTCT of HIV. Both the High Court and the Constitutional Court (on appeal) held that the state's program to prevent MTCT of HIV did not comply with its obligations in terms of sections 27(1) and (2). The Constitutional Court made both declaratory and mandatory orders against the government.

The Constitutional Court considered and rejected the range of reasons advanced by the government for restricting the administration of Nevirapine to the research and training sites.[62] These justifications for its restrictive policy included doubts about the efficacy of Nevirapine where "a comprehensive package of care" could not be made available,[63] the development of resistance to the drug, the drug's safety, a lack of technical and administrative capacity, and budgetary concerns.[64]

---

59 *Ibid.*, para. 99. Order 2(c).
60 The Court also indicated that s. 26(1) imposed a negative obligation "upon the State and all other entities and persons to desist from preventing or impairing the right of access to adequate housing." (para. 34). This negative obligation is further spelled out in s. 26(3), which prohibits arbitrary evictions and demolitions of people's homes. (Ibid). In the recent case of *Jaftha v. Schoeman; Van Rooyen v. Stoltz, supra* note 35, the Court held that such negative violations could only be justified by the state in terms of the stringent requirements of the general limitations clause in the Bill of Rights (s. 36).
61 For more on the Treatment Action Campaign, see its website: www.tac.org.za For an analysis of the strategies embarked upon by the TAC to advance the realization of the right to adequate medical treatment for people living with HIV/AIDS in South Africa, see E. Pieterse and M. van Donk, "Incomplete Ruptures: The Political Economy of Realising Socio-Economic Rights in South Africa," *Law, Democracy and Development* 6 (2002), pp. 193, 213-219; Mark Heywood, "Shaping, Making and Breaking the Law in the Campaign for a National HIV/AIDS Treatment Plan," in P. Jones and K. Stokke (eds.), *Democratising Development: The Politics of Socio-Economic Rights in South Africa* (Dordrecht/Boston/ London: Martinus Nijhoff Publishers, 2005), p. 181.
62 TAC, *supra* note 35, paras. 48-66.
63 This would include counselling, provision of formula milk as a substitute for breast-feeding, antibiotic treatment, vitamin supplements, and the monitoring, during bottle-feeding, of the mother and children who have received Nevirapine. *Ibid.*, para. 49.
64 *Ibid.*, paras. 51-66.

The Court found that the policy of restricting the provision of Nevirapine impacted seriously on a significant group of HIV-positive mothers and children who did not have access to the research sites. As they were too poor to purchase Nevirapine, they were effectively deprived of access to a "simple, cheap and potentially life-saving medical intervention."[65] This restrictive policy was unreasonable because it was inflexible[66] and did not take into account the needs of a particularly vulnerable group.[67] The Court also held that it was implicit that "a policy of waiting for a protracted period before taking a decision on the use of Nevirapine beyond the research and training sites" was also unreasonable.[68] The government was thus ordered "without delay" to "remove the restrictions" that prevent the use of Nevirapine in the reduction of MTCT of HIV at public hospitals and clinics, and to "permit and facilitate" its use.[69] It was specifically ordered to make the drug available for this purpose at hospitals and clinics where this is medically indicated, "which shall if necessary include that the mother concerned has been appropriately tested and counselled."[70]

In relation to the second prong of the attack on government policy (the failure to adopt and implement a comprehensive MTCT prevention plan), the Court held that the rigidity of the government's policy regarding the restrictive use of Nevirapine affected its whole policy on MTCT of HIV.[71] At the time of the commencement of the proceedings, a comprehensive policy for testing and counselling HIV-positive pregnant women was in place, but it was not implemented uniformly.[72] The Court held that the training of counsellors should now include training for counselling on the use of Nevirapine. In addition, the government was ordered to take reasonable measures to extend the testing and counselling facilities at public hospitals and clinics throughout the public health sector "to facilitate and expedite" the use of Nevirapine for the purposes of reducing the risk of MTCT of HIV."[73]

The requirement of transparency was also added as one of the criteria for assessing the reasonableness of a government program.[74] The Court held that the enormous challenge that HIV/AIDS poses to all sectors of society could be met only if there is proper communication, especially by the government.[75] In order for a program to be "implemented optimally," its contents must be made known to all stakeholders. In

---

65   *Ibid.*, at para. 73. In July 2000, the manufacturers of Nevirapine offered to make it available to the South African government free of charge for a period of five years, for the purposes of reducing the risk of mother-to-child transmission of HIV. (para. 19).
66   *Ibid.*, para. 80.
67   The Court considered poverty to be an important indicator of the vulnerability of the group in question: "There is a difference in the positions of those who can afford to pay for services and those who cannot. State policy must take account of these differences." *Ibid.*, para. 70.
68   *Ibid.*, para. 81.
69   *Ibid.*, para. 135 (Orders 3(a) and 3(b)).
70   *Ibid.*
71   *Ibid.*, paras. 82, 95.
72   *Ibid.*, para. 90.
73   *Ibid.*, para. 95. See also para. 135 of Orders 3 (c) and (d).
74   "Indeed, for a public programme such as this to meet the constitutional requirement of reasonableness, its contents must be known appropriately." (*Ibid.*, para. 123).
75   The Court held that the challenge posed by the HIV/AIDS epidemic for the country "calls for a concerted, co-ordinated and co-operative national effort in which government in each of its three spheres and the panoply of resources and skills of civil society are marshalled, inspired and led." (TAC case, para. 123).

this context, the Court regretted the fact that the national government and six provinces had not disclosed any program to extend access to Nevirapine treatment to prevent MTCT of HIV.[76]

The TAC case illustrates how the Grootboom jurisprudence of reasonableness review can be used strategically to support a broader civil society campaign to advance access to socio-economic rights. The TAC had the organizational resources and capacity to demonstrate the unreasonableness of the government's policies relating to MTCT of HIV. They were able to produce an impressive array of expert medical, public health, and economics evidence to support their case. As observed by Geoff Budlender, of the Legal Resources Centre (the attorney for the TAC): "In some ways, the final judgment of the Constitutional Court was simply the conclusion of a battle which TAC had already won outside of the courts, but with the skilful use of the courts as part of a broader struggle."[77]

Implementation of the Judgments

The implementation of the *Grootboom* judgment has been less than optimal. The situation of the community was the subject of a settlement agreement that was made an order of Court (September 21, 2000). In terms of this settlement agreement, the community were permitted to continue to reside on the Wallacedene sport field on a temporary basis until housing became available to them under one of the State's housing programs for the broader Wallacedene. The reported judgment of the Constitutional Court accordingly dealt only with the question of whether the State's housing programme was consistent with section 26 of the Constitution. The judgment was handed down in 2000. It was only in August 2003 that a new program was adopted providing for a program of housing assistance for those in emergency circumstances.[78] The adoption of this program was a direct response to the state's obligations in terms of the Grootboom judgment. It is intended to provide a safety net for communities facing crises, such as natural disasters, evictions, or intolerable conditions posing immediate threats to life, health, and safety.[79]

With regard to the TAC judgment, there has been significant progress in implementing the order, although this is uneven in the various provinces.[80] There are in-

---

76   *Ibid.*, para. 123.
77   G. Budlender, "A Paper Dog with Real Teeth," in *Mail & Guardian*, July 12-18, 2002.
78   *Housing Assistance in Emergency Circumstances*, Chapter 12, National Housing Code. Some scholars have attributed the slow implementation of the Grootboom judgment to the declaratory nature of the order given by the Constitutional Court: See K. Pillay, "Implementation of Grootboom: Implications for the Enforcement of Socio-Economic Rights," *Law, Democracy and Development* 6 (2002): p. 255.
79   Recent High Court cases dealing with evictions in two of South Africa's major cities, reveal that there are still serious problems with the implementation of this program and doubts about its efficacy: See *City of Cape Town v. Rudolph*, 2003 (11) BCLR 1236 (CC); *The City of Johannesburg v. Rand Properties (Pty) Ltd, and Others*, 2006 (6) BCLR 728 (W).
80   Some provinces have remained obdurate in their resistance to implementing the judgment. Mark Heywood (a member of the national executive of TAC) notes: "In provinces where there was already a political commitment to establishing a comprehensive PMTCT programme, the judgment unshackled health departments and politicians and opened the door to implementation. In these provinces there has been an ongoing expansion and improvement." He goes on to say, "By contrast, other provinces have required active engagement and the TAC's advocacy and legal team has focused on improving compliance at this level." M. Heywood, "Contempt or compliance? The TAC case after the Constitutional Court Judgment," *Economic and Social Rights in South Africa Review* 7/4 (2003): p. 9.

dications that capacity constraints in the Department of Health constitute a barrier to the full implementation of the order.[81]

It is important, however, to recognize that the impact of the *Grootboom* and *TAC* judgments are much wider than their immediate implementation. The values and principles articulated in these judgments have both informed a broad range of civil society advocacy and influenced the adoption of pro-poor economic and social policies and legislation.

The Role of the South African Human Rights Commission

The South African Human Rights Commission is one of the "State institutions supporting constitutional democracy" established in terms of Chapter 9 of the Constitution. It has the general mandate to promote human rights and to monitor and assess their observance in South Africa.[82] To this end, it has been given the power to investigate and report on the observance of human rights, to take steps to secure appropriate redress where human rights are violated, to carry out research, and to educate.[83] The Constitution also imposes a special duty on the Commission in relation to socio-economic rights. Each year it must "require relevant organs of state to provide the Commission with information on the measures that they have taken towards the realisation of the rights in the Bill of Rights concerning housing, health care, food, water, social security, education and the environment."[84]

The Commission has, since its institution, compiled five reports on economic and social rights pursuant to its mandate in terms of section 184(3) of the Constitution.[85] The Reports are compiled on the basis of the responses received from relevant organs of state to comprehensive questionnaires ("protocols") sent to them by the Commission. The principles outlined in the *Grootboom* and *TAC* judgments informed the design of the questionnaires. The protocols are intended to provide the Commission with information on policy, legislative, budgetary, and other measures adopted by organs of state toward realizing socio-economic rights. They include questions relating to the access to socio-economic rights enjoyed by vulnerable groups, problems of implementing rights experienced by organs of state, and indicators of progress in fulfilling the rights. The Commission concludes each chapter of its reports with a summary of its conclusions and recommendations relating to the rights in question.

The Commission's recommendations are often far-reaching and aim at ensuring that human rights principles are infused in development processes.[86] The govern-

---

81   See report by Health-E News on "Government's Mother-to-Child HIV Prevention Programme in Trouble," (June 27, 2003), available at www.health-e.org.za/news/article.php?uid=20030618.
82   Section 184 (1) of the Constitution.
83   Section 184(2) of the Constitution. These powers are further regulated in terms of the Human Rights Commission Act 54 of 1994.
84   Section 184(3) of the Constitution. See Dwight G. Newman, "Institutional Monitoring of Social and Economic Rights: A South African Case Study and a New Research Agenda," *South African Journal on Human Rights* 19 (2003): p. 189.
85   Its reports are available at www.sahrc.org.za/esr_report_2002_2003.htm.
86   For example, in its 4th *Economic & Social Rights Report 2000/2002 (Ibid.)*, the Commission's recommendations included the need to adopt measures in the housing sector to give effect to the Grootboom

note continues on following page

ment can use the recommendations of the Commission to devise more effective rights-based strategies and plans of action for the progressive realization of socio-economic rights. The reports are tabled in Parliament and can assist members of Parliament in exercising their oversight function in relation to the Executive. Through this monitoring process the Commission can also attempt to secure appropriate redress for victims of violations of socioeconomic rights[87] and identify issues requiring further research and investigation.[88] Perhaps most significantly, through this mechanism, the Commission can bring systemic abuses of socio-economic rights to the attention of government and the public.

A challenge for the Commission is to achieve more active civil society participation in the process of information gathering, the formulation of recommendations as well as advocacy and monitoring in relation to the Commission's recommendations.

Another similar constitutional institution is the Commission for Gender Equality.[89] Although it does not have an express mandate in relation to socio-economic rights, it has a vital role to play in developing the gender dimensions of these rights. In order to ensure that the impact of gender factors is fully integrated in the monitoring of socio-economic rights, close collaboration between the two institutions is essential.[90]

Pro-Poor Policies and Legislation and the Role of Civil Society

It is important to recognize that human rights-orientated social policies and legislation are not adopted solely, or even primarily, in response to court judgments. There are many examples of social legislation and policies that have been adopted with the aim of giving effect to constitutional rights without the compulsion of a court judgment. Legislation of this nature serves numerous purposes, including:

- Providing greater clarity and definition to the content of socio-economic rights;

- Creating a coherent framework within which the right can be progressively realized;

- Identifying and providing specific protection for especially vulnerable groups;

note continued from preceding page

judgment; the development of a plan to ensure universal access to anti-retroviral drugs for people living with HIV/AIDS; the introduction of a basic income grant; and the need for the budget system to be based on a costed-norms approach. With regard to the latter recommendation, see section on Budgetary Measures below.

87   In terms of the Human Rights Commission Act, the Commission can use alternative dispute resolution mechanisms (mediation, conciliation and negotiation) to attempt to resolve disputes and rectify violations of human rights (s. 8). It can also take cases to court in its own name, or on behalf of a person or a group or class of persons (s. 7(1)(e)).

88   The power of the Commission to conduct investigations is contained in s. 9 of the Human Rights Commission Act.

89   The functions and powers of the Commission for Gender Equality are contained in s. 187 of the Constitution, and in the Commission for Gender Equality Act 39 of 1996.

90   See, in this regard, K. Pillay, "The Commission for Gender Equality: What Is Its Role?" *Economic and Social Rights in South Africa Review* 1/3 (1998), pp. 13-15.

- Allocating responsibilities and tasks to the three spheres of government (national, provincial, and local) in the realization of the rights in question;
- Ensuring that the appropriate financial and human resources are made available; and
- The setting of uniform national norms and standards in order to ensure inter-provincial equity in access to socioeconomic rights.[91]

The following section discusses a number of South African case studies that are illustrative of social policy and legislative initiatives in which a conscious attempt has been made to integrate human rights principles. This discussion also highlights the critical role of civil society organizations in advocating a rights-based approach in social policy and legislative processes.

The Struggle Against the HIV/AIDS Epidemic

The TAC has been campaigning since 1988 for the provision of anti-retroviral therapy in the public and private health care sectors for the treatment of all HIV-positive people. August 2003 represented a turning point in the government's resistant stance to the provision of anti-retroviral therapy in the public health sector. Following the submission of a report by a joint task team of the Department of Health and the Department of Finance,[92] the Cabinet instructed the Minister of Health to prepare a plan for the progressive roll-out of such therapy in the public sector.[93]

Many processes contributed to the reaching of this watershed in the struggle against AIDS, most significantly the extensive social mobilization mounted by the TAC. Coming in the wake of the Constitutional Court judgment in *TAC*, constitutional considerations gave significant impetus both to the development of a national anti-retroviral treatment plan and the substantive content of this plan.[94]

---

91   These are some of the key criteria identified by the Constitutional Court in *Grootboom* for a reasonable government program aimed at realizing constitutional rights (*supra*, paras. 39-40).

92   *Full Report of the Joint Health and Treasury Task Team Charged with Examining Treatment Options to Supplement Comprehensive Care for HIV/AIDS in the Public Health Sector*, August 8, 2003. (Available at www.gov.za/reports/2003/ttr010803final.pdf).

93   See Statement on Special Cabinet Meeting: Enhanced Programme against HIV and AIDS, August 8, 2003. Cabinet decided that "the Department of Health should, as a matter or urgency, develop a detailed operational plan on an antiretroviral treatment programme." Cabinet indicated that this detailed work would be completed by the end of September 2003. On August 22, the Ministry of Health announced a task team to undertake this responsibility, named the "Task Team Charged with Examining Options to Supplement Comprehensive Care for HIV/AIDS in the Public Sector". See L. Altenroxel, "Ministry Confident It Can Meet Month-end Deadline," *Cape Times*, September 23, 2003. Finally at the end of 2003, the government published the *Operational Plan on Comprehensive HIV and AIDS Care, Management and Treatment for South Africa*, November 19, 2003. (Available at http://www.tac.org.za/Documents/TreatmentPlan/OperationalTreatmentPlan.pdf)

94   The Joint Health and Treasury Task Team convened a subgroup of constitutional lawyers and medical ethicists to examine the legal and ethical aspects of various options, "including the possible legal consequences of using different eligibility criteria, and the implications of alternative implementation strategies." *Joint Task Team Report*, *supra*, note 92, p. 61. The Report summarizes the key constitutional principles and considerations that should shape the implementation of an anti-retroviral program:

    1. That there must be provision by the State, in setting policy and legislative frameworks, for mechanisms to address "hard cases" or, as the Constitutional Court has put it, the situation of people "in desperate need."

note continues on following page

In their engagement with the plans to introduce a comprehensive rollout of an anti-retroviral program, the TAC and other civil society organizations drew on the jurisprudence of the Constitutional Court in the *Grootboom* and *TAC* cases. In their joint submission to the Cabinet on this program, TAC and its partners caution against an approach that does not provide for those in urgent need of anti-retroviral treatment:

> We caution against the view that "once a decision to introduce ART is made . . . that six to nine months' preparatory activities are required before the first patients would start to receive medication on the ground." Instead we propose that with immediate effect all sites that can meet the minimum quality of care criteria be designated as "urgent-access treatment sites" and that people who believe they need access to treatment be encouraged to voluntarily test for HIV and are assisted to visit these sites for counselling, diagnosis and treatment.[95]

As the Constitutional Court noted in *Grootboom*, the reasonable design of policy and legislation is insufficient. It must also be reasonably implemented. By the end of 2004, all nine provinces had commenced with the implementation of a general anti-retroviral program in the public sector. However, it is estimated that at the end of 2005, only about 18 percent of all those in the public sector in need of ART therapy were accessing the treatment, and there are still substantial inter- and intra-provincial disparities in patient numbers accessing treatment.[96] A number of civil society organizations have established a Joint Civil Society Monitoring Forum (JCSMF), which aims to monitor and assess the implementation of government's Operational

---

note continued from preceding page

2. There must be flexibility of State policies and programmes to address changing situations and needs.

3. The creation of circumstances in which the rights of the individual may be realised.

4. Transparency and effective communication, which is also used in part as a measure of the reasonableness of a programme.

5 Urgency of the need with special reference to the degree of discrepancy between the "haves" and the "have-nots" with regard to the right in question.

6. Humanitarianism, which relates to human rights of freedom, dignity and equality. *Ibid.*, pp. 61-62.

The Report also considers the constitutional implications of rationing in the provision of health services, particularly in the light of section 9 of the Constitution, which prohibits unfair discrimination "directly or indirectly against anyone on one or more grounds, including race, gender, sex, pregnancy, marital status, ethnic or social origin, colour, sexual orientation, age, disability, religion, conscience belief, culture, language and birth." *Ibid.*, pp. 62-63. The need for inter-provincial equity and co-operative governance in implementing the national treatment program is also emphasized. *Supra*, pp. 63-64. Annexure 4 of the Report contains full details of the constitutional considerations. See also P. de Vos, "So Much to Do, So Little Done: The Right of Access to Anti-retroviral Drugs Post-Grootboom," *Law, Democracy and Development* 7 (2003), p. 83.

95   *Civil Society Submission on the Operational Plan for the Rollout of an Antiretroviral Programme, A People-Centre ARV Programme*, TAC and others, September 16, 2003, (available at www.tac.org.za), p. 7. Annexed to the submission is a memorandum entitled, "Key Elements of an Antiretroviral Treatment Programme That Is Consistent with the Constitution." (Annexure B). This memorandum argues that the implications of the *Grootboom* and *TAC* cases for the program are (amongst others) that "the plan must urgently identify those areas where the need is most pressing, both in terms of HIV prevalence and levels of poverty." It goes on to say: "The magnitude of the urgent need for treatment means that the plan expressly recognise that sites should be able to identify themselves as being ready to provide treatment on whatever scale they can manage. In this way, the plan would ensure that it avoids creating 'missed opportunities.'"

96   *The International Treatment Preparedness Coalition (ITPC) Report*, November 28, 2005, pp. 73-74. (Available at http://www.tac.org.za/Documents/ARVRollout/ITPSTreatmentReportFinal28 nov05.pdf).

Plan on HIV/AIDS treatment from a public health and human rights perspective. This Forum provides the public with valuable information on progress as well as barriers to progress in the implementation of the treatment plan.

The TAC has also focused on the role of the private health care sector in promoting access to treatment for HIV-positive people and on strategies to lower the costs of anti-retroviral and other drugs necessary for treating AIDS-related illnesses. In the latter respect, the TAC actively defended legislation introduced by the state that included measures necessary for lowering the prices of drugs.[97] The three primary measures were provision for generic substitution, parallel importation of patented medicines, and a transparent medicine pricing system through the establishment of a pricing committee. These provisions were challenged by a group of pharmaceutical companies in the High Court (TPD) in the case of *Pharmaceutical Manufacturers' Association and Others v. the President of the Republic of SA and Others.*[98] Their arguments included that the above measures violated their right to property protected in section 25 of the Constitution. The TAC intervened as *amicus curiae* in the case, arguing that these measures were essential to ensuring the right of access to affordable health care for people living with HIV/AIDS. Eventually, after intense national and international public pressure, the companies abandoned their challenge to these legislative provisions.[99]

This case illustrates how civil society organizations were able to mobilize to defend legislative measures adopted by the state to advance the rights of citizens to affordable medicines controlled by powerful multinationals.[100]

Realizing the Right to Education

The right to basic education (including adult basic education) as well as further education are entrenched in section 29 of the Constitution.[101] The courts have not yet interpreted the content of the right to "basic" education.[102] In its White Paper on

---

97   The Medicines and Related Substances Amendment Act 90 of 1997, amending the Medicines and Related Substances Control Act 101 of 1965.
98   Case No. 4183/98, High Court (Transvaal Provincial Division), March 2001.
99   See further, in this regard, M. Heywood, "Debunking 'Conglomo-talk': A Case Study of the Amicus Curiae As an Instrument for Advocacy, Investigation and Mobilisation," *Law, Democracy & Development* 5 (2001): p. 133. See also P. de Vos, *supra*, note 94, p.83.
100   Mark Heywood, Treasurer of the TAC, describes the significance of this intervention as follows:
        …the TAC amicus and the international campaign achieved a great deal. A three-year legal battle had dissolved, freeing the government to implement the Act. Internationally, the intense focus on medicines, prices, patents and rights to health greatly broadened the support-base of an incipient movement that seeks to treat health as a human right and to promote the idea that commodities such as medicines, that are essential for health, should be treated differently under patent law to commodities that do not have any intrinsic link to human dignity and well-being. This conviction undoubtedly had an impact on the negotiations around TRIPS which took place at the World Trade Organisation (WTO) Ministerial Conference in Doha in November 2001. Heywood, *supra*, note 99, p. 156.
101   Section 29(1) (a) and (b) read as follows: "Everyone has the right – (a) to a basic education, including adult basic education; and (b) to further education, which the state, through reasonable measures, must make progressively available and accessible…."
102   The only indication of the Constitutional Court's possible approach to this right is the following obiter statement of Mahomed DP in relation to the similarly drafted s. 32(a) of the interim Constitution. He affirmed that this provision "creates a positive right that basic education be provided for each person and not merely a negative right that such a person should not be obstructed in pursuing his or her basic education," *In re The School Education Bill of 1995* (Gauteng) 1996 (4) BCLR 537 (CC), paras. 8-9. The judge also referred to the right to education being "at public expense."

Education and Training, the Ministry for Education has given the following interpretation to the obligations imposed by this right:

> Appropriately designed education programmes to the level of the pro-
> posed General Education Certificate (GEC) (one-year reception class
> plus 9 years of schooling) whether offered in school to children, or
> through other forms of delivery to young people and adults, would
> adequately define basic education for purposes of the constitutional
> requirement.[103]

In 1996, the South African Schools Act 84 of 1996 was passed to provide for a
uniform system for the organization, governance, and funding of schools. The Act
provides for compulsory schooling from the ages of 7 to 15 years.[104] The state accepts that it must fund public schools on an equitable basis "in order to ensure the
proper exercise of the rights of learners to education and the redress of past inequalities in education provision."[105] However, the Act also provides for the charging of
school fees at public schools.[106] The system of school fees must include equitable criteria and procedures for the total or partial exemption of parents who are unable to
pay school fees.[107] Civil society groups have been concerned about the impact of the
system of school fees on the accessibility of schooling for children from low-income
families.[108] The Department of Education conducted a review of the financing, resourcing, and costs of education in public schools.[109] It acknowledged that the current funding regime creates educational barriers for students from low-income
households and does not provide adequate resources for their education.

In their comments to the Department of Education on this school financing review, the Law and Transformation Project based at the Centre for Applied Legal
Studies (CALS) at the University of the Witwatersrand called for the abolition of
school fees on the basis that they are a barrier to education for poor communities and
run contrary to South Africa's international obligations.[110] They argued that consti-

---

103   *White Paper on Education and Training*, Chapter 7, para. 14.
104   Section 3 of Schools Act, 1996.
105   *Ibid.*, section 34(1).
106   *Ibid.*, section 39. The charging of school fees requires a resolution adopted by the majority of parents attending a general meeting to consider the annual budget of the school.
107   *Ibid.*, section 39(2)(b) read with s. 40.
108   See Report of the National "Speak Out on Poverty Hearings," March to June 1998, *Poverty and
Human Rights*, pp. 30-35. Organizations such as the Education Rights Project (ERP), University of
Witwatersrand, have campaigned for the abolition of compulsory schools fees. South Africa is a party to
the Convention on the Rights of the Child (1989) in terms of which it has undertaken to "make primary
education compulsory and available free to all." (Art. 28(1)(a)) [emphasis added]. The International
Covenant on Economic, Social and Cultural Rights (1966) also requires States parties to provide compulsory primary education, free of charge (Art. 13(2)(a) and Art. 14). As noted above, South Africa has
signed, but is not a party to the latter Covenant. See also F. Veriava and F. Coomans, "The right to education," in D. Brand and C. Heyns (eds.), *Socio-Economic Rights in South Africa* (Pretoria: Pretoria
University Press – PULP, 2005), p. 57.
109   Department of Education's *Report to the Minister on a Review of the Financing, Resourcing and Costs
of Education in Public Schools*. (Available at http://www.education.gov.za/dynamic/dynamic.aspx?pageid=
329&catid=10&category=Reports)According to para. 1.1, the purpose of the Review is to "stimulate and
guide constructive discussion across government structures, in public schools and in society at large with
regard to the resourcing of public schools in South Africa."
110   "Comments on the Department of Education's Report to the Minister on a Review of the
Financing, Resourcing and Costs of Education" Law & Transformation Programme, Centre for Applied
Legal Studies, University of the Witwatersrand, April 30, 2003. (Available at http://www.law.wits.ac.za/
cals/lt/pdf/Minreview_findraft.pdf), p. 34.

tutionally entrenched rights such as the right to basic education require, first, an analysis of the obligations flowing from the particular rights, and then the costing of such obligations so that appropriate budgetary allocations can be made. They contrast this with a "closed-budget approach." This approach "departs from the premise that the available resources for public schools are essentially fixed,[111] and that the only worthwhile discussion that can be held is about what priorities should be followed, and what administrative systems put in place, in deploying these fixed resources."[112] In their submission, they characterize the role of rights in shaping policy as follows:

> The approach adopted by the Court in *Grootboom* makes it clear that constitutional rights are not just tools used by lawyers to force government to accede to awkward political demands. Rather, constitutional rights are policy-structuring devices intended to inform the very way government goes about its business. The Constitution itself (s 2) puts the point in the following terms: "This Constitution is the supreme law of the Republic; law or conduct inconsistent with it is invalid, and the obligations imposed by it must be fulfilled."[113]

Pursuant to its review, the Department published a Plan of Action entitled, "Improving Access to Free and Quality Basic Education for All" (June 14, 2003).[114] The Plan proposed that school fees be abolished in the bottom two quintiles of schools.[115] The constitutional rights to basic education and equality were key considerations in the proposals to address the economic accessibility of education for learners from low-income backgrounds.[116]

Implementation of this Plan commenced in 2006, and it is thus currently too early to assess whether its implementation has improved access to education for children whose families have very limited financial resources.

Protection against Evictions and Demolitions

One of the most pernicious features of apartheid land and housing policies was the use of the law to effect forced removals of people from their land and housing, often summarily without a court order.[117] Largely in response to this history, section

---

111 Barring marginal increases in the allocation to education in any particular fiscal year, within the confines of the MTEF.

112 Law & Transformation Comments, *supra*, note 110, p. 5.

113 *Ibid.*, pp. 5-6.

114 Available at http://www.education.gov.za/dynamic/dynamic.aspx?pageid=329&catid=10&category= Reports. According to the foreword of the Plan, the emphasis "is very much on ensuring that the poorest 40% of learners in South Africa continue to experience improvements in the quality of the schooling they receive, that all barriers to access, be they distance, school fees or some other barrier, be definitively removed in the next three years." See also pp. 4-5 of the Plan entitled, "Access to free and quality education for all: Constitutional imperatives."

115 Schools in these quintiles will be obliged to seek Departmental approval before charging school fees. The Plan suggests a "basic minimum package" for ensuring adequate funding of schools (pp. 15-16). It also proposes an array of reforms to facilitate improved access to schools, such as the regulation of the costs of uniforms and books.

116 *Ibid.*, pp. 4-5. For an evaluation of rights-based strategies in the reform of the South African education system, see Stuart Wilson, "Taming the Constitution: Rights and Reform in the South African Education System," *South African Journal on Human Rights* 20 (2004): p. 418.

117 For a historical overview, see C. Murray and C. O'Regan (eds.), *No Place to Rest: Forced Removals and the Law in South Africa* (Oxford: Oxford University Press and UCT Labour Law Unit, 1990). For an

note continues on following page

26(3) of the Constitution was adopted, which prohibits arbitrary evictions and demolitions without a court order made after considering "all the relevant circumstances." Furthermore "[n]o legislation may permit arbitrary evictions."

The government has adopted important legislation to give substance to this right.
The Prevention of Illegal Eviction From and Unlawful Occupation of Land Act 19
of 1998 (PIE) provides extensive procedural and substantive rights to unlawful occupiers facing evictions.[118] Thus, courts are given discretion to grant eviction orders
"if it is of the opinion that it is just and equitable to do so." Among the relevant factors that a court must consider are whether land can reasonably be made available for
the relocation of the unlawful occupier, as well as "the rights and needs of the elderly, children, disabled persons and household headed by women."[119] The leading
Constitutional Court decision interpreting the provisions of PIE is *Port Elizabeth
Municipality v. Various Occupiers*.[120] This judgment explains how PIE must be interpreted to promote the purposes and values behind s. 26(3) of the Constitution. In
this case the Court held that "a court should be reluctant to grant an eviction against
relatively settled occupiers unless it is satisfied that a reasonable alternative is available, even if only as an interim measure pending ultimate access to housing in the
formal housing programme."[121] Thus, in order to satisfy a court that it is "just and
equitable" to evict people from their homes, organs of state will have to show that
serious consideration was given to the possibility of providing alternative accommodation to the occupiers.[122] The Court also indicated that, in the absence of special
circumstances, "it would not ordinarily be just and equitable to order eviction if
proper discussions, and where appropriate, mediation, have not been attempted."[123]

Similar legislation, applicable to rural land,[124] has been adopted to provide for
state assistance to facilitate long-term security of land tenure[125] and to regulate the
conditions under which the right of people to reside on land may be terminated. For
example, the Act provides that the right of residence of persons who have resided for
10 years on land belonging to an owner and who have reached the age of 60 years or
have had their employment terminated due to ill-health may not be terminated.[126]

---

note continued from preceding page

analysis of the use by the state of legislation such as the Prevention of Illegal Squatting Act to enforce
racially discriminatory land and housing policies, see C. O'Regan, "No More Forced Removals? An
Historical Analysis of the Prevention of Illegal Squatting Act," *South African Journal on Human Rights* 5
(1989): p. 361.
118 See, for example, s. 4 of PIE.
119 The factor relating to the availability of alternative land applies to cases where an unlawful occupier
has occupied the land for more than six months at the time when the proceedings are initiated. See ss.
4(6) and (7), *Ibid.* There has been a range of cases interpreting and applying the provisions of PIE. See,
for example: *Cape Killarney Property Investments (Pty) Ltd v. Mahamba and Others*, 2001 (4) SA 1222
(SCA); *City of Cape Town v. Rudolph*, 2003 (11) BCLR 1236 (C); *Port Elizabeth Municipality v. Various
Occupiers, supra*, note 35.
120 *Supra.*
121 *Ibid.*, para. 28.
122 *Ibid.*
123 *Ibid.*, para. 43.
124 The Extension of Security of Tenure Act 62 of 1997 (ESTA).
125 Section 4 of ESTA gives the Minister of Land Affairs power to grant subsidies to facilitate the planning and implementation of on-site and off-site developments, and to enable occupiers, former occupiers,
and other persons who need long-term security of tenure to acquire land.
126 Section 8(4), ESTA. The only exception permitted is if the occupier has committed a material
breach of his rights and duties.

A set of procedural and substantive rights for those facing evictions from their homes have been created through a combination of constitutional guarantees, legislation, and jurisprudence. The previous legal position where property rights were automatically privileged has been modified. The rights and interests of people who lack security of tenure can no longer be ignored. In this way, human rights institutions have helped to effect some change in the power relations between both public and private landowners and occupiers. However, despite these progressive legal developments, a national survey on evictions in South Africa found that, in the last 21 years, almost 1.7 million people were evicted from farms. Of this figure, 942 303 people were evicted between 1994 to the end of 2004.[127] According to the authors of the study, only one percent of these evictions involved any legal process.[128] This raises the question as to why poor people are not resorting to the courts to protect their constitutional and legislative rights. The reasons for their not doing so are complex and, according to the authors of the study, include unfavorable outcomes in eviction applications brought in terms of ESTA,[129] a lack of access to legal services, and limited knowledge by farm dwellers of their rights and channels of assistance.[130] These factors illustrate that entrenched social power relations, a lack of institutional support for people to exercise their rights, and a judicial culture that is not receptive to socio-economic rights can frustrate the transformative goals of pro-poor legislation and policies.

Toward Universal Access to Social Assistance

Section 27(1)(c) of the Constitution provides that "everyone has the right to have access to social security, including, if they are unable to support themselves and their dependants, appropriate social assistance."

The democratic government inherited a social security scheme that was relatively developed but fundamentally flawed due to its racially discriminatory history and fragmented administration.[131] A key challenge for the government was to establish a comprehensive, national social security system.

In South Africa, social assistance has taken the form of social grants, which are paid in terms of the Social Assistance Act. Currently, the four main means-tested so-

---

127 *Report: Summary of Key Findings from the National Evictions Survey*, (Nkuzi Development Association and Social Services Africa), 2005, p. 7 (Available at http://www.nkuzi.org.za/docs/ Evictions_Summary.pdf); M. Wegerif, B. Russell, and I. Grundling, *Still Searching for Security: The Reality of Farm Dweller Evictions in South Africa* (Nkuzi Development Association and Social Surveys, 2005).
128 *Ibid.*, p. 15.
129 All eviction orders issued in terms of ESTA in the magistrates courts must be reviewed by the specialist Land Claims Court (LCC). However, according to the above study, by the end of 2004, only 25% of eviction orders reviewed by the LCC were set aside. Other research suggests that a large part of the explanation for this is South Africa's formalist legal culture, which restrains a transformative interpretation of the socio-economic rights protected in the Constitution and pro-poor legislation such as ESTA. See in this regard, Theunis Roux, "Pro-poor Court, Anti-poor Outcomes: Explaining the Performance of the South African Land Claims Court," *South African Journal on Human Rights* 20 (2004): p. 511.
130 *National Evictions Survey, supra*, note 127, p. 15.
131 See H. Bhorat, "The South African Social Safety Net: Past, Present and Future," *Development Southern Africa* 12 (1995): p. 595; S. van der Berg, "South African Social Security under Apartheid and Beyond." *Development Southern Africa* 14 (1997): p. 485. The new democratic government inherited a social security system that was fragmented, inequitable, and administratively inefficient. This was an inevitable consequence of a system administered by 14 different departments for the different population groups and homelands. See also *Mashava v. President of the RSA and Others* 2004 (12) BCLR 1243 (CC).

cial grants are the grant for the aged,[132] the grant for the disabled,[133] the foster child grant,[134] and the child support grant (CSG).[135] Together these grants reach almost 12 million vulnerable people in the society. Given the high levels of structural unemployment in South Africa, the government's social assistance program is a vital mechanism of poverty alleviation.[136] It is also the largest single redistributive program of the government.[137]

In its *White Paper for Social Welfare*, released by the Department of Welfare (now the Department of Social Development) in February 1997, the government commits itself to "the provision of a comprehensive national social security system."[138] According to the White Paper, a transformed social security system should be built on two pillars. First, it will require "comprehensive social assistance to those without other means of support, such as a general means-tested social assistance scheme." Second, it will require "the restructuring of social insurance, including the retirement industry, unemployment insurance and health insurance."[139] The ultimate goal, in the words of the White Paper, is "...universal access to an integrated and sustainable social security system. Every South African should have a minimum income, sufficient to meet basic subsistence needs, and should not have to live below minimum acceptable standards. The social security system will also work intersectorally to alleviate poverty."[140]

A number of civil society organizations have since been campaigning for an extension of the social assistance net, particularly the extension of the CSG to all children under the age of 18 years and the phased introduction of a universal basic income grant.[141] They argue that, given the scale of the unemployment problem in South Africa, full employment or significant improvements in the unemployment rates is not likely in the short- to medium term. The existing social security system completely excludes those between the qualifying ages of the child support grant and grant for the aged who have insufficient income to meet their basic needs. They are advocating a universal (non-means-tested) grant of R100 per month payable to every adult and child. The grant would be progressively recouped from higher income earners through the tax system.

---

132   The grant for the aged (a maximum of R820 per month for the 2006/2007 fiscal year) is payable to women at age 60 years, and men at age 65 years.
133   This grant (a maximum of R820 per month for the 2006/2007 fiscal year) is payable to a person, 18 years or older, who is unfit to provide for his or her maintenance because of physical or mental disability.
134   The foster care grant is paid to the foster parents of children under the age of 18.
135   The child support grant (R180 per child) is payable to the primary care giver of a child under the age of 14 years.
136   A. Case and A. Deaton, *Large Cash Transfers to the Elderly in South Africa*, Princeton Research Program in Development Studies Discussion Paper No. 176. The government's macro-economic strategy document acknowledges the vital role of these cash transfers in poverty alleviation, especially in rural areas: *Growth, Employment and Redistribution: A Macroeconomic Strategy* (1996), pp. 14-15.
137   Minister of Finance, Mr. T. Manuel, Budget Speech 2001/2002, available at www.polity.org.za/govdocs/budgets/index.html.
138   Department of Welfare, White Paper for Social Welfare (1997), Chapter 7, para. 26(a).
139   *Ibid.*, Chapter 7, para. 26 (b).
140   *Ibid.*, Chapter 7, para. 27.
141   These include the trade union federation, COSATU, the Churches, Black Sash, and the Alliance for Children's Entitlement of Social Security Rights (ACESS). These organizations and many others, have joined forces in the Basic Income Grant (BIG) Coalition (website at www.big.org.za).

In February 2000, the government appointed a Committee of Inquiry into a Comprehensive Social Security System to review the entire social security system in South Africa, including the feasibility of introducing a basic income grant. The Report of the Committee of Inquiry found that the existing social security programs do not adequately address the problem of poverty: "Half of the poor live in households that receive no social security benefits at all, and the rest remain poor in spite of the benefits that they receive."[142]

Endorsing the approach of the UN Commission on Social Development, the Committee proposed the adoption of a "comprehensive social protection package"[143] comprising a set of measures to address income poverty, capability poverty,[144] asset poverty,[145] and measures to address special needs.[146] It defines the aims of comprehensive social protection (CSP) for South Africa as seeking:

> . . . to provide the basic means for all people living in the country to effectively participate and advance in social and economic life and in turn to contribute to social and economic development . . . It is broader than the traditional concept of social security, and incorporates developmental strategies and programmes designed to ensure, collectively, at least a minimum acceptable living standard for all citizens.[147]

In relation to income poverty specifically, the Committee proposed that the CSP package "should comprise at least one primary income transfer which ensures that all South Africans have some income to mitigate or eradicate destitution or starvation."[148] It also argued that such a basic level of income would have "other developmental spin-offs related to enabling that person to participate more effective in the economy (for example, afford the bus fare to engage in job search)."[149] The Committee recommended a phased introduction of a basic income grant, initially through the extension of the CSG to all children under 18, and thereafter a phased introduction of a basic income grant over the period 2005–2015.[150] The Committee of Inquiry linked the introduction of a basic income grant to the right to social assistance in s. 27(1)(c) as follows:

---

142 *Transforming the Present–Protecting the Future: Consolidated Report of the Committee of Inquiry into a Comprehensive System of Social Security for South Africa*, March 2002, p. 59.
143 In the words of the Committee: "The need for a package derives from an understanding that there are certain basic requirements that should be available for all, and should not be subject to being traded off against each other." Report, *supra*, p. 41.
144 This incorporates the provision of certain basic services to enable people to live and function in society, such as the provision of basic (lifeline tariff) water and electricity, free and adequate health care, free education, food security, and affordable housing and transport. *Report of the Committee of Inquiry, supra*, p. 42. See further in this regard, the section below on Free Basic Services.
145 This includes income-generating assets, such as land, and community infrastructure: This addresses the key underlying structural basis of poverty and inequality in South Africa. *Ibid.*
146 This includes measures to address special needs, such as disability.
147 Report, *supra*, note 142, p. 41.
148 *Ibid.*, p. 42
149 *Ibid.*
150 *Ibid.*, pp. 62-66.

A Basic Income Grant would serve as a social entitlement for all South Africans. Such an entitlement supports the right to appropriate social assistance as entrenched in the South African constitution 27 (1)(c) while furthering the vision of a comprehensive social security system as identified in the White Paper for Social Welfare.[151]

What is remarkable about the Committee's Report is its strong concern that the immediate survival needs of the poor cannot be deferred while pursuing medium- and long-term developmental policies. This resonates strongly with the Constitutional Court's judgments in the *Grootboom* and *TAC* cases, requiring state policy to provide immediate relief for groups in desperate need and living in intolerable conditions.[152] As noted, the Report also argues that the meeting of basic social needs can complement and enhance long-term developmental strategies.

The Committee's Report was considered in public hearings held by the Portfolio Committee on Social Development (National Assembly) in November 2002 and June 2003. The Cabinet also considered it in July 2003. The state, however, has yet to formulate a comprehensive response to the issues raised in the Report. There has not been a clear and transparent policy reform process subsequent to the release of the Committee's Report. The government has instead placed its faith in an expanded public works program as a strategy to address the current crisis of poverty and skills shortages.[153]

Civil society groups have made a range of submissions calling for a systematic policy response to the findings and recommendations of the Taylor Committee Report. In doing so, they have relied on the state's constitutional obligation to formulate a comprehensive, workable plan that is capable of facilitating the realization of the right to social security, as required by the Constitutional Court decision in the *Grootboom* and *TAC* cases.

Groups campaigning for children's rights have achieved notable success.[154] This entailed the extension of the eligible age of the CSG from 7 years to 14 years. This

---

151   *Ibid., supra,* p. 61.
152   This linkage is explicitly dealt with in the Committee of Inquiry Report, *supra*:
> While the Grootboom case has emphasised that it is incumbent on the state to take reasonable measures to give effect to [socio-economic rights], the Committee believes that this should be translated into making available a minimum level or measure of provision to everyone. As a result, it may be advisable for the State to stipulate up front its considered minimum obligations for service delivery, such as it is doing for the free water programme, and its intended schedule for progressively realising this. (pp. 43-44).

For a discussion of the implications of the Grootboom judgment for social security policy reform in South Africa, see S. Liebenberg, "The Right to Social Assistance: The Implications of Grootboom for Policy Reform in South Africa," *South African Journal on Human Rights* 17 (2001): p. 232.
153   Transcript of the Media Briefing by President Thabo Mbeki following the Cabinet Lekgotla, July 29, 2003. In its Notes on the Cabinet Lekgotla, July 23-29, 2003 (dated July 29, 2003), the government said the following in relation to an extended public works program:
> Cabinet was briefed on the preparatory work in identifying projects for an extended Public Works Programme, both as an instrument of poverty alleviation and a basis for skills development. This programme features at the top of government's agenda because it is critical for the inclusion of a great number of South Africans – many of whom have little possibility for immediate absorption into the formal economy – in income-generating activity from which they are also able to acquire skills. (p. 3)

154   A leading role in this regard was played by the Alliance for Children's Entitlement to Social Security Rights (ACESS).

campaign involved extensive reliance on the provision in the Constitution protecting children's socio-economic rights.[155]

Free Basic Services

In 2000, the government adopted a policy of free basic services to ensure that all households have access to at least a basic level of municipal services. Apart from it being a political commitment,[156] the government also used rights-based arguments to support its policy. Thus, the Department of Provincial and Local Government (DPLG) states that this policy is based on "a belief in the right of all South Africans to receive at least a common minimum standard of service, and the constitutional duty of all three spheres of government to achieve it."[157]

In the sphere of water rights, this commitment has found expression in the Water Services Act No. 108 of 1997, which gives everyone "a right of access to basic water supply and basic sanitation."[158] A "basic water supply" is defined as "the prescribed minimum standard of water supply services necessary for the reliable supply of a sufficient quantity and quality of water to households, including informal households, to support life and personal hygiene."[159] This definition is given further specificity in regulations promulgated in terms of this Act. The "minimum standard for basic water supply services" is defined as "a) the provision of appropriate education in respect of effective water use; and b) a minimum quantity of potable water of 25 litres per person per day or 6 kilolitres per household per month."[160] Organizations working in poor communities regard this quota as insufficient to support life and health, however, and are advocating an increased free allocation.[161]

The Act also states that water service must provide for fair and equitable procedures for the limitation or discontinuation of water services. These procedures must "not result in a person being denied access to basic water services for non-payment, where that person proves, to the satisfaction of the relevant water services authority, that he or she is unable to pay for basic services."[162] This constitutes an acknowledge-

---

155   Section 28(1)(c) of the Constitution reads that every child has the right "to basic nutrition, shelter, basic health care services and social services." J. Sloth-Nielsen, *supra*, note 39, p. 210.

156   The policy of free basic services was announced before the municipal elections on December 5, 2000.

157   Department of Provincial and Local Government, Departmental Circular, "Issues to Be Taken into Account When Implementing Free Basic Services," Annexure B, para. 1.

158   Section 3. See also the main objects of the Act, section 2(a).

159   Section 1(3).

160   The regulations further prescribe that this water must be at a minimum flow rate of not less than 10 litres per minutes, within 200 metres of a households, and with "an effectiveness such that no consumer is without a supply for more than seven full days in any year." (Clause 3) The quality of potable water is also prescribed (Clause 5). Regulations Relating to Compulsory National Standards and Measures to Conserve Water, Government Notice No. R. 509, GG No. 22355, June 8, 2001. These levels are based on WHO standards. For a critique of the implementation of the free basic water supply policy, see J. de Visser, E. Cottle, and J. Mettler, "Realising the Right of Access to Water: Pipe Dream or Watershed?" *Law, Democracy and Development* 7 (2003): p. 27.

161   See report of a seminar hosted by the Community Law Centre (UWC) on *Privatisation of Basic Services, Democratisation and Human Rights*, October 2-3, 2003. Available at www.comunitylawcentre.org.za/scr/index/php.

162   Section 4(3)(a) – (c). For a case in which this provision was applied, resulting in a local authority being ordered to restore the water supply to a group of residents they had previously disconnected, see: *Residents of Bon Vista Mansions v. Southern Metropolitan Local Council*, 2002 (6) BCLR 625 (W). This provision is an example of the statutory enforcement of the duty to respect socio-economic rights. See in

note continues on following page

ment that water is a basic right and that the poor should not be denied access to water if they are unable to afford its costs. As of July 1, 2003, there is also a commitment to ensure that low-income households receive a free basic electricity/energy supply of 5kWh/50kWp per household per month.

Budgetary Measures

The Constitutional Court has not clearly defined its approach to the internal limitation in the socio-economic rights sections that require the state to act "within its available resources."[163] In *Grootboom* it indicated that "the availability of resources is an important factor in determining what is reasonable."[164] However, it would undermine a rights-based approach for the state to determine the extent of its own obligations by limiting the budgetary allocations to particular socio-economic rights.[165]

The Constitutional Court, however, has held that the state does have an obligation to ensure that adequate human and financial resources are made available to deal with urgent needs and the management of crises.[166] Although the courts are unlikely to entertain direct challenges to budgetary allocations or macro-economic policy, the Constitutional Court has clearly stated that its orders may have budgetary implications.[167] Where the budgetary implications of expanding access to a socio-economic right are not extensive, however, and the state cannot provide a reasonable justification for restricting access, the Constitutional Court has shown that it would be willing to order the expansion of the particular program. In the *Khosa* case,[168] the Court was faced with a challenge by a group of permanent residents to the provisions of the Social Assistance Act, which provided that only South African citizens were eligible for social grants. The evidence showed that the cost of including permanent residents in the grant system would represent an increase of less than two percent on

---

note continued from preceding page

this regard, General Comment No. 15 of the UN Committee on Economic, Social and Cultural Rights (the right to water, Arts. 11 and 12 of the ICESCR), UN doc E/C.122002/11, paras. 21 and 22. See further A. Kok and M. Langford, "The right to water," in D. Brand and C. Heyns (eds.), *Socio-Economic Rights in South Africa* (Pretoria: Pretoria University Law Press, 2005), p. 191.

163 See sections 26(2) and 27(2).

164 Grootboom, *supra*, Note 35, para. 46.

165 As Darryl Moellendorf argues, "A broader sense of 'available resources' [than those budgeted for the protection of a right] must be employed if socio-economic rights are to guide policy rather than depend on it." "Reasoning About Resources: Soobramoney and the Future of Socio-Economic Rights Claims," *South African Journal on Human Rights* 14 (1998): pp. 330-332.

166 As will be recalled, the Court in *Grootboom* placed an obligation on the State to meet immediate needs in the nationwide housing programme:

> Recognition of such needs in the nationwide housing programme requires it to plan, *budget* and monitor the fulfilment of immediate needs and the management of crises. This must ensure that a significant number of desperate people in need are afforded relief, though not all of them need receive it immediately. Such planning too will require proper co-operation between the different spheres of government. [emphasis added] (para. 68).

In relation to an order handed down, the Court said: "The order requires the State to act to meet the obligation imposed upon it by section 26(2) of the Constitution. This includes the obligation to devise, *fund*, implement and supervise measures to provide relief to those in desperate need." (para. 96) [emphasis added].

167 *Ex parte Chairperson of the Constitutional Assembly: In re Certification of the Republic of South Africa*, (1996) (4) SA 744 (CC) at para. 77. In the TAC case, the Court wrote: "…determinations of reasonableness may in fact have budgetary implications, but are not in themselves directed at rearranging budgets. In this way the judicial, legislative and executive functions achieve appropriate constitutional balance." (para. 38).

168 *Supra*, note 35.

the present cost of social grants.[169] Given the critical role of social grants in protecting a vulnerable group of non-citizens against destitution and fostering their
human dignity, the Court concluded that the state had not produced sufficient
policy or resource-based justifications for their exclusion from the system. It accordingly read the excluded group of "permanent residents" into the provisions of the
Social Assistance Act.

One of the areas of policy formulation that requires a more conscious attempt to
integrate a rights-based approach is that of budget policy. The Budget Reviews display little explicit consideration of the implications of the constitutional rights for
the national budget and intergovernmental resource allocations.[170]

The Financial and Fiscal Commission (FFC) is established in terms of section
220 of the Constitution. It can make recommendations to a range of organs of state
on fiscal and financing matters, including the division of revenue among the different spheres of government. The FFC has displayed a greater awareness of the need
for budgeting to be based on human rights principles. In 2000, the FFC recommended a number of changes to the manner in which the provincial equitable share
is calculated and to other elements of the intergovernmental fiscal system. The central recommendation was the so-called "costed norms approach" to determining
provincial equitable share allocations for basic social services. This approach is based
on establishing basic services levels (in the form of norms and standards) for constitutionally mandated basic services (CMBS), such as health care, education, and social security. Once the norms and standards are established, it is possible to calculate
the resources required for the delivery of the basic services, taking into account the
structure of the provincial populations. According to the FFC "[t]his procedure effectively gives basic social services priority, thereby reflecting constitutional requirements."[171] In addition, the FFC proposes that the government and legislatures
clarify the definition of "progressive realization" of CMBS in order to minimize "the
need for judicial intervention in determining the provision of CMBS."[172] It goes on
to propose a set of policy outcomes, delivery output, and financial input indicators
to measure the progressive realization of norms and standards for the various
CMBS.[173]

In their Report on Social and Economic Rights, the South African Human
Rights Commission indicates that government has not been able to implement the

169   *Ibid.*, para. 62
170   Section 214 of the Constitution provides that an Act of Parliament must provide for "the equitable
division of revenue raised nationally among the national, provincial and local spheres of government." The
Intergovernmental Fiscal Relations Act 97 of 1997 gives effect to s. 214 of the Constitution.
171   Financial and Fiscal Commission Submission on the Medium-Term Expenditure Framework 2004-
2007, *Towards a Review of the Intergovernmental Fiscal Relations System* (April 2003), Part A, pp. 28-30
(available at www.ffc.co.za/docs/submissions/2003/chap 3.pdf). It also points out that these proposals on
CMBS dovetail to a considerable extent with the measures proposed in the *Report of the Committee of
Inquiry into a Comprehensive System of Social Security for South Africa* for alleviating income, capability,
and asset poverty (*supra*, 142, p. 46). Furthermore, it proposes that the costs of poverty targeting "should
be weighed against the costs of providing free basic services universally." (p. 49) It accordingly proposes
that the costs of user fees and tariffs for basic social services in terms of their impact on poverty alleviation should be the subject of careful consideration and further study (p. 50).
172   *Ibid.*, p. 48.
173   *Ibid.*, pp. 48-49.

costed norms approach because it lacks precise information to determine the cost of basic services for each sector, and it has not yet developed a clear definition of constitutionally mandated basic services.[174] It recommends that the Budget Council and Budget Forum do the necessary research so that the costed norms approach can be implemented as soon as possible.[175]

The Human Rights Commission also criticizes public finance processes for being insufficiently participatory and transparent. It calls for more civil society influence in the budgetary process as well as exercise by Parliament of its constitutional right to amend money Bills.[176] Implementation of the costed norms approach will clearly facilitate a more rights-focused approach to budgetary policy and processes.

Conclusion

Social mobilization and political commitment are of primary importance in the adoption of pro-poor developmental policies. This chapter has illustrated how a strong legal commitment to human rights can also play a role in social mobilization and in influencing pro-poor developmental policies. There is a trend in South Africa toward ensuring a package of free basic services to the poor, together with progressive improvements in the quality of social provisioning. We are far from the practical realization of this goal, however. An area that is still relatively undeveloped is the use of rights to challenge the exercise of private power where it operates to exclude the poor from accessing basic services.[177]

If legal strategies are to play a meaningful role in facilitating pro-poor development, however, a number of institutional factors must be addressed and put in place. These include broad-based human rights education, access to legal services for the poor, access to courts, proper guarantees of judicial independence (both vis-à-vis the state as well as independence from powerful business interests in society), changes in the legal culture to make judges and lawyers more receptive to socio-economic rights, proper implementation of judgments, and perhaps most importantly, civil society organizations that are able to mobilize around fundamental reforms and to use litigation strategically to support these goals.[178] The use of rights-based strategies by the TAC discussed in this chapter shows how such strategies can prod the state to give effect to its socio-economic rights obligations, promote knowledge of rights in poor communities, and build organizations.

---

174   South African Human Rights Commission, 4th *Economic & Social Rights Report 2000/2002*, (April 2003), p. 516.

175   *Ibid.*, p. 521.

176   *Ibid.*, Section 77(2) of the Constitution provides that an Act of Parliament must provide for a procedure to amend money Bills before Parliament. This legislation has not yet been enacted.

177   See further in this regard, D. Chirwa, *Obligations of Non-state Actors in Relation to Economic, Social and Cultural Rights under the South African Constitution*, (2002) Research Series of the Socio-Economic Rights Project, Community Law Centre (UWC). See also Report of a Seminar hosted by the Community Law Centre on Privatisation of Basic Services, *Human Rights & Democracy*, October 2-3, 2003. Available at www.communitylawcentre.org.za/ser/index/php.

178   For an excellent analysis of the conditions under which socio-economic rights litigation can have transformative effects, see Siri Gloppen, "Social Rights Litigation as Transformation: South African Perspectives," in P. Jones and K. Stokke (eds.), *Democratising Development: The Politics of Socio-Economic Rights in South Africa* (Dordrecht/Boston/London: Martinus Nijhoff Publishers, 2005), p. 153.

The importance of an integrated approach to human rights cannot be overstated. If human rights norms exclude the basic socio-economic needs of human beings, there is a strong prospect that development processes will neglect the interests of the poor. The inclusion of socio-economic rights on the same terms as civil and political rights in the Constitution facilitates a focus in social policy of building the capacity of the poor and marginalized populations to be active participants in the development process. As holders of rights that protect their fundamental interests, disadvantaged groups have enhanced opportunities to become active beneficiaries of the right to development. As expressed by Budlender, one of South Africa's leading public interest litigators,

> Rights help ensure that people are not mere objects of political policy and government bureaucracies, but the bearers of rights that require their claims to be taken seriously. They fundamentally change the power relations between citizen and State.[179]

In addition, an integrated approach to human rights assists the state in giving effect to its developmental mandate and defending itself against challenges by powerful private entities opposed to transformation.

The South African experience demonstrates that while human rights do not make all the difference to development, they can make a significant difference.

---

179 Comments made at an LLM lecture, University of the Western Cape, September 10, 2003. Geoff Budlender served as Director for many years of the Legal Resource's Centre, which provides free legal services to the poor in public interest cases.

10 | Towards Implementing the Right to Development: A Framework for Indicators and Monitoring Methods

Rajeev Malhotra*

Introduction

The move from advocacy to an implementation framework for universal realization of human rights is inextricably linked to the issue of identifying and devising indicators and monitoring methodologies that are reflective of the relevant human rights norms, standards and principles. At the heart of this is the recognition that, "the bridge between intent and result is built, brick by brick, with information,"[1] or "what gets measured gets done."[2] Indeed, for managing a process of change directed at meeting certain objectives, we need an articulation of targets or benchmarks consistent with the given objectives, mobilization of the required means and identification of policy instruments and mechanisms that translate those means into desired outcomes. In other words, we need indicators for undertaking situational analysis, to inspire public policy, to monitor progress and to measure performance and overall outcomes of the concerned activity. In addition, in case of human rights, and particularly so for the right to development where the debate on its notion and content is far from settled, identification and use of suitable quantitative indicators could also help in clarifying the content of the right, which in turn could facilitate its implementation.[3] It can be argued that appropriate quantitative indicators, by virtue of their definition, presentation, and the data generating methodologies, can provide the means to translate the narrative on the normative content of human rights, as defined in the legal or other relevant instruments, into tools that can help the policy planners and development practitioners in implementing these rights.

However, the task of identifying suitable indicators for facilitating the implementation of human rights, in general, and the right to development, in particular, has its own difficulties. There are at least three issues that need to be addressed. First, the identified indicators that are sensitive and effective in addressing these distinct objectives have to be anchored in an adequate conceptual framework, in this case the

* The author is Development Economist in the Research and Right to Development Branch of the Office of High Commissioner for Human Rights (OHCHR), Geneva Switzerland. The views expressed in the paper are in his personal capacity and do not necessarily reflect the position of the United Nations. This paper is a revised and extended version of a paper presented at a seminar on the right to development in New Delhi 2002. The author has benefited from discussions with Dr. Arjun Sengupta and Nicolas Fasel in writing and revising this paper.

1   Thomas Hammarberg, "Searching the Truth: The Need to Monitor Human Rights with Relevant and Reliable Means," Address at the Statistics, Development and Human Rights conference organized by the International Association for Official Statistics in Montreux, Switzerland, September 4-8, 2000.
2   Douglas N. Daft, Chief Executive Officer of Coca-Cola, United Nations Development Programme, *Human Development Report 2000: Human Rights and Human Development* (New York: UNDP and Oxford University Press, 2000), p. 126.
3   "Information and statistics are a powerful tool for creating a culture of accountability and for realizing human rights," *Id.*, p. 10.

notion of the right to development and an approach to its implementation. Secondly, there has to be an acceptable methodology for generating the required information for defining those indicators. Finally, the selected indicators have to be relevant to the context in which they are applied.

The need for an adequate conceptual basis for indicators lies in having a logic and rationale for identifying and designing them, and not reducing the exercise to an exhaustive listing of possible alternatives. More importantly, it enables an understanding of a linkage between the means and policy instruments, on one hand, and the desired outcomes, on the other. The knowledge of this relationship between outcome and its determinants is particularly important if the concern is to identify indicators that are to help in furthering the implementation of human rights, as against the limited objective of identifying indicators to merely quantify the state of realization of human rights. Consider, for instance, specific information on the number of arbitrary executions in a particular country. While reflecting the magnitude of the human rights violation, this information does not reveal anything about why the right is not being respected, protected or promoted. In this instance, suitably designed indicators could also quantify information on these other aspects of the problem and thereby help in monitoring the implementation of the concerned right. It is important, therefore, to outline a conceptual framework that supports and guides the process of identifying indicators for the right to development. This requires a certain understanding of the definition of the right and how to operationalize it in a rights-based manner.

The foremost consideration in adopting a methodology for identifying and devising right to development indicators, as for any other indicators, is the relevance and effectiveness of selected indicators in addressing the objective(s) for which they are to be used. Most other methodological requirements for developing indicators follow from this consideration.[4] Often, this consideration is overlooked with the result that efficacy of an indicator in its application is invariably compromised. This becomes evident when, for instance, one breaks down a development process into various operational stages, such as appraisal, policy or program formulation, implementation, and evaluation. Each of these stages presents a definitive requirement, often unique, on the nature and choice of indicators. For instance, an indicator seen to be useful in assessing the current status of a particular public service (a state obligation) directed at the fulfillment of a human right need not be the best indicator for measuring the progress of attainment or enjoyment of that service by people. An indicator that is useful for measuring progress in the realization of a human right need not always capture aspects of violation in the implementation of that right. Similarly, the indicator that is suitable for measuring the overall outcomes need not be the best indicator for use in policy prescription.[5] Thus, if indicators are to be

---

4   It includes methodological concerns like validity and statistical reliability of indicators.
5   Consider the right to education: while the prevalent literacy rate may be a good measure of the enjoyment or the fulfillment of the right, it may not be a good indicator for measuring progress in its realization. This may, for instance, be better captured through enrollment rates for children in the school-

note continues on following page

meaningful, they have to measure up to the requirements and criteria relevant for the aspect of the process for which they are being applied. There are at least two important methodological issues that follow from this concern. These relate to the frequency and soundness of data generating methods and, secondly, to the level of required disaggregation in the data and the indicators. For example, should the data for an indicator be collected on an annual basis or at a longer duration of interval? Should it be collected through statistical survey or be based on expert or household opinion?[6] Should the indicator be disaggregated in terms of the region, gender, or other population segments? The answers to these questions have to be resolved in light of the objective(s) for which the indicators are to be used. Once this is done the appropriate methodology for identifying and devising indicators can be selected and applied.

It is equally important that the selected indicators are suitable to the context to which they are applied. The contextual relevance of indicators is a key consideration in their acceptability among the potential users. Countries and regions within countries differ in terms of their social, economic and political attainments. They differ in the level of realization of human rights. These differences are invariably reflected in terms of differences in development priorities. Therefore, it may not be possible to always have a universal set of indictors to assess attainment and progress in the realization of human rights. Having said that, it is also true that certain human rights indicators, for example those capturing attainments or violations in civil and political rights, may well be relevant across all countries and their regions, whereas others that capture realization of economic or social rights — such as the right to education or shelter — may have to be customised, depending on the level of their realization, to be of relevance to different countries. Thus, in designing a set of human rights indicators, as for any other indicators for measuring the process of social change, there is a need to strike a balance between universally relevant indicators and culturally (contextually) specific indicators. Both kinds of indicators are relevant, one for facilitating cross-regional and international comparisons, and the other for reflecting the local concerns and encouraging "ownership" and implementation by the countries.

Against the backdrop of these considerations, this chapter focuses on developing a conceptual framework for anchoring human rights indicators, including those that could be more specifically related to the right to development. It begins, in Section I, by briefly presenting the notion of the right to development based on the 1986 Declaration on the Right to Development and as it has unfolded in recent past, as well as the rights-based approach to its implementation. Section II attempts a defi-

---

note continued from preceding page

going age group. Similarly, in case of the right to a standard of living adequate for the health and well-being of an individual, the indicator life expectancy at birth may be a good summary measure of longevity and to some extent health of individuals, but its usefulness as an indicator for policy prescription may be limited.

6   See for instance, Rajeev Malhotra and Nicolas Fasel, *Quantitative Human Rights Indicators — A Survey of Major Initiatives*, Paper presented at a seminar in Turku, Finland, available at http://www.abo.fi/instut/imr/indicators/index.htm. The paper is a survey of some major initiatives to develop quantitative human rights indicator. It identifies and analyses categories of human rights indicators in terms of their data generating methodologies.

nition of a human rights indicator and uses the outlined notion of the right to development to suggest an approach for identifying indicators that could help in its implementation. Section III puts together a set of principles and criteria for monitoring the implementation of the right to development. The concluding section raises issues and identifies areas where work needs to be further pursued to support the implementation of human rights, including the right to development.

I. The Notion of a Right to Development — A Recap

Article 1 of the Declaration on the Right to Development (DRtD), adopted by the United Nations General Assembly in 1986, states,

> The right to development is an inalienable human right by virtue of which every human person and all peoples are entitled to participate in, contribute to and enjoy economic, social, cultural and political development, in which all human rights and fundamental freedoms can be fully realized.[7]

Such a broad-based notion of development in terms of economic, social, cultural, and political advancement, directed at the full realization of all human rights and fundamental freedoms, transformed the right to development from a mere claim for a supportive international economic order, rooted in the period of decolonization, to a multifaceted and a cross-cutting human right.[8] One can identify a number of features of this right. The DRtD paved the way to bridge the separation of the civil and political rights from the economic, social and cultural rights that had been effected due to the adoption of two separate Covenants in 1966. The right to development thus formalized the notion of "indivisibility of human rights." A second feature of the Declaration was that it not only placed importance on the outcomes of the development process, which could be identified with the realization of other human rights, but also on the process of their realization. It defined the right to development as a right to participate in, contribute to, and enjoy the fruits of multifaceted development. In effect, besides presenting a self-standing human right, the right to development could be seen as an enabling or a framework right. The third feature of the right was its individual and collective aspect. In identifying the "human person" and "peoples" as beneficiaries, it contained elements of both individual and group rights. At the same time, in placing the obligations on the states — individually and collectively — as well as on all peoples to contribute to the realization of the right, the right to development was presented as a progressive right. Finally, while acknowledging the state as the primary duty holder of the right, the DRtD emphasized the importance of international cooperation in the realization of the right to development.

---

7   Declaration on the Right to Development (UN Doc. A/41/128) and the Resolution on the Right to Development (UN Doc. A/41/133) of December 4, 1986.

8   In its early conception in the 1970s and early 1980s, within the confines of the international arena, the right to development was seen as a right of communities, states, and peoples subjugated to colonial domination and exploitation. It was a collective right whose claimholders were the juridical persons at various levels of groupings such as the states, regions, provinces, municipalities, or towns and the duty holders were the state, the developed countries, and the international community. It was not until later that the right was also conceptualized in the municipal law in addition to the international law.

Elaboration at the Global Consultation

After the DRtD, significant clarification on the content and the implementation of the right to development was provided by the "Global Consultation"[9] on the realization of the right to development as a human right held in 1990. The Consultation arrived at conclusions on a number of issues. On *the content of the right* it was observed that the right to development included the right to effective participation in all aspects of development and at all stages of the decision-making process; the right to equal opportunity and access to resources; the right to fair distribution of the benefits of development; the right to respect for civil, political, economic, social and cultural rights; and the right to an international environment in which all these rights could be fully realized. The human person was seen as the central subject, rather than a mere object of the right to development, and the concept of participation was central to the realization of the right. Participation was to be viewed as a means to an end and as an end in itself. While participation was the principal means by which individuals and peoples collectively determined their needs and priorities to ensure protection and advancement of their rights and interests, for it to be effective in mobilising human and natural resources and in combating inequalities, discrimination, poverty and exclusion a genuine ownership or control of productive resources including land, financial capital and technology were seen as necessary. The right to development was related to the right to self-determination in its many aspects.

In *the implementation of the right,* the Consultation favored a development strategy that addressed the issue of not only economic growth but of achieving social justice and the realization of all human rights. While the strategy had to be contextually defined by the people themselves, it had to conform to international human rights standards. In the development strategy, a role was foreseen for affirmative action both at the national level, in favor of disadvantaged groups, and at the international level, in terms of development assistance to countries constrained by limited availability of resources and technical capacities. The removal of barriers to economic activity, such as trade liberalization, was not seen as sufficient in itself. There was recognition of the interdependence between peace, development, and human rights.

Among the possible *criteria to measure progress* towards the realization of the right to development, the Consultation identified a number of categories, including conditions of life (basic material needs such as food, health, shelter, education, leisure, and a safe and a healthy environment, as well as personal freedom and security); conditions of work (employment, extent of sharing in the benefits of work, income and its equitable distribution, and degree of participation in management); equality of access to resources (access to resources needed for basic needs and equality of opportunity); and participation. Since participation was the right through which all other rights in the DRtD were to be exercised and protected, indicators on participation were critical in measuring progress in the realization of the right to development.

---

9   *The Realization of the Right to Development — Global Consultation on the Right to Development as a Human Right.* Report prepared by the Secretary-General, pursuant to the CHR resolution 1989/45; UN Doc. HR/PUB/91/2, p. 44, para. 143.

These included indicators to capture the form, quality, democratic nature, and effectiveness of participatory processes, mechanisms and institutions. At the international level, it included the equality and democratic character of inter-governmental bodies. Moreover, it was concluded that, in assessing participation, there was a need to include the representativity and accountability of decision-making bodies, the decentralization of decision making, public access to information, and responsiveness of decision-makers to public opinion. It was pointed out that effectiveness of participation had to be assessed from a subjective perspective, also — based on the opinion of the affected persons.

Interpretation of the Independent Expert

Following this body of work, the Independent Expert on the Right to Development, Arjun Sengupta, defined the right to development as a right to a particular process of development in which all human rights and fundamental freedoms can be fully realized.[10] The realization of the right to development is seen as a set of claims universally enjoyed by people, principally on their state and also on the society at large including the international community, to a process that permits and sustains improvement in individual capabilities and presents the necessary opportunities for them to realize the outcomes — the rights and freedoms — set forth in the International Bill of Human Rights,[11] in their totality as an integrated whole. The right to development is thus a right of the people to outcomes, which are improved realizations of different human rights. It is also a right to the process of realizing these outcomes facilitated by the concerned duty holders through policies and interventions that conform to the human right norms, standards, and principles.

Indeed, the right to development is seen as a composite right wherein all the economic, social, and cultural rights, as well as the civil and political rights because of their interdependence and indivisibility are realized together. The integrity of the right implies that if any one of the constituent rights is violated, the composite right to development is also violated. The Independent Expert has described this in terms of an improvement of a "vector" of human rights, which is composed of different rights that constitute the right to development. The realization of the right to development implies an improvement of this vector, such that there is improvement of some or at least one of these rights without any other right being violated.

In his interpretation, the Independent Expert attaches importance to economic growth in defining the content of the right. He sees a role for a particular kind of

---

10   The reports of the Independent Expert are available at http://ap.ohchr.org/documents/dpage_e.aspx?m=52. First report: UN Doc. E/CN.4/1999/WG.18/2; second report: UN Doc. A/55/306; third report: UN Doc.E/ CN.4/2001/WG.18/2; fourth report: UN Doc.E/CN.4/2002/WG.18/2; fifth UN Doc.E/CN.4202 /WG.18/6; sixth UN Doc.E/CN.4/2004/WG.18/2; country study UN Doc.E/CN.4/2004/WG.18/3 and the preliminary study UN Doc.E/CN.4/2003/WG.18/2.

11   It mainly comprises the Universal Declaration of Human Rights (UDHR), the International Covenant on Economic, Social and Cultural Rights (ICESCR), and the International Covenant on Civil and political Rights (ICCPR). The other, more recent instruments designed to address the situation of special groups and regions in the promotion and protection of human rights are the Convention on Elimination of Racial Discrimination (CERD), Convention on Elimination of Discrimination Against Women (CEDAW), Convention on the Right of the Child (CRC) and Convention Against Torture (CAT).

economic growth in relaxing the resource constraints on the implementation of the right to development. This role is relevant when the consideration is co-realization of human rights without retrogression in the realization of any right, and when the pace of fulfillment of human rights and their enjoyment by people is also an issue. Some rights — namely the economic, social, and cultural rights — can be realized only progressively due to limitations of resource availability, given the large gaps (particularly in developing countries) in the current attainment levels and the desired development outcomes corresponding to the realization of human rights. There are other human rights, mainly civil and political, which may be realized more directly and immediately, as they do not require significant levels of resources for their fulfillment. For the Independent Expert, economic growth must be consistent with human rights norms and principles. It must satisfy the basic condition of facilitating the realization of all human rights, and policies for economic growth must be equitable, non-discriminatory, and participatory — generally, the features that he identifies with equity. Further, he argues that these policies need to be pursued with accountability and transparency, in order to be in conformity with principles of both equity and justice.[12] In his formulation, economic growth is not only instrumentally relevant but is sufficiently critical for the realization of the right to development to be an end in itself. He therefore suggests that it has to be an element of the vector that defines the composite right to development in any context.[13]

Approach to Implementing Human Rights

The DRtD and its subsequent interpretations emphasizes that the process of implementing the right to development has to be in conformity with the human rights principles. The Independent Expert has also highlighted some of these principles in his reports. Indeed, there is a general understanding now that in the implementation of human rights, adherence to human rights principles constitutes the essence of what has been termed a rights-based approach.[14] A rights-based approach to implementing the right to development (like other human rights) calls for a process based on the following:[15]

- explicit linkages with international human rights instruments;
- universality and inalienability of human rights;
- indivisible, interdependent and co-realizable nature of human rights;

---

12 See the fifth report of the Independent Expert, UN Doc. E/CN.4202 /WG.18/6, para 11.

13 The issue of whether economic growth has an instrumental importance or a constitutive relevance in the notion of right to development can be debated. It could well be argued that a certain kind of economic growth, when seen in terms of the opportunities that it generates for the people to be productively employed and have a life of dignity and self esteem, may also have a constitutive role in the notion of the right to development. However, to the extent that these desired aspects of growth can be reflected in the process and the other outcomes comprising the right to development, it may not be tenable to argue for a "right to economic growth" and reflect it accordingly in the notion of the right to development.

14 The Office of the High Commissioner for Human Rights defines a rights-based approach as a conceptual framework for the process of human development that is normatively based on international human rights standards and operationally directed to promoting and protecting human rights. For details, see http://www.ohchr.org/english/issues/index.htm.

15 For details, see *Report of the Second Interagency Workshop on Implementing a Human Rights-based Approach in the Context of UN Reform.* Available at http://www.undp.org/governance/docshurist/030617Stamford_Final_Report.doc.

- emphasis on participation and inclusion;
- empowerment of people;
- non-discrimination and a process promoting equality;
- accountability and the rule of law;
- recognition that while some human rights can be realized only progressively, others that could be directly guaranteed need to be protected from denial, non-retrogression, and violations; and
- recourse to redress — legal as well as administrative.

The idea of viewing the development process in terms of various rights — as legally enforceable entitlements — in articulating and advancing claims on the duty holders is an essential ingredient to a human rights approach. It makes it necessary for such an approach to forge explicit linkages with the international human rights instruments. These linkages provide the goals and targets for guiding the process, as well as the principles that help in the conduct of the process.

The notion of universality implies that every individual is endowed with human rights by virtue of being human. It means that human rights must be the same everywhere and for everyone. It ensures that the dignity and the worth of the human life is universally respected, is inalienable and protected against actions that interfere with human well-being.

Human rights are indivisible and interdependent. Any two rights are interdependent if the level of enjoyment of one is dependent on the level of realization of the other. The principle of indivisibility requires that improvement in realization of any human right cannot be at the expense of violation or deterioration in the outcomes associated with any other right. For instance, attainments on the right to education cannot be deemed as socially valuable or even acceptable if they are at the expense of improvement in realization of the right to health. At a more general level, improvement in the realization of economic and social rights cannot be at the expense of the realization of civil and political rights. Similarly, the principle of interdependence among human rights makes it necessary that improvement in realization of any one human right is a function of realization in all or at least some of the other human rights, in any context. Thus, for instance, it is futile to talk of the right to information in the absence of a certain minimal realization on the right to education. It is meaningless to talk of the right to work in the presence of violations of the rights to participate and have equal access to public service, and to be considered as an equal on grounds of race, color, sex, language, or religion. These two principles together make it necessary to see the realization of rights-based development as a process of co-realization of all human rights.

The importance of the principle of participation is recognized in the DRtD which, as we have already noted, recognizes the right to participate as the right through which all other rights are to be exercised and protected. For the implementation of the right to development, participation has to be active, free, and meaningful. It has to be inclusionary such that people, including those from different communities, minorities, indigenous groups, women, other special interest groups, and civil society, are a part of the process to implement the right. It has to be empowering for the participants, enabling them to decide and act for themselves. Moreover, the process for the implementation of human rights has to be non-discriminatory in all respects with equal opportunities for "the equal." It permits the use of special and differential treatment, including the use of affirmative action at both national and international level to address, respectively the vulnerabilities and the inequities of the marginalized groups in the society and the constraints faced by the developing countries in pursuing their development at a desired pace.

Accountability and the rule of law is the cornerstone of a rights-based approach. The implementation process has to be accountable to the people at large. It requires the identification of the claim-holders and their entitlements and the corresponding duty-holders and their obligations. The duty holders primarily include the state, local organizations and authorities, private companies, aid-donors, multilateral institutions and international organizations, and individuals. They have positive obligations (to protect, promote and provide) as well as duties that require abstaining from violations of human rights. Accountability also requires that the process is *transparent* and *credible* in the eyes of people so that it encourages their unfettered participation.

Under the International Covenant on Economic, Social and Cultural Rights (ICESCR), states are required to take immediate steps for the progressive realization of the concerned rights, so that a failure to take the necessary steps, or any retrogression, will flag a breach of the state's duties. Similarly, under the International Covenant on Civil and Political Rights (ICCPR), states are bound to respect the rights concerned, to ensure respect for them, and to take the necessary steps to put them into effect. This recognition that some human rights are subject to progressive realization while others that could be directly guaranteed need to be protected *ad infinitum* against denial, non-retrogression, and violation, brings into play a certain notion of sustainability in following a rights-based approach to the imple-mentation of the right to development. In fact, it can be argued that the rights-based approach addresses sustainability of human wellbeing and freedom, inter-temporally as well as spatially in any context. This aspect is further reinforced with an emphasis in the approach to provide for a genuine recourse to redress — legal as well as administrative — to people who are denied the capacity to realize their human rights.

Some Considerations for a Framework for Indicators

The notion of the right to development as outlined in the DRtD, its subsequent interpretation and elaboration, as well as the approach to its implementation raises some obvious considerations that need to be kept in mind as one moves to outlining a framework for right to development indicators. These could be summarized along the following lines:

- as a composite of all human rights, the right to development indicators would need to capture the attainment levels of people or target groups on specific human rights, as well as the effort being made by the duty holders in furthering the realization of those rights;

- the selection of specific human rights for implementing the right to development would depend on the country context, the development priorities, and the aspirations of its people;

- the necessity of the implementation process to be in conformity with human rights principles would require the right to development indicators to include measures that reflect the extent of operationalization and the adherence of the process to such principles; and

- if feasible, summary measures that provide an indication of the overall realization of the right to development in a given context.

While the right to development, like any other human right, has to follow a rights-based approach in its implementation, it would be necessary to keep in mind the two characteristics of this right that distinguish it from other substantive human rights. This relates to the notion of indivisibility and interdependence of human rights as well as the critical importance of international cooperation in furthering its implementation. These principles are critical in devising the relevant polices and strategies for the implementation of the right to development and, by that virtue, would need to be reflected in the set of indicators identified for facilitating the implementation and monitoring of this right.

Secondly, though it may not be feasible to have a universal composite measure or an index to reflect the realization of the right to development, as the countries would differ in terms of their external and domestic development contexts and prevailing attainments levels on human rights, and on account of legitimate difference in development priorities and aspirations of the people, it may still be possible and even desirable to have an overall summary measure for the right that could be identified at the national level. For instance, an overall indicator on the degree of inequality in the distribution of wealth and/or income or the incidence of poverty (particularly for vulnerable segments of the population) could be good summary measures for tracking improvements in the realization of the right to development in some contexts. In others, one could look at measures that capture the extent of participation encouraged and exercised in decision making on issues that have a significant bearing on the lives and well being of people. Such right to development summary measures at country level would have to be identified by an assessment of what constitutes the essence of the right in a given country context. One could also think of composite measures that bring together some relevant indicators of a particular kind (namely, "outcome" or "process" indicators) at the country level. However, it would have its share of pitfalls and limitations. On the whole, if a summary measure is feasible and appropriate in reflecting the right to development concerns it could do wonders in improving advocacy, as well as implementation of the right.[16]

---

16 A good example of this consideration is the Human Development Index (HDI) brought out by UNDP in its annual *Human Development Reports.*

In the literature, there is an absence of adequate consensus on what could be considered as human rights and right to development indicators. The Independent Expert on the Right to Development has focused on various commonly used socioeconomic indicators to monitor and assess the development process for the realization of the right to development in his reports. While these attempts are useful starting points, they do not comprise an adequate framework for any approach to identify and design indicators for facilitating the implementation and monitoring of the right to development.

II. A Framework for Indicators

The general notion of the word "indicator" constrains all indicators to have a common purpose, namely to provide specific information on the state or condition of an event, activity or an outcome. However, it allows indicators to assume various forms, of a qualitative or a quantitative nature. This in turn creates the scope for plurality in the understanding of the concept and methodologies to build indicators, which sometimes can be a source of confusion. It is necessary, therefore to have a minimum common understanding of the types of indicators that are a focus of this chapter and are seen as being useful in monitoring the implementing of the right to development.

In the context of this chapter, it is useful to look at human rights indicators as specific information on the state of an event, activity, or outcome that can be related to human rights norms and standards; that addresses and reflects human rights concerns and principles; and that is used to assess and monitor promotion and protection of human rights. Defined in this manner, there could be some indicators that are uniquely human rights indicators because they owe their existence to certain human rights norms or standards, and are generally not used in other contexts. This could be the case, for instance, with an indicator like the number of extra-judicial summary or arbitrary executions, or the reported number of victims of torture by the police and the paramilitary forces, or the number of children who do not have access to primary education because of discrimination exerted by officials. At the same time, there could be a large number of other indicators, such as socio-economic statistics (for example, the UNDP's human development indicators), that could meet (at least implicitly) all the definitional requirements of a human rights indicator as laid out here. In all these cases, to the extent that such indicators relate to the human rights standards and principles and are used for human rights assessment, it would be helpful to consider them as human rights indicators.

Quantitative and Qualitative Indicators

Indicators can be *quantitative* or *qualitative*. The first category views indicators narrowly as an equivalent of "statistics" and the latter, a broader usage covering any information relevant to observance or enjoyment of a specific right. In this chapter the term "quantitative indicator"[17] is used to designate any kind of indicators that

---

17   The three expressions, namely, quantitative, statistical, or numerical indicators, are often used interchangeably.

are or can be expressed in quantitative form, such as numbers, percentages, or indices. In this tradition there have been attempts to identify and develop quantitative indicators, such as enrollment rates for the school-going age group of children, indicators on ratification of treaties, proportion of seats held by women in national parliament, and incidence of enforced or involuntary disappearance. At the same time, one finds a widespread use of "checklists," or a set of questions as indicators, which sometimes seek to complement or elaborate numerical information on the realization of human rights. In this instance, the usage of the word "indicator" refers to information beyond statistics. In the agencies of the United Nations system and in the human rights community, experts have often favored such an interpretation of the word indicator. It is important to note that these two main usages of the word "indicator" in the human rights community do not reflect two opposed approaches. Given the complexity of assessing compliance with human rights standards, all relevant qualitative and quantitative information is potentially useful. Quantitative indicators can facilitate qualitative evaluations by measuring the magnitude of certain events. Reciprocally, qualitative information can complement the interpretation of quantitative indicators.

Objective and Subjective Indicators

In addition to this distinction between a quantitative and a qualitative indicator, human rights indicators could also be categorized as *objective* or *subjective* indicators. This distinction is not necessarily based on the consideration of using, or not using, reliable or replicable methods of data collection for defining the indicators. Instead, it is ideally seen in terms of the information content of the concerned indicators. Thus, objects, facts, or events that can, in principle, be directly observed or verified (for example, weight of children, number of violent deaths, or nationality of a victim) are categorized as objective indicators. Indicators based on perceptions, opinions, assessment, or judgments expressed by individuals are categorized as subjective indicators.[18] In practice and in the context of certain human rights, this distinction between objective and subjective information is often difficult to make. Elements of subjectivity in the identified category of objective indicators cannot be fully excluded or isolated. The characterization of the nature of information captured can in itself be seen as a subjective exercise. Nevertheless, use of transparent, specific and universally recognized definitions for particular events, facts and objects contribute, in a general sense, to greater objectivity when identifying and designing any type of indicator, be it a quantitative, qualitative, subjective, or an objective indicator.

The use of these indicators, whether quantitative/qualitative or objective/subjective, in undertaking human rights assessments represent options that are in most instances complementary and mutually supportive. In that sense no single indicator or single category of indicator can provide a complete assessment of a given situation. Just as one ends up looking at information and analysis beyond a given indicator to

---

18   The distinction between objective and subjective indicators has its origin primarily in the literature on development economics; see, for instance, UNDP's *Human Development Report 2002* (New York: Oxford University Press and UNDP, 2002), pp. 36-37.

assess a situation adequately, one has to consider the information content of different kinds of indicators related to a situation to assess the essence of that situation.

Indicators for the Right to Development

In outlining a framework for identifying and devising indicators for the implementation and monitoring of the right to development, we may need to consider two sets of indicators. The first of these is general in the sense that it does not relate exclusively to the realization of any specific human right, but is meant to capture the quality of process in terms of its adherence to the principles that define a rights-based approach to implementing a human right. The indicators in this category, for instance, would capture the extent to which the development process is participatory, inclusionary, accountable, non-discriminatory, sustainable, or empowering. The second set of indicators is more specific and directed at capturing the attainments of individuals on all those human rights (for example the right to adequate food, the right to adequate housing, or the right to life) the progress in which is considered critical for the fulfillment and enjoyment of right to development, in a given context. As noted earlier, this basket of rights may vary from one country to another depending on its level of development, the priorities and the aspirations of the people. The indicators identified for a human right have to be anchored in the normative content of that right, as enumerated in relevant articles of the treaties and concerned General Comments of the Committees. It calls for a well thought-through approach to translate the legal standards of the human rights framework into operational elements that could directly contribute to identification and selection of suitable indicators for human rights implementation and monitoring. These two sets of indicators are complementary and between them are expected to potentially cover the conduct of the process and the outcomes that it generates for realizing the right to development.

Indicators for Human Rights Principles

There are some issues that need to be kept in mind while identifying indicators for the principles that define a rights-based approach to implementing and monitoring human rights. For example, it may not be always possible to identify indicators for each of the principles uniquely. Given the inter-relatedness and the mutually reinforcing nature of these principles, we may have to look at indicators that capture the operationalization of the concerned principle in the most appropriate manner. There could be instances where the same indicator captures more than one principle of the rights-based process. It would be desirable to work with as many of such indicators as possible as it would ease the requirement of data collection for the implementing and monitoring agencies. Secondly, it is possible that in the absence of a direct measure of any principle that informs the process of a rights-based approach to implementing human rights, there may be a need to use proxy indicators, which, though being only indirect measures of the concerned principle are nonetheless useful in assessing the conformity of the process to the desired path. Finally, it is also possible that, depending on the level of disaggregation of the indicators such as national, regional, or local project level, different indicators may have to be considered to capture these principles or even the same principle.[19] Let us now identify the possible indicators for the different principles.

Consider the necessity for an indicator to have an explicit linkage with the international human rights instruments. We have seen that this is very much a definitional requirement of any indicator to be used in human rights monitoring. It enables and ensures that the indicators are uniquely defined with respect to the normative content of the rights. Among the human rights, there are some that are "substantive rights," such as the right to life or right to education, that have a relatively clear content and may also have a "level" or "progressive" component in realizing them. There are others that are "procedural rights,"[20] like the right not to be discriminated against, or the rights in the administration of justice (including the right to a fair trial), the realization of which may be critical to the process of realizing the substantive rights. It is necessary that indicators for the procedural as well as the substantive rights are anchored in the relevant human rights standards. We come back to this issue more centrally in elaborating the second set of indicators for substantive rights that are seen as being critical for implementing the right to development in a given context.

The principles of universality, indivisibility, and interdependence of human rights encourage the need to have a common approach to identifying indicators for both civil and political rights, as well as the economic, social, and cultural rights. Indeed, the recognition that there is an element of protection, as well as promotion, in the implementation of all human rights, and that the underlying processes in the implementation of both sets of rights have to be in conformity to the relevant human rights standards and principles, reinforces the need to have a common approach to human rights implementation and monitoring. More importantly, in the context of implementing the right to development, the principle of indivisibility and interdependence requires that the set of indicators selected cover all facets of the right — the civil and political as well as the economic, social, and cultural.

The emphasis on participation and having an inclusionary and empowering approach has two aspects. The first one is to ensure that there are at least some indicators selected that capture the essence of these principles in the implementation process of the right and, secondly, that the process of identifying the indicators and using them for monitoring the implementation of the right is itself based on participation and inclusion of all stakeholders of that process. Indeed, identification of specific indicators for these principles may not be as important as the application of these principles in undertaking a rights-based process to monitor the implementation of human rights. However, there may be instances where summary outcome indicators, like Gini Coefficient of income, as a measure of how outcome of a

---

19   For instance, an indicator on the principle of participation at the country or regional level may be different from the one that captures participation at the level of a project or a development program.
20   See Maria Green, "What We Talk About When We Talk About Indicators: Current Approaches to Human Rights Measurement," *Human Rights Quarterly*, Vol. 23, No. 4, (November 2001), p. 1071.

development process flows to different segments of a population in terms of their re-spective income shares, could be used as a proxy for assessing the participatory na-ture of the development process. Such inequality indicators can also be used in conjunction with changes in the incidence of poverty. A move towards greater equality and a lower incidence of poverty would imply that the fruits of the develop-ment process are being distributed evenly and to a larger number of people and thus, the process is participatory at least in its outcomes. These indicators could also be presented at a higher level of aggregation, including provincial or even regional levels. Moreover, they could also be seen in terms of a process rather than only as out-come indicators. In such a case, we could also look at indicators that capture the in-equality in growth rates for Gross Domestic Product at the regional or province level. The process part of the participation could also be captured by bringing in indica-tors on civil and political rights, particularly related to participation in the political affairs, decision making, and government.

It is not easy to identify indicators that directly capture the notion of empower-ment, as it is commonly understood. However, if empowerment is thought of as a state of being that enables a person to have a say and exercise choice in decisions re-lated to the self, or at the level of households or community, it may be possible to identify some proxy indicators. Indicators on work participation rates of the popu-lation, in general, and of specific sections, in particular (such as women, minorities, and other social groups); location-specific work-participation rates; and work partic-ipation rates by type of employment could be useful indicators in this context. These indicators, when tracked over time, would reveal the extent to which a development process generates employment, hence incomes and opportunities for people to exer-cise choice. In certain contexts, where lack of literacy is seen as a bottleneck to aware-ness, information, and empowerment, the notion of empowerment could be related to the degree of educational attainments. Similarly, indicators on decision-making processes, electoral participation, recourse to redress, and financial and administra-tive decentralization within countries at regional and sub-regional levels are also useful indicators in capturing the notion of empowerment. Some of these indicators could also reflect the extent to which the process is participatory.

In seeking indicators to capture principles of non-discrimination and equality in the implementation of human rights necessitates a specific focus on disaggregation of data, to reflect the situation of the vulnerable and marginalized population groups vis-à-vis the rest of the population. More importantly, it implies an emphasis on in-dicators that capture the nature of access, and not just availability, to goods and serv-ices that allow an individual to realize his or her rights. It is, perhaps, also useful to view the principles of non-discrimination and equality, as well as those related to the rule of law and recourse to redress mechanisms, as "procedural rights" that have a bearing on the realization of all the "substantive rights." Indeed, it may be easier to define procedural rights in the context of a substantive right. Thus, the human rights principle of non-discrimination or the notion of recourse to redress could be incor-porated in the design of indicators for monitoring a substantive right. For instance, compliance with the principle of non-discrimination in the context of the right to education could be captured using an indicator like the proportion of girls in the school-going age group enrolled in school to the proportion of boys in the same age group enrolled in school.

The principle of accountability is, perhaps, the most difficult to quantify in terms of indicators, and particularly so if the aim is to objectively track the notion over time in the process of implementing human rights. This is so because all human rights are not justiciable everywhere and at all times. Moreover, the notion of accountability could be interpreted in different ways. The fact that the content of a human right is clarified and even quantified with the use of appropriate indicators and, by virtue of that, the obligations of the duty holder become more apparent and concrete, is already a step in the direction of improving accountability in the process of implementing human rights. The notion of accountability could also be viewed in terms of selecting indicators that establish an unambiguous linkage between duties of the State parties (through identification and application of specific public policy instruments) and the corresponding targets or desired outcomes for a right, which are seen as milestones in the realization of that human right. One has to then simply track indicators on those milestones to assess the extent to which the state can be held accountable for its acts of commission or omission in implementing the right. In the following section on the framework of indicators for substantive human rights, a possible approach to address such an interpretation of the accountability principle is outlined. The suggested framework, as we shall shortly see, is also useful in capturing the essence of the principle of progressive realization. The key concern, in this case, is to identify indicators that are able to monitor the realization of the right at periodic intervals of time.

Indicators for Substantive Human Rights

The indicators on substantive human rights (identified as constituting the composite right to development in a given context) could reflect outcomes — both positive, such as the literacy attainment of a population group, and negative, as in the number of extra-judicial killings — and the underlying processes relevant for the realization of the concerned human right. In each case, as a starting point, there is a need to translate the narrative on the legal standard of the right into a limited number of characteristic attributes that facilitate the identification of the appropriate indicators for monitoring the implementation of the right. Such a step is prompted primarily by the need to establish a clear linkage between the identified indicators and the relevant human rights standards. It also contributes to the analytic convenience of having a structured approach with which to read the normative content of the right. Often, one finds that the enumeration of the right in the relevant articles and their elaboration in the concerned general comments are quite general and even overlapping, and not quite amenable to the process of identifying indicators. By identifying the major attributes of a right, the process of selecting suitable indicators or clusters of indicators is facilitated. Consider the case of right to life: following this approach, and taking into account Article 6 of the ICCPR and General Comment 6 of the Human Rights Committee, one could, for example, identify at least four attributes of the right to life — namely, "arbitrary deprivation of life," "disappearances of individuals," "health and nutrition," and "death penalty." Similarly, in the case of the right to food, based on Article 11 of ICESCR and General Comment 12 of the Committee on Economic, Social, and Cultural Rights (ESCR), one could identify "nutrition," "food safety and consumer protection," "food availability," and "food accessibility" as the relevant attributes.[21]

To the extent feasible, for all substantive rights, the attributes have to be based on an exhaustive reading of the legal standard of the right and identified in a mutually exclusive manner. It may be argued, for instance, in the case of most economic, social, and cultural rights, to adopt a generic approach to the identification of attributes based on the notion of "adequacy," "accessibility," "availability," "adaptability," and "quality." While such an approach may not be feasible for most civil and political rights, even in the case of economic, social, and cultural rights it may not be easy to follow consistently. Moreover, the notion of adequacy for each economic, social, and cultural right would have unique manifestation anchored in the respective standard. It may, therefore, be best to adopt a flexible approach in the identification of the attributes of the rights, the only consideration being that attributes should reflect the essence of the normative content of the right and should be in the nature of a step closer to identifying the relevant indicators.

In the second stage, a configuration of structural, process and outcome indicators would be identified for the selected attributes of a human right. A key concern in proposing such a configuration of indicators is to facilitate a simple, systematic and a comprehensive approach to the identification of indicators for monitoring the implementation of each right. It enables a common approach to the organization of specific information for monitoring the civil and political rights, as well as the economic, social, and cultural rights. The approach highlights the importance of the nature and conduct of the process in the realization of human rights. Further, as pointed out in the previous section, by establishing an unambiguous linkage, to the extent feasible, between duties of the State parties (policy instruments) and the desired targets or milestones in the realization of human rights, the approach brings out the value-added of a rights-based approach — in particular, the importance of accountability in the implementation and monitoring of human rights. In fact, the implicit causality between the structural, process, and outcome indicators enables the identification and assessment of the effort that a State party is expected to take or is

---

21   In undertaking this exercise, one could take into account, for example, Articles 10, 11, and 12 of the ICESCR, 6 of the CRC, and 9 of the CMW in the context of the right to life, and Articles 6(1) of ICCPR, 5(e-iii) of ICERD, 14(2-h) of CEDAW and 27(3) of CRC for the right to food. Moreover, General Comment No. 17 of the HRC on the rights of the child, General Comment No. 12 of the CESCR on the right to food, the United Nations Principles on the Effective Prevention and Investigation of Extra-Legal, Arbitrary and Summary Execution, the United Nations Code of Conduct for Law Enforcement Officials, the Convention on the Prevention and Punishment of the Crime of Genocide and reports of the Special Rapporteur on Extrajudicial, Summary, or Arbitrary Executions are also relevant sources for the right to life. Similarly, General Comment No. 15 of the CESCR on the right to water, General Comment No. 6 of the HRC on the right to life and the reports of the Special Rapporteur on the Right to Food are other examples of sources that may be taken into account for the second right.

taking in addressing its obligations — an issue that should legitimately be the prime concern in monitoring the implementation of human rights.

The *structural indicators* are those indicators that reflect the ratification or adoption of legal instruments by a country, and the existence of basic institutional mechanisms deemed necessary for facilitating realization of the concerned human right. For example, the structural indicators in the context of the right to food would include information on the legal status of the right; legal status of related rights (rights of women to agricultural land); the existence of institutional mechanisms, including the policy and regulatory frameworks; and agencies mandated to address and monitor the issue of food availability and accessibility. Similarly, in the case of the right to legal remedies, the structural indicators could include information on ratification of relevant international instruments; establishment of requisite judicial institutions; and a supportive framework of laws, rules, and regulations seen as necessary to implement the right.

The *process indicators* relate the state policy instruments with development milestones which cumulate into outcomes that could be more directly related to realization of human rights. Such indicators could not only capture the notion of accountability but, at the same time, help in directly monitor the progressive fulfillment of the right or the process of protecting the right, as the case may be for the realization of the concerned right. Unlike the outcome indicators the process indicators are more sensitive to reflecting changes; hence, instead of a series of outcome indicators over a number of years, they are better at capturing progressive realization of the right or reflecting the progress in the efforts of the State parties in protecting the rights. In case of the right to food, process indicators could include the various state policy instruments such as indicators on land tenure system, land reforms, public investment in irrigation, agriculture extension, subsidy on agriculture inputs, indicators on trade regime; population covered by the public distribution system, food subsidy; and indicators on capacity of the state to undertake relief work. Similarly, in case of the right to life, some of the relevant process indicators covering the identified attributes could include proportion of reported cases of arbitrary deprivation of life taken-up by independent reporting/investigating mechanisms; average time spent by an under-trial in police custody before judicial examination; and proportions of convicts exercising the right to review by higher court.

The *outcome indicators* capture attainments that reflect the enjoyment of the right at an individual level, as well as the collective level, in a given context. Some outcome indicators in case of the right to food could be the share of monthly household expenditure on food, average calorie intake of the people vis-à-vis applicable norms or anthropometric measures for women and children. In case of the right to life these could be proportion of death sentences commuted or the reported incidence of arbitrary loss of life. There are at least two important features of an outcome indicator. First of all, as mentioned above, these indicators could be more directly related to the realization of the corresponding right and secondly, there may be a number of processes contributing to the attainment of a single outcome. It therefore becomes useful to make a distinction between the process and outcome indicators. Thus, for instance, if life expectancy at birth is used as an outcome indicator for the realization of right to health, it may be useful to look at process indicators on infant mortality, public hygiene, nutrition, and education as milestones that need to be progressively attained for the fulfillment and the realization of this human right. Identically, if reported incidence of disappearances or arbitrary detentions is an outcome indicator for the realization of the right to life, it may be useful to monitor the process of training programs for police personnel, to improve their awareness and sensitivity to respect human rights, the creation of independent investigating mechanisms at the country level, like National Human Rights Institutions, or access of the individuals to a judicial review of their detention, as means to protect and promote the right.

It may be argued that an approach based on identification of indicators in each of these three categories may lead to a large number of indicators required for monitoring human rights. While this is partially true, there are ways to overcome this concern. One could set aside some criteria to limit the final selection of indicators for a specific right. Sometimes a single indicator may be seen as adequate to cover more than one attribute of a right; in other cases, a few indicators may be required to cover just one attribute of a right. Given that it may not be always easy to find a unique indicator for a given attribute of a right, it may be desirable to select indicators that can potentially capture more than one attribute of the concerned right; thereby economizing on the total number of indicators. Moreover, the configuration of the structural, process, and outcome indicators should be seen as a framework to systematically cover all aspects of the realization of a right — from the perspective of duty holders and their obligations, as well as the right holder and his or her rights. The actual choice of indicators could be made taking into account the country context and its implementation priorities. In most instances, statistical considerations and data availability will also have a role in arriving at the list of indicators suitable for monitoring the implementation of human rights. Finally, in the context of implementing the right to development, it may be desirable to keep in mind that, depending on the country context, there may be a specific need to identify some indicators that capture the essence and importance of international cooperation in facilitating the implementation of the right to development. It would also be necessary to keep in mind the need for the selected indicators to be suitable for temporal and spatial comparison and amenable to disaggregation and decomposition in terms of gender and specific population groups.

Merits of the Framework

Ultimately, it may not matter if an indicator is identified in one or the other suggested category. However, working with such an approach simplifies the selection of indicators; encourages the use of contextually relevant information; facilitates a more comprehensive coverage of the different attributes or aspects of the realization of the right; and, perhaps, also minimizes on the overall number of indicators required to monitor the realization of the concerned right in any context. Moreover, though there is no one-to-one correspondence between the three categories of indicators and the state obligations to respect, protect, and fulfill human rights, an appropriate combination of structural, process, and outcome indicators, particularly the process indicators, could help in assessing the implementation of the three obligations.[22]

Through such a configuration of indicators, there is also an attempt at capturing both the "flow" and the "stock" aspects of the process of social change and development that underpins the protection and the promotion of the human rights. A "flow" indicator allows monitoring of momentary changes (from year to year — for example, per capita availability of food grains or number of reported entries in and releases from arbitrary deprivation of liberty during a reference period), while a "stock" indicator reflects summary outcomes that consolidate such changes over successive years (for example, anthropometric measures for school-going children or the number of reported persons arbitrarily deprived of their liberty at the end of a reference period). An appropriate mix of such indicators could potentially overcome some of the constraints associated with availability of suitable information and data-lags in monitoring human rights.

III. Rights-Based Approach to Monitoring

Having outlined a framework for identifying indicators for facilitating the implementation of the right to development, it would be desirable to apply and interpret such indicators appropriately and undertake the assessment process in a rights-based manner, that is, in conformity human rights standards and principles. A rights-based monitoring is not divorced from other existing monitoring approaches such as those followed by any administrative agency at national or sub-national level to monitor, for instance, agricultural production and food security, or administration of justice, or even project-level outcomes and impacts. However, it necessitates a certain institutional arrangement for collection of information and a focus on specific data that embodies and reflects the realization of human rights for the most vulnerable and marginalized groups of a population. A shift in focus from national averages to status of vulnerable groups, ideally going down to the individual level, permits an assessment of the extent of discrimination, lack of equality, or even violation of the right for some — a principal concern in monitoring the realization of human rights. This, however, does not mean that rights-based monitoring is all about disaggregated information and indicators. Indeed, as has been outlined above, rights-based monitoring requires an appropriate set of indicators as tools to facilitate a credible assessment of the realization of human rights.

---

22   This is particularly so if one is using socio-economic and other administrative data for inferring the implementation of the three kinds of obligations. While an outcome indicator may reveal the overall failure of the State party in meeting the three obligations, it may not be able to distinguish which of the three obligations are indeed violated. In case of the process indicators it may be easier to identify the specific obligations that are being violated. However, if we consider events-based data on human rights violations given the nature and the methodology for collection of relevant information, it may be the easiest way to derive indicators that capture specifically the violations to respect, protect, or fulfill. For details see Malhotra and Fasel, "*Quantitative Human Rights Indicators — A Survey of Major Initiatives, supra,* note 6."

Rights-based monitoring often builds on existing monitoring systems by bringing in the human rights perspective through recognition of various stakeholders — the duty-bearers and the claim-holders — and the kind of information that is particularly relevant for each of them. It involves a distinction to be made between institutions with responsibility for implementing programs and providing information on progress in meeting their obligations for realization of the relevant human rights, and the institutions that represent independent monitoring mechanisms. For instance, in case of a monitoring system for the right to food, the Ministry of Agriculture or Health and Family Welfare, on one hand, and an independent national human rights institution or a human rights nongovernmental organization (NGO), on the other, may have distinct though complementary roles to play in monitoring the realization of the right to food. In devising a rights-based monitoring system, it is necessary that the approach to identifying institutions, their responsibilities, and the methods to collect information adhere to the principles of participation, transparency, and accountability. More importantly, it is essential that the process is country-owned, country-implemented, sufficiently decentralized, and inclusive for the different stakeholders to reflect their concerns.

In setting up a rights-based monitoring mechanism at the country level or strengthening an existing mechanism to monitor the realization of a particular human right, one can identify, among others, the following steps or guiding principles. These steps could help in putting together the requisite institutional arrangements for monitoring and in identifying the specific capacity gaps that may have to be addressed in improving the implementation of human rights.

Identification of Stakeholders for Monitoring Human Rights

As a first step, it would be necessary to identify the various institutional and non-institutional stakeholders who would be contributing to the monitoring process, either as information providers or independent interpreters of the available information, or as the ultimate users of that information for articulating their claims and monitoring the realization of human rights. This may involve, *inter alia*, the administrative agencies including the relevant line ministries, the National Human Rights Institution, relevant civil society organizations engaged in monitoring human rights, consumer groups, other social groups — including parliamentary committees — and claim holders at large. Once the monitoring stakeholders have been identified at the country level, it would be necessary to bring together the different monitoring stakeholders in a participatory process, where their respective competencies and perspectives, based on complementarities in objectives (such as focus on different aspects of the right) and methods of information collection, contributes to the monitoring process. An important element of this process is the identification of an independent institution that takes a lead in interpreting the available information from a human rights perspective, and perhaps also coordinates the assessment of other partners. It could well be the National Human Rights Institution or human rights NGO. This would facilitate the creation of a country-owned monitoring mechanism.

Identification of Major Vulnerable Groups

It is possible that one could identify different segments of the population as being vulnerable on different attributes or elements of the core content of a specific human right. For instance, considering the right to adequate food, in some cases children could be more likely to suffer form dietary inadequacy or malnutrition, whereas working or migrant populations may be more vulnerable from the point of food safety and consumer protection. In each country, it would be desirable to assess the major vulnerable and marginalized groups by population segments and by region. The process of identifying the vulnerable groups using appropriate criteria also has to be based on the human rights principles of participation and transparency, allowing for potential self-selection by individuals, if required. This would yield the focus group for rights-based monitoring and, at the same time, help in assessing the disaggregation requirement of information and data for the identified indicators.

Focus on Non-Discrimination and Accessibility Indicators

Given that human rights are universal and inalienable, it is imperative in the context of undertaking rights-based monitoring that special attention be given to such information, data and indicators that capture the extent to which discrimination of individuals and population groups influences the level of realization of their human rights. Thus, the notion of "accessibility" as against mere "availability" has a particular importance in the human rights framework and in the context of rights-based monitoring. It is not sufficient, for instance, to ensure the availability of such commodities and services that correspond to the realization of human rights; it is equally important to ensure the accessibility of these commodities and services to all individuals, in keeping with the human rights principles of non-discrimination and equality.[23] Accordingly, in undertaking rights-based monitoring or human rights assessments, it is necessary to identify relevant information on discrimination and tailor the data generating mechanisms to collect, compile, and present such information as appropriate indicators.

Reporting Periodicity, Publication, Access to Information, and Follow-Up

Given that the realization of human rights is not a one-time event, both protection and promotion of human rights have to be continuously pursued. It would be necessary to have information or data to monitor the concerned human right at different points of time, at least, or ideally through an appropriate time-series of observations. This would facilitate monitoring of the progressive realization of the right and the incidence of violation of the right over time. A rights-based monitoring mechanism also requires access of all stake-holders, in particular the claim holders, to available information and data on realization of the right. This necessitates a framework with a schedule of publication and dissemination of relevant information. As a follow-up to the monitoring process, it also implies a framework that enables use of available

---

23   The notion of accessibility has dimensions like physical and economic access that may have to be monitored.

information as an advocacy tool — to raise awareness on entitlements and duties, help in better articulation of claims by the right holders and in monitoring the progress in discharge of obligations by duty holders.

Conclusion

This chapter has made an attempt to outline a framework for identifying and devising indictors to facilitate the implementation and monitoring of the right to development. In building this framework, it has addressed the conceptual basis for such indicators by summarizing the notion of the right to development as presently understood in the debates in the various mechanisms of the United Nations Commission on Human Rights. An approach has been suggested to identify indicators on the "substantive" human rights that may constitute the composite right to development in any context, as well as the on the human rights principles that must be adhered to in any process to implement the right to development. The chapter also identifies the elements of a rights-based framework for monitoring the implementation of the right to development.

It has to be recognized that having suitable indicators to facilitate the implementation of human rights is just one element, though perhaps a critical one, in the realization of the rights. The other, equally important element is to use indicators, other relevant information, and suitable tools to formulate the required policies and programs to implement the human rights. This chapter does not enter into any discussions about the nature of policies and programs that could help in the implementation of the right to development. While appropriate indicators may help in identifying development outcomes and goals that embody the normative human rights concerns and correspond to the realization of the right to development, the policies that could help in reaching such goals and outcomes still need to be worked out. In general, while it is true that there is no unique model for the implementation of the right to development as it is largely context-determined, there is considerable scope in analyzing the development experience of both developed and developing countries to identify the elements that can facilitate the operationalization of the right to development. It would be interesting, for instance, to identify the strategies that some countries may, if at all, have adopted to address the issue of enforceability of the right to development or its constituent rights in their respective contexts. It may also be desirable to study the approaches employed to provide redress, not necessarily through legal recourse alone, to the perceived denial or violation of the right. Insights from such analysis could help in furthering the implementation of the right to development.

Finally, the issue of priority-setting in the context of implementation of such human rights as are subject to progressive realization and define the composite right to development in a given context has not been addressed in this paper. Indeed, this issue is yet to be addressed in the debate on the right to development. The issue is all the more important where it matters the most. In some poor, developing countries, where gaps in the realization of rights are equally large for most human rights, the resource constraints may make the issue of priority-setting, and the implicit trade-offs in the fulfillment of various rights, potentially intractable for the duty holders. In such instances, though human rights principles could be invoked to help address the issue, a formal analysis of the process of priority setting and formulation of a more rigorous approach may be necessary for furthering the implementation of the right to development.

Part IV. International Institutions and Global Processes

11 | Human Rights-Based Development in the Age of Economic Globalization: Background and Prospects
Asbjørn Eide

We live in an age of accelerating globalization. This process should have been one of inclusion, expanding effective human freedom for all through multilateral cooperation based on shared commitments towards common goals. That, indeed, was an inspiring vision for those who took the initiative after World War II to establish the United Nations and to include the realization of human rights for all among its aims. For many, however, the globalization we have witnessed during the past quarter century is a process of expanding power by dominant actors in the global economy, bringing vastly increased fortunes to some, causing growing inequalities between and within nations and causing outright impoverishment for the most vulnerable. The economic pattern of globalization has become deeply conflictual. It is the purpose of this chapter to show that the pattern deviates from global cooperation as envisaged in the establishment of the United Nations and the adoption in 1948 of the package of universal standards for human rights. I argue in this chapter that the only way to ensure a constructive and consensual globalization is through human rights-based development, where economic and social rights are given their position as equals with civil and political rights.

Visions and Commitments:
Setting Out the Visions: 1941 to 1948

When the then President of the United States, Franklin D. Roosevelt, made his State of the Union Address to the US Congress on January 6, 1941 — the so-called Four Freedoms Address — he was the first politician to present a vision of worldwide development based on human rights and freedoms. In this address, he projected a world founded upon four freedoms: the freedom of speech and expression, the freedom of worship, the freedom from want, and the freedom from fear. His vision was endorsed in the Atlantic Declaration[1] made by President Roosevelt and the then-Prime Minister of the United Kingdom, Winston Churchill, in August 1941, and repeated in what was called the Declaration by United Nations, a meeting of governments (many of them in exile) in January 1942.[2] It captured the imagination of people around the world during the war years and laid the groundwork for the preparation of the United Nations and the elaboration of a declaration of human rights that should have global application.

---

1 The text of the Atlantic Charter is found in Ruth Russell, *The History of the United Nations* (Washington, DC: The Brookings Institution, 1958), p. 975.
2 *Ibid.*, p. 976.

The preparation took place against a somber background: the lights of democracy had largely been extinguished on the continent of Europe, Japanese militarist aggression was rampant in East and Southeast Asia, and massive violations of human rights were carried out with impunity. Large parts of the world were still under colonial rule.

There was a growing recognition that the political upheavals and the emergence of authoritarian regimes in Europe had been caused by the social and economic chaos resulting from the great economic depression in the 1930s and the lack of adequate economic and social policies to address that chaos; consequently, there was a perceived need for a more cooperative approach to economic, social, and humanitarian affairs at the global level.

The outcome of World War II made it possible to envisage a fundamental change of the international order, from one of coexistence between self-centered, sovereign states, watching each other as potential threats to one of cooperation, which could make it possible to solve common problems of the world community. The future United Nations was envisioned as the forum and the main institution for this purpose.

The Charter of the United Nations, adopted in May 1945, set as one of its three main purposes achieving, "international co-operation in solving international problems of an economic, social, cultural, or humanitarian character, and . . . promoting and encouraging respect for human rights and for fundamental freedoms for all without distinction as to race, sex, language, or religion."[3] In 1948, these rights were spelled out in the Universal Declaration of Human Rights (UDHR). In its Preamble, the Declaration refers to the Four Freedoms Address as its source of inspiration. The fundamental starting point of the Declaration is that human rights are for everyone, everywhere in the world; everyone is, "born free and equal in dignity and rights,"[4] and a broad list of rights was included to ensure that human beings should remain free and equal. Civil, political, economic, social, and cultural rights were made part of a composite package, which today constitutes the normative system of human rights.

Taken together, that interrelated and indivisible system of human rights norms was proclaimed by the United Nations General Assembly as

> a common standard of achievement for all peoples and all nations, to the end that every individual and every organ of society, keeping this Declaration constantly in mind, shall strive by teaching and education to promote respect for these rights and freedoms and by progressive measures, national and international, to secure their universal and effective recognition and observance.[5]

The UDHR did not spell out in detail whose responsibility it should be to ensure that these rights could in fact be enjoyed, but this became clearer with the sub-

---

3   United Nations Charter, Article 1(3). Available at www.un.org/aboutun/charter/.
4   *Ibid.*, Article 1.
5   Universal Declaration of Human Rights (UDHR), Preamble of the Declaration. General Assembly Resolution 217 A (III) (December 10, 1948). Available at www.unhrc.ch/udhr/.

sequent adoption of the main international covenants on human rights. Yet there were already some important points in the Declaration. While each state would, by necessity, have the primary responsibility to ensure and realize these rights, the Preamble in the UDHR shows that rights-based development is a responsibility to which everyone should contribute. This is also reflected in Article 29 (1) of the Declaration: every person has duties to the community in which the free and full development of his or her personality is possible.

The call for global action is set out in UDHR, Article 28, which provides that, "everyone is entitled to a social and international order in which the rights and freedoms set forth in this Declaration can be fully realized."[6] The "social order" refers to the national society; the "international order" refers to the international community. From the very beginning, it was clear that the realization of rights requires action at both levels.

Establishing Responsibility

Expressions of commitments to universal human rights could have remained empty rhetoric. The movers of the human rights project were aware that duty-bearers had to be identified and their responsibility clarified, but it took time. Due in part to the onset of the Cold War, it took nearly two decades before the United Nations General Assembly was able to adopt the two Covenants that spell out the duties of states to respect, ensure, and fulfill the human rights initially set out in the Universal Declaration of Human Rights. The International Covenant on Economic, Social and Cultural Rights (ICESCR) and the International Covenant on Civil and Political Rights (ICCPR) were finally adopted in 1966.

Under ICESCR Article 2, each State party

> undertakes to take steps, individually and through international assistance and co-operation, especially economic and technical, to the maximum of its available resources, with a view to achieving progressively the full realization of the rights recognized in the present Covenant by all appropriate means, including particularly the adoption of legislative measures.[7]

This is probably the clearest expression of the obligation to pursue human rights-based development. Under ICCPR Article 2, each State party "undertakes to respect and to ensure to all individuals within its territory and subject to its jurisdiction the rights recognized in the present Covenant."[8] Taken together, these express a clear duty for all States parties to the Covenants to combine respect for and realization of all rights listed in the two covenants. The Covenants have been supplemented by other conventions and declarations, including ICERD (International Convention on the Elimination of all Forms of Racial Discrimination, 1965), CEDAW

---

6   *Ibid.*, Article 28.
7   International Covenant on Economic, Social and Cultural Rights (ICESR), Article 2. General Assembly Resolution 2200A (XXI) (December 16, 1966). Available at www.unhchr.ch/html/menu3/b/a_cesr.htm.
8   International Covenant on Civil and Political Rights (ICCPR), Article 2. General Assembly Resolution 2200A (XXI) (December 16, 1966). Available at www.unhchr.ch/html/menu3/b/a_ccpr.htm.

(International Convention on the Elimination of Discrimination against Women, 1979), CAT (Convention against Torture, 1984), CRC (Convention on the Rights of the Child, 1989), and the International Convention on the Protection of Migrant Workers and Their Families, 1990. Human rights conventions were also adopted by regional organizations in Europe, the Americas, and Africa.

Recognizing Responsibility for the Implementation of Human Rights

It took another decade before the two main human rights covenants entered into force in 1976, which required 35 ratifications. By becoming parties to the Covenants, State parties explicitly recognize their responsibility to implement the rights in their domestic legal, administrative, and social order, and to engage in a dialogue with the United Nations on their fulfillment of that responsibility. Their main responsibility is to respect the freedoms set out and to protect and to fulfill the rights contained in the conventions for everyone on their territory. As of 2005, the vast majority of states have ratified the main conventions, although some notable exceptions remain.

Duties of International Cooperation?

The adoption and ratification of human rights conventions and the establishment of international machineries for the monitoring of their implementation was part of the elaboration of the intended international law of cooperation which, as set out in Article 1(3), was one of the main purposes of the United Nations Charter. Under Article 55 of the Charter, the United Nations shall promote:

a. higher standards of living, full employment, and conditions of economic and social progress and development;

b. solutions of international economic, social, health, and related problems; and international cultural and educational cooperation; and

c. universal respect for, and observance of, human rights and fundamental freedoms for all without distinction as to race, sex, language, or religion.[9]

Under Article 56, all members of the United Nations pledged themselves to take joint and separate action in cooperation with the Organization for the achievement of the purposes set forth in Article 55.

In 1986 the General Assembly adopted the Declaration on the Right to Development, which builds on UDHR Article 28 and on the obligations of States under the UN Charter to engage in international cooperation as set out in the UN Charter Articles 55 and 56.

The normative origins and legal foundation for a human rights-based approach to development should therefore be relatively clear. It took considerable time, however, before serious and systematic integration of human rights penetrated international development thinking and practice.

---

9   UN Charter, Article 56, *supra*, note 3.

From Visions of Cooperation to Post-War Confrontation

While the visions for a human rights-based cooperative process of development were implied in the UN Charter and the UDHR, hard political and economic reality made it inoperative during much of the post-World War II period. Proclamations of good intentions were soon submerged by conflicting forces in the global political economy.

The initial euphoria of cooperation sparked by the experiences of World War II soon gave way to the East-West systemic conflict. Fundamentally different approaches to political economy struck at the core conceptions of development. Between the centrally planned Socialist countries and the market-oriented countries, there was little space for cooperation. The Soviet notion of a proletarian dictatorship, allegedly intended to create the conditions for the future Communist society of ultimate freedom and abundance, was imposed on Eastern European countries while home-grown Communists took power in former Yugoslavia, in China in 1950 and later also in Vietnam.

The East-West confrontation is now history, but it had a profoundly negative impact on global development policies for nearly 40 years. Both the Soviet Union and the United States sought to expand their respective areas of influence, and became directly or indirectly involved in conflicts which, at their origin, reflected tensions about social and economic policies in the countries concerned.

The United States became at an early stage predominantly concerned with the prevention and containment of communism. For this purpose the US developed a combination of "carrot" and "stick" policies. The carrots included some economic assistance, while the sticks included, among other things, training and indoctrination by the United States of many Third World military forces, which were activated when there were fears of left wing economic policies taking over. An important example of the carrot is the Alliance for Progress, introduced by President John F. Kennedy in 1961, shortly after his election. It was presented as a project to assist Latin American countries to achieve important social reforms, undoubtedly a genuine commitment by President Kennedy. In the background, however, were fears of growing anti-United States sentiments in Latin America, vividly demonstrated when the then-Vice President of the United States, Richard Nixon, toured Latin American countries in 1958 and was met with mass demonstrations and displays of hostility. The US was also shaken by the take-over of Cuba by Fidel Castro. The fears gave rise to a program to provide military assistance and training to other Latin American — and many other Third World — countries, which was later to be a factor in US support for several authoritarian regimes in Latin America and Asia. The carrot, the economic assistance intended for Latin America, in the end did not amount to much and yielded limited results. It met resistance both in the US, where corporations were suspicious of the social reform elements of the package, and also from the conservative forces in Latin America — the big landowners — who were strongly opposed to land reform and who threatened with a nationalist reaction if pursued by the US.[10]

---

10   John Toye and Richard Toye, *The UN and Global Political Economy: Trade, Finance and Development* (Bloomington and Indianapolis: Indiana University Press, 2004), p. 175.

On the Western side, even if the countries were all basically market-oriented, there were considerable differences of approach. As a response to the severe depression starting in 1929 in the United States and spreading to Europe, many Western countries had given the state a considerably stronger role in the economy. The justification for doing so was strengthened by the publication in 1935 of John Maynard Keynes' *The General Theory*, which dealt a near-fatal blow to classic economic theory as it had evolved from the time of Adam Smith's *Wealth of Nations* (1776).[11] During the first quarter century after the adoption of the UN Charter, economic life in Western Europe and Canada was characterized by cooperation between capital, labor, and the state, with welfare innovations and state interventions in the economy along Keynesian lines. While Keynesian thinking had received backing in the United States during the presidency of Franklin D. Roosevelt, it never took the same hold there as it did in Europe, and it started to erode when World War II ended, particularly after the Republican Dwight D. Eisenhower's presidential victory in 1951.

Keynesians Face Neo-Liberals in the West

In the West, disagreements emerged between politicians and economists favoring Keynes' prescriptions and those ascribing to updated versions of classical economics, later called the neo-liberals. This was not mainly a discussion about economic theories, but about political and economic priorities, even if sometimes presented as debates about the "right" economic solutions.

The controversies had a spill-over effect on the debate within the United Nations, as shown in the eminent historical work of John Toye and Richard Toye.[12] Very simply put, the Keynesians argued in favor of policies aimed at full employment, which had wide-ranging consequences for the role of the state in the economy. The state would have to be both an entrepreneur and a guarantor of welfare. As an entrepreneur, the state would play together with private enterprises, taking measures which could open future possibilities, initiating structural improvements, and investing in enterprises that were beyond the capacity of the private sector. The state would also create protection for infant industries against competition from corporations of more advanced countries.

Keynesian approaches required regulated economies in which the state could have some control over factors that would determine the process of industrialization and employment. In the early years, the United Kingdom (under Prime Minister Clement Attlee) strongly favored this approach, as did the governments of many Western countries, including the Scandinavian states.

This policy quickly lost appeal in the United States as it ran counter to the dominant interests of the major private corporations, most of which had their headquarters there. They wanted maximally open economies around the world. With their increasingly dominant power in the emerging global market, they favored policies re-

---

11   John Maynard Keynes, *General Theory of Employment, Interest and Money* (1935); reprint included in *Collected Writings of John Maynard Keynes, Vol. 7 — The General Theory*, Donald Moggridge (ed.) (London: Macmillan for the Royal Economic Society, 1973).
12   Toye and Toye, *supra*, note 10.

ducing political, economic, and social barriers to worldwide access. Communism was the worst barrier to such access. The remaining colonies held by European powers were also seen as barriers because the metropolitan countries tended to treat "their" colonies as preserves both for delivery of raw material and for purchase of their finished products. The United States in the 1950s and early 1960s was therefore pushing for decolonization, while seeking to ensure that governments of newly independent states joined the global market rather than go the Communist way. Regulated national economies, with a strong role for the state as entrepreneur and guarantor, were also looked upon with suspicion, because they would constitute barriers to global access for corporations in terms of trade and investment.

The legacy of thinking in the Western world since the time of Locke, Montesquieu, Rousseau, and Smith had given rise to different strands of liberal ideologies: On the one hand, extreme economic liberalism, in the past associated with "Manchester liberalism" and in the 1970s resurfacing as "neo-liberalism," rejecting state intervention in the economy; and, on the other, socially conscious liberalism, which saw the private market as essential but recognized the need for public measures to facilitate the functioning of the market, ensure more equal sharing of benefits, and create or restore of equal opportunity for all.

North-South and the Quest for a New International Economic Order

Within and outside the United Nations, the countries of the Third World began in the early 1960s to form a coalition, making demands for substantial changes in the global economic structures, and to develop their own thinking about development and their role in the international economic system. While the Latin American countries had become independent from European colonial rule a century earlier, many African and Asian countries become independent only after World War II, and some not until the 1960s. The colonial system had blocked the possibility for colonized peoples to develop their own economic and political systems based on indigenous cultures and traditions. The emphasis of the UN Charter on the right to self-determination, together with the Declaration on Non-Self-Governing Territories contained in the Charter, helped to speed up the decolonization process. It was largely completed during the 1960s, but tensions over relations between the industrialized North and the formerly colonized South were not thereby over. The newly independent states faced enormous difficulties, and expectations that could not be met in the face of unrealistic domestic promises and considerable irresponsibility. Extensive external interference added to the difficulties.

Many newly independent states faced great difficulties in developing appropriate and responsive governance after having long been subjected to alien domination where there had been minimal attention to principles of accountability or responsiveness to the needs of the colonized peoples. When, at independence, human rights were nominally included in many of the constitutions of the new states, the political practices often turned in authoritarian directions, unable to ensure mechanisms for peaceful accommodation of differences or broad, effective participation and the creation of social justice. The colonial period had also caused profoundly unequal links between the newly independent country and the colonial metropolis. The established asymmetric economic relations were often aggravated in the postcolonial period. These and other factors explain why governments of newly independent states faced considerable difficulties in elaborating healthy economic and social policies and functioning political systems.

Using the UN Charter's principle of sovereign equality as the foundation of international cooperation, the "non-aligned" movement in the 1960s started a drive for a "New International Economic Order," intended to be more egalitarian in nature than the one prevailing. The intellectual origin is partly found in the so-called "Prebisch-Singer Thesis."[13] Raul Prebisch, an Argentinean economist, became the Executive Secretary of the UN Economic Commission for Latin America (ECLA) in 1950, and the first Secretary-General of the United Nations Conference on Trade and Development (UNCTAD) in 1963. Hans Singer, a German-born refugee from Nazi Germany, conducted research under Keynes in Britain during World War II, and was one of the first economists appointed to the UN Secretariat in 1953.[14] Their joint thesis argued that the cause of the persistent deficit in the balance of payment between industrialized and developing countries was caused by the disparity in the rate of growth of earnings from the export of primary products and the rate of costs of the import of industrial goods needed for investment and growth as well as for consumption.[15] The essence of the argument was that unless significant changes were made in economic policies at the national and international level, the rich countries would get richer and the poor countries would get poorer.

Measures recommended to rectify this situation corresponded to concerns within Keynesian thinking for policies towards full employment. Due to the disparity in prices, agricultural productivity in developing countries would have to be raised, but that could be done only by improvements in technology. That would require import of costly machinery, for which the agricultural products could not pay. From there it was concluded that import substitution would be required for these countries to develop their own infant industries, including machinery and other equipment for agricultural intensification. Industrialization would be necessary to break out of dependency and to absorb as workers those who became redundant in the agricultural sector due to increased mechanization.

The thesis was further elaborated by several Third World scholars into the so-called dependency theory. In its strongest forms, some writers argued for a delinking from the economies of the developed countries.[16] The more moderate version was to demand significant changes in the international economic order, later to be called a New International Economic Order.

---

13   *Ibid.*, p. 111.
14   Louis Emmerij, Richard Jolly, and Thomas G. Weiss, *Ahead of the Curve? Ideas and Global Challenges* (Bloomington and Indianapolis: Indiana University Press, 2001), p. 51.
15   The history of the emergence of this thesis, which had enormous impact on the debate within and outside the UN for more than two decades, is described in Toye and Toye, *The UN and Global Political Economy*, pp. 111-116.
16   Richard Jolly, et al., *UN Contributions to Development Thinking and Practice* (Bloomington and Indianapolis: Indiana University Press, 2004), pp. 100-102.

As a result of these debates, UNCTAD was established in 1964 to promote fairer terms of trade and better terms for financing development. Encouraged by the initial success of the joint action by the major oil-producing countries (OPEC) in increasing the petroleum prices in 1973, proposals for changes in the international economic system were vigorously pursued by the developing countries at the UN. The Sixth Special Session of the UN General Assembly in 1974 adopted the Declaration and Program of Action of the New International Economic Order (NIEO),[17] followed in December 1974 by General Assembly approval of the Charter of Economic Rights and Duties of States.[18]

The NIEO Declaration envisaged substantial changes in the international system, allowing developing countries significant opportunities to improve their economy to escape out of poverty.[19] It included an integrated approach to price supports for an entire group of developing country commodity exports, indexation of developing country export prices to tie them to rising prices of developed countries' manufactured exports, attainment of official development assistance to reach the target of 0.7 percent of GNP of the developed countries, linkage of development aid with the creation of the International Monetary Fund's (IMF) Special Drawing Rights (SDRs), a negotiated redeployment of some developed countries' industries to the developing countries, lowering of tariffs on the exports of manufactures from the developing countries, the development of an international food program, and the establishment of mechanisms for the transfer of technology to developing countries separate from direct capital investment.

The Charter of Economic Rights and Duties of States affirmed each state's full permanent sovereignty over its natural resources and economic activities, including the right to nationalize foreign property. It also stipulated that primary product producers should have the right to join in producers' cartels and that other countries had the duty to refrain from efforts to break these cartels.

The adoption of the NIEO Declaration and the Charter of Economic Rights and Duties of States were major symbolic victories of the developing countries. However, increasing differences of interest between them made it difficult to maintain a common bargaining position in their negotiation with the powerful industrialized countries. For this and other reasons, they did not have the necessary economic power to enforce implementation of the programs implied. By the end of the 1970s, the vision — or dream — of a fair and egalitarian international economy was largely over.

The Power Over Capital and Credit

A major problem for developing countries was their lack of savings that could be invested for industrial and other development. Their very limited capacity for saving made them look to the United Nations for solutions. Under its Charter, the United

---

17   UN General Assembly Resolution 3201 (S-VI) (1974). Available at http://daccessdds.un.org/doc/RESOLUTION/GEN/NR0/071/94/IMG/NR007194.pdf?OpenElement
18   UN General Assembly Resolution 3281 (XXIX) (December 12, 1974). Available at www.un.org/documents/ga/res/30/ares30.htm.
19   Jolly et al., *UN Contributions to Development Thinking and Practice,* pp. 120-124.

Nations had been given the task of promoting higher standards of living, full employment, and conditions of economic and social progress and development,[20] and all of its members had pledged themselves to take joint and separate action in cooperation with the UN for the achievement of that purpose.[21] With their influence in the UN General Assembly, they hoped that the UN would be the forum to establish funds, with which they could overcome the difficulty of access to investment capital.

Very soon, however, they met an obstacle which has remained with the UN throughout its history. The Bretton Woods conference, which preceded the establishment of the United Nations (it was held near Washington, DC, in July 1944), had decided to establish the monetary and financial organizations that became the International Monetary Fund (IMF) and the World Bank. The structure of these organizations differs fundamentally from the UN in that voting power is based on the monetary contribution to the organizations, which in effect means that they are controlled by the rich countries and dominated by the United States. While nominally these institutions are specialized agencies of the UN, in practice the UN has no power over them. From the very start, the United States was determined to prevent the UN from "telling the IMF and the World Bank what to do." This was already the position of the US Secretary of the Treasury under President Roosevelt, Henry Morgenthau, and has been firmly maintained since that time.[22]

During the 1950s, efforts were made within the UN General Assembly to establish a facility for soft-loan credit to developing countries, called SUNFED (Special United Nations Fund for Economic Development). The main spokesperson for it was Hans Singer, one of the key economists within the UN. His proposal drew enormous hostility among rightwing forces in the United States, alleging that this was a Socialist plot to undermine the United States. Singer was personally attacked in a very vicious way and eventually withdrew.[23] In 1957 ECOSOC nevertheless recommended to the General Assembly to establish SUNFED, against strong opposition not only from the US, but also from the UK and Canada. When it came before the General Assembly, the project was seriously weakened. SUNFED was given a very limited role and budget, while the intended soft-loan institution was eventually placed under the World Bank and called the International Development Association (IDA). The final outcome, therefore, was to place the capacity to make such loans firmly under the voting control of the rich countries still dominated by the US. The efforts of the developing countries to have a fund controlled by the UN therefore came to very little; what remained was a mandate to, "create conditions which would make investments either feasible or more effective",[24] which was understood to engage in what was called pre-investment activities. SUNFED and the Expanded Technical Assistance Program (EPTA), established in 1949, were subsequently merged into UNDP. As a result there is one development program (UNDP) inside

---

20   UN Charter, Article 55, *supra,* note 3.
21   UN Charter, Article 56, *supra,* note 3.
22   Toye and Toye, *supra,* note 10, p. 23.
23   *Ibid.,* p. 173.
24   UNGA resolution 1240(XIII) quoted by Toye and Toye, *supra,* p. 174 at note 56.

the UN, with very limited funds but with a high profile on human development and human rights, and another set of development actors outside the control of the UN (the World Bank and the IMF) with substantial resources and power but with a low or non-existing profile on human rights.

The Debt Crisis and the Resurgence of the Neo-Liberals

The major factor which broke the backbone of collective action by developing countries was the debt crisis. From the beginning of the 1980s, this crisis brought into focus their glaring powerlessness in the world economy at about the same time as the entry of neo-liberalist governments in the major Western states.

In 1982, Mexico became the first country to default on its debt payment. The default was perceived among creditor nations as a threat to the international credit system. The IMF and the World Bank, strongly influenced by the US treasury during the Reagan administration, became the primary agent of international finance capital by establishing requirements of harsh "structural adjustment" to ensure debt repayment.[25] Blocked from any possibility of credit unless the criteria were accepted, developing countries had no option but to submit.

With the NIEO dead, the old and established economic order became even more unequal than before due to the impact of the debt crisis and its handling by the financial institutions. It was further aggravated by the corruption of some governments in the South, many of which were not had not been democratically elected and offered minimal transparency in their administrations. Lending institutions in the North were also to blame. They had not given much attention to the ability of the borrowers to pay back, as they assumed that their home countries would bail them out if the debtor countries defaulted on payment.

The negotiating power of the developing countries received a final blow with the collapse of the Soviet Union and the end of the Cold War. Through the Non-Aligned Movement, they were previously able to obtain some concessions, due to the competing efforts of the West and the East to have influence in the South. When the East-West competition ended, that leverage disappeared.

In the middle of the 1970s, the approaches to political economy in the West underwent considerable changes. A precursor was the 1975 selection of Margaret Thatcher as leader of the Conservative Party in the United Kingdom. She became Prime Minister after the Conservatives' election victory in 1979 and remained in office until 1990. When Ronald Reagan was elected President of the United States in 1980, the two major Western countries embraced a neo-liberal ideology, slightly modernizing the 19th-century "laissez-faire" political economy that since World War II had been seen as archaic and obsolete. They devoted their energy to breaking the influence of the trade union movements, substantially reducing public spending in the social and health fields, adopting tax cuts to benefit the rich, and engaging in extensive deregulation.

---

25 Joseph E. Stiglitz, *Globalization and its Discontents* (London: Allan Lande and the Penguin Press, 2002).

The neo-liberal ideology was fed by a variety of normative theories and assumptions. These included the writings of libertarian philosophers who, on the basis of their particular versions of social contract theory, sought to reduce human rights to rights of personal autonomy and protection of property;[26] the "public choice" theoreticians who asserted that public servants were led in whole or in part only by their own self-interest, and therefore engaged in or supported "rent-seeking,"[27] or a combination of these,[28] combined with resurrection of classical economic theory asserting the benefit of free international trade and exchange.

The Bretton Woods Institutions at the Forefront of Development Policies

The re-emergence of laissez-faire ideologies after decades of socially conscious policies had their own internal reasons in the US and UK, but what gave it a global dimension was that it coincided with the debt crisis, which broke the back of the Third World movement for a new international economic order. This gave the Bretton Woods institutions an entirely different role than what had previously been envisaged. The IMF and the World Bank became in the 1980s the central actors in global economy, with an unprecedented power to prescribe and to implement economic and monetarist policies for developing countries and — from the 1990s — also for the so-called countries-in-transition emerging from the breakdown of the Soviet Union and the fall of the Berlin Wall. Governmental decision-making concerning social issues related to regulations, taxation, public spending, and social security arrangements were closely watched, particularly by the IMF, which had considerable economic sanctions at its disposal should a developing country stray from the neo-liberal agenda.

The IMF and the World Bank were the main institutions to which states could turn when they needed funding, whether to service debt or take new development initiatives. They — particularly the IMF — have also come to function as gatekeepers for foreign private investment. If the IMF finds that a developing country's macroeconomic policy is not sufficiently disciplined, potential private investors are likely to abstain from investing there.

The Washington Consensus

The links between the US Treasury and the international financial institutions during the Reagan/Thatcher era led to the emergence of the "Washington Consensus." Reflecting the neo-liberal agenda, the concrete measures it proclaimed can be summarized as encompassing privatization of public enterprises, deregulation of the economy, liberalization of trade and industry, massive tax cuts, monetarist measures to keep inflation in check, strict control of labor, reduction of public expenditures (particularly social spending), downsizing of government, expansion of international markets, and removal of controls on global financial flows.[29]

---

26   Robert Nozick, *Anarchy, State and Utopia* (Oxford: Blackwell, 1974).
27   Milton Friedman and Rose Friedman, *Free to Choose* (Harmondsworth, UK: Penguin, 1980).
28   F. A. Hayek, The Road to Serfdom (1944; reprint, London: Routledge and Kegan Paul, 1978).
29   Manfred B. Steger, *Globalization: A Very Short Introduction* (Oxford: Oxford University Press, 2003), p. 41.

The structural adjustment policies pursued by the IMF and the World Bank ostensibly had the purpose of promoting sustainable macroeconomic policies in the countries affected, but the adjustments were also tailored to serve the interests of major corporate interests and foreign investors. Privatization was encouraged or made a requirement for credit. Reduced protection of domestic industries was requested. Currency devaluation was called for, as were increased interest rates. "Flexibility" of the labor market, consisting of reduction or elimination of protection for labor rights under the heading of "labor discipline" was another part of the packages. A termination of food subsidies was requested. Regulations and standards relating to investment were to be reduced or removed. These structural adjustments were almost the reverse of the structural changes in the global economy demanded by the Non-Aligned Movement in the 1960s and 1970s.

The economists in the IMF do not simply give economic advice; their conditionality affects a wide range of national policies in areas such as social security, education, health, and labor relations, and their prescriptions are practically binding. They have, in effect, taken over what should be the area of democratic decision-making by elected politicians in the affected countries. Above all, for these economists, human rights appear to be non-factors, in particular the economic and social rights.

While some measures demanded by the Bretton Woods institutions might make good sense in given contexts, the generalized and persistent demands for these structural adjustments had crippling effects on many poorer countries, making them increasingly dependent on the rich states. Governments needed to increase exports to keep their currencies stable and earn foreign exchange with which to help pay off debts, but the value of their primary commodities was falling relative to the cost of their imports. Governments therefore had to spend less, reduce consumption, and remove or decrease financial regulations. In some countries, particularly in East and South East Asia, there was already an industrial base to offset the shocks and to facilitate the emergence of a new entrepreneurial class, which greatly benefited from the new conditions of profit extraction. Others paid the price through decreased attention to labor rights, access to education, health services, and other aspects of social and economic rights.

WTO: Trade, But Not Necessarily Development

The 1948 Havana Charter on Trade and Employment had envisaged the establishment of an International Trade Organization, which would have followed the then-prevailing model of inter-state cooperation. The idea failed, due in particular to rejection by the US Congress. While the General Agreement on Tariffs and Trade (GATT) served some of the needs, there was a gap that had to be filled by better institutional mechanisms. UNCTAD, which was set up in 1964, was established to promote fairer terms of trade and better terms for financing, which would have facilitated selective industrial and trade policies by developing states and thereby making it possible to improve their relative position on the international market.

Since 1994, however, UNCTAD has been marginalized by the WTO, which, resulting from the conclusion of the so-called "Uruguay round" from 1986 to 1994, sought to overcome a crisis in GATT arising from the new neo-liberal economic policies.

That WTO differs significantly from UNCTAD appears already from its name: the "W" stands for "World," as opposed to the "UN" ("United Nations") in UNCTAD. This was deliberate: the major industrial countries did not want the trade organization to be part of the UN system. Secondly, while the "TAD" in UNCTAD stands for "Trade and Development," the "T" in WTO stands only for "Trade," excluding the "D" for "Development." Neither in name nor in practice is the WTO a development organization.

Most trade at the international level is conducted between corporations, or even between different branches of the same corporation. Research indicates that multinational corporations account for up to 70 percent of international trade.[30] The WTO serves to facilitate the export orientation that is an essential component of the Washington consensus and essential to corporate expansion.

Concepts of Development in the UN Discourses

Rarely did the participants in the debates on political economy clarify what they meant by "development." It was often more implicit than explicit. Many aspects needed clarification: What is the primary and secondary purpose of development? Who decides what should be achieved by development? Who should be the actors — the driving forces — of development? Who should be the participants? Who should be the beneficiaries?

In hindsight, it is possible to make a distinction between "intended development" and "immanent development."[31] Much of the UN debate until 1980 was about "intended development," measures taken by defined actors to achieve goals considered to be desirable and positive. "Intended development" raises all the questions above: Who sets the aims or values, who executes the measures envisaged, and who monitors the impact of the measures?

"Immanent development," on the other hand, has been used to describe assumptions of what will happen when private actors are free to do what they want in the economic field. It is, as I understand it, a reference to the likely outcomes of "the invisible hand," as described by Adam Smith. The neo-liberal ideology, and many of the activities of the World Bank and the IMF since 1980, have focused on the perceived benefit of facilitating the free operation of private corporations with minimal state interference, and with support mainly given to make the market function better, by overcoming infrastructural and other obstacles. This is essentially a faith whose "truth" cannot be tested any more than the truth of religious beliefs. Whenever the economic processes in the market fail to give the results presumed to flow from free market operations, it is shrugged off as market failure.

---

30   David Held, et al., *Global Transformation* (Stanford: Stanford University Press, 1999).
31   First introduced by M. Cowan and R. Shenton, 1995; here taken from K.G. Nustad, "The Development Discourse in the Multilateral System," in *Global Institutions and Development: Framing the World,* Morten Bøas and Desmond McNeill, (eds.) (London and New York: Routledge, 2004), pp. 3-14.

Richard Jolly, et al., argue that the following stages can be seen in the evolution of UN ideas and action on development: The 1940s and 1950s set the foundations for UN development thinking and practice; the 1960s was the UN Development Decade, when there was mobilization for development; in the 1970s, the focus was on equity in development; while in the 1980s there was a loss of UN control (when the Bretton Woods institutions took over) and a marginalizing of the poorest. During the 1990s, a human vision was rediscovered, particularly through the UNDP, focusing on "human development" and "development as freedom."[32]

Death of the Washington Consensus?

Criticism of the IMF and the World Bank dramatically increased during the 1990s. The human rights bodies of the United Nations conducted studies and adopted resolutions pointing to the incompatibility of their policies with human rights requirements.[33] Implicit criticism came from the UNDP, through its emphasis on human development and its link with human rights. When James Wolfensohn became President of the World Bank Group in 1996, efforts were made to diversify lending in ways that were more compatible with human rights concerns — gender equality, participation, civil society involvement, good governance, and environmental conservation.[34] When Joseph Stiglitz was appointed the Chief Economist of the Bank in 1997, after having been Chairman of President Clinton's Council of Economic Advisers, he brought in better financial-sector regulation and technology-transfer policies, and wanted to incorporate democratization and more egalitarian distribution. This angered the US Treasury Department (under Lawrence Summers), and forced Wolfensohn to ensure the departure of Stiglitz from the Bank as a condition for a second term of Presidency for Wolfensohn.[35] Stiglitz resigned in 1999. He received the Nobel Prize for Economics in 2001. In 2002, he published his path-braking book, *Globalization and its Discontents*, revealing the power of the US Treasury over the IMF and through it, indirectly as well as directly, on the World Bank. He also argued forcefully that opposition to globalization is not opposition to increased global cooperation, but to the particular set of doctrines under the heading of the Washington Consensus, which is offered as the only possible policy. That, he said, "flies in the face both of economics, which emphasizes the notion of trade-offs, and of ordinary common sense."[36]

In 2004, at a conference on poverty reduction in Shanghai, China, Wolfensohn declared that the Washington Consensus was dead:

> This is not a conference for teaching the Washington Consensus. The Washington Consensus has been dead for years. It's been replaced by all sorts of other consensuses. But today we're approaching our discus-

---

32   F Jolly, et al., *UN Contributions to Development Thinking and Practice*, pp. 49-246.
33   See, for example, J. Oloka-Onyanga and Deepika Udagama, *Globalisation and its Impact on the Full Enjoyment of Human Rights*. Final report for the United Nations Sub-Commission on Promotion and Protection of Human Rights. UN Doc. E/CN.4/Sub.2/2003/14, 2003.
34   Toye and Toye, *The UN and Global Political Economy*, p. 286.
35   *Ibid.*
36   Stiglitz, *supra*, note 24, p. 221.

sions with no consensuses. We're approaching our discussion with an interchange of ideas, with the opportunity to share experiences, with the opportunity to learn from each other.[37]

If this becomes future World Bank practice, it would open the development debate to considerable improvements. One of the most persistent criticisms of the World Bank — and even more of the IMF — is that they essentially prescribe what countries should do, rather than pursue a dialogue with them. Whether the assertion by Mr. Wolfensohn (who, at the end of his second term in June 2005, was replaced by Mr. Wolfowitz), will hold true for the future remains to be seen, but there is no doubt that the neo-liberal agenda is in serious disarray. This is one reason why there is at present a return to the original intentions in the United Nations Charter and the UDHR in favor of a human rights-based development.

The normative origins and legal foundations for a human rights-based approach to development should therefore be relatively clear and well-embedded in the major UN instruments, including the Charter. However, it took considerable time before serious and systematic integration of human rights penetrated international development thinking and practice. The following section addresses this issue.

Values and Contents of Rights-Based Development: Why Now?

Issues relevant to human rights were often present in past UN discourses on development, but were submerged under conflicting approaches to global political economy. In the early years, when memories of the great depression of the 1930s were still fresh, there was talk about full employment and, through it, the enjoyment for all of an adequate standard of living. When this was subordinated to a discussion about industrialization and growth, there emerged a critical dissent requesting growth with distribution. During the onslaught of the conservative, neo-liberal counter-revolution in the 1980s, imposing structural adjustment based on the principles of the Washington Consensus, UNICEF took the lead in demanding adjustment with a human face. But it was the UNDP's introduction in 1990 of the notion of "Human Development," inspired and later elaborated by Amartya Sen's focus on "Development as Freedom,"[38] which has helped to turn the tide toward a human rights-based development.

This coincided with the status of the UN human rights project. By around 1990, a significant number of states had become parties to the main human rights conventions and had thereby undertaken legal obligations to implement them. The international monitoring bodies — the Human Rights Committee; the Committee on Economic, Social and Cultural Rights; the Committee on the Elimination of Racial Discrimination; the Committee on the Elimination of Discrimination against Women; and soon thereafter the Committee on the Rights of the Child — were

---

37   James Wolfensohn, Opening Address at the Scaling Up Poverty Reduction Conference (Shanghai, China, May 25, 2004). Available at info.worldbank.org/etools/docs/reducingpoverty/doc/134/file/JDWShanghaiOpening.pdf.
38   Amartya Sen, *Development as Freedom* (Oxford: Oxford University Press, 1999).

more effectively formulating requests for states to better implement their obligations. The international human rights system has now been comprehensively developed; the standard-setting is complete and substantial practice already exists, including detailed guidelines by the international treaty bodies to states on how they shall conduct their human rights-based development.

Non-governmental human rights organizations have become increasingly influential, playing an important role in pushing the UN to develop its human rights machinery. They also have a growing presence and role within states, promoting awareness of human rights and helping victims and neglected groups to bring their claims forward. Within the international civil society, human rights organizations and development organizations play a growing role, and are increasingly interacting and cooperating with each other.

The Cold War is definitely over. Its tragic consequences, resulting from efforts from the East and West to pervert democratic and social developments in the Third World, are slowly being overcome. Andrea Cornwall and Celestine Nyamu-Musembi also point to one reason that donor agencies have taken greater interest in human rights-based development: the shift in aid delivery from sector-specific or project-based intervention to budget support makes it important to ensure that the budget support is spent accountably. For this purpose, public institutions in recipient countries need to reform and bolster the capacity of civil society to hold the public sector to account.[39]

The extreme neo-liberal direction taken by globalization in the 1980s has been so thoroughly criticized that it has opened up for some modification of its course. It is revealing that even Mr. Wolfensohn, when still President of the World Bank, could declare in 2004 that the Washington Consensus was dead.

The Values of Human Rights-Based Development

The concept of "development" is, at its base, a normative question, as distinct from "social change," which is a descriptive term. It is therefore essential to know who sets the norms for what constitutes development. It has been a deeply contested issue during the history of the United Nations, and remains so today. Various conceptions of development have emerged and had a dominant role for some time, but then lost much of their appeal, only to be followed by new conceptions. They have all since been challenged as insufficient and misdirected. The different approaches to development also had implications regarding the choice of international development agencies.

Not "Value Added" but Value Change

Adherents of present orthodoxy in development thinking often ask what is the value added by using a human rights-based approach to development. The question is wrongly put. It is not a question of value added: a human rights-based approach

---

39   Andrea Cornwall and Celestine Nyamu-Musembi, "Why Rights, Why Now?" *IDS Bulletin* 36, No.1 (January 2005), pp. 13f.

is a fundamental value change, when compared to some of the other notions of development, in particular those which use growth through market expansion as the dominant criteria.

Combining Outcome and Process

The essence of human rights-based development is set out in the Declaration on the Right to Development, Article 1:

> The right to development is an inalienable human right by virtue of which every human person and all peoples are entitled to participate in, contribute to, and enjoy economic, social, cultural and political development, in which all human rights and fundamental freedoms can be fully realized.[40]

The two foundational values therefore are the following:

> (a) that the aim of economic, social, cultural and political development is to achieve an outcome where all human rights and freedoms can be fully realized. It is therefore a direct application of the Universal Declaration, Article 28.

> (b) that the process of development has to include every person and all peoples. Everyone is entitled to participate in, contribute to and benefit from that development.

To make this even clearer, Article 1 of the Declaration states, "The human person is the central subject of development and should be the active participant and beneficiary of the right to development."[41]

Human rights-based development is therefore different from other conceptions of development in the identification of the desired outcome and the participation in and process by which to reach that outcome.

Rights and Responsibility, Not Needs and Charity

A human rights-based approach differs fundamentally from the needs-based approach that is sometimes a supplement to growth-oriented development policies. While the needs-based approach focuses on the delivery of services to marginalized groups that are likely to remain marginal, and their delivery is often justified as charity by the powerful in society, the rights-based approach calls for ensuring effective entitlements to all as a right, for which no person need feel any shame, but can effectively demand.

In a human rights-based approach, rights are matched with responsibilities. The approach clearly places responsibilities on the state in which the individual lives, but it also implies an authorization to adopt the regulations necessary to ensure due participation, and an adequate process of development to reach outcomes that give higher-level human rights realization.

---

40   Declaration on the Right to Development, Article 1. General Assembly Resolution 41/128 (December 4, 1986). Available at 193.194.138.190/html/menu3/b/74.htm.
41   *Ibid.*

State responsibility also includes an accountability requirement, transparency, rule of law, effective remedies, and other aspects of due process. Domestic requirements for responsibility and accountability are matched by international monitoring mechanisms, generating a dialogue with each state on its compliance with the responsibilities that it has undertaken by becoming party to the international human rights instruments.

Freedom of Self Is Linked to the Freedom of Others

Since human rights are for everyone, the freedoms and rights of one person must take into account the necessary conditions for the enjoyment of rights by others. The enjoyment of human rights for all implies that one also accepts a set of duties — duties of constraint in the exercise of freedoms, and duties of contribution to facilitate the enjoyment of rights by others. This is the concern underlying the formulation in Article 29 (1) of the Universal Declaration of Human Rights: "Everyone has duties to the community in which alone the free and full development of his personality is possible."[42]

The interconnection between one's own freedom and that of others is one of the main reasons that the normative system of human rights is indivisible and interdependent — rights have to be balanced against each other.

In the human rights instruments adopted by the United Nations, there is otherwise no explicit mention of duties. But it is implicit, and sometimes explicit, that the state has to adopt and enforce a number of duties or obligations in order to ensure, in a balanced way, human rights for all. These may be duties of omission (constraints) or duties of commission (contributions to be made, actions to be taken). It is explicitly provided in the International Convention on the Elimination of All Forms of Racism, Article 4, that states must prohibit and punish certain activities which otherwise would have been covered by freedom of expression or association. Such provisions apart, the normal pattern is that states decide for themselves what duties they must impose, such as taxation to fund the right to education or the right to health services, so that all people can enjoy their human rights. Underlying the Universal Declaration and the subsequent human rights instruments is the assumption that states will impose such duties as are required. It therefore limits itself to point out that in doing so,

> Everyone shall be subjected only to such limitations (in the exercise of their rights) as are determined by law solely for the purpose of securing due recognition and respect for the rights and freedoms of others and of meeting the just requirements of morality, public order and the general welfare in a democratic society.[43]

In assessing what is required to ensure the rights of others and to meet the just requirements of general welfare, it is essential to take into account the interdependence of rights — the economic, social, and cultural, as well as the civil and political.

---

42   UDHR, Article 29(1), *supra*, note 5.
43   *Ibid.*, Article 29(2).

Human Rights-Based Development and Poverty Reduction

The recent focus by the World Bank and the IMF on poverty reduction, with all its weaknesses, should be taken as a signal of change away from the Washington Consensus, towards a more socially conscious development. Yet these policies are still far from a practical application of a human rights-based approach.

The notion of "poverty reduction" tends to overlook one very important aspect, namely the process of impoverishment, or poverty production. What is described as development has often caused extensive impoverishment of part of the population, while others have benefited greatly. Sometimes those who benefited most were already well off, while those who were impoverished were weak before. Such is often the result of market-oriented development activities that weaken the resources and space of indigenous peoples.

There are many forms of impoverishment or poverty production. Much of it is not intended, but is nevertheless foreseeable. Some is even intended as a contribution to progress. When capital-intensive trawlers are allowed to catch the fish outside the coastal waters, the artisanal fishers lose their livelihood. When agriculture is mechanized, farm workers become redundant.

Much development has an exclusionary effect: The rapid growth of digital technology has generated enormous benefits, but has caused many to be left further behind, even more remote from the networks of those who are "in."

This is not a reason to block progress and change. Human rights do not encourage luddism,[44] but do make it necessary to take into account the situation of those who are negatively affected by technical and other change, involve them in discussions on how to minimize the negative consequences, and to find other meaningful alternatives.

Conventionally, poverty reduction tends to be an add-on to growth-oriented, technology-aided market expansion. A human rights-based approach to development, in contrast, sees development as an inclusive approach that expands freedom for all — particularly for those whose freedoms and rights have been most restricted due to material need, deprivation of access to health or education services, dependency on the power of others, or other limitations on the rights they should enjoy under the human rights system.

At the request of the UN Committee on Economic, Social and Cultural Rights, the Office of the High Commissioner for Human Rights (OHCHR) developed guidelines for the integration of human rights into poverty reduction strategies, prepared by legal scholars Manfred Nowak and Paul Hunt and economist Siddiq Osmani. The Draft Guidelines insist that poverty reduction should be based explicitly on the norms and values set out in international human rights instruments, and argue that this normative framework is the only existing normative system with global acclaim. But it also argues that the human rights framework is compelling in

---

44   The Luddites, or Ludds, were a social movement of English workers in the early 1800s who protested — often by destroying textile machines — against the changes produced by the Industrial Revolution that they felt threatened their jobs.

the context of poverty reduction because it has the potential to empower the poor. Empowerment of the poor and their organizations (where they exist) through rights of participation, public insight, and the right to make legal claims (individually, but more importantly through organizations) are key ingredients of the Draft Guidelines' human rights approach to development. This is not just a moral framework, but a legally committing framework for any State party to human rights conventions, and most countries are legally obliged by ratification of core human rights instruments.

The Draft Guidelines states that a human rights approach has the potential to advance the goal of poverty reduction in a variety of ways:

> (a) by urging speedy adoption of a poverty reduction strategy, underpinned by human rights, as a matter of legal obligation;

> (b) by broadening the scope of poverty reduction strategies so as to address the structures of discrimination that generate and sustain poverty;

> (c) by urging the expansion of civil and political rights, which can play a crucial instrumental role in advancing the cause of poverty or education;

> (d) by confirming that economic, social and cultural rights are binding international human rights, not just programmatic aspirations;

> (e) by adding legitimacy to the demand for ensuring meaningful participation of the poor in decision-making processes;

> (f) by cautioning against retrogression and non-fulfillment of minimum core obligations in the name of making trade-offs; and

> (g) by creating and strengthening the institutions through which policy-makers can be held accountable for their actions.[45]

The Content and Indivisibility of the Human Rights System

UDHR Article 28 can be seen as the initial call for rights-based development by requiring the transformation of social and international order to ensure the full realization of all rights contained in the Declaration. This concern has been frequently repeated by the United Nations. The states assembled at the World Conference on Human Rights in Vienna in 1993 adopted by consensus the Vienna Declaration, which states:

> All human rights are universal, indivisible, interdependent and interrelated. The international community must treat human rights globally in a fair and equal manner, on the same footing, and with the same emphasis. While the significance of national and religious back-

---

45   Office of the High Commissioner for Human Rights (OHCHR), Draft Guidelines, para. 24, p. 3. Available at http://www.unhchr.ch/development/povertyfinal.html.

grounds must be borne in mind, it is the duty of States, regardless of their political, economic and cultural systems, to promote and protect all human rights and fundamental freedoms.[46]

What, then, are the different components of the international human rights system? The UDHR starts with the classical civil rights: integrity rights, freedom of action, and rights pertaining to fair trial and due process. There cannot be unlimited freedom of action in any society. Indeed, one of the purposes of state formation is to maintain law and order, to ensure that persons do not act towards others in ways which destroy the integrity and freedom of others, or block the necessary measures taken to ensure welfare in society. The state is bound, therefore, to set some restrictions and impose some duties. In order to ensure that penal prosecution and the law on which it is based are compatible with human rights requirements, the right to a fair trial and due process is therefore also important.

The UDHR states that "the will of the people shall be the basis of authority of the government."[47] It implies a right for all to participate, directly or through freely chosen representatives, in the exercise of government, and equal rights for all of access to public service. It consolidates, therefore, the notion of freedom with and through participation.

Moreover, the greatest innovation made by the UDHR is the inclusion of economic, social, and cultural rights.[48] It refers to the economic, social, and cultural rights as "indispensable for (one's) dignity and free development of (one's) personality," and to "the right to social security," which entitles everyone access to welfare state provisions.[49] It precedes five subsequent articles which declare the rights to work (Article 23), to rest and leisure (Article 24), to an adequate standard of living (Article 25), to education (Article 26), and to participate freely in the cultural life of the community (Article 27).

At the core of social rights is the right to an adequate standard of living (Article 25). In order to enjoy these social rights, there is also a need to enjoy certain economic rights. These are the right to property (Article 17), the right to work and other work-related rights (Articles 23 and 24), and the right to social security (Articles 22 and 25).

The combination of economic and social rights serves the dual function of freedom and equality to which human rights-based development is aimed. Under the heading of cultural rights fall several categories of rights, including the rights of minorities and indigenous peoples to maintain and develop their own culture, which has been further developed in other instruments.

---

46   Vienna Declaration and Programme of Action (July 1993). UN Doc. A/CONF.157/23 (July 12, 1993), para. 5.

47   UDHR, Article 21, *supra*, note 5.

48   On the economic, social, and cultural rights in the UDHR, see the chapters on Articles 22-27 in Gudmunder Alfredsson and Asbjørn Eide, *The Universal Declaration of Human Rights: A Common Standard of Achievement* (Dordrecht, Boston, and London: Martinus Nijhoff Publishers, 1999). On the further development of those rights, see Asbjørn Eide, Catarina Krause, and Allan Rosas, eds., *Economic, Social and Cultural Rights: A Textbook* (Dordrecht, Boston and London: Martinus Nijhoff Publishers, 1995).

49   UDHR, Article 22, *supra*, note 5.

Not Only Freedom From the State, But Also Freedom Through the State

It is important to recognize and to avoid a fundamental mistake often made: one very widespread myth has been that human rights are solely intended as protection from the state. While this is part of the function of human rights, it gives a much-distorted picture. Almost all human rights require an active state to protect and facilitate the enjoyment of the rights. The right to life, freedom from torture and maltreatment, freedom from slavery, and many others are not only protection from the state, but require protection by the state against private individuals and non-state actors. Human rights require measures by the state to prevent violence against women or brutality against children, within the family and by other actors. Economic and social rights also require active measures by the state in order to be protected and fulfilled. Without an understanding that human rights are more than protection from the state, the significance of rights-based development will not be grasped.

Responsibilities for Human Rights-Based Development

The primary responsibility under international human rights law is placed on the state, a point to which we return below. But that is not the whole story. The Declaration on the Right to Development states that, "All human beings have a responsibility for development, individually and collectively, taking into account the need for full respect for their human rights and fundamental freedoms as well as their duties to the community, which alone can ensure the free and complete fulfillment of the human being, and they should therefore promote and protect an appropriate political, social and economic order for development."[50]

It is important to recognize that human rights-based development starts from the premise that the human person is not only the subject of development, but that she or he is expected also to do what they can to take care of their own needs and to contribute to the common process of development. The reference above to the duty of all human beings to the community stems from the Universal Declaration of Human Rights Article 29. There are at least three levels of community to take into account: The local or ethnic, the national, and the world community. There should be an awareness of responsibilities to all three levels, which in practical terms may be difficult for the individual but which can be administered by the state and international organizations

The role of the state under the human rights system is, therefore, on the one hand, to respect and to protect the individuals in their efforts to meet their own needs, and, on the other hand, to facilitate those efforts by appropriate policies and to be a provider where the capabilities of the individual do not suffice to ensure an adequate standard of living in freedom.

The Declaration goes on to say that, "States have the right and the duty to formulate appropriate national development policies that aim at the constant improve-

---

50   Declaration on the Right to Development, Article 2(2), *supra*, note 39.

ment of the well-being of the entire population and of all individuals, on the basis of their active, free and meaningful participation in development and in the fair distribution of the benefits resulting there from."[51]

This corresponds to the general obligations of states under international human rights law. The state cannot, however, implement its responsibility unless generally supported in its national society. Human rights are often expressed as freedoms: freedom from the state and freedoms in relation to other actors in society — private persons, corporations, and movements of various kinds. There is a need for a general culture of human rights in society, where most actors not only assert their own rights but also the rights of others. The state has not only an obligation to respect, but also to protect and to fulfill human rights; to be able to do so, the state generally needs broad support for its measures, it will otherwise either have to use harsh measures of compulsion and control, or to neglect its human rights obligations — violation by omission.

However, the state must recognize the general validity of the notion of subsidiarity, starting with the principle that everyone has the primary responsibility to take care of its own needs and should be given the necessary freedom to do so. This does not mean unlimited freedom, which is impossible if the rights of others shall also be guaranteed, but as much freedom as is possible, while the state protects and fulfills the rights of others.

Subsidiarity also relates to minorities and indigenous peoples, in varying degrees. Where possible, indigenous peoples should have sufficient self-determination to organize their own ways of caring for their own needs, including their right to control the natural resources on which they traditionally have made their living. This should also be applicable to minority groups that live in conditions similar to indigenous peoples, and have maintained a separate way of life from that of the dominant groups in society.[52]

National human rights institutions are essential to human rights-based development. Such institutions have become important in recent years. Under the Paris Principles, they shall have a broad mandate; this implies that they should deal with all human rights and therefore be faced with the issues of interdependence and indivisibility. The major issue is whether, and to what extent, they address economic and social rights. The predominant trend has been to focus on civil rights, taking up cases where there are apparent violations of such rights, since violations are more easily detected. But several national institutions in different parts of the world are already on record to address the whole broad range of human rights. This includes the South African Human Rights Commission, the National Human Rights Commission in India, and the Danish Institute for Human Rights.

The UN World Conference on Human Rights, held in Vienna in 1993, recommended that each state should consider the desirability of drawing up a national ac-

---

51   *Ibid.*, Article 2(3).
52   Margot E. Salomon with Arjun Sengupta, *The Right to Development: Obligations of States and the Rights of Minorities and Indigenous Peoples* (London: Minorities Rights Group International, 2003).

tion plan, identifying steps whereby that state would improve the promotion and protection of human rights.[53] This amounts to a call for human rights-based development. The World Conference also called for the implementation of strengthened advisory services and technical assistance activities by the then-Centre for Human Rights (now the Office of the High Commissioner for Human Rights), in order for states to prepare and implement coherent and comprehensive plans of action for the promotion and protection of human rights.

This can serve as a very useful mechanism to ensure, in practice, an integrated and systemic implementation of human rights, taking their interdependence fully into account. A number of states have already prepared such plans of action, with somewhat varying contents.

Strategies for Rights-Based Development

At the 1993 World Conference on Human Rights, the governments of the world agreed that, "The promotion and protection of human rights is the first responsibility of governments."[54] This responsibility overrides and takes priority over other commitments by the state.

In the Millennium Declaration, states resolved themselves, "To respect fully and uphold the Universal Declaration of Human Rights," to "strive for the full protection and promotion in all our countries of civil, political, economic, social and cultural rights for all," and "to strengthen the capacity of all our countries to implement the principles and practices of democracy and respect for human rights, including minority rights."[55]

The guidance for human rights-based development is found in the instruments themselves, and has since been elaborated by the monitoring bodies. Article 2 of the ICCPR requires each State party to respect and ensure the civil and political rights of all individuals within its territory and subject to its jurisdiction, without discrimination. Under Article 2 of the ICESCR, states have obliged themselves to take steps to the maximum of their available resources with a view to progressively achieving economic, social, and cultural rights. Under the Convention on the Rights of the Child, States parties "shall undertake all appropriate legislative, administrative, and other measures for the implementation of the rights recognized in the present Convention. With regard to economic, social and cultural rights, States parties shall undertake such measures to the maximum extent of their available resources and, where needed, within the framework of international cooperation."[56] States parties are required to give effect to the obligations under these conventions in good faith, as set in Article 26 of the Vienna Convention on the Law of Treaties.

---

53 Declaration and Programme of Action, Article 1. Available at www.unhchr.ch/html/menu5/vwchr.htm.
54 *Ibid.*
55 United Nations Millennium Declaration, General Assembly resolution 55/2 (September 8, 2000), Section V. Available at www.ohchr.org/english/law/millennium.htm.
56 Convention on the Rights of the Child, General Assembly resolution 44/25 (November 20, 1989), Article 4. Available at www.unhchr.ch/html/menu3/b/k2crc.htm.

The obligations of the human rights conventions are binding for every State party as a whole, including all branches of government (executive, legislative, and judicial), at national, regional, or local levels. The Human Rights Committee, in its General Comment 31 (adopted in 2004), has pointed out that the positive obligations on States parties to ensure Covenant rights will only be fully discharged if individuals are protected by the state, not just against violations of Covenant rights by its agents, but also against acts committed by private persons or entities that would impair the enjoyment of Covenant rights insofar as they are amenable to application between private persons or entities.

Under Article 2 of the ICCPR, States parties have to take the necessary steps to give effect to the Covenant rights in the domestic order.[57] Unless Covenant rights are already protected by their domestic laws or practices, States parties are required on ratification to make such changes to domestic laws and practices as are necessary to ensure their conformity with the Covenant. This means that States parties to that Covenant are obliged to establish the civil and political rights frameworks for a human rights-based development.

The UN Committee on Economic, Social and Cultural Rights has elaborated the guidelines for the progressive realization of the economic, social, and cultural rights, which are at the core of what is here understood as rights-based development. The Committee has given general guidelines in General Comments 3 and 9, while specific guidelines have been given in General Comments 4 and 7 (concerning the right to housing), General Comments 11 and 13 (on the right to education), General Comment 12 (concerning the right to food), General Comment 14 (on the right to education), and General Comment 15 (on the right to drinking water).

While the full realization of economic, social, and cultural rights may not be possible immediately, steps toward that goal must be taken as soon as the Covenant enters into force for the state concerned. The Committee has requested that such steps should be deliberate, concrete, and targeted at meeting the obligations recognized in the Covenant. The Committee also underlines the fact that, even in times of severe resources constraints, whether caused by a process of adjustment, of economic recession, or by other factors, the vulnerable members of society can and indeed must be protected by the adoption of relatively low-cost, targeted programs.[58] The Committee is also of the view that every State party is obliged to ensure the satisfaction of, at the very least, minimum essential levels of each of the rights. "Thus, for example, a State party in which any significant number of individuals is deprived of essential foodstuffs, of essential primary health care, of basic shelter and housing, or of the most basic forms of education is, prima facie, failing to discharge its obligations under the Covenant." The Committee has also called on states to ensure that remedies exist in cases of violations or neglect of the rights.[59] A similar approach has been taken by the UN Committee on the Rights of the Child in its General

---

57 ICCPR, Article 2, para. 2, *supra*, note 8.
58 UN Committee on Economic, Social and Cultural Rights, General Comment 3, paras. 9 and 12. Available at www.unhchr.ch/html/menu2/6/cescr.htm.
59 *Ibid.*, General Comment 9, para. 10.

Comment 5, including an insistence that economic and social rights, as well as civil rights, in the Child Convention must be regarded as justiciable.

Both the Committee on Economic, Social and Cultural Rights and the Committee on the Rights of the Child have called on states to adopt strategies for the implementation of the various rights contained in the relevant convention. These guidelines set for the preparation and implementation of such strategies can indeed be seen as guidelines for a rights-based development in relation to each of the rights addressed.

For purposes of illustration, the realization of the right to food (from General Comment 12 of the Committee on Economic, Social and Cultural Rights) will here be examined in more detail. The Committee has pointed out that the right to adequate food, like any other human right, imposes three types or levels of obligations on States parties: the obligations to respect, to protect, and to fulfill. In turn, the obligation to fulfill incorporates both an obligation to facilitate and an obligation to provide. The obligation to respect existing access to adequate food requires that States parties not take any measures that prevent such access. The obligation to protect requires measures by the state to ensure that enterprises or individuals do not deprive other individuals of their access to adequate food. The obligation to fulfill, or facilitate, means the state must pro-actively engage in activities intended to strengthen people's access to, and utilization of, resources and means to ensure their livelihood, including food security. Finally, whenever an individual or group is unable, for reasons beyond their control, to enjoy the right to adequate food, states must fulfill that right directly. This obligation also applies for persons who are victims of natural or other disasters.

As the Committee points out, the most appropriate means of implementing the right to adequate food will vary significantly among State parties. However, the Covenant clearly requires that each State party take the necessary steps to ensure that everyone is free from hunger and, as soon as possible, can enjoy the right to adequate food. This requires the adoption of national strategies, policies, and corresponding benchmarks to ensure food and nutrition security for all, based on human rights principles that define the objectives. States should also identify the resources available to meet the objectives, and the most cost-effective way of using them. The strategies should be based on a systematic identification of policy measures and activities relevant to the situation and context, facilitating coordination between ministries and regional and local authorities, and ensuring that related policies and administrative decisions are in compliance with the obligations under Article 11 of the Covenant. The formulation and implementation of national strategies for the right to food requires full compliance with the principles of accountability, transparency, people's participation, decentralization, legislative capacity, and the independence of the judiciary. Good governance is essential to the realization of all human rights, including the elimination of poverty and ensuring a satisfactory livelihood for all.[60]

---

60   *Ibid.*, General Comment 14, paras. 22-24.

The Committee further details the adoption of institutional mechanisms that would secure a representative process in the formulation of a strategy, sets out the responsibilities and time-frame for the implementation of the necessary measures, and gives particular attention to the need to prevent discrimination in access to food or resources for food. These steps should include guarantees of full and equal access to economic resources, particularly for women — including the right to inheritance; the ownership of land and other property; credit, natural resources, and appropriate technology; measures to respect and protect self-employment and work that provides a remuneration ensuring a decent living for wage earners and their families (as stipulated in Article 7 (a) (ii) of the Covenant); and maintaining registries on rights in land, including forests.

As part of their obligations to protect people's resource bases for food, States parties should take appropriate steps to ensure that activities of the private business sector and civil society are in conformity with the right to food.

Even where a state faces severe resource constraints, whether caused by a process of economic adjustment, economic recession, climatic conditions or other factors, measures should be taken to ensure that the right to adequate food is fulfilled, especially for vulnerable population groups and individuals.

In implementing such strategies, states should set verifiable benchmarks for subsequent national and international monitoring and provide the goals, as well as a time-frame for the achievement of those targets; the means by which the goals could be achieved described in broad terms (in particular, the intended collaboration with civil society, the private sector, and international organizations); institutional responsibility for the process; and the national mechanisms for its monitoring, as well as possible recourse procedures. In developing the benchmarks and framework legislation, States parties should actively involve civil society organizations.

States parties are also called upon to develop and maintain mechanisms to monitor progress on the realization of the right to adequate food for all, to identify the factors and difficulties affecting the degree of implementation, and to facilitate the adoption of corrective legislation and administrative measures. They should also ensure the availability of remedies for persons or groups who are victims of a violation of the right to adequate food, and who must be given adequate compensation, satisfaction, or guarantees of non-repetition. Judges and other members of the legal profession should therefore pay greater attention to violations of the right to food.

It would be possible, through a review and analysis of these and similar guidelines adopted by the relevant committees, to elaborate a comprehensive set of strategies for rights-based development. On the basis of General Comment 12, the UN Food and Agricultural Organization adopted a set of practical guidelines for the implementation of the right to food in November, 2004.[61] This has been seen as a landmark commitment to human rights and provides, in the field of food and nutrition, a clear roadmap for human rights-based development. It is hoped that similar processes will

---

61 Food and Agriculture Organization of the United Nations, "FAO Council adopts Right to Food Guidelines." Available at www.fao.org/newsroom/en/news/2004/51653/.

be carried out by other agencies (among others, by the World Health Organization [WHO] for health and the United Nations Economic, Scientific and Cultural Organization [UNESCO] for education and cultural rights), and thereby create a broad set of guidelines and recommendations for human rights-based development.

In the future application of human rights-based development, the role of the UN human rights treaty bodies will be increasingly important. In their dialogue with states, they are in a position to discuss whether the measures taken are optimal to the task, and their concluding observations containing country-specific recommendations are directly relevant for the advancement of the human rights-based road to development. The conclusions of the treaty bodies will therefore also be an important source for external donors, since they result from a dialogue with the concerned states and reflect the views of diverse independent experts from all parts of the world. Their legitimacy is therefore considerably higher than the narrow and Western-dominated expertise of the international financial institutions.

Enabling and Assisting: Desirable Roles for International Actors

Human rights talk has become more common in development assistance, which indeed is welcome. It is important to recognize that it may fail, however, if larger factors, which determine conditions for development, are neglected.

Dialogue between developed states and developing states, whether bilateral or through multilateral donor organizations, will not by itself lead to a meaningful human rights-based development if the government does not have the will or interest to pursue it. International actors can seek to persuade but cannot impose a human rights-based development. Most states have ratified the relevant international institutions, however, and have therefore undertaken a legal obligation to implement the rights contained in the conventions. Pushed by actors in the civil society of their own countries, they may be willing to embark on rights-based development even if this changes power relations within the country, but their will to do so depends greatly on conditions at the international level.

What donors and the international community at large can do is to help create an enabling international environment, which makes it more feasible and more attractive to pursue a human rights-based approach. They can also provide assistance that increases the capacity of governments to pursue such development. The Declaration on the Right to Development and the Millennium Declaration have made it clear that this is a shared responsibility. Management of worldwide economic and social developments as well as threats to international peace and security must be shared among the nations of the world and should be exercised multilaterally. As the most universal and most representative organization in the world, the United Nations must play the central role.

While this chapter has focused mainly on the domestic implementation of human rights-based development, it should be obvious that much depends on decisions made in the global political economy, including changes in the development approaches of the international financial organizations, a stronger role for the UN itself, and a more development-focused approach within the World Trade Organization.

There is a strong need for improved governance of the global economy. At present, globalization has global consequences, but does not have global governance. Regulatory mechanisms are missing, and cannot be put in place with the present international system of governance. The most important decisions are made by the IMF and the World Bank, which do not have democratic legitimacy due to their voting rules. The WTO is based on consensus in decision-making, but has so far been unable to have a real impact in ensuring a more equitable North-South relationship.

All actors in the international community need to cooperate. The United Nations, the financial institutions, regional organizations, national and local authorities, as well as the organizations of civil society, must be encouraged to contribute in their own ways and with their own resources to reduce inequalities and promote genuine freedom for all — freedom from want and from fear, as well as freedom of speech and belief. It is essential to narrow the gap between developed and developing countries, and overcome the social tensions that undermine social and economic stability and security.

In paragraph 2 of the Millennium Declaration, the leaders of the world stated:

> We recognize that, in addition to our separate responsibilities to our individual societies, we have a collective responsibility to uphold the principles of human dignity, equality and equity at the global level. As leaders we have a duty therefore to all the world's people, especially the most vulnerable and, in particular, the children of the world, to whom the future belongs . . . .

In paragraph 5, they added . . .

> We believe that the central challenge we face today is to ensure that globalization becomes a positive force for all the world's people. For while globalization offers great opportunities, at present its benefits are very unevenly shared, while its costs are unevenly distributed. We recognize that developing countries and countries with economies in transition face special difficulties in responding to this central challenge. Thus, only through broad and sustained efforts to create a shared future, based upon our common humanity in all its diversity, can globalization be made fully inclusive and equitable. These efforts must include policies and measures, at the global level, which correspond to the needs of developing countries and economies in transition and are formulated and implemented with their effective participation.[62]

Human rights-based development, with recognition of the corresponding international obligations, is the road to achieve this goal.

---

62   United Nations Millennium Declaration, *supra*, note 55.

In Place of Conclusion: 11 Propositions

Proposition 1: From Neglect to Rhetoric —
But Not Much Rights-Based Action

The human rights-based approach to development was largely neglected in development thinking until the second part of the 1990s. It has since received increasing attention, but more on the rhetorical level than in practical implementation of development polices.

Commitment to rights-based development is expressed in important documents, particularly by agencies in the UN Development Group, led by the UNDP, and by Nordic, British, Dutch, and German development ministries and agencies.[63] But the operationalization of a rights-based approach tends to disappear or become very vague in the body of the same reports. This is not surprising: it reflects a problem of disparate values and interests in economics, politics, and human rights law, both nationally and internationally.

Proposition 2: The Agents of Rights-Based Development —
Clarification Required

A human rights-based approach cannot be driven solely by donors or development agencies. The primary responsibility must be borne by the recipient country. A human rights-based approach must not merely be internalized and grudgingly accepted, but preferably be self-generated by the recipient nation. The potential role for international civil society is substantial, but must be better clarified. Multinational corporations have an ambiguous role in the process. There is uncertainty as to whom the international financial institutions serve — the corporations, the rich countries, or the developing countries. If mixed, whose interests are given the greatest attention?

Proposition 3: Distinctions Are Necessary

Distinction 1: Rights-based development is different from needs-based development. Needs are met, if at all, by charity, which is a marginal supplement to enrichment in centers of growth and global processes of accumulation; rights are entitlements, which can be claimed and must be met by those who have a duty towards the rights-holder.

Distinction 2: Human rights-based development is more than and often quite different from "simple" rights-based development. "Rights" can cover any kind of rights and are locally determined as a result of power relations; rights can include established property rights irrespective of whether their origin, use or inheritance principles are "just" ; human rights-based development builds on the international normative system of rights and the obligations undertaken by (most) states, which makes possible a growing international consensus on the content of the rights and the corresponding responsibility of the duty-holders.[64]

---

63   L. H. Piron, "Rights-Based Approaches and Bilateral Aid Agreements: More than a Metaphor?" IDS Bulletin 36, No.1, p. 25.
64   This point is also made by Piron, "Rights-Based Approaches," *supra,* note 63, p. 23.

Distinction 3: A human rights-based approach to development is different from both a state-centric economic command system, even when the aim is protective and intended to eliminate social inequality, and from neo-liberal economic ideology, even if the aim is liberative and intended to assert the freedom to choose. Human rights are both protective (by the state and its agencies) and liberative (from the state and its agencies), and a core function is to facilitate empowerment of those who are otherwise weak, to make them able to participate effectively and thereby promote a well-functioning society.

Proposition 4: Indivisibility Should Be Maintained, But Human Rights Fundamentalism Avoided

A human rights-based approach generally places civil, political, economic, social, and cultural rights on the same level. And yet priorities at particular points in time and in particular countries have to depend on which set of rights is most neglected then and there.

Proposition 5: Foundations in International Law Should Be Recognized and Used

Foundations in international law for a human rights-based approach is found in the UN Charter (Articles 1 and 55-56), the UDHR (Articles 1 and 28, combined with preamble, para. 2, second period), and given legal detail in ICCPR, ICECR, ICERD, ICEDAW and CRC — among others. Relevant is also the UN Declaration on Social Development (1969), the Declaration on the Right to Development, the Vienna Declaration, and the Millennium Declaration.

Proposition 6: Strategies for Human Rights-Based Development Exist and Should Be Further Developed

Components of the necessary strategies have increasingly been elaborated by human rights treaty bodies in their general comments. Many of them explicitly require states to adopt sectoral strategies (in food, health, housing, education, and other areas by the CESCR); many of the general comments of the Human Rights Committee, CEDAW, and the CRC Committee are also building blocks for a comprehensive, human rights-based approach to development.

Proposition 7: Not Value Added, But Value Change

A human rights-based approach to development is not a matter of "value added" to traditional development policies, nor is it about doing slightly better "what we always have done." It requires a basic value change in conceptualizing and prioritizing development. It requires attention both to process and to outcomes.

The process requires broad participation in development, particularly for those who most need the development; freedom of expression and information; freedom of assembly and association; effective participation by those affected; attention to minority rights and to those of indigenous peoples; and freedom in the choice of work or other income-generating activity.

It requires attention to outcomes, particularly for those who do not have social security, those who presently live below the level of adequate standard of living, and those who do not have satisfactory access to health or to education. This requires preset benchmarks, monitoring at national and international levels, advance identification of those responsible for ensuring that process is respected and the benchmarks are achieved, and effective remedies when these responsibilities are not met. It requires, in particular, avoidance of negative outcomes, in the sense of poverty production (impoverishment). Much of what passes as "poverty reduction strategies" does not meet these criteria.

Proposition 8: Still Absent: Value Consensus

A full-fledged human rights-based approach by development agencies would require a broad value consensus between donors and recipients. It also requires consensus between the different donors. As of today, there are only fragments of such consensus. However, the United Nations Development Group made an important step forward at its Second Interagency Workshop on Implementing a Human Rights-Based Approach, when it adopted a document entitled *A Common Understanding among UN Agencies on a Human Rights-Based Approach.*[65]

Proposition 9: Testing Commitment to Human Rights-Based Development

Several ongoing activities within human rights bodies can be used to test states' commitment or non-commitment to human rights-based development. The following examples illustrate how state commitment could be tested:

- The attitudes of different states toward the proposal in the UN Human Rights Commission for the adoption of an optional protocol making possible complaints against violations of economic, social, and cultural human rights.

- The attitudes of different states toward the voluntary guidelines adopted under FAO auspices on the implementation of the right to food.

- The attitudes of different states toward various general comments of the human rights treaty bodies, in particular to those of the Committee on Economic, Social and Cultural Rights, which provide the most detailed guidance on human rights-based development.

- The attitudes about international obligations for human rights, on the basis of United Nations Charter 55 and 56 and corresponding provisions in human rights treaties.

---

65 *The Human Rights Based Approach to Development Cooperation — Towards a Common Understanding Among UN Agencies.* In the Report of the Second Interagency Workshop on Implementing a Human Rights-based Approach in the Context of UN Reform (Stamford, CT: May 5-7, 2003). Available at www.undg.org/documents/3404-Inter Agency_Workshop_on_Implementing_A_ Human_Rights-based_Approach_to_Development_-_Stanford_Workshop_May_03.doc.

Proposition 10: A Human Rights-Based Development Is Desirable and Possible, But Not Yet Probable

Increasing attention to a human rights-based approach is desirable. It is also possible, but doubts persist whether it is probable. It is unfair for agents of rich countries to demand a rights-based approach by the governments of the poor countries, when the international economic system is structured in a way that gives highly unequal benefits to the rich and the poor, and rich countries do not seem to want to meaningfully change that.

Proposition 11: Broadening an Overlapping Consensus Is Possible

Deep value changes are unlikely, because different actors have different interests. But broadening an overlapping consensus is possible when different interests can be promoted by the same policies. An historical example in economics was the Keynesian General Theory, which reconciled labor and capital interests and fundamentally changed (for some time) social and economic thinking.[66]

Perhaps the most important challenge ahead for a human rights-based approach to development is the following issue: can a broader, overlapping consensus be achieved between private capital interests and the interests of people at large, for the public good (education, health, and, at least partly, social security) and the fullest possible employment or income generation for all, facilitated by state intervention, and in recognition of international obligations?

---

66 *The Human Rights Based Approach to Development Cooperation — Towards a Common Understanding Among UN Agencies.* In the Report of the Second Interagency Workshop on Implementing a Human Rights-based Approach in the Context of UN Reform (Stamford, CT: May 5-7, 2003). Available at www.undg.org/documents/3404-Inter Agency_Workshop_on_Implementing_A_Human_Rights-based_Approach_to_Development_-_Stanford_Workshop_May_03.doc.

12 | Globalization and the Human Rights Approach to Development
Siddiq Osmani

This chapter examines the implications of the current wave of globalization for the pursuit of a human rights approach to development. It is now widely recognized that broad-based development is not possible without empowering the people — especially the poor. The human rights approach to development is essentially about such empowerment. The notion that individuals have rights, which they can claim, and that there are some actors who are obliged to meet those claims, is an immensely empowering one. Once policy-making is required to conform to the human rights framework, the rationale of development policies changes in a fundamental way. Policies are no longer driven merely by the recognition that people have needs that ought to be fulfilled but that they have rights that entail legal obligations on the part of the state and other relevant actors.

In this approach, the nation states bear the primary obligation for ensuring that the human rights are realized in full for everyone within their jurisdiction. The question has arisen, however, about whether the wave of globalization that is currently sweeping the world weakens or strengthens the ability as well as incentives of nation states to discharge their obligations. This question is the object of scrutiny of this chapter.[1]

The central argument of the chapter is that there is nothing deterministic about the impact of globalization on the ability or incentives of nation states to discharge their human rights obligations. As in all spheres, globalization entails both constraints and opportunities, and much depends on how national and international policies attempt to deal with them. The second section of the chapter scrutinizes some of the potential constraints, and the third section examines potential opportunities. The fourth section lays out some principles that national policy-making ought to follow in order to render globalization not only compatible with the human rights approach to development but also conducive to it.[2]

Some Potential Constraints to the Human Rights Approach to Development in the Age of Globalization

In both popular and academic discussions, globalization is thought to pose a number of constraints to the fuller realization of human rights — so much so, in the opinion of some, that globalization is not deemed to be compatible with human rights at all. This concern with a potential conflict between globalization and human rights is scrutinized below in the context of three sets of issues. These are (1) how the

---

1 The definition of globalization can be quite elastic, going beyond economic integration of the world to encompass political and cultural integration as well. This chapter focuses only on the economic dimension of globalization and its implications for the human rights approach to development.
2 It is recognized that national-level policy-making must be supplemented by policies at the international level in order to be fully effective, but limitation of space prevents an examination of the international dimension of the human rights approach to development in this chapter.

force of competition engendered by globalization might affect workers' rights, (2) how the drive towards liberalization of trade and capital flows might undermine the fiscal powers of nation states to discharge their human rights obligations, and (3) how changes in the structure of production and employment induced by globalization might threaten the rights of the poorer and weaker segments of the society.

Globalization and Labor Standards: A "Race to the Bottom"?

One area where globalization is sometimes seen to be incompatible with, or even inimical to, human rights is that of labor standards. The working class has come a long way since the early days of the industrial revolution to secure various rights through a long process of political struggle. The world community has come to accept, at least in principle, that workers have certain fundamental human rights that must guide their relationship with employers and governments. The International Labor Organization (ILO) has defined them as core "labor standards," which include (1) prohibition of forced labor, (2) freedom of association, (3) the right to organize and bargain collectively, (4) elimination of the exploitation of child labor, and (5) non-discrimination in employment. There are other standards — related to wages, health and safety conditions, rules of dismissal, among others — that are not treated as core but are nevertheless considered important enough to be part of the conditions for "decent work." The struggle to achieve these rights is still incomplete — some of these rights have been achieved less than others and workers in some countries have achieved them less than in others. Globalization is seen by many to be an enemy of this struggle. It is feared that globalization will not only stand in the way of fuller achievement of workers' rights but will actually cause a regression of rights by inducing governments to lower the level of labor standards.

The basis of this fear lies in the force of competition unleashed by globalization. As more and more nations begin to integrate with the world economy, they will have to compete with each other ever more fiercely in order to survive and prosper. It is feared that this intensification of competition might undermine labor standards in at least two ways. First, since higher labor standards are likely to entail higher cost of employing labor, countries wishing to compete in the world market might let their standards fall to the level of competitors with lower standards in order to keep their cost and prices competitive. Second, countries might be tempted to lower their labor standards in order to attract foreign investors who might otherwise go to countries where the standards are less stringent. Both these compulsions — remaining competitive in the world market and attracting foreign capital — might thus lead to a "race to the bottom" among countries as they engage in a process of competitive degradation of labor standards.

Although this fear has a superficial plausibility, theoretical arguments are by no means unambiguous and the empirical evidence is far from supportive.[3] There are a

---

3   For an overview of the theory and empirical evidence, see K. E. Maskus "Should Labour Standards be Imposed Through International Trade Policy?" Policy Research Working Paper 1817 (Washington, DC: World Bank, 1997) and R. M. Stern, "Labour Standards and International Trade," Discussion Paper no. 430. Research Seminar in International Economics. (Ann Arbor: University of Michigan, 1998).

number of reasons why higher labor standards need not erode competitiveness. First, in a competitive labor market workers may have to trade off some cash rewards in order to achieve higher labor standards, in which case the overall cost of labor need not rise for the employers. Second, in order to be competitive in the world market and attractive to foreign capital, what matters is not just the cost of employing labor but the relationship between cost and productivity of labor. Even if a high level of labor standards entails higher costs, it may also help raise productivity — by boosting workers' morale, incentive, loyalty, and sheer physical ability. If the gain of productivity outweighs any rise in costs, higher labor standards will not entail any loss of competitive advantage. Third, even if higher costs are not matched by higher productivity, thereby forcing prices up, competitiveness will not be lost if consumers are willing to pay a premium for the products produced under better labor standards.

On the empirical front, too, there is no convincing evidence of any systematic relationship between competitive advantage and labor standards. In a comparative study across a large number of countries, Rodrik found no effect of labor standards on a country's competitiveness in the export market, after controlling for other factors (such as productivity and factor endowments) that have a bearing on exports.[4] A study of imports into the US market from 10 major developing countries found that countries with lower labor standards did not enjoy a higher share of the market and that within those developing countries the more export-oriented firms enjoyed higher or similar labor standards as compared with the less export-oriented ones.[5] In a similar vein, an Organization for Economic Co-operation and Development (OECD) study concluded that "there is no evidence that lower standards countries enjoy a better global export performance than higher standard countries").[6] Thus, there is no reason to suspect, on the basis of existing evidence, that the drive to gain competitiveness in the world market has induced a general tendency to devalue labor standards.

The evidence on the relationship between labor standards and the direction of foreign capital flow also provides no reason to support the "race to the bottom" hypothesis. An analysis of US foreign direct investment in the 1980s found that countries with a poorer record of civil and political rights in general and workers' rights in particular actually received less investment from the US than would have been predicted by their other characteristics.[7] In other studies, labor standards in recipient countries were found to have no systematic relationship with the size of foreign direct investment (FDI) coming from the USA[8] and from the OECD countries as a whole.[9] In popular discussion, the link between foreign investment and labor stan-

---

4   D. Rodrik "Labor Standards in International Trade: Do They Matter and What Do We Do About Them?" in Robert Lawrence, Dani Rodrik, and John Whalley, *Emerging Agenda for Global Trade: High Stakes for Developing Countries* (Washington, DC: Overseas Development Council, 1996).
5   M. Aggarwal, "International Trade, Labor Standards, and Labor Market Conditions: An Evaluation of the Linkages," Working Paper 95-06-C (Washington, DC: US International Trade Commission, 1995).
6   OECD, *Trade, Employment, and Labour Standards: A Study of Core Workers' Rights and International Trade* (Paris: Organization for Economic Co-operation and Development, 1996), p. 12.
7   Rodrik, *supra*, note 4.
8   Aggarwal, *supra*, note 5.
9   OECD, *supra*, note 6.

dards has focussed mainly on the so-called export processing zones (EPZ), where labor standards, especially those relating to the right to collective bargaining, sometimes tend to be poor. There is, however, no evidence that EPZs with lower standards have in general succeeded in attracting more foreign capital than those with higher standards. On the contrary, a recent study has concluded that "Countries that pursue more integrated policy approaches for attracting export-oriented FDI — for example by encouraging tripartite representation (employers, workers and public authorities) on EPZ committees, guaranteeing workers' rights (including freedom of association and collective bargaining), and upgrading skills and working conditions — have tended to attract higher quality FDI)."[10] Moreover, as a result of combined efforts of the ILO, workers' associations and civil society organisations, labor standards seem to be improving in several EPZs over time rather than going down.[11]

The point of all this is not to deny that some countries may sometimes be tempted to compromise on their labor standards in the hope of stealing a march over others. Rather the point is that deliberate and competitive degradation of workers' rights is neither an inescapable consequence nor a general tendency of countries trying to integrate with the world economy.

Fiscal Autonomy of Nation States

One of the essential features of globalization is liberalization of trade and capital flows that helps integrate an economy more closely with the global economy. Trade liberalization involves elimination or at least substantial reduction of trade barriers such as tariffs and quotas. Tariff reduction, however, has consequences not just for trade flows but also for government budgets. In most developing countries, the domestic base of revenue collection is rather skimpy, and governments tend to rely heavily on tariffs on internationally traded goods as a major and, in some cases, the most important source of budgetary revenue. Trade liberalization might, therefore, entail considerable loss of revenue for the government. Something similar may happen with the liberalization of capital flows. Governments may be tempted to reduce taxes on the income earned by foreign capital in order to induce foreign investors to come to their shores in preference to other countries. The resulting loss of revenue may seriously constrain the government's ability to undertake essential expenditures that directly or indirectly help realize the human rights of the people, by ensuring better access to food, health, education, and so on.

Apart from possible loss of revenue, there is another way in which free flow of capital may constrain a government's fiscal powers. Governments in developing countries often resort to deficit financing in order to carry out expenditures that cannot be financed fully by the small amount of revenues they can manage to collect. Deficit financing, however, can lead to inflation, which in turn can lead to pressures for depreciation of the currency in the foreign exchange market. Any such

10 UNCTAD, *World Investment Report 2002: Transnational Corporations and Export Competitiveness* (Geneva: United Nations Conference on Trade and Development, 2002), p. 244.
11 ILO, "Employment and Social Policy in Respect of Export Processing Zones (EPZs)," GB.286/ ESP/3. Committee on Employment and Social Policy, Governing Body (Geneva: International Labor Organization, 2003), p. 15.

pressure for depreciation is bound to be viewed with concern by foreign investors, as a depreciated currency would mean a fall in the real value of their assets and income. Foreign capital would, therefore, tend to shy away from countries whose governments have a propensity to indulge in excessive deficit financing. As a result, if a government is keen to keep foreign capital within its shores, it would be seriously constrained in taking recourse to deficit financing.

Liberalization of trade and capital flows may thus limit a government's ability to undertake desired expenditures by reducing the amount of revenue on the one hand and constraining the use of deficit financing on the other.[12] It is conceivable that this will impair a government's ability to undertake fiscal expenditures that are essential for better realization of human rights.

It is important, however, to recognize that the fiscal constraint is not an inevitable consequence of globalization. There are a number of reasons for avoiding excessive pessimism in this regard. The first point to note is that many aspects of fuller realization of human rights do not make any substantial demand on budgetary resources. In this context, it is useful to note a three-fold classification of State obligations that has been discussed extensively in the human rights literature — namely, the obligation to *respect*, the obligation to *protect*, and the obligation to *fulfill* human rights.

The obligation to *respect* entails that the State must not do anything that would violate the rights of people. In the civil and political sphere, this means for example that the State must not deny people their freedom of speech, or must not put them into jail without following the due process of law, and so on. In the economic sphere, it means for example that the State must not deny any individual or group access to their means of livelihood, or to health care, or to education, etc.

The obligation to *respect* is a kind of negative obligation — it specifies what the State must not do. The other two obligations are positive in nature — they specify what the States must do. To obligation to *protect* emanates from the possibility that even though the State itself may not violate the rights of anyone, some third party might try to do so. The State in that case has an obligation to protect those whose rights are being violated or being threatened by others. For example, if an oppressive landlord is violating a tenant farmer's right to food by unlawfully evicting him from the only piece of land on which the latter's subsistence depends, then the State must protect the farmer by taking appropriate punitive actions on the landlord.

The third and final obligation — namely, the obligation to *fulfill* rights — is subdivided into two parts — to *facilitate* and to *provide*. The obligation to *facilitate* means that the State must proactively engage in activities that would strengthen people's ability to meet their own needs. For example, while it is true that every in-

---

12 See B. Khatri and M. Rao, "Fiscal Faus Pas? An Analysis of the Revenue Implications of Trade Liberalization," *World Development* 30(8), 2002, and B. Khatri,"Trade Liberalization and the Fiscal Squeeze: Implications for Public Investment," *Development and Change* 34(3), 2003, on the analytical and empirical issues regarding the impact of liberalization on revenues and expenditure of governments in the developing countries.

dividual must be responsible for maintaining his or her own health, the State has an obligation to facilitate this process either by creating the conditions in which market can supply the healthcare demanded by the people, or, in case the market fails, by supplying it through the State machinery.

The obligation to *provide* goes one step further. It requires the State not just to create the conditions in which people would be able to provide for themselves but actually transfer the necessary resources to those who for one reason or another cannot provide for themselves. Thus, the State must directly provide food whenever an individual or a group is unable, for reasons beyond their control, to provide for themselves the food they need (for example, the old and the infirm, people displaced by wars or natural disasters, and so on).

One of the distinctions among these different categories of obligations is that not all of them are equally dependent on the availability of resources. For instance, the "respect" obligations with regard to most rights would require political will more than economic resources. The "protect" and "fulfill" obligations would typically be more dependent on resources, but even there rapid progress can be made by improving the efficiency of resource use — for example, by scaling down expenditure on unproductive activities and by reducing spending on activities whose benefit goes disproportionately to the privileged groups of the society. Very often when governments plead inability to realize human rights because of resource constraint the real problem is not so much the lack of resources as such but the propensity to waste resources and to pander to powerful vested interests. If globalization can pressure delinquent governments to cut down on such wasteful use of resources by constraining their fiscal powers, that won't be such a bad thing for the cause of human rights after all.

This is not to deny that there is no genuine problem of resource constraint that stands in the way of full realization of human rights in most developing countries. Even after wasteful expenditures have been cut to the minimum, it is still possible that governments will not have enough resources at their disposal to discharge their human rights obligations fully. In that case, any curtailment of fiscal powers will have to be viewed with concern. It is, therefore, important to consider whether, and to what extent, globalization is actually likely to constrain the fiscal autonomy of developing countries.

There are a number of reasons to suspect that the fear about globalization's impact on fiscal powers may be grossly exaggerated. Consider first the effect of tariff reduction. What typically happens in the course of trade liberalization is not a sudden drop to zero tariff across the board but a change from a regime of high and variable tariff rates to a regime of low and relatively uniform rates. The average rate of tariff invariably goes down as a result, but this does not necessarily mean that total tariff revenue must go down as well. This is because the tax base tends to expand at the same time.

First, since tariff reduction leads to greater volume of trade, total tariff revenue may increase even if the average rate goes down, depending on price elasticities of import and export. Secondly, since trade liberalization typically involves replacing quantitative restrictions on imports by tariff restriction (the so-called tariffication of quotas), many more commodities get subjected to tariff payments than before. As a result, there can be no general presumption that trade liberalization will necessarily lead to a loss of revenue. A similar argument applies to the liberalization of capital flows. Even if a government reduces the income tax rate in order to attract foreign capital, total tax revenue may still increase if the inflow of foreign capital rises enough to generate more than proportionate increase in income by employing such capital to productive use.

It is also important to note that the revenue impact of trade liberalization cannot be judged simply from the effect on tariff revenue because tariffs may be replaced by other taxes. The problem with tariff is that it is a discriminatory tax — that is, it discriminates against imports compared with domestic goods. Such discriminatory taxes distort the incentive structure and thereby induce economic inefficiency.[13] That is why trade liberalization, whose objective is to improve economic efficiency, requires the reduction and eventual elimination of tariffs. But this objective does not require elimination of taxes on imports altogether. It is perfectly admissible to replace tariff with a tax that is neutral between imported and domestic goods. Such a tax would continue to raise revenue from imports — as well as from domestic goods — while being perfectly consistent with the principle of trade liberalization. Total tax revenue may not thus fall, and may in fact increase, even if tariff revenue falls. Therefore, if a government is concerned about the revenue effect of trade liberalization, it has the option of imposing such a neutral tax (such as the value-added tax).

Clearly, then, the fiscal constraint impact of globalization cannot be taken for granted. Governments are not entirely helpless in this matter. They have policy options available at their disposal that may in fact enhance their fiscal powers. These options include tariffication of quotas, setting the average rate of tariff at a level that avoids serious loss of tariff revenue, replacing tariffs with neutral taxes, and generally improving the efficiency of revenue collection, which happens to be pretty low in developing countries. To what extent developing countries are actually making use of these policy instruments along with their attempt at trade liberalization is not yet known — research on this topic is still very limited. But there is some evidence to support the argument that trade liberalization can go hand in hand with improved fiscal powers provided appropriate policy options are adopted.

The experience of Bangladesh is instructive in this regard.[14] Bangladesh adopted sweeping measures of trade liberalization in the late 1980s and early 1990s. Tariff revenues as a proportion of GDP have fallen slightly as a result, but total revenue from imported goods has not. This is because the government of Bangladesh partially replaced tariffs with the neutral value-added tax (VAT) in 1992, applied uniformly on domestic and imported goods. On the domestic front, the new tax replaced the old-style excise duties, and on the import front it (partly) replaced cus-

---

13 Except in special cases where tariffs may be justified on the ground of externalities.
14   S. R. Osmani, W. Mahmud, B. Sen, H. Dagdeviren, and A. Seth, *The Macroeconomics of Poverty Reduction: The Case Study of Bangladesh* (Dhaka: UNDP, 2003).

toms duties and sales tax on imports. In addition, the government introduced the so-called Supplementary Duty, which is also meant to be imposed equally on import and domestic production.

As a result of these tax reforms, the overall collection of indirect taxes did not actually suffer in Bangladesh following trade liberalization. As a proportion of GDP, total revenue from indirect taxes in fact increased from 4.6 percent in the late 1980s to 5.6 percent in the first half of the 1990s and further to 6.3 percent in the second half of the decade.

Increased revenue from indirect taxes has been supplemented by a move towards better collection of direct taxes that proved quite successful up to the mid-1990s (but tapered off since then). As a result, total revenue as a percentage of GDP went up from 6.3 percent in the second half of the 1980s to 9.2 percent in the second half of the 1990s. Correspondingly, public expenditure as a percentage of GDP also went up — from 12.9 percent to 13.6 percent of GDP. While this increase is quite small, it is significant that it happened despite a secular decline in the inflow of foreign aid during the same period. Finally, it is worth noting that the share of public expenditure going to sectors that benefit the poor proportionately more — such as health, education, and basic infrastructure — has also increased. For instance, the combined share of health and education in total budgetary expenditure has gone up from 14 percent in the first half of the 1980s to 23 percent in the second half of the 1990s While the evidence from a single country is by no means conclusive, this is enough to make the point that there is nothing inevitable about globalization making it harder for governments to discharge their human rights obligations by constraining their fiscal powers. Much depends on the details of the policy package that is implemented in the course of liberalization.

Winners and Losers from Structural Change

Integration with the global economy inevitably brings about structural changes within an economy, opening up new opportunities for enhancing employment and income but also closing down, or at least diminishing, many existing means of livelihood. To use economic jargon, opportunities open up in those activities in which a country has comparative advantage, and diminish in those in which it has comparative disadvantage. All this may have profound implications for pursuing the human rights approach to development.

Economic theory suggests that generally speaking gains will outweigh losses, so that a nation as a whole should gain in the form of an overall increase in welfare. The problem, however, is that gains and losses may not be distributed evenly across the population. Much depends on who happens to be engaged in the expanding activities and who in the contracting ones, and who has the skills and other means of access to the new opportunities that are being opened up. Evidence as well as common sense suggests that losses will generally be felt disproportionately more by the weaker segments of the society. They would suffer more simply because they lack the flexibility to cope with the changing winds of market forces owing to the various impediments they face in accessing new skills and resources. There is a real danger that some of them might face a reversal in the achievement of a range of human rights such as the rights to food, work, health, and shelter. This is one reason for concern regarding the compatibility of globalization with human rights.

While recognizing that globalization has the potential to make some of the poor more vulnerable in the face of changing structure of opportunities, it is necessary, however, to avoid excessive alarmism in this regard. A couple of points are worth noting here.

First, it is often suggested almost in an axiomatic fashion that globalization has widened income inequality in the world, which is seen as prima facie evidence for the view that the poor have been hurt by the process. However, quite apart from the fact that widening inequality can easily go in hand with absolute improvement in the living conditions of the poor, the very notion that globalization has widened inequality is deeply problematic. The empirical evidence on what has happened to income distribution in the world in the current phase of globalization is inconclusive.[15,16] More importantly, no one has yet found a satisfactory way of separating out the effect of globalization from the effects of other factors that might have a bearing on income distribution in the world.

In any case, even if it can be shown that globalization has indeed contributed to widening of inequality in the world, it does not follow that globalization must necessarily do so. In the 1950s and 1960s, it used to be believed that when a backward economy begins to develop along the capitalist line income distribution necessarily worsens at the initial stage, before improving much later. Known as the Kuznets hypothesis, this belief has now come to be belied by empirical evidence. What happens to income distribution at any stage of development depends very much on the nature of policies pursued by governments. With appropriate policies, distribution can actually improve as an economy grows — there is nothing inevitable about the Kuznets hypothesis. The same is true in principle about the effect of globalization. Policies — at both national and international level — can make a difference. As will be argued below, this is precisely the reason for taking the human rights approach to development even more seriously in the age of globalization.

The second point to bear in mind is that even without globalization structural changes do occur in any economy except in the most moribund ones. Owing to changes in technology, tastes, demographic structure, and so on, new opportunities open up in the sphere of production and old ones close down all the time. The effects of these home-grown structural changes are not qualitatively dissimilar to those induced by globalization. They too create new uncertainties and vulnerabilities along with new opportunities, and in this case too the cost of negative effects tends to fall disproportionately more on the weaker segments of the population, and for much the same reasons. If this is not seen as a reason for avoiding structural changes in general, it should not be seen as a reason for shutting the door to globalization either.

---

15   B. Milanovich, "Can We Discern the Effect of Globalization on Income Distribution? Evidence from Household Surveys," Policy Research Working Paper 2876 (Washington, DC: World Bank, 2002).
16   M. Ravallion, "Debates on Globalization, Inequality and Poverty: Why Measurement Matters," Policy Research Working Paper 3038 (Washington, DC: World Bank, 2003).

There is, however, a very good reason for being especially concerned with the possible negative effects of globalization and for trying to do something about it. The problem is that unlike home-grown structural changes, which typically unfold incrementally over a long haul allowing a breathing space for necessary adjustments, the current phase of globalization is bringing about sweeping structural changes within a short period of time. The sheer pace of change can entail serious problems of adjustment, especially when it comes to setting up an adequate social protection scheme for those suffering most from the disruptions caused by structural changes. What is worse, this problem can be compounded by two other factors.

One of these can be described as the problem of shifting comparative advantage. As noted earlier, when a country integrates with the world economy, the structure of production begins to shift away from activities with comparative disadvantage towards those with comparative advantage. The problem, however, is that structural changes caused by this shift may not be a once-for-all affair because the nature of comparative advantage may itself undergo rapid change during the process of globalization. Comparative advantage, it must be remembered, is inherently comparative in nature – that is, it depends not just on the characteristics of a particular country but also on those of other countries that participate in a trading network. As a result, any country that has already embraced globalization may find that its comparative advantage keeps changing as the net of globalization spreads, bringing in new countries within the trading network. Thus, countries such as Malaysia and Taiwan have discovered to their dismay that the comparative advantage they have enjoyed in labor-intensive garment industries for a number of years was suddenly eroded as Bangladesh, Sri Lanka, and Vietnam enter the export market with even cheaper labor. Similarly, the Latin American countries that once found comparative advantage in labor-intensive activities when they first embraced globalization now find that they no longer have comparative advantage in those activities as populous countries such as China and India have entered the scene. In each case, a country that loses comparative advantage in one sphere will eventually find it elsewhere. But the problem is that shifting comparative advantage of this kind can keep the structure of an economy in a constant state of flux for a prolonged period of time.[17] The disruptive effects of globalization may, therefore, be quite serious.

The other problem stems from the erratic behavior of international finance. One of the presumed gains from globalization is that free flow of capital will ensure efficient use of resources by moving finance from regions with low marginal rate of return to regions with higher returns. In reality, however, capital does not always behave in such efficient manner because of various kinds of market failures arising from imperfect and asymmetric knowledge that is inherent in capital markets. In the absence of perfect knowledge, flow of capital in and out of countries is often guided by "herd behavior," as an initial move by some investor is blindly imitated by hordes of others. The magnitudes of capital movement can thus be quite out of proportions

---

17 In theory, the economic structure will eventually settle down to some kind of steady state as the net of globalization engulfs the whole world, but that could take a very long time indeed.

with the underlying rates of return. In that case, what should have been an orderly and limited movement of capital becomes a stampede, plunging a country into a crisis that is deeper than what it probably deserved in terms of its economic fundamentals. Even the direction of flow can sometimes be erratic, for example, when the "contagion effect" takes hold — that is, when capital moves out of a country not necessarily because anything is fundamentally wrong with it but because some other country of similar type is experiencing a crisis. The series of financial crises that rocked Asia and Latin America in the past decade and a half bear clear hallmarks of such erratic behavior of international finance.

This is not to suggest that the countries that experienced crises did not get many of their economic policies seriously wrong or that they didn't need to bring about fundamental structural changes in their economies in order to make them more efficient. They generally did, but it is also undeniable that the erratic movement of international finance forced some additional structural changes that were not needed on efficiency grounds and were probably quite harmful (for example, when drying up of capital forced even potentially efficient activities to be closed down).[18] Many of these uncalled for changes were probably reversed as the countries emerged out of crises and international finance resumed business as usual. But the harm done during the crisis in terms of unnecessary human sufferings caused by disruptions and dislocations, not all of which were efficiency enhancing, was real and extremely painful.

Globalization can thus have both an accentuating and a distorting effect on structural changes, even though some of these changes would in any case occur in an economy even without it. The potential for creating new uncertainties and vulnerabilities (along with new opportunities) is, therefore, correspondingly greater in the context of globalization than without. As such, the potential for hurting the weaker segments of the population is also greater in the age of globalization, unless conscious efforts are made to protect them.[19]

This is where the human rights approach to development can play a vitally important role. The international human rights normative framework has a particular pre-occupation with individuals and groups that are vulnerable, marginal, disadvantaged, or socially excluded. That is why it can act as an effective counterweight to the disruptive effects of globalization whose burden is likely to fall disproportionately on these very categories of people. Two elements of the international human rights normative framework are especially relevant here. These are the twin principles of non-discrimination and equality and the principle of non-retrogression of rights.

The principles of non-discrimination and equality are among the most fundamental elements of international human rights law. These are elaborated in numerous human rights instruments, including the Universal Declaration of Human

---

18 The problem was compounded by policy errors made by the Bretton Woods institutions. For a searching analysis of these issues, see J. E. Stiglitz, *Globalization and Its Discontents* (London: Allen Lane, 2002).

19 The empirical evidence on the uneven impact of globalization on the poor is discussed by P. R. Agenor, "Does Globalization Hurt the Poor?" Policy Research Working Paper 2922 (Washington, DC: World Bank, 2002) and M. Ravallion, "Looking Beyond Averages in the Trade and Poverty Debate," Policy Research Working Paper 3461 (Washington, DC: World Bank, 2004).

Rights, the two International Covenants on civil-political rights and economic-so-cial-cultural rights, the International Convention on the Elimination of All Forms of Racial Discrimination (ICERD), Convention on the Elimination of All Forms of Discrimination against Women (CEDAW), and the Convention on the Rights of the Child. Recognizing the fundamental importance of these twin principles, the international community has established two treaty bodies, under ICERD and CEDAW, that are devoted exclusively to the promotion and protection of non-discrimination and equality.

If left unattended, the uneven burden of adjustments to globalization can fall foul of the principles of non-discrimination and equality. The problem is not just that globalization will not have a neutral or uniform effect on everyone in the society — no policy or economic change can be expected to have such an ideal effect. The problem arises when there is a systematic bias against some groups or individuals. If the adverse effects of a policy or economic change were to be distributed randomly among the population, the question of discrimination would not arise. But this is unlikely to be the case. Since the brunt of the burden is likely to be borne by the weaker segments of the population, the possibility of discrimination is very real. Two considerations are important to bear in mind in this context.

First, it needs to be recognized that discrimination and inequality may take many different forms and stem from many different sources. They may arise from explicit legal inequalities in status and entitlements. But they can also arise from policies that disregard the needs of particular people, or from social values that shape relationships within households and communities in a manner that discriminates against particular groups of people. Second, it is important to look at the effects of policies, not just intentions. For example, if the effect of a policy regime is to impoverish disproportionately women, or indigenous peoples, or some other marginalized group, it is prima facie discriminatory, even if the policy-makers had no intention of discriminating against the group in question.

Adherence to the human rights approach to development will, therefore, require that those who are systematically hurt by the disruptions caused by globalization be accorded special attention. In particular, efforts will have to be made to equip them with the skills and resources necessary to take advantage of the new opportunities being opened up by structural changes and to remove the impediments they face in getting access to productive employment so that their loss from adjustments can be minimised and the scope for gaining from new opportunities maximized.

The principle of non-retrogression of rights can also play a vitally protective role for the vulnerable people. This principle states that nobody should be allowed to suffer an absolute decline in the enjoyment of any right at any time. The human rights approach to development acknowledges that full enjoyment of all the rights may only be possible over a period of time, and that as time passes some rights may be advanced faster than others.[20] But it does not permit the level of enjoyment of any right to decline in comparison with the past. Globalization can clearly lead to a vio-

---

20 This is known as the principle of progressive realization of rights, which is discussed further below.

lation of this principle if the rapid and overlapping structural changes it brings about lead to such a serious disruption that the weak and vulnerable individuals suffer an absolute decline in their living standard. Such a decline clearly occurred in a spectacular manner for a large number of people during the financial crises of the recent past. But even in normal times, many individuals and groups have suffered a decline in living standards in a manner that was perhaps less spectacular but no less real for them. The human rights approach to development demands that an adequate social protection scheme be put in place to prevent such a decline.

Globalization and Growth: Opportunities for the Human Rights Approach to Development

Globalization not only entails potential constraints to the quicker realization of human rights, it also creates new opportunities — principally by helping to promote faster rate of economic growth. Just as the constraints are only potential that can be handled with appropriate policy response, the opportunity that growth creates is also potential — one that must be harnessed in the service of human rights with the support of the right kind of policies and institutions. Some of the principles that must underlie the supportive regime of policies and institutions are discussed below. At this point, we first elaborate on the links between globalization, growth, and human rights.

In much of the traditional discourse on human rights as well as a large part of the development discourse, economic growth tends to be viewed with a good deal of suspicion. This is not entirely surprising in view of the fact that many enthusiasts of economic growth tend to be so obsessed with it as to almost disregard the adverse human consequences of wrong kinds of economic growth. But one needs to distinguish between economic growth in general and wrong kinds of economic growth in particular. The kind of growth that either neglects, or, worse still, curtails and violates human rights has, of course, no place in the human rights approach to development. But that does not mean that the need for economic growth can be neglected by this approach. The power of economic growth can and should be harnessed for the speedy realization of the right to development.

One could even argue that economic growth is not just compatible with the human rights approach but is an integral part of it. One of the salient features of the human rights approach to development is the recognition that the existence of resource constraint might call for progressive realization of rights over a period of time. But in order that the leeway offered by the idea of progressive realization does not induce the duty-holders to relax their efforts, the human rights approach also requires that measures be taken to fully realize all the rights "as expeditiously as possible." Once the speed of realization of rights is accorded due importance, it is easy to see why rapid economic growth is essential for the human rights approach to development. The point is made most forcefully by Sengupta:[21] "It is of course pos-

---

21 A. Sengupta, Fifth Report of the Independent Expert on the Right to Development, Report submitted to the Open Ended Working Group on the Right to Development (Geneva: Commission on Human Rights, UN Economic and Social Council, 2002).

sible, by reallocation and redistribution of existing resources, to improve the realization of some of the rights, separately and individually, for a limited period and to a limited extent, without economic growth . . . However, it must be recognized that all rights, including civil and political rights, involve using resources to expand the supply of the corresponding goods and services and, possibly, public expenditure. Therefore, if all or most of these rights have to be realized fully and together and in a sustainable manner, steps have to be taken to relax the resource constraint by ensuring economic growth." In short, since realization of rights involves resources, speedy realization of rights calls for softening the resource constraint, which in turn calls for economic growth.

A related reason why growth is essential for the pursuit of a right-based approach to development is that it will ease the pain of making trade-offs among rights. The idea of trade-offs among rights sits uneasily with the notion of indivisibility of rights, which has a hallowed position in the literature on human rights. Strictly speaking, however, trade-offs need not be inconsistent with indivisibility of rights when one recognizes that there are actually two kinds of trade-offs one can think of. One kind of trade-off refers to actually reducing the level of some kind of right from the existing level in order to raise the level of some other right. This notion of trade-offs is obviously incompatible with indivisible rights.

But there is another kind of trade-off that is not only compatible with the notion of indivisibility but also unavoidable. When a government is trying to improve the levels of various rights under resource constraint, it is necessarily faced with the choice of allocating scarce resources among alternative rights. We can either spend more on the improvement of right X and less on right Y, or the other way round. But if we do decide to spend a bit more on X, we necessarily decide to spend a bit less on Y — that's the trade-off. In this case, however, no single right needs be diminished compared to the existing situation, and yet there is a trade-off in terms of how much improvement we can achieve in some right relative to some other. This kind of trade-off at the margin — which might be called incremental trade-off — is unavoidable in a world of scarce resources, which is the real world we live in.

Incremental trade-offs do not violate the principle of indivisibility of rights because they do not require that the level of any particular right be diminished from the existing level in order to promote another nor do they require that promotion of some right be put completely on hold while trying to advance another. Nonetheless, they do present painful choices to the policy-makers who might be keen to improve rapidly the realization of all rights at the same time but unable to do so because of resource constraint. In this situation, faster rate of growth will help ease the pain of making unavoidable trade-offs by making more resources available.

A strategy for promoting economic growth must, therefore, constitute an integral part of the human rights approach to development. Globalization can be a powerful ally in this regard because of its growth-promoting potential.[22]

---

22   For a thorough analysis of the theory and evidence on the links between globalization and growth, see J. Bhagwati, *In Defense of Globalization* (Oxford: Oxford University Press, 2004).

There is, of course, no guarantee that by embracing globalization a country will automatically accelerate the rate of growth. Things can go wrong for many reasons. Some of these reasons could be external — such as collapse of the international financial system; but many could be internal — such as poor governance, civil war, deteriorating environment, and so on. Other things remaining the same, however, globalization will enhance the growth potential by bringing about a more efficient allocation of resources, by fostering competition, and by spurring technological diffusion. This potential must be harnessed for advancing the cause of human rights.

It must be realized, however, that ensuring faster growth is one thing and harnessing its potential for the cause of human rights is quite another. All that growth does is to make it easier to advance the human rights approach to development — by speeding up progressive realization of rights and by easing the pain of unavoidable trade-offs. But it does not ensure that the realization of human rights will in fact be advanced for the simple reason that the resources made available by growth may not actually be used for the purpose of promoting rights.

For growth to be an ally of human rights, any strategy of growth must be embedded in a comprehensive framework of policies and institutions that is consciously designed to convert resources into rights. The precise details of policies and institutions will, of course, vary from one situation to another, but some general principles can be derived from the normative framework laid down by the international law of human rights. The more important among these principles are elaborated below.

The Principles of the Human Rights Approach to Development

In order to delineate the major principles of the human rights approach to development, it is first necessary to appreciate what exactly is demanded by the human rights norms — that is, what goals they set and what obligations they entail about how to go about realising those goals.

Any approach to development must be underpinned by some set of values and norms, whether explicit or not. The human rights approach to development is based on an explicit framework of norms and values — one that has been universally accepted and codified through a series of international covenants, treaties, declarations, and conventions. To begin with, this approach adopts a particular view of what constitutes development. This is best exemplified by the following formulation of the concept of the "right to development" recently adopted by the international community. "The Right to Development is an inalienable human right by virtue of which every human person and all peoples are entitled to participate in, contribute to and enjoy economic, social, cultural and political development, in which all human rights and fundamental freedoms can be fully realized."[23]

This formulation clearly implies that development is to be defined broadly as "economic, social, cultural and political development," in which "all human rights and fundamental freedoms" can be fully realized. The human rights approach thus

---

23   This is from Article 1 of the Declaration of the Right to Development, 1986.

demands broadening the concept of development from the narrowly economic one that has dominated much of the development literature in the past. The narrow concept of economic development still remains important, but it is no longer enough. Development must entail fuller realization of economic, social, and cultural rights on the one hand and civil and political rights on the other. By postulating that the pursuit of one set of rights to the neglect of others does not constitute development, this concept of development thus embraces the notion of "indivisibility of rights," which the human rights community has long championed.[24]

The human rights approach not only offers a comprehensive notion of development, but it also lays out a number of principles that must guide the policies and institutions to be designed for promoting development. For convenience of exposition, these principles may be classified into three categories: (1) those informing the process of policy formulation, (2) those shaping the content of policies, and (3) those guiding the monitoring of policy implementation.[25]

The Rights-Based Process of Policy Formulation

One of the most important principles of the human rights approach to policy formulation is that it should be participatory in nature. In particular, the population groups that are affected directly or indirectly by a particular policy should be able to play an effective role in the process of formulating that policy. One may distinguish four stages of participation: preference revelation; policy choice; implementation; and monitoring, assessment and accountability.

The stage of *preference revelation* is the initial stage of any process of policy formulation. Before policies can be formulated, people must be enabled to express what their preferences are, i.e. what objectives they want to achieve. The stage of *policy choice* refers to the stage at which policies are formulated and decisions taken regarding the allocation of resources among alternative uses. As different patterns of resource allocation will serve the interests of different groups of people differently, a conflict of interest is inherent in any process of policy formulation. Traditionally, the poor and the marginalized groups lose out in this process, as they do not possess enough political or financial power to make their interests count. The human rights approach must take steps to alter this situation by creating a legal-institutional framework in which these groups can participate effectively in policy formulation.

Opportunities must be created to enable the people to exercise their right to participate in the *implementation* stage as well, even though implementation of policies

---

24 This is entirely consistent with the notion of "development as freedom," as propounded by A. Sen, *Development as Freedom* (New York: Alfred A. Knopf, 1999). Sen defined freedom broadly to encompass both negative and positive freedoms — in the sense of Berlin. See I. Berlin, "The Two Concepts of Liberty," in his *Four Essays on Liberty*, 2nd Edition (Oxford: Clarendon Press, 1969). Since negative freedoms correspond broadly to civil and political rights and positive freedoms correspond broadly to socio-economic rights, the notion of development as freedom correspond closely to the notion that development consists in the realization of the whole range of human rights.
25 The following discussion draws heavily on S.R. Osmani, "An Essay on the Human Rights Approach to Development" in A. Sengupta, A. Negi, and M. Basu (eds.), *Reflections on the Right to Development* (New Dehli: Sage Publications, 2005). In the specific context of the human rights approach to poverty reduction strategies, many of these principles are also discussed in OHCHR, *Guidelines for A Human Rights Approach to Poverty Reduction Strategies* (Geneva: Office of the High Commissioner for Human Rights, 2005):.to which the present author was one of the contributors.

is primarily the responsibility of the executive arm of the State. The final stage of participation is the stage of *monitoring and assessment* of the success or failure of policies so that the State and other duty-bearers can be held accountable for their obligations.[26]

For genuine participation to be possible some preconditions must be met and certain other rights must be fulfilled. The essential precondition is that the ordinary people must be empowered to claim their rights and to participate effectively in the decision-making process. The process of empowerment can itself be quite complex and time-consuming because of the deep-rooted nature of the asymmetries of power that exist in most societies.

To begin with, the character of the polity must be democratic in nature. Though by no means sufficient, democratic governance is a necessary condition for creating a space in which all groups of people can effectively participate in national decision-making processes. The second precondition is to strengthen the bargaining power of the marginalized groups so that they are able to participate effectively in potentially conflictual situations. Capacity-building activities are also essential for this purpose, and civil society can play a very constructive role in this sphere. For this to be possible, the State must create the necessary legal and institutional environment in which an independent civil society can flourish. In turn, the creation of such an environment requires simultaneous efforts to promote a range of civil and political rights. These include the right to information, the right to freedom of expression, the right of association, and the right of equal access to justice. Without the fulfillment of these rights, empowerment is not possible; and without empowerment, effective participation is not possible. Therefore, taking measures to fulfill these rights is an essential component of the human rights approach to development.

Principles Shaping the Contents of Policies Under the Human Rights Approach

The contents of policies refer to the goals and targets that are set by the State, the resources that are committed for the realization of those targets, and the methods that are adopted to achieve them. It is recognized that setting targets and committing resources for them will necessarily involve setting priorities, which in turn will involve considering trade-off among alternative goals. These acts of setting priorities and accepting trade-offs must necessarily involve some value judgements. For a policy regime to be consistent with the human rights approach, these value judgements must be shaped by the human rights norms. This has several implications for the characteristics of policy contents.

First, the goals and targets set by the State must conform to those set by various human rights instruments and elaborated by the relevant treaty bodies.

Second, policies must take cognisance of people's rights to equality and non-discrimination, which are among the most fundamental tenets of international human rights law.

---

26   The issue of accountability is discussed further below.

The third set of principles relates to the possible trade-offs among rights. The existence of resource constraint that gives rise to the idea of progressive realization of rights also makes it inevitable that policy-makers will have to face trade-offs among alternative rights — that is, some rights may have to be given priority over others — because all rights cannot be fulfilled at the same time or at the same pace. While the human rights approach recognizes the inevitability of trade-offs, it also imposes certain conditions on it.

The first condition is imposed by the principle of indivisibility of rights, which demands that no human right can be considered intrinsically inferior to any other. If a certain right is to be given priority, it can only be done on practical grounds — for example, because a certain right has remained historically more under-realized than others, or because it is likely to act as a catalyst towards the speedy fulfillment of others, and so on.

Another condition is imposed by the principle of non-retrogression of rights — the idea that no right can be deliberately allowed to suffer an absolute decline in its level of realization. This condition implies that, while allocating more resources to the rights that have been accorded priority at any given point in time, care must be taken to ensure that the rest of the rights maintain at least their initial level of realization.

Finally, the priorities and trade-offs must be decided in a genuinely participatory manner, so that interests and values of the weaker segments of the society do not get lost through the pressure of powerful interest groups.

The Human Rights Approach Towards Monitoring of Policy Implementation

Monitoring and evaluation of performance is a necessary part of any kind of development strategy, whether rights-based or otherwise. But the characteristic feature of the human rights approach is that it emphasises the notion of accountability in a way that traditional approaches do not.

The very notion of rights implies the notion of duties or obligations. But a duty can only be meaningful if the duty-bearer can be held accountable for failing to perform its duty. The need to ensure accountability is, therefore, centrally important for the human rights approach to development.

There must exist mechanisms through which the culpability of the State can be ascertained in case of failure to adopt and implement appropriate policies so that sanctions can be imposed if it is indeed found culpable. These accountability mechanisms can be of various kinds — judicial, administrative, community-based, and so on. It must be noted that holding the duty-bearers to account does not necessarily imply taking recourse to the court of law. There can be both judicial and non-judicial means of accountability — the latter might involve quasi-judicial (for example, ombudsman, treaty bodies), political (for example, parliamentary process), administrative, and civil society institutions. The human rights approach to development would require the setting up of an appropriate mix of accountability mechanisms. Each State must decide for itself which accountability mechanisms are most appropriate in its particular case, but all mechanisms must be accessible, transparent, and effective. Most importantly, accountability procedures must be participatory in nature so that people are able to hold the State accountable for its actions.

Once these principles are accepted as the foundation of policy-making for all-round development of the society, it should be possible to harness the forces of globalization for advancing the cause of human rights and to guard against any adverse consequences.

Concluding Observations

The nation state has been accorded a central role in the human rights discourse. It is the state that has the primarily responsibility of discharging the obligations arising from commitment to human rights. Fears have been expressed in recent times, however, that the wave of globalization that is sweeping the world might undermine both the ability and the incentive of nation states to advance the cause of human rights. These fears are grounded in a large part, but not solely, on the nature of economic forces supposed to be unleashed by globalization. This paper has examined some of the economic forces that are discussed most frequently in this context and has argued that while the fears are not entirely groundless they tend to be severely exaggerated.

Three common hypotheses have been scrutinised in this context. First, globalization might impair the state's ability to fulfil its human rights obligations by constricting its command over fiscal resources. Second, globalization might compromise the rights of workers by giving the state an incentive to reduce labour standards in the face of competition for markets and capital. Third, the changes in economic structure brought about by globalization might militate against the rights of the economically weak and disadvantaged sections of the society.

An examination of both theory and evidence suggests that neither of the first two hypotheses has general validity, although the possibility that they might turn out to be true in specific cases cannot be ruled out. The paper argues, however, that there is nothing inevitable about the tendencies highlighted by these hypotheses and that a genuine commitment to human rights can indeed act as a bulwark against them.

The third hypothesis, by contrast, has a greater degree of plausibility. A couple of points are, however, worth bearing in mind in this context. First, that some of the weaker segments of the society may be harmed by structural changes in the economy is true of any kind of structural change, not just those brought about by globalization. Second, while some the weaker segments may be harmed, others may gain, and the society as a whole might gain too, especially as globalization unleashes the forces of economic growth through multiple channels. It is, in principle, within the powers of the state to harness this potential for higher growth to the service of human rights – in particular to the protection of the economic and social rights of those who bear the brunt of structural change. For this to be possible in practice, however, the policies and institutions of the state must be designed in conformity with the principles of a human rights approach to development. This paper has examined some the major considerations that ought to guide the designing of policies and institutions based on human rights principles.

13 | Advocating the Right to Development Through Complaint Procedures Under Human Rights Treaties

Martin Scheinin

Introduction

This chapter addresses the capacity of international monitoring mechanisms under existing human rights treaties to deal with claims related to the right to development. Above all, the intention is to refute the contention that these mechanisms would not be suited for such claims. The methodology applied is to demonstrate through selected cases that many human rights treaties actually have potential in relation to the operationalization of the right to development. Rather than look at the mainstream of international case law for the establishment of "The Law" in the issue, this chapter examines promising cases or even certain underdeveloped dimensions in existing cases to demonstrate the *potential* within the framework of existing human rights treaties.

Another methodological point to be made at the outset is that development-related cases brought by indigenous peoples to international bodies should not be seen as involving a marginal dimension of the overall issue of the right to development. Rather, it is precisely groups that identify themselves as distinct peoples within a given state that are the *most likely* claimants of the right to development when it comes to the utilization of judicial or quasi-judicial procedures under human rights treaties. We cannot even expect cases where the whole population of a country would institute a case against their state, simply because there usually is no other legitimate representative of the population than the government — that is, the respondent in any such case. The second scenario with some probability to materialize is an international case brought by the government of a developing country against one or more developed states for failure to meet their transnational obligations.[1] However, as long as states, including governments of developing countries, feel reluctant to resort to the existing procedures for inter-state complaints under human rights treaties, it is more likely that such a case would be taken to the International Court of Justice than before a human rights body.

Third, the point of departure of this chapter is that human rights lawyers should not accept the assumption that the right to development represents merely "imperfect obligations" — that is, moral obligations with no corresponding rights entitlements invocable by the beneficiary of the right. It is submitted that it might be a viable option to strive for the realization of the right to development also under existing human rights treaties and through their monitoring mechanisms, provided that an interdependence-based and development-informed reading can be given to

---

1 Reference is made to Article 2, para. 1 of the International Covenant on Economic, Social and Cultural Rights, which refers to "international assistance and co-operation" as one dimension of state obligations under the treaty.

the treaties in question. If this is possible, then one need not accept the contention that the right to development is (only) about "imperfect obligations."

Additionally, if this interim conclusion is justified, then there is no need to prioritize the creation of a separate new procedure for the right to development in comparison to the utilization of existing human rights treaties, their monitoring mechanisms, and the added value provided by the potentials of cross-fertilization among existing treaties in pursuing the composite right to development. Existing human rights bodies are quite capable of taking the interdependence of human rights duly on board when interpreting the provisions of one treaty. Hence, the presumed lack of such interdependence is not as such a valid ground to propose a new monitoring mechanism for the right to development.

Experiences from Existing Mechanisms
The International Covenants of 1966

It goes without saying that neither the International Covenant on Economic, Social and Cultural Rights (ICESCR) nor the International Covenant on Civil and Political Rights (ICCPR) includes a separate provision on the right to development. Within the framework of the two Covenants of 1966, the "home" of the right to development is to be found in their Common Article 1 on all peoples' right to self-determination. Paragraph 1 of Article 1 actually employs the notion of development as a constituent element of self-determination,[2] while paragraph 2 is even more important for the operationalization of the economic or resource dimension of self-determination, intimately connected with the right to development.[3] And paragraph 3, with its reference to the solidarity dimension of self-determination — that is, the obligation of states to promote self-determination in other parts of the world — brings the dimension of so-called transnational obligations into the framework of the ICCPR, where it is otherwise absent. In all, Common Article 1 of the two Covenants is broad and ambitious and comprises important elements of the right to development.

It is worth noting in this regard that Article 1, paragraph 2, of the 1986 Declaration on the Right to Development makes this connection by using the notion of self-determination and repeating some of the language in Common Article 1, paragraph 2 of the 1966 Covenants:

> The human right to development also implies the full realization of the right of peoples to self-determination, which includes, subject to the relevant provisions of both International Covenants on Human Rights, the exercise of their inalienable right to full sovereignty over all their natural wealth and resources.[4]

---

2   "All peoples have the right of self-determination. By virtue of that right they freely determine their political status and freely pursue their economic, social and cultural development."
3   "All peoples may, for their own ends, freely dispose of their natural wealth and resources without prejudice to any obligations arising out of international economic co-operation, based upon the principle of mutual benefit, and international law. In no case may a people be deprived of its own means of subsistence."
4   Declaration on the Right to Development, General Assembly Resolution 41/128 of December 4, 1986.

Despite this potential link between self-determination and the right to development, it must at the same time be emphasized that the practical effect of Common Article 1 of the two Covenants is greatly weakened by three *procedural* shortcomings: 1) so far, there is no complaint procedure under the ICESCR; 2) states have made no use of the inter-state complaint procedure under the ICCPR, applicable also in respect of Article 1; and 3) the individual complaints procedure under the ICCPR is restricted to cases where there is an individual victim, hence excluding the genuine collective right of self-determination from the scope of the right of complaint.[5]

The procedural shortcomings just mentioned have not deprived Common Article 1 of its meaning for the right to development. With respect to the ICCPR, there are two approaches through which the Human Rights Committee, as the monitoring body under the ICCPR, has been able to build upon the right of self-determination and its link to economic development: 1) growing recognition of the importance of Article 1 in the reporting procedure under ICCPR Article 40 and 2) emerging use of Article 1 standards in the interdependence-based interpretation of other provisions of the ICCPR, notably Article 27 on minority rights.

In considering the periodic state reports under Article 40 of the ICCPR — the only mandatory monitoring mechanism of the Covenant — the Human Rights Committee has relied also on Article 1 in its assessment of countries' compliance. Paragraph 2 on the economic or resource dimension of self-determination, which is of particular relevance in the context of development, has been addressed in relation to such indigenous groups that appear to qualify as "peoples." For instance, in its concluding observations on Canada in 1999, the Committee emphasized:

> . . . that the right to self-determination requires, *inter alia*, that all peoples must be able to freely dispose of their natural wealth and resources and that they may not be deprived of their own means of subsistence (Art. 1, para. 2). The Committee recommends that decisive and urgent action be taken towards the full implementation of the [Royal Commission on Aboriginal Peoples] recommendations on land and resource allocation.[6]

The applicability of Article 1 on self-determination to indigenous peoples was first recognized by the Committee when dealing with the report by Canada after the country's own Supreme Court had first implied that several "peoples" may exist within one state.[7] The Committee has followed the same approach with respect to other countries with distinct indigenous peoples within their boundaries. Explicit references to either Article 1 or to the notion of self-determination have been made in the Committee's concluding observations on Mexico,[8] Norway,[9] Australia,[10]

---

5   *Lubicon Lake Band v. Canada* (Communication 167/1984), Views adopted March 26, 1990, Report of the Human Rights Committee, GAOR, Thirty-eighth session, Suppl. No. 40 (A/38/40), pp. 1-30, para.13.3.
6   Concluding Observations on Canada, UN Doc. CCPR/C/79/Add.105 (1999), para. 8.
7   *Reference re Secession of Quebec* (1998) 2 S.C.R., p. 217.
8   Concluding Observations on Mexico, UN Doc. CCPR/C/79/Add.109 (1999).
9   Concluding Observations on Norway, UN Doc. CCPR/C/79/Add.112 (1999).
10   Concluding Observations on Australia, UN Doc. CCPR/CO/69/AUS (2000).

Denmark,[11] Sweden,[12] and Finland.[13] As in the case of Canada, paragraph 2 of Article 1 — that is, the resource dimension of self-determination — has received particular emphasis in the context of indigenous peoples. For instance, in its concluding observations on Australia, the Committee stressed that the state party "should take the necessary steps in order to secure for the indigenous inhabitants a stronger role in decision-making over their traditional lands and natural resources."

It is true that use of Article 1, paragraph 2, of the ICCPR has so far been limited to dealing with reports by developed countries. When the same approach is applied to indigenous or otherwise distinct peoples in developing countries, however, the provision may prove highly relevant for pursuing claims related to the right to development.

Another dimension of the growing importance of that provision is the recognition of the interpretive effect of the right of self-determination in cases brought before the Human Rights Committee under the Optional Protocol to the ICCPR. As previously mentioned, the position of the Committee is that, as individuals cannot claim the status of "victim" in relation to the right of a people to self-determination, the Optional Protocol does not allow cases to be brought directly under Article 1 of the Covenant. However, the Committee's case law under the minority rights provision in Article 27 and, in particular, the notion of "culture" in that provision, have been able to incorporate much of the substance of the right of self-determination — or, if one wants to put it that way, even the right to development. Sami reindeer herding cases against Finland have been important in this respect, as the Committee developed its combined test of participation by the group and sustainability of the indigenous economy in its assessment of what kind of competing resource use is permissible under Article 27.[14]

The later case of *Mahuika et al. v. New Zealand* builds on the Committee's earlier case law and demonstrates, by being related to a nationwide fisheries settlement in New Zealand and the share of the indigenous Maori in that settlement, that Article 27 claims by indigenous groups need not pertain to romanticized images of isolated pockets of traditional indigenous life but may very well involve major economic activities that are important for the national economy of a country. For the purposes of the current discussion, another important dimension of the case is that, in its Views, the Human Rights Committee finally recognizes the link between Article 27 and Article 1 through the interpretive effect of the right of self-determination when addressing the application of Article 27.[15] This dimension of interde-

---

11   Concluding Observations on Denmark, UN Doc. CCPR/CO/70/DNK (2000).
12   Concluding Observations on Sweden, UN Doc. CCPR/CO/74/SWE (2002).
13   Concluding Observations on Finland, UN Doc. CCPR/CO/82/FIN/Rev.1 (2004).
14   See *Länsman et al. v. Finland* (Communication 511/1992), Views adopted October 26, 1994, Report of the Human Rights Committee, Vol. II, GAOR, Fiftieth Session, Suppl. No. 40 (A/50/40), pp. 66-76 and *Länsman et al. v. Finland* (Communication No. 671/1995., Views adopted October 30, 1996, Report of the Human Rights Committee, Vol. II, UN Doc. A/52/40 (Vol. II), pp. 191-204. For a discussion of the combined test of participation and sustainability, see Martin Scheinin, "The Right to Enjoy a Distinct Culture: Indigenous and Competing Uses of Land," in Theodore S. Orlin, Allan Rosas, and Martin Scheinin (eds.), *The Jurisprudence of Human Rights Law: A Comparative Interpretive Approach* (Åbo: Åbo Akademi University Institute for Human Rights, 2000), pp. 159-222.
15   *Mahuika et al. v. New Zealand* (Communication No. 547/1993), Views adopted October 27, 2000, Report of the Human Rights Committee, Vol. II, UN Doc. A/56/40 (Vol. II), pp. 11-29. "Furthermore,
note continues on following page

pendence between Articles 1 and 27 was already present in the *Lubicon Lake Band* case and in the combined test of sustainability and participation developed in the *Länsman* cases. It was only in *Mahuika*, however, that the Committee formally recognized the relevance of Article 1 in addressing Article 27 claims, explicitly recognizing that although Article 1 cannot itself be the basis for a claim by an individual, the right of self-determination may affect the interpretation of other provisions of the Covenant, including the right of members of a minority to enjoy their own culture (Article 27). The same approach as in *Mahuika* was followed in the case of *Diergaardt et al. v. Namibia.*[16]

Further light on the issue of interdependence between the right of self-determination and other provisions of the Covenant is shed by the case of *Gillot et al. v. France*, decided in 2002.[17] The complaint was related to restrictions in the right to participate in referendums in New Caledonia, allegedly in violation of Article 25 of the Covenant (right of public participation). Interpreting Article 25 in light of Article 1, the Committee considered that, in the context of referendums arranged in a process of decolonization and self-determination, it was legitimate to limit participation to persons with sufficiently close ties with the territory whose future was being decided. Since the residence requirements for participation in the referendums in question were neither disproportionate nor discriminatory, the Committee concluded that there was no violation of Article 25.

The American Convention on Human Rights

Under the American Convention on Human Rights, our example is the case of *Awas Tingni Community v. Nicaragua.*[18] The case related to the failure of the state to demarcate the communal lands of the indigenous Awas Tingni Community, to the failure to afford effective measures to ensure the property rights of the community to its ancestral lands and natural resources, and also to interference by the state because it had granted a logging concession on community lands. As usual, the case was initiated in the Court by the Inter-American Commission on Human Rights. The report of the Commission underlined the potential of an interdependence-based approach to human rights, since it relied quite heavily on Article 27 of the ICCPR, understood in light of the practice of the Human Rights Committee in issues related to indigenous peoples' land and resource rights. However, once the Awas Tingni case made it to the Court, the Court restricted itself to findings of violation of two provisions of the American Convention itself, namely those on property rights (Article 21) and the right of judicial protection (Article 25). It would be wrong, however, to

note continued from preceding page
the provisions of Article 1 may be relevant in the interpretation of other rights protected by the Covenant, in particular article 27." para. 9.2.
16   "Furthermore, the provisions of Article 1 may be relevant in the interpretation of other rights protected by the Covenant, in particular Articles 25, 26 and 27." para. 10.3 in *J.G.A. Diergaardt et al. v. Namibia* (Communication No. 760/1997), Views adopted July 25, 2000, Report of the Human Rights Committee, Vol. II, GAOR, Fifty-fifth Session, Suppl. No. 40 (A/55/40), pp. 140-160.
17   *Marie-Hélène Gillot et al. v France* (Communication No. 932/2000), Views Adopted July 15, 2002, Report of the Human Rights Committee, Vol. II, GAOR, Fifty-seventh Session, Suppl. No. 40 (A/57/40), pp. 270-293.
18   Inter-American Court of Human Rights, *The Case of the Mayagna (Sumo) Awas Tingni Community v. Nicaragua*, Judgment of August 31, 2001.

say that the Court would have lost sight of interdependence. Rather, the two provisions mentioned were addressed in a way that gives full attention to the specificity in indigenous land rights and also demonstrates how the right to development can be made present and effective within the framework of a relatively traditional human rights treaty centered around civil and political rights. In its discussion on Article 21, the Court stated, *inter alia:*

> Indigenous groups, by the fact of their very existence, have the right to live freely in their own territory; the close ties of indigenous people with the land must be recognized and understood as the fundamental basis of their cultures, their spiritual life, their integrity, and their economic survival. For indigenous communities, relations to the land are not merely a matter of possession and production but a material and spiritual element which they must fully enjoy, even to preserve their cultural legacy and transmit it to future generations.[19]

The same approach is visible in the pronouncements by the Court of the remedy required. For instance:

> . . . the State must carry out the delimitation, demarcation, and titling of the corresponding lands of the members of the Mayagna (Sumo) Awas Tingni Community and, until that delimitation, demarcation and titling has been done, it must abstain from any acts that might lead the agents of the State itself, or third parties acting with its acquiescence or its tolerance, to affect the existence, value, use or enjoyment of the property located in the geographic area where the members of the Mayagna (Sumo) Awas Tingni Community live and carry out their activities . . . .[20]

African Charter of Human and Peoples' Rights

What makes the African Charter a special case in the analysis of development-related claims is its emphasis on collective (peoples') rights, in addition to the standard approach of individual human rights. Of particular relevance for our discussion is the cluster of provisions in Articles 19-24 on collective rights of peoples, starting with the equality of peoples (Art. 19), their right to existence and self-determination, with references to "economic and social development" and "the right to the assistance of the States parties to the present Charter in their liberation struggle against foreign domination" (Art. 20), a separate provision on the economic/resource dimension of self-determination (Art. 21),[21] a more general provision explicitly on the right to development (Art. 22), the right to peace and security (Art. 23), and the right to a satisfactory environment, with an explicit reference to development (Art. 24).

It is clear that these provisions overlap with each other to a high degree, so that the right to development is not merely protected by the relatively abstract provision

---

19   *Ibid.*, para. 149.
20   *Ibid.*, para. 173(4).
21   The provision starts with a clause quite similar to Common Article 1 (2), of the two UN Covenants: "All peoples shall freely dispose of their wealth and natural resources."

of Article 22 but gets much of its substance from more concrete or otherwise complementary dimensions in other articles, including Articles 20, 21, and 24.

The potential of the substantive law of the African Charter in respect to the right to development is demonstrated through the case of *The Ogoni People v. Nigeria*, decided by the African Commission of Human and Peoples' Rights in October 2001.[22] The case was centered around a claim that the military government of Nigeria had been directly involved in oil production through the state oil company, the Nigerian National Petroleum Company (NNPC), the majority shareholder in a consortium with Shell Petroleum Development Corporation (SPDC), and that these operations had caused environmental degradation and health problems resulting from the contamination of the environment among the Ogoni People.[23]

Thereafter, the complaint was expanded to fields like arbitrary executions, destruction of villages, impunity, and destruction of food resources and farmlands. To make a long and complex story short, the African Commission established violations of Articles 2, 4, 14, 16, 18(1), 21, and 24 of the African Charter. In addition to the individual rights to nondiscrimination (Art. 2), life (Art. 4), and property (Art. 14), the right to health (Art. 14) and the right to protection of the family (Art. 18) were found to be violated. In the present context the most interesting dimension of the case relates to the establishment of violations of Articles 21 and 24, which are two right-to-development-related provisions mentioned above. The Commission was not very clear as to who were the beneficiaries of all the rights that were found to have been violated, but from the formulation of Articles 21 and 24 as peoples' collective rights and the frequent references in the Commission's report to the Ogoni people (or, occasionally, "the Ogoni population" or "the Ogonis"), one may draw the conclusion that it was the development-related rights of the Ogoni people that were violated by Nigeria as a state.

Under Article 24 of the African Charter, the Commission describes the provision as requiring the State "to take reasonable and other measures to prevent pollution and ecological degradation, to promote conservation, and to secure an ecologically sustainable development and use of natural resources."[24] Furthermore:

> Government compliance with the spirit of Articles 16 and 24 of the African Charter must also include ordering or at least permitting independent scientific monitoring of threatened environments, requiring and publicizing environmental and social impact studies prior to any major industrial development, undertaking appropriate monitoring and providing information to those communities exposed to hazardous materials and activities and providing meaningful opportunities for individuals to be heard and to participate in the development decisions affecting their communities.[25]

---

22 Communication No. 155/96, *The Social and Economic Rights Action Center and the Center for Economic and Social Rights v. Nigeria*.
23 *Ibid.*, para. 1.
24 *Ibid.*, para. 52.
25 *Ibid.*, para. 53.

In its discussion of Article 21, in turn, the Commission refers, *inter alia*, to the purpose of the provision as to "restore co-operative economic development"[26] and proceeds to a finding of a violation:

> Contrary to its Charter obligations and despite such internationally established principles, the Nigerian Government has given the green light to private actors, and the oil Companies in particular, to devastatingly affect the well-being of the Ogonis. By any measure of standards, its practice falls short of the minimum conduct expected of governments, and therefore, is in violation of Article 21 of the African Charter.[27]

The Commission continues with a discussion on the general right-to-development provision in Article 22 of the Charter, not as an independent right but as an element in the implicitly recognized right to food.[28] Although the Commission does not include a finding of a violation of Article 22 in its recapitulation of findings, its conclusion under this heading is quite clear:

> The government's treatment of the Ogonis has violated all three minimum duties of the right to food. The government has destroyed food sources through its security forces and State Oil Company; has allowed private oil companies to destroy food sources; and, through terror, has created significant obstacles to Ogoni communities trying to feed themselves. The Nigerian government has again fallen short of what is expected of it as under the provisions of the African Charter and international human rights standards, and hence, is in violation of the right to food of the Ogonis.[29]

The European Convention on Human Rights

Among regional human rights treaties, the European Convention on Human Rights is known for its efficient monitoring mechanism based on the combination of the legally binding force of the judgments of the Court and the systematic and unconditional backing given to their implementation by the Committee of Ministers, the main political body of the Council of Europe. However, due to its age and traditional Western European geographic constituency, the treaty is also known for its failure to address collective rights, including constituent elements of the composite right to development.

Nevertheless, a remarkable potential application of the right to development can be found in three cases related to environmental harm and their assessment under Article 8 (right to private life, family, and home).

G. and E. v. Norway (the Alta River Dam Case). In a case brought by members of the indigenous Sami people, the European Commission of Human Rights recognized that "under Article 8 a minority group is, in principle, entitled to claim the

---

26 *Ibid.,* para. 56.
27 *Ibid.,* para. 59.
28 *Ibid.,* para. 64.
29 *Ibid.,* para. 66.

right to respect for the particular life style it may lead as being 'private life', 'family life' or 'home'." However, through quantitative assessment of the size of the area of land to be flooded, compared to the total area of reindeer herding lands, in addition to references to majority decision making and the economic well-being of the country, the case was declared inadmissible as manifestly ill-founded.[30]

López Ostra v. Spain. The European Court of Human Rights established a violation of Article 8 due to environmental harm caused by the establishment and operation of a plant for the treatment of waste from leather tanneries. In the view of the Court, by allowing the establishment of the plant in a residential area, the state had failed to strike a proper balance between the economic well-being of the broader community and the respect for individual rights under Article 8.[31]

Hatton and Others v. the United Kingdom. Although the Chamber Judgment of October 2, 2001, finding a violation of Article 8 was later overturned by a 12-5 majority of a Grand Chamber Judgment of July 8, 2003, its reasoning on a human rights assessment of projects with environmental implications deserves attention as a potentially important approach to environmental harm in a development context. With respect to a new scheme for night flights at Heathrow airport, the Chamber reasoned:

> The Court would, however, underline that in striking the required balance, States must have regard to the whole range of material considerations. . . . It considers that States are required to minimize, as far as possible, the interference with these rights, by trying to find alternative solutions and by generally seeking to achieve their aims in the least onerous way as regards human rights. In order to do that, a proper and complete investigation and study with the aim of finding the best possible solution which will, in reality, strike the right balance should precede the relevant project.[32]

Taken together, these three cases show, if not more, a plausible line of argument for potential claimants that wish to address dimensions of the composite right to development through the European Convention on Human Rights. As to the practical potential of such an approach, the reader is reminded of the fact that the Convention is a part of applicable domestic law within the Russian Federation and could also give rise to international complaints to the European Court of Human Rights by indigenous peoples within that country.

Some Conclusions

On the basis of the above stock-taking of existing case law under human rights treaties, the following conclusions are proposed:

---

30   *G. and E. v. Norway*, European Commission of Human Rights, *Decisions and Reports*, Vol. 35 (1984), pp. 30-45.
31   *López Ostra v. Spain*, European Court of Human Rights, Judgment of December 9, 1994.
32   *Hatton and Others v. the United Kingdom*, European Court of Human Rights, Chamber Judgment of October 2, 2001, para. 97. See also para. 106.

1) Irrespective of whether a specific human rights treaty includes an explicit provision on the right to development (the African Charter) or not (all other treaties discussed above), most, if not all, human rights treaties provide at least some potential for claims related to the right to development. Due to the composite nature of the right to development, this should not come as a surprise.

2) Which particular rights provisions will prove most dynamic for their application in respect to development-related claims depends both on the catalog of rights in a specific treaty and on the traditions built within the institutionalized practices of interpretation under that treaty. For example, Article 8 of the European Convention (private and family life), Article 21 of the American Convention (property), and Article 27 of the ICCPR (minority cultures) appear quite different from one another but may lead to quite similar outcomes with respect to development-related claims.

3) Many of the case law examples provided above illustrate a high level of interdependence among human rights. The interaction between Articles 1 and 27 of the ICCPR, the implicit reliance on ICCPR Article 27 case-law in the Inter-American system, and the link between the right to development and the right to housing in our example from the African system all demonstrate this point.

4) Claims by indigenous groups for land and resource management have much more than marginal importance for the operationalization of the right to development through claims brought before international human rights courts and treaty bodies.

5) Due to the underdeveloped acceptance of international complaint procedures for economic and social rights, the dimensions of the right to development related to these rights have had less opportunity to develop under existing mechanisms than certain other dimensions. The African Charter may be an exception in this respect and deserves more attention.

6) Another weakness of existing mechanisms is related to their general nature as mechanisms for addressing state responsibility under human rights treaties where only states are parties. Other actors, such as inter-governmental organizations, international financial institutions, and transnational corporations are not subject to these procedures.

Through the prism of state responsibility, the cases discussed above have focused on acts or omissions of states in relation to various peoples' right to development. Nevertheless, the facts of this limited selection of cases illustrate that other types of actors were also involved in the actual chain of events, giving rise to state responsibility for human rights violations, such as foreign or multinational forestry or oil corporations. It would be worthwhile to discuss arrangements through which actors other than states could be made internationally accountable under the same substantive norms that are today applicable in respect to states.

14 | The Role of the International Financial Institutions in a Rights-Based Approach to the Process of Development

Sigrun I. Skogly

Introduction

In recent years, much has been written on the international financial institutions (IFIs)[1] and their relationship to international human rights law.[2] The debate has moved from a very strong separation of the activities of the IFIs from human rights in the 1980s and early 1990s, to much more acceptance of a link,[3] recognizing that a development process (and that the IFIs are part of this process) ultimately is about people[4] — and their living conditions. A significant body of literature points to the positive and negative impact on human rights of the policies and programs[5] of the IFIs, and the institutions themselves have moved toward an acceptance that a human rights conducive policy may be a positive way of fulfilling their mandates,[6] even if no specific acceptance of obligations in this sphere has been explicitly voiced.[7]

---

1 When using the term, International Financial Institutions, I am referring to the International Bank for Reconstruction and Development (IBRD) and the International Monetary Fund (IMF) unless otherwise specified. The IBRD will be referred to as the "World Bank." Much of the general discussion in this chapter will, nevertheless, be applicable to other financial institutions, such as the regional development banks, and to a certain extent, also the World Trade Organization (WTO).

2 Katarina Tomaševski, *Development Aid and Human Rights Revisited* (London: Pinter, 1993), pp. 59-70; Clarence Dias, "Influencing the Policies of the World Bank and the International Monetary Fund," in Lars Adam Rehof and Claus Gulmann (eds.), *Human Rights in Domestic Law and Development Assistance Policies of the Nordic Countries* (Dordrecht: Martinus Nijhoff Publishers, 1989); Philip Alston, "The International Monetary Fund and the Right to Food," 30 *Howard Law Journal*, 1987, pp. 473-482; Jack Donnelly and Rhoda Howard, *Human Rights Self-Monitoring: A Proposal for the Northern European Democracies* (Bergen: Christian Michelsen's Institute, 1996); Lawyers Committee on Human Rights, *The World Bank, Governance and Human Rights* (New York: August 1993); Sigrun I. Skogly, *The Human Rights Obligations of the World Bank and the International Monetary Fund* (London: Cavendish, 2001); Jason Morgan-Foster, "The Relationship of IMF Structural Adjustment Programs to Economic Social and Cultural Rights: The Argentine Case Revisited," *Michigan Journal of International Law, Vol. 22 (2003)*; Mac Darrow, *Between Light and Shadow: The World Bank, the International Monetary Fund, and International Human Rights Law* (Oxford: Hart Publishing, 2003).

3 See, for instance, World Bank, *Development and Human Rights: The Role of the World Bank* (Washington, DC: The World Bank, 1998).

4 See, generally, Clarence Dias, "Mainstreaming Human Rights in Development Assistance: Moving from Projects to Strategies." in H. H. and E. Borghese (eds.), *Human Rights in Development Co-operation*, SIM Special No. 22 (Utrecht: Netherlands Institute for Human Rights, 1998), p. 189.

5 See Morgan-Foster's article (note 2) in which he demonstrates how the structural adjustment policies of the Bank and the Fund have influenced the human rights enjoyment in Argentina.

6 The acceptance of a positive contribution has been made more specifically by the World Bank than the IMF. This is evidenced through the World Bank's publication on their role in development and human rights, referred to in note 3. The Bank has also entered into dialogue with the UN High Commissioner of Human Rights and other branches of the UN human rights system. See Mary Robinson, *Bridging the Gap between Human Rights and Development: From Normative Principles to Operational Relevance* (Washington, DC: Presidential Fellows' Lecture, 2001). See also UN High Commissioner for Human Rights, *Human Rights in Development: Draft Guidelines: A Human Rights Approach to Poverty Reduction Strategies* (Geneva: 2002). (Hereinafter referred to as"Draft Guidelines, 2002").

7 This statement should be qualified. When the IMF's General Counsel addressed the UN Committee on Economic, Social and Cultural Rights in 2001, he clearly refuted the proposition that the Fund was

note continues on following page

This chapter will not revisit this debate.[8] It will assume that IFIs are international legal subjects and are therefore under an obligation to perform their functions within the limits of international law, including international human rights law.

The role of IFIs in a rights-based approach to the process of development becomes highly apparent in a globalized world. In a report to the UN Commission on Human Rights, Arjun Sengupta, the Independent Expert on the Right to Development, expressed the challenges that globalization poses to the right to development, and not least how global actors such as IFIs figure in that equation. In this report, he states that ". . . realizing the right to development implies the fulfillment of the obligations of States, the international community and other agents to carry out appropriate development policies."[9]

Earlier in his report, Sengupta qualifies the development policies needed for the right to development to include a process "of step-by-step progressive realization of all the [human] rights, the implementation of a development policy to realize these rights, and the relaxation of resource constraints on these rights through economic growth."[10] In his recommendations, the Independent Expert states:

> . . . the claim of the right to development approach is that it is feasible to design and implement a development policy that can achieve the right to development while respecting the constraints of the process of globalization and making maximum use of the opportunities provided. Such a policy should be based on a coordinated programme of different policies to realize the individual rights (to food, health, education, work, social security, etc.) with policies to realize sustainable and participatory economic growth with equity.[11]

In this report, however, despite pointing to the challenges that globalization represents for the right to development, Sengupta does not reflect in any detail on the actual role of the international institutions. Most of the focus is still on the role of the individual state to "fit into" a globalized world, rather than on the role of the international community and its institutions in the right to development process.[12]

---

note continued from preceding page

bound by the International Covenant on Economic, Social and Cultural Rights, but accepted that the Fund is bound by customary international law. One should be able to extrapolate from this opinion that the Fund has accepted that they are bound by customary international human rights law. See François Gianviti, "Economic, Social and Cultural Human Rights and the International Monetary Fund," working paper submitted to the UN Committee on Economic, Social and Cultural Rights, UN Doc. E/C.12/2001/WP.5, May 7, 2001 (hereinafter "Gianviti: 2001"). In private meetings between the author and representatives of the Legal Department in the World Bank in May 2001, the lawyers did not seem to have any problem with the proposition that the Bank was under international law obligations not to violate human rights.

8   For a comprehensive elaboration of the obligations that the IFIs have based on international human rights law, see my earlier work, *The Human Rights Obligations of the World Bank and the International Monetary Fund* (London: Cavendish, 2001).

9   Arjun Sengupta, *Preliminary Study of the Independent Expert on the Right to Development on the Impact of International Economic and Financial Issues on the Enjoyment of Human Rights* (Geneva: United Nations, Commission on Human Rights, 2003), para. 41.

10   *Ibid.*, para. 3.

11   *Ibid.*, para. 42.

12   *Ibid.*, para. 43. This statement should be qualified. Although the report focuses most on what the individual state should do in terms of the process of the right to development in times of globalization, the Independent Expert clearly also recognizes the obligations of the international community. He states: "When the right to the process of development is being implemented by a country, the obligation of the international community to facilitate that implementation becomes paramount."

This is where the focus of this chapter lies. It will address the role of IFIs in a rights-based approach to the process of development. The chapter will analyze the qualitative characteristics of a rights-based approach to development that have bearings on the role of the IFIs, and it will then examine the challenges that this approach will pose to them. These challenges will be divided into two separate areas: namely, those faced by IFIs as entities with separate international legal personality, and those faced by states that constitute the membership of these institutions. The chapter will conclude with a discussion of the ways in which a rights-based approach may be used to improve the result-oriented work of the IFIs.

Qualitative Characteristics of a Rights-Based Approach to Development

Like many other labels given to the focus of the international development process, a rights-based approach to development has become a common label in the last decade or so.[13] A rights-based approach to development has been endorsed by international organizations,[14] non-governmental organizations (NGOs),[15] and governments[16] alike. Despite this rather general acceptance in recent years, however, there is no clear agreement on the actual content or definition of a rights-based approach to development. Some of the most common characteristics included by commentators are that 1) it implies a law-based, or, at least, a normative framework for the policy choices;[17] 2) it provides a predictable framework for action with the "advantage of objectivity, determinacy and the definition of appropriate legal limits;"[18] 3) it entails an empowering strategy[19] that may result in a real participatory approach;[20] and 4) it is accompanied by legal means to secure redress for violations[21] and a wider and stronger accountability not only for states, but also intergovernmental and non-governmental actors.[22] Professor Sengupta has defined the right to development in the following terms:

> The right to development refers to a process of development which leads to the realization of each human right and of all of them together and which has to be carried out in a manner known as rights-

---

13 For a discussion on the importance of the various concepts used to describe the development process and the compelling difference it makes to use a human rights concept, see Philip Alston, "What's in a Name: Does it Really Matter if Development Policies Refer to Goals, Ideals or Human Rights?", in H. H. and E. Borghese, *Human Rights in Development Co-operation*, SIM Special No. 22 (Utrect: Netherlands Institute for Human Rights, 1998), p. 189.
14 The Secretary-General of the UN, Kofi Annan, has called for mainstreaming of human rights into all UN activities; a rights-based approach to development has become a central focus of UNICEF's work, and other organizations are following suit.
15 This is, for instance, the case for Oxfam and Save the Children.
16 Many governments have now expressed their support for a rights-based approach to development, including Sweden, Norway, the Netherlands, and New Zealand. For an interesting, although possibly slightly out-of-date review of states' commitment to a rights-based approach to development, see appendix in H. H. and E. Borghese, *Human Rights in Development Co-operation*, SIM Special No. 22 (Utrecht: Netherlands Institute for Human Rights, 1998).
17 Dias, *op. cit.* p. 80; Darrow, *op. cit.* p. 5.
18 Darrow, *Ibid.*, p. 5.
19 Alston, *op. cit.* p. 105.
20 *Ibid.*
21 Darrow, *op.cit.* p. 5.
22 Alston, *op. cit.* p. 104.

based, in accordance with the international human rights standards, as a participatory, non-discriminatory, accountable and transparent process with equity in decision-making and sharing of the fruits of the process.[23]

These points can be generally summarized as an approach that provides a normative foundation, sets legal limits for acceptable behavior on parts of governments and international institutions, and entails a participatory process toward the end goal of human rights fulfillment in regions and states that are participants in the development process.

To the present author, there is therefore a strong convergence between a rights-based approach to development and the right to development itself, in the understanding of it that the Independent Expert has purported over the last few years. This implies that the right to development is about the fulfillment of all human rights as laid down in the International Bill of Human Rights, and that there is a right to a process of development, based on human dignity, participation, and non-discrimination.

This emphasis on the fulfillment of human rights and the process is — as shall be shown later — vital to the discussion of the role of IFIs in a rights-based approach to the process of development. However, in all of the approaches to the right to development, there seems to be a strong emphasis on the involvement of those affected by the development activities (either beneficially or adversely, in the words of Clarence Dias.)[24] This is laudable. Some rights, such as freedom of information, the right to participation, or the right to an effective remedy are rights in themselves, in addition to being instrumental to the enjoyment of other rights, such as the rights to food or health or education. Nevertheless, there has been a trend to emphasize the former at the expense of the latter. This will be further discussed below in relation to the IFIs.

Additionally, it is important to emphasize that, although a rights-based approach to development is about empowerment and participation, it also provides limitations and requirements for acceptable developmental policies. These limitations and requirements relate to governments, NGOs, and international organizations' actions in that the policies, programs, and strategies that are implemented should have certain qualitative characteristics that are defined by the material content of international human rights law. The limitations and requirements also relate to the empowered, participating population, however, in that international human rights law provides protection for vulnerable groups or groups that are not necessarily successful in taking part in the participatory structures, such as people living in poverty, minorities, indigenous peoples, children, and women. Thus, in situations in which human rights violations take place, it would not be an acceptable defense for a government or an international institution to claim that, through participatory practices, the

---

23 Arjun K. Sengupta, ("The Theory and Practice on the Right to Development," *Human Rights Quarterly* 24(4) (2002), p. 845.
24 Dias, *op. cit.* p. 75.

people decided on the policy that violated human rights.[25] The state and the international actors remain responsible for violations of international human rights law, even if a participatory and informed process has taken place.

It is crucial that IFIs become involved and contribute constructively to the process of the right to development. For the fulfillment of the right to development, this process cannot be completed through the actions of minor actors alone or through "lip-service" or "add-on" commitments to human rights. As a process, the right to development needs the full commitment of the major players in the international community to achieve its stated purpose. Although states are recognized as the main obligation holders in the process of the right to development, the strong influence on national policies by the forces of globalization and the institutions that carry them forward merit special attention.

The International Monetary Fund (IMF) and the World Bank play a significant part in the determination of development policies and the creation of development conditions for states. This significant role is based on at least three separate factors:

1) They provide financial support to countries in the process of development. This financial support is determined on the basis of a quality assessment of the developmental/financial policies — an assessment undertaken by the financial institutions themselves.

2) They act as catalysts for other public and private transfer of money through foreign investment and other private/public support for developing countries.

3) They are major players in the globalized, neo-liberal international community. Together with the G-8 states and organizations such as the WTO, the IMF and the World Bank form the "trend-setters" in international financial and development environments.

These three factors imply that IFIs play a crucial role in the international community and ultimately penetrate national borders. They have vital impact on the ability of individual states to carry out the process of the right to development.

Challenges Faced by the IFIs As Separate Entities

For IFIs, the human rights component of the right to development sets qualitative limitations and requirements on the content of legitimate policies. As the IFIs are bound to respect international human rights law (at least those parts of it that represent international customary law),[26] the substantive content of these norms represents the limitations and framework within which the IFIs may operate. Thus, the institutions are faced with a dual challenge: 1) to carry out mandates and functions

---

25   A parallel can here be drawn to the discussion on right to self-determination, in which some authors — notably Rosalyn Higgins — have claimed that respect for human rights is a material limitation upon the right to self-determination. Rosalyn Higgins, *International Law: Problems and Process* (Oxford: Clarendon Press, 1995), Chapter 7.

26   The IMF's Legal Counsel, François Gianviti, indirectly recognized in his paper on the Fund's relationship to the International Covenant on Economic, Social and Cultural Rights, that the IMF is bound by customary international law (although he argued that human rights provisions are not part of this element of international law). Gianviti 2001, paras. 18-20.

as laid down in the constituent treaty and 2) to do this in a manner consistent with international law.

As mentioned above, IFIs, and in particular the World Bank and the IMF, enjoy international legal personality separate from that of its members.[27] This status carries rights and obligations stemming from international law and internal law of the institutions. Generally speaking, international law sets the limits for permissible behavior by the institutions, while their internal law lays out the positive mandate that the institutions shall strive to fulfill. However, in their work to fulfill the mandate, the institutions need to observe international law to avoid acting unlawfully. Thus, the norms provided by international customary law, by general principles of law, and in the treaties to which the institutions are parties create legal obligations for the institutions.[28] These obligations may be both of a negative and positive nature — to refrain from certain acts or to take positive steps to achieve a certain result. In regard to international human rights law, the negative obligations would imply that IFIs should refrain from conduct that may violate the customary human rights law or general principles of international human rights law. With regard to more positive obligations, this may, for instance, imply taking steps to regulate their subcontractors in project implementation to ensure that these do not violate human rights.

These positive and negative obligations, however, may also be addressed with regard to obligations of conduct and obligations of result.[29] Ultimately, one would strive toward the fulfillment of obligations of result — that is, the activities of the IFIs would lead to respect for human rights. This is only part of the story, however. The obligations of conduct are equally important for the IFIs and the people who benefit from their policies. *How* certain results are obtained is a crucial factor. It is not acceptable that these institutions pursue policies that, in the long run, will lead to an improved human rights situation, but in the short term involve severe restrictions or violations of human rights. It is possible to argue, for example, that the situation in Chile with respect to economic and social human rights has improved over the past 40 years. The massive violations of civil and political rights committed by the Pinochet regime in the 1970s and 1980s cannot be justified, however, by the end result of an improved human rights situation at the end of the century. The ways in which certain policy goals are achieved are as important as the goals themselves.

---

27 See, generally, Sigrun Skogly, 2001, *op. cit.*

28 H. G. Schermers and N. M. Blokker, *International Institutional Law: Unity within Diversity*, 3rd rev. (The Hague: Martinus Nijhoff, 1995), p. 984; Jan Klabbers, *An Introduction to International Institutional Law* (Cambridge: 2003), p. 310 (on responsibility for breach of international law); Sigrun Skogly, 2001, *op. cit.*

29 The recognition of the importance of obligations of conduct and obligations of result is now firm in general international law. In the final drafts of the Articles on State Responsibility, the International Law Commission deleted the specific reference to this distinction in its articles. However, it was recognized that the distinction is now included in the "character of obligation" as provided in Article 12. James Crawford, *The International Law Commission's Articles on State Responsibility: Introduction, Text and Commentaries* (Cambridge, UK: Cambridge University Press, 2002). In the field of human rights, this distinction is clearly recognized in the *Maastricht Guidelines on the Violations of Economic, Social and Cultural Rights*, adopted in Maastricht, January 1997; para. 7. Available at: http://www.uu.nl/uupublish/home-rechtsgeleer/onderzoek/onderzoekscholen/sim/english/instruments/22884main.html). The relevance of the distinction between obligations of conduct and obligations of result has also been recognized by the Independent Expert in this 2003 report. Sengupta, 2003, *op. cit*, para. 4.

Thus, a participatory process in determining development policy will, from a human rights perspective (if it is a real process and not window-dressing), be far better than one determined by the Washington-based institutions (with or without member state involvement), even if the result of the content of the policies may be the same.

The Process of the Right to Development Incorporated into Policies and Programs

There is therefore a need to ensure that the process of the right to development is incorporated into policies and programs of the IFIs. This emphasis in itself will entail respect for a number of specific human rights, in addition to the procedural aspects.

Participation

Participation has become a common focus within the development discourse in the last few years, emphasizing the right to participation as a human right[30] and, outside the rights framework, participation as an essential component of a "bottom-up" approach to development.[31]

Participation as a human right builds on Article 21 in the Universal Declaration on Human Rights (UDHR) and Article 25 of the International Covenant on Civil and Political Rights (ICCPR). These provisions guarantee the right to take part in the conduct of public affairs (ICCPR) or to take part in the government of the country (UDHR). Additionally, Common Article 1 of the two Covenants on the right to self-determination may be seen as an expression of a collective right to participation.

In the recent past, IFIs have put much emphasis on a participatory approach to development policy, particularly through the Poverty Reduction Strategy (PRS) process.[32] This is a positive initiative that should be welcomed and acknowledged. However, in order to ensure that the process is in accordance with human rights principles, any institution that attempts a participatory process should 1) recognize participation as a right, and not as another policy tool and 2) ensure that the participation is real — that is, that people affected have a real say in the priorities, design, and implementation of development policies that affect them.

---

30   See, for instance, Dominic McGoldrick, *The Human Rights Committee: Its Role in the Development of the International Covenant on Civil and Political Rights* (Oxford: Oxford University Press, 1991), p. xxxiii; James C. N. Paul, "Law and Development into the 1990s: The Need to Use International Law to Impose Accountability to People on International Development Actors," *Third World Legal Studies — 1992*, p. 7; Matthew Craven, *The International Covenant on Economic, Social and Cultural Rights: A Perspective on its Development* (Oxford: Clarendon Press, 1995), pp. 120-22.
31   Sarah C. White, "Depoliticising Development: The Uses and Abuses of Participation," *Development in Practice* 6 No. 1, 1996.
32   The Poverty Reduction Strategy was introduced by the World Bank and the International Monetary Fund in 1999, and according to the Bank's own information: " Poverty Reduction Strategy Papers are to provide the basis for assistance from the World Bank and the IMF as well as debt relief under the HIPC initiative. PRSPs should be country-driven, comprehensive in scope, partnership-oriented, and *participatory.* A country only needs to write a PRSP every three years. However, changes can be made to the content of a PRSP using an Annual Progress Report." (emphasis added). Quote taken from the World Bank website at http://www.worldbank.org/poverty/strategies/define.htm#prsp.

Difficulties may arise with this approach, however, as it involves a complex process of "trial and error." It is difficult, for example, to establish exactly who will be affected by a certain program, project, or policy, and it is, likewise, difficult to determine which groups (grass-roots organizations or NGOs) adequately represent the people. This is where a focus on the obligation of conduct becomes important. Even though it is virtually impossible to guarantee that a right-to-participation approach is going to be successful, an emphasis on "best practices" and an attempt to implement a right to participation are imperative.

Information and Expression

Another right that is necessary for the process of the right to development to be effective is the right to information — both to receive and to impart information. This is guaranteed in Article 19 of the UDHR and Article 19 of the ICCPR. It is an important right in itself but is also a prerequisite for the right to participation. The right to participation becomes an illusion if information is not available, or if individuals and groups are not able to impart information received. For instance, when the World Bank was involved in the privatization of the copper mines of Zambia, the process of privatization was far from open and transparent, and the lack of information to the population has been duly documented.[33] Lack of openness, transparency, and information suggested that groups adversely affected by the privatization process were unable to effectively participate and to propose amendments to the process itself. It may well be that the Zambian government expressed a desire to retain the details of this information. However, the Bank, if fulfilling its human rights obligations, should have insisted that the information be released to the population on the basis of the internationally agreed human rights provisions.

A closely related right, which is also imperative in terms of the right to participation, is the freedom of expression. The ability to express one's views, including opposition to proposed policies, without fear of persecution or intimidation otherwise, is a strong and necessary condition for the process of the right to development. The IFIs should ensure that the policies agreed to with national authorities are made known to the population, and that anyone who seeks further information, or expresses opposition to the plans, will be protected against censorship and persecution.

Non-Discrimination

The prohibition of discrimination is a fundamental principle in international human rights law. Included in the UN Charter[34] and a central element in all subsequent human rights instruments,[35] this principle is often considered to represent ob-

---

33 *Zambia, Deregulation and the Denial of Human Rights*, Submission to the UN Committee on Economic, Social and Cultural Rights, 2000. Submitted by Inter-African Network for Human Rights and Development (Afronet), Citizens for a Better Environment, and Rights and Accountability in Development (RAID); Executive Summary, p. 13ff.
34 UN Charter, Article 1(3).
35 The Universal Declaration on Human Rights, Article 2; The International Covenant on Civil and Political Rights, Article 2; The International Covenant on Economic, Social and Cultural Rights, Article 2(2). All other major human rights instruments, both of universal and regional characters contain similar non-discrimination provisions.

ligations *erga omnes* in international law.[36] There is therefore no doubt that the IFIs are under an international law obligation to respect the non-discrimination principle in its broad application. Thus, ensuring that people do not face discrimination in their access to the benefits of the development process is an end in itself in the development process. It is also a means to achieve the fulfillment of other rights, as the non-discrimination element will ensure equal access to services and benefits from other policies in the development process. It is pertinent to note that human rights law favors affirmative action, or positive discrimination, employed to remedy human rights violations suffered by parts of the population in the past, resulting in unequal access to benefits or enjoyment of services. Therefore, IFIs would be justified in supporting policies of positive discrimination in the process of the right to development.

Accountability

A central element in any discussion on human rights is the opportunity for redress in case of breaches of obligations. A wide variety of remedies may be applicable within international human rights law, and judicial remedies, or access to court, represent only some of the many options. With respect to IFIs, it should be possible to hold accountable those that fail to comply with the requirements of a human rights approach to the development process (to the extent that they are compatible with the obligations to comply). Although redress cannot readily be obtained through national or international courts due to the current immunities and jurisdictional limitations of these judicial institutions,[37] adapting existing structures specifically for this purpose might prove successful. One such structure is the World Bank's Inspection Panel. As the mandate of the Panel is currently formulated, it is by no means an ideal way of addressing human rights breaches. First of all, the Panel may only deal with breaches of the World Bank's own stated policies. Since the Bank does not have an operational policy on human rights, this represents a clear limitation.[38] Secondly, the Panel, although independent of the Bank's internal structures, does not have the final say, as the Board of Governors receives recommendations from the Panel and may or may not act on these recommendations.[39] Nevertheless, the Inspection Panel could be developed into a structure that could effectively deal with breaches of human rights — but this would require an amended mandate and that the Bank adopt a human rights policy for its operations. The Panel should also be extended to cover the operations of the IMF.

---

36 Theodor Meron, *Human Rights and Humanitarian Norms as Customary Law* (Oxford: Clarendon Press, 1989), pp. 193-94.
37 For further discussion on these issues, see Skogly, 2001 *op. cit.*; H. F. Bekker, *The Legal Position of Intergovernmental Organizations: A Functional Necessity Analysis of Their Legal Status and Immunities* (Dordrecht: Martinus Nijhoff Publishers,1994).
38 There are, nevertheless, certain areas where the Bank has stated human rights policies. This is most notably in the area of indigenous peoples. Operational Directive 4:20 on Indigenous Peoples provides in para. 6 that the Bank must "ensure that the development process fosters full respect for their dignity, human rights and cultural uniqueness."
39 An example in which the Board of Executive Directors has not acted upon the recommendations of the Panel was in the Itapartica Resettlement and Irrigation project in Brazil. For further details, see World Bank, "World Bank Board Agrees to Action Plan for Itaparicia Resettlement and Irrigation Project" (Brazil: Press Release, September 10, 1997).

Expanding the role of the Inspection Panel still focuses on the violation aspect, however, without giving due consideration to the promotional aspect of the process of the right to development. It is crucial that the IFIs themselves accept accountability for this process with respect not only to the member states and their creditors, but also to the millions of individuals who are affected by their policies. IFIs' accepting this responsibility would represent an active approach in assessing human rights effects (both positive and negative) of past and current policies, programs, and projects, with the aim to learn from errors and to improve the process in the future. Institutions would therefore be able to incorporate an accountability aspect that goes beyond the prospect of litigations in case of violations.

Substantive Aspects of Human Rights Incorporated into Policies and Programs

All of the above variables are important in the process of the right to development. Respect for the right to participation, to information and expression, to be free from discrimination, and to ensure the accountability of the IFIs with regard to the quality of their own policies, is important in terms of the rights that they themselves represent, but also important for the ability of people to realize the substance of other human rights. Often, in a human rights debate on the development process, the right to participation is seen as an end in itself, with a view that if this right is fulfilled, then all other rights will naturally follow.

This opinion, however, is misguided, since although the right to participation does represent a right to participate in the determination of the manner in which other human rights are implemented, it does not, in and of itself, guarantee that all rights will be implemented for all individuals. The obligation holders — in our case the IFIs — have to ensure that policies designed to improve the development process also contribute equally to the fulfillment of the substantive elements of other human rights. Additionally, a reliance on internationally agreed standards to which the member states have voluntarily and publicly agreed will enable the IFIs to avoid criticism for taking politically motivated positions. To insist on the adherence to the international law obligations of the member states will not represent political interference, and particularly not if such insistence is done consistently. In this context, it could be reasonable to argue that the IFIs should adopt a similar policy on human rights treaties that the Bank has adopted for project and programs that may impact the environment. The Bank should not agree to programs that may run counter to the provisions of environmental treaties by which their members are bound.[40]

Since it is not possible in this chapter to provide an exhaustive account of all rights, only a few examples will be discussed. Development will be viewed in light of Amartya Sen's understanding of it in his book, *Development as Freedom,* in which these concepts are considered a way of achieving capabilities to further personal choices.[41]

---

40   Ibrahim Shihata, *The World Bank Inspection Panel* (Oxford: Oxford University Press, 1994), p. 141.
41   Amartya Sen, *Development and Freedom* (Oxford: Oxford University Press, 1999), p. 89.

Health

In the process of the right to development, the right to health is seen as crucial. Respect for the right to the highest attainable standard of mental and physical health[42] is imperative for an individual's ability to take part in and benefit from the process of development. When IFIs are involved in infrastructural projects within the health services or in the discussions on the allocation of limited funds for national health care, the core content of the right to health should give guidance to policy-makers. Notably, the UN Committee on Economic, Social and Cultural Rights expressed the view in their General Comment on the right to health:

> In conformity with articles 22 and 23 of the Covenant, WHO, The International Labour Organization, the United Nations Development Programme, UNICEF, the United Nations Population Fund, the World Bank, regional development banks, the International Monetary Fund, the World Trade Organization and other relevant bodies within the United Nations system, should cooperate effectively with States parties, building on their respective expertise, in relation to the implementation of the right to health at the national level, with due respect to their individual mandates. In particular, the international financial institutions, notably the World Bank and the International Monetary Fund, should pay greater attention to the protection of the right to health in their lending policies, credit agreements and structural adjustment programmes.[43]

Food

In the areas of food and agriculture, in addition to focusing on the financial goals of providing foreign exchange earnings from the agricultural business, institutions should view the individual's right to adequate food as an equal or possibly prioritized variable when determining agricultural policies. This approach would involve analyzing changes in production on a micro, food-security level as well as from a macro income-earnings perspective. According to Sengupta et al., "development as freedom consists of expansion of capabilities and freedom of people to realize what they value."[44] The expansion of capabilities covers resources available for the enjoyment of human rights. A restriction of this enjoyment is permissible only to ensure the protection of rights of others and general welfare in society.[45] With regard to the right to food, it would therefore follow that the IFIs should consider changes in agricultural production with a view to fulfilling the right to food. To enhance income-generating agricultural production, they should avoid limiting the resources available for the population while, at the same time, protecting the already existing resource base within the local population. Doing so would render the actions consistent with a right-to-development approach. Added to this, the policies should be non-discrim-

---

42   International Covenant on Economic, Social and Cultural Rights, Article 12.
43   UN Committee on Economic, Social and Cultural Rights, General Comment No. 14 on the Right to Health, para. 66.
44   Sengupta et al., 2003, *op. cit.* p. 15.
45   Article 29 of the Universal Declaration of Human Rights.

inatory, implying that no group (including women) should bear the heavier burden of change, and that all groups should share the benefits from the new policies.

Again, the core content of the right to food and the ways in which this can be affected by the policies of the IFIs should be a central part of the determination of food and agricultural policies. As was the case for the right to health, the UN Committee on Economic, Social and Cultural Rights has expressed the following view:

> The international financial institutions, notably the International Monetary Fund (IMF) and the World Bank, should pay greater attention to the protection of the right to food in their lending policies and credit agreements and in international measures to deal with the debt crisis. Care should be taken, in line with the Committee's General Comment No. 12, paragraph 9, in any structural adjustment programme to ensure that the right to food is protected.[46]

Access to Justice

Since the early 1990s, IFIs have recognized the importance of a functioning judicial system for the development process. This has been emphasized in the institutions' approach to "good governance," in which the rule of law plays a central part. The difference, however, between their approach to the rule of law and a human rights approach to the rule of law and access to justice is a qualitative one. While the good governance debates within the IFIs in the early 1990s emphasized creating a stable and predictable environment for business to operate,[47] a human rights approach also emphasizes equal and effective access to the courts for cases involving human rights violations as well as civil claims. There are important arguments in favor of using the international standards for independence of the judiciary and other human rights aspects of access to justice in the international support work — also undertaken by the IFIs.[48] This would enable consistency and predictability for states during the process of improving their justice sector. It would also represent a means to overcome political concerns.[49]

Equality before the law, access to the justice system, fair trial guarantees, and the independence of the judiciary are central aspects of the International Bill of Human Rights and all the regional human rights instruments. The IFIs would contribute to a functioning judicial system, which is paramount for the protection of all human rights, through active support for legal aid schemes, legal education, and the prevention of corruption. The World Bank is already involved in these efforts, and its contribution should be enhanced and strengthened. It is, nevertheless, important to recognize that there are significant differences among legal traditions and cultures,

---

46   UN Committee on Economic, Social and Cultural Rights, General Comment No. 12 on the Right to Adequate Food, para. 41.
47   *World Bank Managing Development: The Governance Dimension — A Discussion Paper* (Washington, DC: The World Bank, 1991). See also, Ibrahim Shihata, *The World Bank in a Changing World: Selected Essays,* Franziska Tscofen and Antonio R. Parra (eds.) (Dordrecht: Martinus Nijhoff Publisher, 1991).
48   The World Bank has engaged actively in supporting judicial and legal reform in its member states. Information about these activities can be accessed at http://www4.worldbank.org/legal/leglr/.
49   International Council on Human Rights Policy *Local Perspectives: Foreign Aid to the Justice Sector,* (1999), p. 85.

and the way in which external support for access to justice is designed will need to take these local circumstances into consideration.

Poverty Reduction Strategies

Leaving the previous examples from codified human rights law, this section will end in a consideration of how strategies such as those discussed above may have an impact on the poverty reduction strategies. The process of the right to development in this context can be seen as a strategy for achieving the goals of poverty reduction. The understanding of development as a process to improve and increase the capabilities of people living in poverty to realize their own aspirations and choices denotes a recognition and respect for these people's fundamental rights. Sen holds that "poverty must be seen as the deprivation of basic capabilities rather than merely a lowness of incomes, which is the standard criterion of identification of poverty."[50] Therefore, the process of the right to development involves more than economic growth if it is to relate to poverty eradication; it additionally implies the creation of circumstances in which these basic capabilities may be fulfilled.

The IFIs have a stated purpose of addressing poverty issues and working toward poverty reduction, the essential elements of the 1999 Poverty Reduction Strategies.[51] The policies applied by the IFIs in the 1980s and 1990s were seen as having failed to achieve the poverty reduction initially envisaged, and different approaches needed to be tried. One of these was the Poverty Reduction Strategy Papers (PRSP), which is combined with the debt reduction programs contained in the Heavily Indebted Poor Countries Initiative (HIPIC). These strategies were also inspired by the emphasis in the 1990s on democratization and accountability, which were seen as essential elements of a good governance strategy. In this, the national or local "ownership" of policies, programs, and projects became an essential part of the new approach — and particularly a call for much larger popular participation in the definition of developmental goals. We can, therefore, at this preliminary stage, see a convergence between the participation element of the process of the right to development and the participation element of the PRS process.

If the PRS process is to be seen as creating the necessary environment for the process of the right to development, however, the IFIs will need to consider a number of additional aspects of the PRS process. In the Draft Guidelines on a Human Rights Approach to Poverty Reduction Strategies, developed by a group of experts for the UN High Commissioner for Human Rights in 2002, the importance of establishing structures to monitor compliance with human rights principles in the PRSP process is emphasized. According to these Guidelines,

> ... global actors must be subject to accessible, transparent and effective monitoring and accountability procedures. If global actors fail to establish appropriate monitoring and accountability mechanisms

---

50 Sen (1999), *op. cit.* p. 87.
51 Further information about the PRSP process can be accessed at the World Bank website at http://www.worldbank.org.

in relation to their poverty reduction and human rights responsibilities, others should take steps to do so.[52]

It is, however, interesting to observe that although the PRSPs were developed by the IFIs to enhance their effectiveness toward the goal of poverty reduction, most of the guidelines developed to safeguard economic, social, and cultural rights in this process are addressed the states and what they should do.

Challenges Faced by States Members of the International Financial Institutions

All of the previous comments have related to the institutions as separate legal entities from those of the member states, and the challenges that these institutions face in the process of the right to development. The institutions are composed of states, however, and these individual states have human rights obligations that, to a certain extent, extend to their behavior within the institutions. In this section, I will address how states' human rights obligations may be expressed in their behavior through IFIs.

The traditional approach to international human rights law implies that states are the main obligation holders and that they are primarily obligated to ensure that individuals within their jurisdiction do not suffer human rights violations.[53] This understanding of human rights obligations is based on a respect for the *comity*[54] principle and general principles of states territorial sovereignty. This approach to human rights respect, however, is built on a traditional view of the state as the dominant actor in the international community and asserts that each individual state is endowed with complete sovereignty over its own territory and its subjects. If such complete sovereignty exists, it makes sense to allocate all responsibility for human rights respect to the state as well. What this approach does not take into account, however, are the changed realties of the international community at the beginning of the third millennium. We are today witnessing a world where the globalizing effects of technology, capital movement, the economic power of transnational corporations, significant international regulation, and a *de facto* unequal position of states themselves, limit states' domestic policy choices. The role of the state in domestic policies is significantly reduced, particularly in poorer states, in great part as the result of policy insistence from the IFIs themselves.

We are also witnessing a world in which the actions of states have significant impact on other states and on individuals within other states. Recent events of sanctions, the war on terrorism, and more conventional wars are examples of how foreign policy decisions may affect people in other countries. It is therefore necessary to take a new look at the theory limiting human rights obligations to states. There are provisions in international human rights law that support a wider understanding of ob-

---

52 Draft Guidelines, see note 6, para. 245.
53 What is implied by "within their jurisdiction" is the subject of intense debate, particularly after the European Court of Human Rights gave its ruling of inadmissibility in the *Bankovic* case. See *Bankovic and Others v. Belgium and 16 Other Contracting States* (Application No. 52207/99).
54 The *comity* principle reflects states' reciprocal respect for each other's sovereignty including their legislation, judicial system, and territorial integrity.

ligations. The provisions of Articles 55 and 56 of the UN Charter, Article 28 of the UDHR indicate that international cooperation and efforts are part of the requirements of human rights law.[55] More concretely, the states that are parties to the International Covenant on Economic, Social and Cultural Rights (ICESR)[56] undertake to "take steps, *individually and through international assistance and cooperation, especially economic and technical,* to the maximum of its available resources . . ." for the full realization of the rights of the Covenant. Whether this passage implies an obligation to provide international development assistance, or indeed a right for poorer countries to receive assistance, has been debated.[57] What is less controversial is that states that become parties to this Covenant undertake certain responsibilities that go beyond their national borders, including acting through international organizations.[58]

These responsibilities imply that when states participate in the work of the IFIs, they retain their human rights obligations. For debtor states, this means that they should raise their obligations based on the Covenant in negotiations with the institutions.[59] Just as international human rights law sets limitations for permissible behavior by the IFIs themselves, so do these norms set limits for states when agreeing on policies, programs, and projects funded by or co-financed by the IFIs. It is not only the debtors that retain human rights obligations, however. Based on the provisions in the Covenant, as well as customary international law,[60] creditor states are equally required to take into account the human rights effects in third countries of the decisions that they make within the IFIs. These states, therefore, are obliged to consider how individual projects, programs, and policies may affect the population in the countries where they are to be implemented[61] and to alter them when necessary to avoid possible human rights violations.

---

55   Draft Guidelines, Guideline 15, see note 6; see also Sigrun I. Skogly, "The Obligation of International Assistance and Cooperation in the International Covenant on Economic, Social and Cultural Rights," in Morten Bergsmo, (ed.) *Human Rights and Criminal Justice for the Down Trodden: Essays in Honour of Asbjørn Eide* (Leiden: Martinus Nijhoff Publishers, 2003), pp. 403-421; Sigrun I. Skogly and Mark Gibney, "Transnational Human Rights Obligations of States," 23 *Human Rights Quarterly,* No. 3, 2002. For a more in depth analysis of Articles 55 and 56, see Sigrun I. Skogly, *Beyond National Borders: States' Human Rights Obligations in International Cooperation* (Antwerp: Intersentia, 2006).
56   As of October 2005, 151 states are parties to the Covenant.
57   For a fuller discussion of this issue, see Sigrun I. Skogly, 2006, *op. cit.*
58   UN Committee on Economic, Social and Cultural Rights, General Comment No. 3 (199), paras. 14 and 15; General Comment No. 8 (1997); General Comment No. 12 paras. 36-39 (1999); General Comment No. 15 (2002) paras. 30-36; Maastricht Guidelines, paragraph 19; Draft Guidelines 2002, Guideline 15.
59   The UN Committee on Economic, Social and Cultural Rights has on several occasions raised this question when examining reports by states that receive financial assistance from IFIs. See, *inter alia,* UN/Economic and Social Council, Committee on Economic, Social and Cultural Rights, Concluding Observations on Report by Egypt, UN Doc. E/C.12/1/Add 44, May 23, 2000, paras. 10, 14, and 28.
60   For a further elaboration of how the various sources of international human rights create extraterritorial obligations, see Sigrun Skogly, *Beyond National Borders: States Human Rights Obligations in International Cooperation* (Antwerp: Intersentia, forthcoming, 2005).
61   Again, the UN Committee on Economic, Social and Cultural Rights now regularly requests information from states that are members of the IFIs about how they ensure that their human rights obligations inform their behavior within the IFIs. See *inter alia* UN/Economic and Social Council, Committee on Economic, Social and Cultural Rights, *Concluding Observations on Report by Italy*, UN Doc. E/C.12/1/Add 43, May 23, 2000, para. 20.

Obligations Related to the Human Rights-Based Approach to the Process of Development

Just as the organs of the IFIs are limited in their policy choices by the qualitative content of human rights, the states members of these institutions will individually be limited in what kind of policies, programs, or projects they can support. These limitations have been described above in terms of procedural and substantive content and also in terms of obligations of conduct and obligations of result. It would be naïve to think that all problems would be solved merely by telling states that they needed to incorporate human rights concerns into their policies toward the IFIs. Just as for the institutions themselves, states will face situations of trial and error in ascertaining that their policies do not adversely affect human rights enjoyment for individuals in other states. This would be a similar approach to that taken by the UN Committee on Economic, Social and Cultural Rights, in that they do not expect full realization of all the rights in the Covenant immediately, but they do expect states to show that they have made attempts and that there are positive developments.[62]

One of the immediate requirements in this respect is national coordination and education among staff responsible for the states' policies within the IFIs and the people representing them in these institutions. Unless a comprehensive approach is taken, and people within the Foreign Office and within the circles representing the state in the IMF (most commonly, representatives of the central banks) are fully informed as to how international human rights obligations should impact upon the state's behavior in these institutions, it is highly unlikely that such an approach will be followed.

Thus, in the process of the right to development, states members of the IFIs should ensure that their behavior through these institutions results in the fulfillment of "all the human rights and fundamental freedoms and achieve[s] a process of economic growth, with equity and justice, which eradicates poverty, illiteracy, malnutrition and ill-health and protects the marginalized and the vulnerable groups of the society."[63]

Sources of International Human Rights Law Obligations

As with many discussions on states or other institutions' human rights obligations, it is necessary to identify the content of these obligations. I have concluded in earlier work that, based on international human rights law, it is not possible to argue that the IFIs themselves have the full set of human rights obligations — as they are not parties to the Covenants that establish the most elaborate obligations.[64] This is, however, not the case for the states members of the IFIs. Of the approximately 180

---

62   UN Committee on Economic, Social and Cultural Rights, General Comment No. 3 (1990), paras. 9 and 10.

63   Arjun K. Sengupta, *Preliminary Study of the Independent Expert on the Right to Development on the Impact of International Economic and Financial Issues on the Enjoyment of Human Rights* (Geneva: United Nations, Commission on Human Rights, 2003), para. 7.

64   In this regard, I agree with the IMF's legal counsel, Mr. François Gianviti (Gianviti, 200, *op. cit.*), that the provisions of the Covenant do not bind the IMF per se, as the Fund is not, and indeed cannot, be a party to the Covenant. This does not imply that I agree with the General Counsel in the implications of this fact for the Fund's obligations with regard to other sources of international human rights law.

members of the IFIs, 151 have ratified the ICESCR. Therefore, these 153 states are bound by the obligations as contained in this Covenant, as well as other obligations stemming from other sources of international human rights law. It is therefore pertinent to look somewhat closer at these obligations with regard to their behavior through the IFIs.[65]

In terms of the obligation to *respect*, states shall ensure that policies, programs, or projects that they support do not violate the human rights of people to the extent that they are already enjoying them. For instance, if a proposed program or project shows that there is great likelihood that girls will be unable to continue to attend primary schools because of the introduction of school fees that are prohibitive for the parents, then such a program would be unsustainable from a human rights perspective. Likewise, the obligation to *protect* people from human rights abuses committed by third parties would imply that states need to ascertain that subcontractors or other private actors engaged by the IFIs to carry out their programs are not likely to engage in activities that were counterproductive in terms of individuals' human rights. This could, *inter alia,* be done through conditions added to project/program approvals for the institutions to the effect that they should ensure that appropriate human rights appraisals are carried out in the project proposals and the vetting of subcontractors.

The obligation to fulfill is perhaps more interesting than the other obligations. In this respect, it is doubtful whether the IFIs themselves have a firm obligation,[66] and the extraterritorial obligations of states may also be weaker.[67] Since human rights obligations generally are strongest for the territorial state, questions may be asked as to whether it is contrary to principles of sovereignty to demand that foreign states, through their actions in IFIs, are obligated to actively fulfill human rights. If we base this discussion on the ICESCR, the question becomes whether the provision in Article 2(1) — and indeed, the four other references to international cooperation in the Covenant — imply an obligation to avoid violations, to protect from violations by third parties, and to promote the fulfillment of human rights through international cooperation.

The answer to this question may be negative — that it is only the territorial state that has these far-reaching obligations — but the question could also be answered in a different manner. Given the very strong interdependence among states and the unequal partnerships among them, if the obligation to fulfill were a requirement for extraterritorial behavior, this would respond to the reality that it is not possible for many states to fulfill human rights obligations by themselves. This was indeed the

---

65   For a discussion of the extraterritorial obligations in relationship to the ICESCR see Sigrun I. Skogly, "The Obligation of International Assistance and Co-operation in the International Covenant on Economic, Social and Cultural Rights," in Morten Bergsmo, (ed.) *Human Rights and Criminal Justice for the Downtrodden* (Dordrecht: Martinus Nijhoff, 2003); Fons Coomans, "Some Remarks on the Extraterritorial Application of the International Covenant on Economic, Social and Cultural Rights;" and Rolf Künneman, "Extraterritorial Application of the International Covenant on Economic, Social and Cultural Rights;" both contributions in Fons Coomans and Menno T. Kamminga, *Extraterritorial Application of Human Rights Treaties* (Antwerp: Intersentia, 2004).
66   Skogly, 2001, *op. cit.* Chapter 7.
67   For further reflections on this question, see Skogly, 2006, *op. cit.*

view of many delegations to the United Nations during the drafting of the Covenant in the 1950s and 1960s.[68] The money transfers that result from the activities of the IFIs, either directly or through guarantees, through policy approval that leads to other funds, are so substantial that if states acting through the institutions carried out their obligations to fulfill, real improvements in human rights might be expected. This should then be related not only to the ICESR, but also to the Declaration on the Right to Development and the process that this right entails. One could argue that it would be a legitimate policy for states that are members of the IFIs to further their human rights obligations through the institutions' policies. This argument would be even stronger if there were a convergence of the views between creditor and debtor states, even if the institutions themselves did not favor such a policy. The policy options available to states in promoting human rights by using the IFIs as a vehicle would likely be limited by the mandates of the IFIs as defined by the Articles of Agreement. Or, in other words, if states were to promote human rights through projects, programs, and policies developed by the creditor and debtor states, these projects, programs, and policies should not have a content that would be contrary to the mandates of the institutions through which they are applied.

States that engage in the process of the right to development or a rights-based approach to development could therefore, through their behavior in and support for the IFIs, aim to fulfill human rights and fundamental freedoms and achieve a process of economic growth that includes the qualifications as stipulated by the Independent Expert.[69]

The Merger of the Challenges for the IFIs and Their Members

The question that results from the analysis of the various actors' involvement in the process of development is obviously: how do the challenges of these actors merge? I have identified at least three separate sets of actors that interact in the process — namely debtor states, the IFIs, and the creditor states. Both the debtor and the creditor states are members of the IFIs. Merging the responsibility or the obligations of these three sets of actors in any given policy, program, or project context might be very difficult. All of these actors, however, have human rights obligations according to international law — although to varying degrees. The debtor state that seeks assistance from the IFIs will have the full set of human rights obligations, particularly if the country has ratified human rights treaties. As separate legal personalities, the IFIs have obligations based on general principles of international human rights law and customary international human rights law, while the creditor state have extraterritorial human rights obligations to varying degrees, determined by the number and content of the human rights treaties they have ratified.[70]

---

68 For instance, Chile (E/CN.4/SR.216, 21 May 1951), France (E/CN.4/L.55), India (E/CN.4/SR.231), Greece (E/CN.4/SR.236), Egypt (E/CN.4/SR. 236), and Denmark (E/CN.4/ SR. 236); India, E/CN.4/SR.231.
69 See notes 9, 10, and 11.
70 It should be noted that the obligation to cooperate internationally is contained in the ICESCR as well as in other human rights treaties, most notably the Rights of the Child Convention, Article 4, and in the Convention on the Abolition of all forms of torture.

Yet, if we approach these obligations from the perspective of the process of the right to development, there should be little difficulty in merging the challenges faced by these three actors working toward the common goal. This can be addressed in terms of "mutuality of obligations,"[71] or in terms of partnership built on equity. The partnership notion should be emphasized, as much of what separates the right to development from a fulfillment of the rights contained in the International Bill of Human Rights may still be perceived as *imperfect obligations,* as discussed by Sen, building on Kant's philosophy.

The fact that, as of yet, the breaches of the obligations pertaining to the process of the right to development may not be easily processed through courts with clear duty-holders, does not imply that there are no obligations. The obligations should be addressed through a constructive partnership, however, in which the three actors work together toward the common goal of achieving the process of the right to development through equity of the parties involved. If the parties fail to achieve these common goals, it might be necessary to address the question of shared responsibility and shared accountability in relationship to the intended beneficiaries of the right to development.

The final points concern the value added by applying this approach to the activities of the IFIs and states through their actions within the IFIs. If the right to development becomes key guidance to the operations of these institutions, this would represent a constructive approach for the IFIs. A rights-based approach to the process of development will imply qualitative limitations upon certain policies, while at the same time direct the policy decisions in a constructive way toward the goal of ensuring that all individuals will benefit from the process of development.

Through the active participation of people to determine their development priorities, within the limits set by international human rights law, and in particular UDHR Article 29, the policies, programs, and projects will reflect the developmental goals much more clearly. It is, however, necessary that the limitations set by the human rights approach are made clear from the outset and that these are related to the specific policies, programs, or projects proposed in order to avoid the impression that new conditions are being established. If it is perceived in a manner such that national policy change, determined by external actors, needs to be implemented before the development priorities may be acted upon, the danger is that it is resisted by the very people that should benefit from the changes. On the other hand, this can be avoided if the participatory process is clearly developed within the framework of each actor's human rights obligations.

Conclusion

If states and IFIs are to take the right to development seriously, an attitude shift is necessary. With respect to the IFIs, their approach in regard to human rights is far too often to minimize their obligations. If we abandon this negative and limited

---

71   See *supra,* note 9, para. 46. Sengupta explains "mutuality of the obligations" as "the obligations of developing countries to carry out these rights-based programmes are matched with reciprocal obligations of international community to cooperate to enable the implementation of the programmes."

thinking and turn the approach around, however, the questions become: how can these actors positively contribute to the process of the right to development, and how can a rights-based approach to development improve the work of the IFIs? It is time that the IFIs and their member states see human rights not as an obstacle but rather as an opportunity to develop policies particularly effective in reaching the final goal of human development — the increase in resources available for constructive, vibrant societies that contribute to the furthering of human kind. If the process of the right to development through growth, non-discrimination, and participation is seen as an opportunity rather than an obstacle, the IFIs will enhance their efficiency in fulfilling their own mandates. Such an approach implies consistency, while at the same time it requires and accepts national and regional variations. It would also ensure that those most vulnerable and exposed to human rights violations are brought into the focus of development.

Part V. Conclusions

Conclusions
The Editors

The contributors to this volume have provided a wealth of analysis and insights about human rights in development, rights-based approaches to development, and the right to development. From these studies and the deliberations of the Nobel Symposium, we have reached several conclusions regarding the present state of the debate on these complex issues.

The first — and fairly obvious — conclusion is the general proposition that the theory and practice of development may be enriched by the introduction of normative dimensions of a human rights framework and that development and human rights are mutually reinforcing strategies for the improvement of human well being. However, there remains considerable uncertainty regarding the content and practical value of human rights in development practice.

There are several approaches to human rights in development, ranging from concern for duties under human rights treaties within specific sectors of the economy (such as health or education) to more systematic efforts to apply human rights norms to the entire process of development. United Nations resolutions and declarations on human rights in development, including those on the right to development, have endorsed the more systematic linkage.

The meaningful application of human rights concepts to the process of development requires linking the essentially legal and political approach of the former to the essentially economic and social context of the latter. Several chapters of this book provide core definitions as used both in the literature and among practitioners. Other chapters examine how human rights obligations apply to relations among states in the development field.

Definitions

Human rights in development — or the human rights-based approach to development — refers to the means and methods of fulfilling human rights obligations through development policies and practices. Governments and international institutions have recently developed, clarified, and applied their own definitions and policies in this area, a promising trend in development discourse, which, in some cases, is generating new models for development interventions and programs.

Summarizing the definition in the 1986 Declaration on the Right to Development and in the work of Arjun Sengupta as UN Independent Expert, we define the right to development as a right to a process as well as to progressive outcomes aiming at the full realization of all human rights in the context of equitable growth. More broadly, it involves the general improvement of the capabilities of the population in ways that are compatible with human rights.

The right to development and human rights in development are related in the sense that the implementation of the former requires that governments and development partners apply human rights in their development policies and practices in an integrated way, along with the other requirements stipulated in or implied by the 1986 Declaration. Thus the right to development includes, but is not coterminous with, a human rights approach to development insofar as this approach may be applied in a single sector of the economy or in a localized development project. Taken in its broadest sense of the integrated and systematic promotion and protection of human rights in the context of development, the human rights-based approach to development is essentially the same as the right to development although the latter has the additional requirement that the process itself be regarded as a right. Because this broadest interpretation is rarely used, the concept of the right to development is useful to underscore the systematic and integrated approach to human rights in development.

The greatest challenge is to translate abstract definitions into useful tools for the development practice. Indeed, describing the component elements of the right to development does not specify the steps required to implement it. At the current stage of experience with the right to development, this right cannot be implemented with the same rigor as other human rights norms, nor can appropriate measures of accountability and remedial action be put in place to respond to instances of failure to implement this right. Unless it is associated with appropriate measures of accountability, this right will remain primarily rhetorical.

Legal Status of the Right to Development

Governments have taken widely varying positions regarding the legal status of the right to development, ranging from the outright rejection of the claim that it is a human right at all to the position that it is a core right that should be legally binding and central to all efforts to promote and protect human rights. Our view is an intermediary one, according to which the right to development is grounded in international law, but the extent to which it constrains states legally is in the process of evolution. The official statements of governments since the mid-1970s, especially their support for the 1986 Declaration on the Right to Development, the 1993 Declaration of the Vienna Conference on Human Rights, and other resolutions of the General Assembly and summits, attach legal significance to this human right. The 1986 Declaration, like other declarations adopted by the General Assembly, creates an enhanced expectation that governments will move from political commitment to legal obligations. The Declaration, therefore, is a legitimate reference by which to hold governments at least politically accountable as an international norm crystallizes into law.

Insofar as the human right to development reaffirms rights that are already contained in legally binding instruments, such as the International Covenants on Human Rights, it builds on and integrates binding norms. Taken as a composite right, the right to development involves "perfect obligations" of its component rights. The duty-bearers, therefore, may be easily identified, and claims of conforming action may be legally enforced. However, the right to development establishes the obligation to integrate those components into a coherent development policy. This is an "imperfect obligation," the realization of which requires complex sets of actions and allocation of resources to develop and apply policies at national and international levels. Governments have a moral obligation to establish such policies to ensure that development is advanced in a way that systematically integrates the five core human rights principles enumerated by Sengupta, namely, equity, nondiscrimination, participation, transparency, and accountability. In this sense, it is an aspirational right to which governments may be politically committed but for which there are not yet legal remedies. Beginning as an imperfect obligation, the right to development should be progressively translated into more specific obligations. The current role of the Open-Ended Working Group on the Right to Development and its high-level task force and the review of their mandates by the Human Rights Council offer an opportunity to move in that direction.

Obligations of States Regarding Their National Policies and Practices of Development Based on Human Rights

The primary responsibility for the realization of human rights and development rests with the state, although other states and civil society are vital agents for that purpose. The state is legally bound by its international human rights obligations and politically bound by its commitment to the right to development. The cumulative effect is that states have an obligation to impose on their agents duties to respect human rights in the development process and to protect people from violations of these rights by third parties (non-state actors). Furthermore, they have a duty to see that steps are taken to promote, facilitate, and provide for all aspects of the right to development to the limits of their capacity, including by drawing on external support and assistance. According to this reasoning, the right to development follows the same analytical framework of its normative content as other rights examined by treaty bodies. It would help if governments and independent national and international groups conducted national assessments of progress achieved and difficulties encountered in implementing the right to development. Peer review of such assessments should occur at the level of the Human Rights Council in the context of the "universal periodic review." The credibility of this process depends on the quality of the data and the analysis of indicators and benchmarks, the openness of governments to inputs from civil society and development partners, and their willingness to accept constructive criticism and recommendations for improvement, considering that all countries have a long way to go in order to reach the full potential of the right to development.

International Cooperation to Support the Right to Development and Human Rights in Development

According to human rights law, exemplified by Article 2 of the International Covenant on Economic, Social and Cultural Rights, members of the international community (states and intergovernmental and non-governmental organizations) are obliged to assist one another in progressively fulfilling the above responsibilities through international cooperation. However, whether the obligation of international assistance and cooperation includes introducing human rights and the right to development into development policy is a matter of dispute. A strict interpretation limits the legal obligation of assistance to the minimal contribution to policies and programs of international institutions and bilateral agencies, without implicating the structures of the international political economy. A broader interpretation extends the responsibility of countries and other entities — including non-state actors — to the creation, in the words of the Declaration on the Right to Development, "of national and international conditions favourable to the realization of the right to development" and, therefore, to structural transformation of the international political economy. The commitment of the international community to meeting the Millennium Development Goals (MDGs) and the recent assessments of the human rights dimensions of the MDGs may be invoked in this context, notwithstanding the low probability that the MDGs will be reached by 2015.

The process of globalization and the trend favoring free markets and free trade may exacerbate the disparities and injustices of unequal development and weaken human rights protections. It is equally true that free movement of ideas, peoples, goods, images, technology, capital, and labor offers enormous opportunities for equitable growth and poverty alleviation that are essential to the realization of the right to development. The predatory trends and negative impact of globalization should be seen as the result of the failure of states to create "national and international conditions favourable to the realization of the right to development" and "to formulate appropriate national development policies," as required by the Declaration on the Right to Development. Thus, the right to development perspective offers a normative toolkit for assessing processes of globalization through the lenses and principles of international distributive justice.

International mechanisms for the implementation of the right to development involve responsibilities of multilateral and bilateral agencies, including human rights bodies, development agencies, and financial institutions. The challenge remains to develop some concrete principles, mechanisms, and guidelines for an operational model to implement the right to development. In each of these institutional settings, there is at best an embryonic mechanism to implement and monitor the right to development. Indicators and benchmarks can be developed with scientific rigor, and their further development merits sustained attention, as underscored in the chapter by Malhotra.

The reference in the Declaration on the Right to Development to the responsibility of states for the creation of "international conditions favourable to the realization of the right to development" applies primarily to affluent countries, which have "the duty to take steps, individually and collectively, to formulate international development policies with a view to facilitating the full realization of the right to development." Accordingly, we consider that donor countries — acting through their development cooperation programs or through the international institution to which they belong — have a duty to facilitate the efforts of developing countries to advance the right to development by relaxing constraints on productive resources and supporting institutional development.

This duty, expressed in the non-binding Declaration, is reinforced by the legally binding obligations on member states under Articles 55 and 56 of the United Nations Charter and of States Parties to the International Covenant on Economic, Social and Cultural Rights under Article 2 of that instrument. This duty to act jointly and separately to achieve the development and human rights purposes of the UN and to contribute through international cooperation to the realization of economic, social, and cultural rights provides the most solid legal footing for the right to development. Although the same obligation of international cooperation is not present in the International Covenant on Civil and Political Rights, both Covenants refer to the need to create "conditions . . . whereby everyone may enjoy his civil and political rights, as well as his economic, social and cultural rights" and the Universal Declaration of Human Rights called, in Article 28, for a social and international order in which all rights can be fully realized. These universally accepted standards reinforce the idea of an obligation to cooperate internationally for the realization of the right to development.

Transforming International Economic Relations

It is understandable that the political climate in which the right to development emerged continues to place this right in the political realm of rhetoric rather than in the normative domain of priority setting and allocation of resources. The right to development requires that development partners put in place bilateral facilities or country-specific arrangements, such as the "development compacts" proposed by the Independent Expert, or similar mechanisms. Such arrangements offer an alternative to human rights conditionality in that they institutionalize mutual responsibility. Developing countries would fulfill their obligations to apply human rights-consistent development policies, and affluent countries and international institutions would support the right to development through aid, debt relief, trade, and finance.

Both of these dimensions of multilateral and bilateral international cooperation open up new possibilities for realizing the right to development, ultimately transforming international economic relations on the basis of equity, partnership, and shared responsibilities between the developed and developing countries. Such an approach will also give substance to the otherwise grandiloquent commitment of the Millennium Summit "to making the right to development a reality for everyone and to freeing the entire human race from want."

Contributors

Bård A. Andreassen is Associate Professor at the Norwegian Centre for Human Rights, University of Oslo. He holds a PhD in political science and a Diploma in international human rights law. His research focuses on human rights in processes of democratization in ethnically divided societies (Eastern Africa), human rights-based development, development assistance and human rights, international election monitoring, economic and social rights, and transitional justice. He has been Editor of the international research and documentation project, Human Rights in Developing Countries (project of cooperation among European human rights institutes), and Editor in Chief of the *Nordic Journal of Human Rights*. From 1991-2001, he was head of the Research Program on Human Rights and Development at the Norwegian Centre and is currently Research Director of the Research Group on Human Rights and Development at the Law Faculty, University of Oslo.

David Beetham is Professor Emeritus, University of Leeds, Fellow of the Human Rights Centre, University of Essex, and Associate Director of Democratic Audit. He has served as a consultant to international organizations and development agencies on democracy and human rights assessment. Recent publications include *Democracy and Human Rights* (Polity Press, 1999), *Democracy: a Beginner's Guide* (Oneworld Publications, 2005), *Parliament and Democracy in the Twenty-first Century* (Inter-Parliamentary Union, 2006), *Human Rights: a Beginner's Guide* (Oneworld Publications, forthcoming 2007).

Asbjørn Eide is Senior Fellow at the Norwegian Centre for Human Rights, formerly Torgny Segersted Professor of Human Rights at the University of Gothenburg, and presently visiting Professor at the University of Lund, Sweden. He was the Director of the Norwegian Institute (now Centre) of Human Rights since its inception in 1987 to 1998. He has been a member of the United Nations Sub-Commission on the Promotion and Protection of Human Rights for 20 years, Chairman of its working group on Minorities, and President of the Council of Europe's Advisory Committee on National Minorities. His main publications deal with the development of the international system for the protection of human rights, in general, and on economic and social rights and minority rights, in particular.

Yash Pal Ghai recently retired from is the Sir YK Pao Chair of Public Law at the University of Hong Kong, where he is now Honorary Professor. He is now mainly engaged in writing and in consulting on constitutional matters in various countries. He was the chair of the Kenya Constitution Review Commission and chair of the Kenya National Conference (equivalent of a constituent assembly) between 2000 and 2004. He is Special Representative of the UN Secretary-General on Human Rights in Cambodia. Ghai has written several books and articles on constitutions, ethnic relations, human rights, and sociology of law. His most recent books are *Ethnicity and Autonomy: Negotiating Competing Claims in Multi-ethnic States* and *Hong Kong's New Constitutional Order: Basic Law and Chinese Resumption of Sovereignty* (2nd ed. — work is in progress on a 3rd edition).

Jakob Kirkemann Hansen is Program Manager at the Danish Institute for Human Rights. He holds a master's degree in Social Anthorpology and in Human Rights and Democratization. He is currently involved in a long-term cooperation program focusing on the practical implementation of rights-based policies and has been co-responsible for a series of lectures on human rights and democracy at the Institute of Anthropology, University of Copenhagen. He as worked in Central Asia, the Balkans, Turkey, East Timor, Cambodia, South Africa, Sudan, Malawi, and Ethiopia. He has been a consultant for the World Bank, the European Union, Danida, and Sida.

Sandra Liebenberg was appointed in 2004 to the HF Oppenheimer Chair in Human Rights Law at Stellenbosch University in South Africa. She served as a convener of the Technical Committee advising the Constitutional Assembly on the Bill of Rights in the 1996 Constitution. She was also employed as a researcher at the Community Law Centre, UWC, where she served as head of the Women and Human Rights Project, and subsequently founded the Socio-Economic Rights Project at the Center. She is currently appointed as a trustee of the South African Institute for Advanced Constitutional, Public, Human Rights, and Constitutional Law (SAIFAC) and is a board member of the Centre on Housing Rights and Evictions (COHRE). She also serves on the editorial board of the *South African Journal on Human Rights* and the *African Human Rights Law Journal.* She has published widely in the field of socio-economic rights.

Rajeev Malhotra is a Development Economist, working presently with the United Nations at the Office of the High Commissioner for Human Rights in Geneva. Previously, he was Deputy Adviser at the Planning Commission, Government of India. He was trained as a macro-economist and has more than 10 years of experience working on macro-econometric as well as planning models and the planning process in India. He was associated with the preparation of India's national development budget during the period 1998-2002. He has worked and published on methodological issues in estimation of poverty, human rights indicators, right to development, and specific issues on Indian economy. He was the principal author of the first *National Human Development Report for India* (2002). He has studied at Delhi University and at the London School of Economics.

Stephen P. Marks is François-Xavier Bagnoud Professor of Health and Human Rights in the Department of Population and International Health at the Harvard School of Public Health and a Senior Fellow at the University Committee on Human Rights Studies at Harvard. The emphasis of Professor Marks's work is on human rights, public health, international law, international politics, international organizations, economic development, peace, and conflict studies. He has been a consultant to the United Nations Development Program, the World Health Organization, UNESCO, and UNICEF, as well as to several foundations. He co-directed, with Arjun Sengupta, a project on the right to development and is the current Chair of the UN High-Level Task Force on the Implementation of the Right to Development. His other current research interests include human rights and tobacco control, poverty and human rights, and access to essential medicines, and human rights indicators to advance the rights of the child in the context of poverty reduction.

Siddiq Osmani is Professor of Development Economics, University of Ulster, United Kingdom. He is the coordinator of the Bangladesh Country Study of the Right to Development Project at the FXB Center for Health and Human Rights at the Harvard School of Public Health. He was a member of a team set up by the UN Office of the High Commissioner for Human Rights to prepare the *Guidelines for Implementing the Human Rights Approach to Poverty Reduction.*

Margot E. Salomon is a Lecturer in Human Rights at the Center for the Study of Human Rights and the Department of Law at the London School of Economics and Political Science. From 1999-2004, Salomon was Legal Officer and Representative to the United Nations and to the African Commission on Human and Peoples' Rights for the NGO Minority Rights Group International. She holds visiting lectureships at the University of Essex, UK, where she teaches Human Rights and Development within the LLM in International Human Rights and at the UN University in Tokyo. She is a member of the Advisory Group to the UN High-Level Task Force on the Implementation of the Right to Development. Salomon's primary research interests include the legal dimensions of poverty; the rights of minorities and indigenous peoples; and the protection of human rights in Africa. She is currently working on a book addressing world poverty and the re-conceptualization of the purposes of international law to be published by Oxford University Press in 2006 and is co-editing an anthology on the responsibilities approach to human rights and development. Recent publications include "Towards a Just Institutional Order: A Commentary on the First Session of the UN Task Force on the Right to Development," *Netherlands Quarterly of Human Rights,* and *The Right to Development: Obligations of States and the Rights of Minorities and Indigenous Peoples* (with Argun Sengupta).

Hans-Otto Sano is Research Director at Danish Institute for Human Rights. He holds a PhD in economic history and a Diploma in organization sociology. He has focused for more than 20 years on development issues, especially poverty dimensions, agricultural change, and policy and good governance. He has worked in development research institutions, in universities, in consulting, and most recently at the Danish Institute of Human Rights. During the past six years, he has focused his research on human rights and development with an emphasis on rights-based development, human rights and good governance, and human rights indicators. He is currently involved in a research project on rights-based development, examining the issue from conceptual and practical angles. He has done field work in rural eastern Africa in Zambia and Tanzania and has been working in rural Niger in West Africa for more than a year. He has been a consultant for Danida, Norad, Dutch Mede European Consultancy, the European Union, and the World Bank.

Martin Scheinin is Professor of Constitutional and International Law and Director of the Institute for Human Rights at Åbo Akademi University, Finland. In addition, he is the leader of the Nordic Network of Human Rights Research and Adjunct Professor (Professor II) in Indigenous Peoples' Rights at University of Tromsø (Norway). He is United Nations Special Rapporteur on the protection and promotion of human rights and fundamental freedoms while countering terrorism. From 1997-2004, he served as a member of the Human Rights Committee established under the International Covenant on Civil and Political Rights.

Amartya Sen is Lamont University Professor and Professor of Economics and Philosophy at Harvard University and was until recently the Master of Trinity College, Cambridge, UK. He has served as President of the Econometric Society, the Indian Economic Association, the American Economic Association and the International Economic Association. He was formerly Honorary President of OXFAM and is now its Honorary Advisor. Born in Santiniketan, India, Amartya Sen studied at Presidency College in Calcutta, India, and at Trinity College, Cambridge. He is an Indian citizen. He was Lamont University Professor at Harvard also earlier, from 1988–1998, and previous to that he was the Drummond Professor of Political Economy at Oxford University and a Fellow of All Souls College (he is now a Distinguished Fellow of All Souls). Prior to that, he was Professor of Economics at Delhi University and at the London School of Economics. He was the winner of the Nobel Prize in Economics in 1998.

Amartya Sen's books have been translated into more than thirty languages and include *Collective Choice and Social Welfare* (1970), *On Economic Inequality* (1973, 1997), *Poverty and Famines* (1981), *Choice, Welfare and Measurement* (1982), *Resources, Values and Development* (1984), *On Ethics and Economics* (1987), *The Standard of Living* (1987), *Inequality Reexamined* (1992), *Development as Freedom*

(1999), *Rationality and Freedom* (2002), *The Argumentative Indian* (2005), and *Identity and Violence: The Illusion of Destiny* (2006), among others. His research has ranged over a number of fields in economics, philosophy, and decision theory, including social choice theory, welfare economics, theory of measurement, development economics, public health, gender studies, moral and political philosophy, and the economics of peace and war.

Arjun Sengupta holds a PhD in economics from the Massachusetts Institute of Technology and has served as Member Secretary to the Indian Planning Commission and as Executive Director of the International Monetary Fund. He is currently a member of Parliament, Adjunct Professor at the Harvard School of Public Health, UN Independent Expert on Extreme Poverty and Human Rights, and member of the High-Level Commission on the Economic Empowerment of the Poor. In his previous capacity as Independent Expert on the Right to Development for the UN, he reported extensively to the Human Rights Commission and the General Assembly on the current state of progress in the implementation of the right to development. He is also the Chairman of the National Commission for Enterprises in the Unorganized Sector of the Government of India.

Sigrun I. Skogly is Reader in Human Rights Law at Lancaster University Law School in the UK. She is the author of a number of articles on human rights obligations; economic, social, and cultural rights; and the relationship between human rights and poverty. Her current research concerns states' extraterritorial human rights obligations. She published the book *The Human Rights Obligations of the World Bank and the International Monetary Fund* in 2001 and *Beyond National Borders: States' Human Rights Obligations in International Cooperation* in 2006.

Index